SOUL OF AMERICA

SOUL OF AMERICA

DOCUMENTING OUR PAST
1492–1974

ROBERT C. BARON
SENIOR EDITOR

Fulcrum, Inc.
Golden, Colorado

Cover Illustration: From the painting *Drafting the Declaration of Independence* by J. L. G. Ferris ©
J. L. G. Ferris, Archives of '76, Bay Village, Ohio.

Interior Illustrations: page xvi, *Signing of the Mayflower Compact,* courtesy of the Pilgrim Society,
Plymouth, Massachusetts; page 25, Benjamin Franklin, courtesy of The Library Company of Phila-
delphia, Philadelphia, Pennsylvania; page 26, J*oin or Die* editorial cartoon, courtesy of The Library
Company of Philadelphia; page 41, John Adams, courtesy of the White House Historical Association,
Washington, D.C.; page 109, James Madison, courtesy of the White House Historical Association;
page 121, George Washington, courtesy of the White House Historical Association; page 141,
Thomas Jefferson, courtesy of the White House Historical Association; page 146, Lewis and Clark,
courtesy of the Oregon Historical Society, Portland, Oregon; page 182, James Monroe, courtesy of
the White House Historical Association; page 184, *Negro laborers,* courtesy of the National Archives,
Washington, D.C.; page 214, Elizabeth Cady Stanton, courtesy of the National Women's Party, Wash-
ington, D.C.; page 219, Frederick Douglass, courtesy of the National Archives; page 245, Abraham
Lincoln, courtesy of the National Archives; page 267, *Wounded Soldier,* courtesy of the National
Archives; page 295, Booker T. Washington, courtesy of the Tuskegee Institute National Historical Site,
Tuskegee, Alabama; page 314, Theodore Roosevelt, courtesy of the White House Historical
Association; page 344, Franklin D. Roosevelt, courtesy of the White House Historical Association;
page 355, *Members of the Mochida Family,* courtesy of the National Archives; page 356, *Victory,*
courtesy of the National Archives; page 360, Harry Truman, courtesy of the White House Historical
Association; page 378, Dwight Eisenhower, courtesy of the White House Historical Association;
page 389, Martin Luther King, Jr., courtesy of the National Archives; page 393, Lyndon B. Johnson,
courtesy of the White House Historical Association; page 400, courtesy of the National Organization
for Women, Washington, D.C.; and page 412, Richard M. Nixon, courtesy of the White House
Historical Association.

Library of Congress Cataloging-in-Publication Data

Soul of America : documenting our past / edited by Robert C. Baron . . .
    [et al.] .
        p.   cm.
    Bibliography: p.
    Includes index.
    ISBN 1-55591-047-5
    1. United States--History--Sources. I. Baron, Robert C.
E173.S687   1989   89-7920
973--dc20   CIP

Printed in the United States of America

0   9   8   7   6   5   4   3   2   1

Fulcrum, Inc.
Golden, Colorado

TABLE OF CONTENTS

INTRODUCTION

THIS book is about America; it presents the ideas and writings of the men and women who have shaped our nation.

America has always been a special place, a place unlike any other. We are a nation of immigrants and descendants of immigrants. From the villages and towns of Europe, Africa, Asia and the Americas, immigrants sailed and steamed across the ocean to reach this country's shores. And once in the new world, they walked and rode across the continent, heading west, toward new opportunities, jobs and the open land—marching on to the leadership of the free people of the world.

Our leaders have recognized the special place that is America. Included in this book are basic American ideas, eloquently expressed in their words:

> Thomas Jefferson in the "Declaration of Independence": "We hold these truths to be self-evident, that all men are created equal, that they are endowed by their Creator with certain unalienable Rights, that among these are Life, Liberty and the pursuit of Happiness. That to secure these rights, Governments are instituted among Men, deriving their just powers from the consent of the governed."

> John Adams in his "Inaugural Address": "Employed in the service of my country abroad during the whole course of these transactions, I first saw the Constitution of the United States in a foreign country. . . . I read it with great satisfaction, as the result of good heads prompted by good hearts, as an experiment better adapted to the genius, character, situation, and relations of this nation and country than any which had ever been proposed or suggested."

> Abraham Lincoln in the "Address at Gettysburg": "That this

nation, under God, shall have a new birth of freedom—and that government of the people, by the people, for the people, shall not perish from the earth."

Herbert Hoover in an October 1928 speech: "And what have been the results of the American system? Our country has become the land of opportunity to those born without inheritance, not merely because of the wealth of its resources and industry but because of this freedom of initiative and enterprise."

Franklin Delano Roosevelt in the "Four Freedoms" speech: "Since the beginning of our American history we have been engaged in change—in a perpetual peaceful revolution—a revolution which goes on steadily, quietly adjusting itself to changing conditions."

John F. Kennedy in his "Inaugural Address": "The torch has been passed to a new generation of Americans—born in this century, tempered by war, disciplined by a hard and bitter peace, proud of our ancient heritage—and unwilling to witness or permit the slow undoing of those human rights to which this nation has always been committed."

Lyndon B. Johnson in his November 1963 address to Congress: "Our American unity does not depend upon unanimity. We have differences; but now, as in the past, we can derive from those differences strength, not weakness, wisdom, not despair."

America is a country born of an ideal, an idea of freedom—religious freedom, political freedom, economic freedom, the freedom to speak and think as one wishes—and the opportunity to grow and change and to provide a better world for their families and for their descendants.

Change has come slowly at times, but it has come. It was more than a century between the time when Roger Williams and William Penn demanded freedom of religion and the time that the Bill of Rights was ratified. The first amendment states: "Congress shall make no law respecting an establishment of religion, or prohibiting the free exercise thereof; or abridging the freedom of speech or of the press; or the right of the people peaceably to assemble, and to petition the government for a redress of grievances."

It has taken time, often far too much time, for woman suffrage and black equality to be achieved, for political and economic rights to be extended to all citizens. But progress has been and continues to be made. This change has occurred because of individuals.

Hear their words. Hear the words of Coronado; William Penn and Roger

Williams; Benjamin Franklin, George Washington, John Adams, Thomas Jefferson, Thomas Paine, Patrick Henry and James Madison; John C. Calhoun, Daniel Webster and Henry Clay; Abraham Lincoln and Robert E. Lee; Frederick Douglass, Booker T. Washington and Martin Luther King, Jr.; Abigail Adams, Elizabeth Cady Stanton, Susan B. Anthony and Jane Addams; Theodore Roosevelt, Woodrow Wilson, Franklin Delano Roosevelt and John Kennedy. Hear their words.

The native people who resided in this land had much to teach us. We have too infrequently listened. Hear their words as well. Listen to Red Jacket and Tecumseh. Let Chief Joseph of the Nez Percé speak: "Treat all men alike. Give them the same laws. Give them all an even chance to live and grow. All men were made by the same Great Spirit Chief. They are all brothers. The earth is the mother of all people, and all people should have equal rights upon it."

In the five centuries since Columbus and his ships sailed on to a new world, in the four centuries since Coronado led an expedition of discovery and exploration across the southwest, in the three centuries since Roger Williams and William Penn wrote so strongly about religious freedom, in the two centuries since Jefferson's immortal words proclaimed our independence, in the century since Lincoln with his courage held the country together and helped heal the nation's wounds, and in this century of wars and depression, economic growth and the movement of the United States onto center stage as a world power— throughout all that time, political and economic rights have been extended to an ever-increasing share of our population.

How did the wilderness described by Columbus and Coronado become the leading nation in the world? How did the dreams of freedom—freedom of religion, of political beliefs, of expression, of opportunity—develop? What are some of the ideals and hopes of this country? What are some of its principles? The documents, Supreme Court decisions, speeches and songs collected here provide some answers to these questions.

The origin of *Soul of America* was in watching television, a rather dangerous pastime for a historian. In noting the anniversary of the death of President John F. Kennedy, each network showed a three-minute summary of Kennedy's life, focusing on his inaugural address and the "ask not what your country can do for you" quote. No television program or, for that matter, any newspaper ever reproduced more than a few sentences from his inaugural address. There were numerous commentaries, reports, historical analyses and opinions about the speech, but only fragments of the actual text.

A few weeks later, the editors and others began to discuss the most important documents in American history as well as some of the most beautiful speeches. Eventually we decided to prepare a book of documents and developed a list of items to be included. We discussed the documents and their influence on people and history.

Sometimes choices were obvious—the Constitution or the Declaration of Independence. Some choices were based on their long-term influence—the Seneca Falls Declaration or Thoreau's speech "Civil Disobedience," which influenced Ghandi in South Africa and India and later, Martin Luther King, Jr., and the civil rights movement. Some selections were made based on the beauty of the language and the expression of major ideas—the selections by Thomas Paine, Frederick Douglass, Sojourner Truth and Chief Joseph.

The volume is organized in chronological order. But certain themes often extend over many decades. A reader can study each document in order or read all writings on a particular subject.

Suggestions were made by each editor, but ultimately, I am responsible for the final selections. I am also responsible for the introductions to all material from the fifteenth century to the early nineteenth century.

I would like to thank the associate editors: Maxine Benson, former State Historian for Colorado, an editor, author and friend who assisted in the organization and editing of this book; Chris Bierwirth of the University of Wisconsin, who wrote the introductions to those pieces from the mid to late nineteenth century; Cathy Lavender-Teliha of the University of Colorado, who wrote the introductions to the selections from the twentieth century; and Kay Baron, who aided in selecting the material and organizing the book and who typed all the documents. I would also like to thank Carmel Huestis, Karen Groves and Jay Staten of Fulcrum for their editing, suggestions and encouragement.

Robert C. Baron
Summer 1989

Signing of the Mayflower Compact, artist unknown.

1

COLONIAL AMERICA

PRIVILEGES AND PREROGATIVES GRANTED TO COLUMBUS

April 30, 1492

Christopher Columbus was born at Genoa, Italy, in 1451 and went to sea at the age of fourteen. Early in his life he conceived the idea of reaching India by sailing westward and began to seek a patron for such an expedition. He applied to John II of Portugal, by letter to Henry VII of England, and to Isabella, Queen of Castille. Based on adverse recommendations from her advisors, Isabella initially rejected Columbus's plans. Columbus was on his way to France when he was called back to Castille, where King Ferdinand and Queen Isabella agreed to sponsor the expedition on the terms described here. On Friday, August 3, 1492, Columbus set sail with three small ships and 120 adventurers. After a stop in the Canary Islands, they reached land in the New World on October 12, 1492.

FOR as much of you, Christopher Columbus, are going by our command, with some of our vessels and men, to discover and subdue some Islands and Continent in the ocean, and it is hoped that by God's assistance, some of the said

Islands and Continent in the ocean will be discovered and conquered by your means and conduct, therefore it is but just and reasonable, that since you expose yourself to such danger to serve us, you should be rewarded for it. And we being willing to honour and favour you for the reasons aforesaid; Our will is, That you, Christopher Columbus, after discovering and conquering the said Islands and Continent in the said ocean, or any of them, shall be our Admiral of the said Islands and Continent you shall so discover and conquer; and that you be our Admiral, Vice-Roy, and Governour in them, and that for the future, you may call and stile yourself, D. Christopher Columbus, and that your sons and successors in the said employment, may call themselves Dons, Admirals, Vice-Roys, and Governours of them; and that you may exercise the office of Admiral, with the charge of Vice-Roy and Governour of the said Islands and Continent, which you and your Lieutenants shall conquer, and freely decide all causes, civil and criminal, appertaining to the said employment of Admiral, Vice-Roy, and Governour, as you shall think fit in justice, and as the Admirals of our kingdoms use to do; and that you have power to punish offenders; and you and your Lieutenants exercise the employments of Admiral, Vice-Roy, and Governour, in all things belonging to the said offices, or any of them; and that you enjoy the perquisites and salaries belonging to the said employments, and to each of them, in the same manner as the High Admiral of our kingdoms does. And by this our letter, or a copy of it signed by a Public Notary: We command Prince John, our most dearly beloved Son, the Infants, Dukes, Prelates, Marquesses, Great Masters and Military Orders, Priors, Commendaries, our Counsellors, Judges, and other Officers of Justice whatsoever, belonging to our Household, Courts, and Chancery, and Constables of Castles, Strong Houses, and others, and all Corporations, Bayliffs, Governours, Judges, Commanders, Sea Officers; and the Aldermen, Common Council, Officers, and Good People of all Cities, Lands, and Places in our Kingdoms and Dominions, and in those you shall conquer and subdue, and the captains, masters, mates, and other officers and sailors, our natural subjects now being, or that shall be for the time to come, and any of them, that when you shall have discovered the said Islands and Continent in the ocean; and you, or any that shall have your commission, shall have taken the usual oath in such cases, that they for the future, look upon you as long as you live, and after you, your son and heir, and so from one heir to another forever, as our Admiral on our said Ocean, and as Vice-Roy and Governour of the said Islands and Continent, by you, Christopher Columbus, discovered and conquered; and that they treat you and your Lieutenants, by you appointed, for executing the employments of Admiral, Vice-Roy, and Governour, as such in all respects, and give you all the perquisites and other things belonging and appertaining to the said offices; and allow, and cause to be allowed you, all the honours, graces, concessions, prehaminences, prerogatives, immunities, and other things, or any of them which are due to you, by virtue of your commands of Admiral, Vice-Roy, and Governour, and to be observed completely, so that nothing be diminished; and that they make no objection to this, or any part of it, nor suffer it to be made; forasmuch as we from this time forward, by this our letter, bestow on you the employments of Admiral, Vice-Roy, and perpetual Governour forever; and we put you into possession of the said offices, and of every of them, and full power to use and exercise them, and to receive the perquisites and salaries belonging to them, or any of them, as was said above. Concerning all which things, if it be requisite, and you shall desire it, We command our Chancellour, Notaries, and other Officers, to pass, seal, and deliver to you, our Letter of Privilege, in such form and legal manner, as you shall require or stand in need of. And that none of them presume to do any thing to the contrary, upon pain of our displeasure, and fortfeiture of 30 ducats for each offence. And we command him, who shall show them this our Letter, that he summon them to appear before us at our Court, where we shall then be, within fifteen days after such summons, under the said penalty. Under which same, we also command any Public Notary whatsoever, that he give to him that shows it him, a certificate under his seal, that we may know how our command is obeyed.

Given at Granada, on the 30th of April, in the year of our Lord, 1492.

I, the King, I, the Queen

LETTER FROM
FRANCISCO VAZQUEZ DE CORONADO
TO HIS MAJESTY

October 20, 1541

Francisco Vazquez de Coronado was born in 1510 at Salamanca, Spain. A soldier, he was appointed governor of New Galicia, Mexico, by Don Antonio de Mendoza. In 1540, Coronado was appointed to lead the greatest Spanish frontier expedition. In his search for the Seven Cities of Gold, Coronado took with him more than 200 cavalrymen, seventy foot soldiers, five friars and over 1,000 Indians on a two-year march across the Southwest. His party explored the Colorado River, discovered the Grand Canyon of the Colorado, and traveled from western Mexico along the Rio Grande valley of New Mexico through Texas to the great plains of eastern Kansas.

HOLY Catholic Caesarian Majesty: On April 20 of this year I wrote to Your Majesty from this province of Tiguex, in reply to a letter from Your Majesty dated in Madrid, June 11 a year ago. I gave a detailed account of this expedition, which the viceroy of New Spain ordered me to undertake in Your Majesty's name to this country which was discovered by Friar Marcos of Nice, the provincial of the order of Holy Saint Francis. I described it all, and the sort of force I have, as Your Majesty had ordered me to relate in my letters; and stated that while I was engaged in the conquest and pacification of the Indians of this province, some Indians who were natives of other provinces beyond these had told me that in their country there were much larger villages and better houses than those of the natives of this country, and that they had lords who ruled them, who were served with dishes of gold, and other very magnificent things; and although, as I wrote Your Majesty, I did not believe it before I had set eyes on it, because it was the report of Indians and given for the most part by means of signs, yet as the report appeared to me to be very fine and that it was important that it should be investigated for Your Majesty's service, I determined to go and see it with the men I have here. I started from this province on the 23d of last April, for the place where the Indians wanted to guide me.

After nine days' march I reached some plains, so vast that I did not find their limit anywhere that I went, although I traveled over them for more than 300 leagues. And I found such a quantity of cows in these, of the kind that I wrote Your Majesty about, which they have in this country, that it is impossible to number them, for while I was journeying through these plains, until I returned to where I first found them, there was not a day I lost sight of them. And after seventeen days' march I came to a settlement of Indians who are called Querechos, who travel around with these cows, who do not plant, and who eat the raw flesh and drink the blood of the cows they kill, and they tan the skins of the cows, with which all the people of this country dress themselves here. They have little field tents made of the hides of the cows, tanned and greased, very well made, in which they live while they travel around near the cows, moving with these. They have dogs which they load, which carry their tents and poles and belongings. These people have the best figures of any that I have seen in the Indies. They could not give me any account of the country where the guides were taking me. I traveled five days more as the guides wished to lead me, until I reached some plains, with no more landmarks than as if we had been swallowed up in the sea, where they strayed about, because there was not a stone, nor a bit of rising ground, nor a tree, nor a shrub, nor anything to go by. There is much very fine pasture land, with good grass. And while we were lost in these plains, some horsemen who went off to hunt cows fell in with some Indians who also were out hunting, who are enemies of those that I had seen in the last settlement, and of another sort of people who are called Teyas; they have bodies and faces all painted, are a large people like the others, of a very good build; they eat the raw flesh just like the Querechos, and live and travel round with the cows in the same way as these. I obtained from these an account of the country where the guides were taking me, which was not like what they had told me, because these made out that the houses there were not built of stones, with stories, as my guides had described it, but of straw and skins, and a small supply of corn there.

This news troubled me greatly, to find myself on these limitless plains, where I was in great need of water, and often had to drink it so poor that it was more mud than water. Here the guides confessed to me that they had not told the truth in regard to the size of the houses, because these were of straw, but that they had done so regarding the large number of inhabitants and the other things about their habits. The Teyas disagreed with this, and on account of this division between some of the Indians and the others, and also because many of the men I had with me had not eaten anything except meat for some days, because we had reached the end of the corn which we carried from this province, and because they made it out more than forty days' journey from where I fell in with the Teyas to the country where the guides were taking me, although I appreciated the trouble and danger there would be in the journey owing to the lack of water and corn, it seemed to me best, in order to see if there was anything there of service to Your Majesty, to go forward with only 30 horsemen until I should be able to see the country, so as to give Your Majesty a true account of what was to be found in it. I sent all the rest of the force I had with me to this province, with Don Tristan de Arellano in command, because it would have been impossible to prevent the loss of many men, if all had gone on, owing to the lack of water and because they also had to kill bulls and cows on which to sustain themselves. And with only the 30 horsemen whom I took for my escort, I traveled forty-two days after I left the force, living all this while solely on the flesh of the bulls and cows which we killed, at the cost of several of our horses which they killed, because, as I wrote Your Majesty, they are very brave and fierce animals; and going many days without water, and cooking the food with cow dung, because there is not any kind of wood in all these plains, away from the gullies and rivers, which are very few.

It was the Lord's pleasure that, after having journeyed across these deserts seventy-seven days, I arrived at the province they call Quivira, to which the guides were conducting me, and where they had described to me houses of stone, with many stories; and not only are they not of stone, but of straw, but the people in them are as barbarous as all those whom I have seen and passed before this; they do not have cloaks, nor cotton of which to make these, but use the skins of the cattle they kill, which they tan, because they are settled among these on a very large river. They eat the raw flesh like the Querechos and Teyas; they are enemies of one another, but are all of the same sort of people, and these at Quivira have the advantage in the houses they build and in planting corn. In this province of which the guides who brought me are natives, they received me peaceably, and although they told me when I set out for it that I could not succeed in seeing it all in two months, there are not more than 25 villages of straw houses there and in all the rest of the country that I saw and learned about, which gave their obedience to Your Majesty and placed themselves under your royal overlordship.

The people here are large. I had several Indians measured, and found out they were 10 palms in height; the women are well proportioned and their features are more like Moorish women than Indians. The natives here gave me a piece of copper which a chief Indian wore hung around his neck; I sent it to the viceroy of New Spain, because I have not seen any other metal in these parts except this and some little copper bells which I sent him, and a bit of metal which looks like gold. I do not know where this came from, although I believe that the Indians who gave it to me obtained it from those whom I brought here in my service, because I can not find any other origin for it nor where it came from. The diversity of languages which exists in this country and my not having anyone who understood them, because they speak their own language in each village, has hindered me, because I have been forced to send captains and men in many directions to find out whether there was anything in this country which could be of service to Your Majesty. And although I have searched with all diligence I have not found or heard of anything, unless it be these provinces, which are a very small affair.

The province of Quivira is 950 leagues from Mexico. Where I reached it, it is in the fortieth degree. The country itself is the best I have ever seen for producing all the products of Spain, for besides the land itself being very fat and black and being very well watered by the rivulets and springs and rivers, I found prunes like those of Spain [or I found everything they have in Spain] and nuts and very good sweet grapes and mulberries. I have treated the natives of this province, and all the others whom I found wherever I went, as well as was possible, agreeably to what Your Majesty had commanded, and they have received no harm in any way from me or from those who went in my company. I remained twenty-five days in this province of Quivira, so as to see and explore the country and also to find out whether there was anything beyond which could be of service to Your Majesty, because the guides who had brought me had given me an account of other provinces beyond this. And what I am sure of is that there is not any gold nor any other metal in all that country, and the other things of which they had told me are nothing but little villages, and in many of these they do not plant anything and do not have any houses except of skins and sticks, and they wander around with the cows; so that the account they gave me was false, because they wanted to persuade me to go there with the whole force, believing that as the way was through such uninhabited deserts, and from the lack of water, they would get us where we and our horses would die of hunger. And the guides confessed this, and said they had done it by the advice and orders of the natives of these provinces. At this, after having heard the account of what was beyond, which I have given above, I returned to these provinces to provide for the force I had sent back here and to give Your Majesty an account of what this country amounts to, because I wrote Your Majesty that I would do so when I went there.

I have done all that I possibly could to serve Your Majesty and to discover a country where God Our Lord might be served and the royal patrimony of Your Majesty increased, as your loyal servant and vassal. For since I reached the province of Cibola, to which the viceroy of New Spain sent me in the name of Your Majesty, seeing that there were none of the things there of which Friar Marcos had told, I have managed to explore this country for 200 leagues and more around Cibola, and the best place I have found is this river of Tiguex where I am now, and the settlements here. It would not be possible to establish a settlement here, for besides being 400 leagues from the North sea and more than 200 from the South sea, with which it is impossible to have any sort of communication, the country is so cold, as I have written to Your Majesty, that apparently the winter could not possibly be spent here, because there is no wood, nor cloth with which to protect the men, except the skins which the natives wear and some small amount of cotton cloaks. I send the viceroy of New Spain an account of everything I have seen in the countries where I have been, and as Don Garcia Lopez de Cardenas is going to kiss Your Majesty's hands, who has done much and has served Your Majesty very well on this expedition, and he will give Your Majesty an account of everything here, as one who has seen it himself, I give way to him. And may Our Lord protect the Holy Imperial Catholic person of Your Majesty, with increase of greater kingdoms and powers, as your loyal servants and vassals desire. From this province of Tiguex, October 20, in the year 1541. Your Majesty's humble servant and vassal, who would kiss the royal feet and hands:

FRANCISCO VAZQUEZ CORONADO.

THE MAYFLOWER COMPACT

Pilgrim Leaders   *November 11, 1620*

In the fall of 1620 a group of thirty-five Separatists from the Church of England, called Pilgrims, and seventy non-Pilgrims set out on the ship Mayflower *for the mouth of the Hudson River, then within the boundaries of Virginia. Because of weather and currents, when the ship reached North America these people found themselves at what is now Cape Cod, far from their destination. The Pilgrims drew up the Mayflower Compact as a set of laws to be followed until a legal charter could be obtained from England. This document was signed by almost all the adult men in the group.*

IN The Name of God, Amen. We, whose names are underwritten, the Loyal Subjects of our dread Sovereign Lord King James, by the Grace of God, of Great Britain, France, and Ireland, King, Defender of the Faith, etc. Having undertaken for the Glory of God, and Advancement of the Christian Faith, and the Honour of our King and Country, a Voyage to plant the first colony in the northern Parts of Virginia; Do by these Presents, solemnly and mutually in the Presence of God and one another, covenant and combine ourselves together into a civil Body Politick, for our better Ordering and Preservation, and Furtherance of the Ends aforesaid; And by Virtue hereof do enact, constitute, and frame, such just and equal Laws, Ordinances, Acts, Constitutions, and Offices, from time to time, as shall be thought most meet and convenient for the general Good of the Colony; unto which we promise all due Submission and Obedience. IN WITNESS whereof we have hereunto subscribed our names at Cape Cod the eleventh of November, in the Reign of our Sovereign Lord King James of England, France, and Ireland, the eighteenth and of Scotland, the fifty-fourth. Anno Domini, 1620

Mr. John Carver
Mr. William Bradford
Mr. Edward Winslow
Mr. William Brewster
Isaac Allerton
Miles Standish
John Alden
John Turner
Francis Eaton
James Chilton
John Craxton
John Billington
Joses Fletcher
John Goodman
Mr. Samuel Fuller
Mr. Christopher Martin
Richard Gardiner
Mr. John Allerton
Thomas English
Edward Doten
Edward Liester.

Mr. Stephen Hopkins
Digery Priest
Thomas Williams
Gilbert Winslow
Edmund Margesson
Peter Brown
Richard Bitteridge
George Soule
Edward Tilly
John Tilly
Francis Cooke
Thomas Rogers
Thomas Tinker
John Ridgate
Edward Fuller
Richard Clark
Mr. William Mullins
Mr. William White
Mr. Richard Warren
John Howland

ORDINANCE FOR THE
VIRGINIA HOUSE OF BURGESSES

July 24, 1621

In 1606 King James of England granted the first charter to the Virginia Company, which settled 120 people in Jamestown. A second charter was granted in 1609, and a third in 1612, giving more independence to the company. The first Assembly of these settlers was held seven years later, and marks the beginnings of representative government in America. On July 24, 1621, the following ordinance for Virginia was issued.

AN ordinance and Constitution of the Treasurer, Council, and Company in England, for a Council of State and General Assembly. Dated July 24, 1621.

To all People, to whom these Presents shall come, be seen, or heard The Treasurer, Council, and Company of Adventurers and Planters for the City of London for the first colony of Virginia send Greeting. Know ye that we, the said Treasurer, Council, and Company, taking into our careful Consideration the present State, of the said Colony of Virginia, and intending, by the Divine Assistance, to settle such a Form of Government there as may be to the greatest Benefit and Comfort of the People, and whereby all Injustice, Grievances, and Oppression may be prevented and kept off as much as possible from the said Colony, have thought fit to make our Entrance, by ordering and establishing such Supreme Councils, as may not only be assisting to the Governor for the time being, in the Administration of Justice, and the executing of other Duties for this office belonging, but also, by their vigilant care and Prudence, may provide, as well for a Remedy of all Inconveniences, growing from time to time, as also for advancing of Increase, Strength, Stability, and Prosperity of the said Colony:

II. We therefore, the said Treasurer, Council, and Company, by Authority directed to us from his Majesty under the Great Seal, upon mature Deliberation, do hereby order and declare, that, from hence forward, there shall be two supreme councils in Virginia, for the better Government of the said Colony aforesaid.

III. The one of which Councils, to be called the Council of State . . . shall be chosen, nominated, placed, and displaced, from time to time, by us the said Treasurer, Council, and Company, and our Successors: . . . Which said Counsellors and Council we earnestly pray and desire, and in his Majesty's Name strictly charge and command, that (all Factions, Partialities, and sinister Respect laid aside) they bend their Care and Endeavors to assist the said Governor; first and principally in the Advancement of the Honour and Service of God, and the Enlargement of his Kingdom amongst the Heathen People; and next, in erecting of the said Colony in due obedience to his Majesty, and all lawful Authority from his Majesty's Directions; and lastly, in maintaining the said People in Justice and Christian Conversation amongst themselves, and in Strength and Ability to withstand their Enemies. And this Council, to be always, or for the most Part, residing about or near the Governor.

IV. The other Council, more generally to be called by the Governor, once yearly, and no oftener, but for very extraordinary and important occasions, shall consist, for the present, of the said Council of State, and of two Burgesses out of every Town, Hundred, or other particular Plantation, to be respectively chosen by the Inhabitants; Which Council shall be called The General Assembly, wherein (as also in the said Council of State) all Matter shall be decided, determined, and ordered by the greater Part of the Voices then present; reserving to the Governor always a Negative Voice. And this General Assembly shall have free Power to treat, consult, and conclude, as well of all emergent Occasions concerning the Publick Weal of the said Colony and every Part thereof, as also to make, ordain, and enact such general Laws and Orders, for the Behoof of the said Colony, and the good Government thereof, as shall, from time to time, appear necessary or requisite:

V. Whereas in all other Things, we require the said General Assembly, as also the said Council of State, to imitate and follow the Policy of the Form of Government—Laws, Customs, and Manner of Trial, and other Administration of Justice, used in the Realm of England, as near as may be, even as ourselves, by his Majesty's Letters Patent, are required.

VI. Provided, that no Law or Ordinance, made in the said General Assembly, shall be or continue in Force or Validity, unless the same shall be solemnly ratified and confirmed, in a General Quarter Court of the said Company here in England, and so ratified, to be returned to them under our Seal: It being our Intent to afford the like Measure also unto the said Colony, that after the Government of the said Colony shall once have been well framed, and settled accordingly, which is to be done by Us, as by Authority derived from his Majesty, and the same shall have been so by Us declared, no Orders of Court afterwards shall bind the said Colony, unless they be ratified in like Manner in the General Assemblies. IN WITNESS whereof we have here unto set our Common Seal, the 24th of July 1621, and in the Year of the Reign of our Sovereign Lord, James, King of England, etc.

HISTORY OF PLYMOUTH PLANTATION

William Bradford   *1630*

William Bradford was born in Austerfield, County Yorkshire, England, in 1589. He joined the Separatist congregation near his home and in 1608 escaped to Holland to avoid religious persecution. He became a leader of the Pilgrims and helped organize their trip to Massachusetts on the Mayflower. *In 1621 Bradford succeeded John Carver as governor of the Plymouth Colony, and over a twenty-year period starting in 1630, wrote* Of Plymouth Plantation, *from which the following*

selection is taken. A private manuscript, the book was first
published by the Massachusetts Historical Society in 1856, more
than 200 years after it was written.

BEING thus arrived in a good harbor and brought safe to land, they fell upon their knees and blessed the God of Heaven who had brought them over the vast and furious ocean and delivered them from all the perils and miseries thereof, again to set their feet on the firm and stable earth, their proper element.

But here I cannot but stay and make a pause and stand half amazed at this poor people's present condition; and so I think will the reader too, when he well considers the same. Being thus past the vast ocean and a sea of troubles before in their preparation (as may be remembered by that which went before), they had now no friends to welcome them, nor inns to entertain or refresh their weatherbeaten bodies, no houses or much less towns to repair to, to seek for succor. It is recorded in Scripture as a mercy to the apostle and his shipwrecked company, the barbarians showed them no small kindness in refreshing them, but these savage barbarians, when they met with them (as after will appear) were readier to fill their sides full of arrows than otherwise. And for the season, it was winter, and they that know the winters of that country know them to be sharp and violent and subject to cruel and fierce storms, dangerous to travel to known places, much more to search an unknown coast. Besides, what could they see but a hideous and desolate wilderness full of wild beasts and wild men? And what multitudes there might be of them they knew not. If it be said they had a ship to succor them, it is true; but what heard they daily from the master and company but that with speed they should look out a place with their shallop where they would be at some near distance; for the season was such as he would not stir from thence till a safe harbor was discovered by them where they would be and he might go without danger; and that victuals consumed apace but he must and would keep sufficient for themselves and their return. Yea, it was muttered by some that if they got not a place in time they would turn them and their goods ashore and leave them. Let it also be considered what weak hopes of supply and succor they left behind them that might bear up their minds in this sad condition and trials they were under; and they could not but be very small. It is true, indeed, the affections and love of their brethren at Leyden was cordial and entire towards them, but they had little power to help them or themselves; and how the case stood between them and the merchants at their coming away hath already been declared. What could now sustain them but the spirit of God and His grace? May not and ought not the children of these fathers rightly say: "Our fathers were Englishmen which came over this great ocean, and were ready to perish in this wilderness; but they cried unto the Lord, and he heard their voice and looked on their adversity, etc. Let them therefore praise the Lord, because he is good and his mercies endure forever. Yea, let them which have been redeemed of the Lord show how he hath delivered them from the hand of the oppressor. When they wandered in the desert wilderness out of the way, and found no city to dwell in, both hungry and thirsty, their soul was overwhelmed in them. Let them confess before the Lord his loving kindness, and his wonderful works before the sons of men."

MASSACHUSETTS SCHOOL LAW

April 14, 1642

The Massachusetts Bay Colony School Law of 1642 is one of the earliest laws on education in the American colonies. It reflected a concern with establishing a uniform code of education in the colony and showed an awareness that family responsibility for education had been a failure without minimum standards and public financial support.

THIS Cort, taking into consideration the great neglect of many parents and masters in training up their children in learning and labor, and other implyments which may be proffitable to the common wealth, do hereupon order and decree that in euery towne ye chosen men appointed for managing the prudentiall affajres of the same shall henceforth stand charged with the care of the redresse of this evill, so as they shalbee sufficiently punished by fines for the neglect thereof, upon presentment of the grand iury, or other information or complaint in any Court within this iurisdiction; and for this end they, or the greater number of them, shall have power to take account from time to time of all parents and masters, and of their children, concerning their calling and implyment of their children, especially of their ability to read and understand the principles of religion and the capitall lawes of this country, and to impose fines upon such as shall refuse to render such accounts to them when they shall be required; and they shall have power, with consent of any Court or the magistrate, to put forth apprentices the children of such as they shall (find) not to be able and fitt to employ and bring them up. They shall take . . . that boyes and girles be not suffered to converse together, so as may occasion any wanton, dishonest, or immodest behavior; and for their better performance of this trust committed to them, they may divide the towne amongst them, appointing to every of the said townesmen a certaine number of families to have special oversight of. They are also to provide that a sufficient quantity of materialls, as hemp, flaxe, etc., may be raised in their severall townes, and tooles and implements provided for working out the same; and for their assistance in this so needfull and beneficiall imploymt, if they meete with any difficulty or opposition which they cannot well master by their own power, they may have recorse to some of the magistrates, who shall take such course for their help and incuragmt as the occasion shall require according to iustice; and the said townesmen, at the next Cort in those limits, after the end of their year, shall give a briefe account in writing of their proceedings herein, provided that they have bene so required by some Cort or magistrate a month at least before; and this order to continew for two yeares, and till the Cort shall take further order.

THE BLOODY TENET OF PERSECUTION

Roger Williams   *1644*

> *Roger Williams was born in London in 1604 and*
> *educated at Pembroke College, Cambridge. He became a*
> *Puritan and emigrated to Massachusetts in 1630. His opposition*
> *to the New England theocracy and his defense of the Indians*
> *were unpopular with the authorities there, and in 1635 he was*
> *banished from the Massachusetts Bay Colony. He moved south,*
> *where he purchased land from the Indians and founded the*
> *town of Providence. He was president of Rhode Island from*
> *1654 to 1658. Williams's belief in religious tolerance led Rhode*
> *Island to become the first colony to offer religious freedom.*
> *Williams's writings include* A Key to the Language of America,
> *a study of Indian languages;* Queries of Highest Consideration;
> *and* The Bloody Tenet of Persecution for Cause of Conscience,
> *from which the following is taken.*

FIRST, that the blood of so many hundred thousand souls of Protestants and Papists, spilt in the wars of present and former ages, for their respective consciences, is not required nor accepted by Jesus Christ the Prince of Peace.

Secondly, pregnant scriptures and arguments are throughout the work proposed against the doctrine of persecution for causes of conscience.

Thirdly, satisfactory answers are given to scriptures, and objections produced by Mr. Calvin, Beza, Mr. Cotton, and the ministers of the New English churches and others former and later, tending to prove the doctrine of persecution for cause of conscience.

Fourthly, the doctrine of persecution for cause of conscience is proved guilty of all the blood of the souls crying for vengeance under the altar.

Fifthly, all civil states with their officers of justice in their respective constitutions and administrations are proved essentially civil, and therefore not judges, governors, or defenders of the spiritual or Christian state and worship.

Sixthly, it is the will and command of God that (since the coming of his Son the Lord Jesus) a permission of the most paganish, Jewish, Turkish, or antichristian consciences and worships, be granted to all men in all nations and countries; and they are only to be fought against with that sword which is only (in soul matters) able to conquer, to wit, the sword of God's Spirit, the Word of God.

Seventhly, the state of the Land of Israel, the kings and people thereof in peace and war, is proved figurative and ceremonial, and no pattern nor president for any kingdom or civil state in the world to follow.

Eighthly, God requireth not a uniformity of religion to be enacted and enforced in any civil state; which enforced uniformity (sooner or later) is the greatest occasion of civil war, ravishing of conscience, persecution of Christ Jesus in his servants, and of the hypocrisy and destruction of millions of souls.

Ninthly, in holding an enforced uniformity of religion in a civil state, we must necessarily disclaim our desires and hopes of the Jew's conversion to Christ.

Tenthly, an enforced uniformity of religion throughout a nation or civil state, confounds the civil and religious, denies the principles of Christianity and civility, and that Jesus Christ is come in the flesh.

Eleventhly, the permission of other consciences and worships than a state professeth only can (according to God) procure a firm and lasting peace (good assurance being taken according to the wisdom of the civil state for uniformity of civil obedience from all sorts).

Twelfthly, lastly, true civility and Christianity may both flourish in a state or kingdom, notwithstanding the permission of divers and contrary consciences, either of Jew or Gentile.

THE GREAT CASE OF LIBERTY OF CONSCIENCE

William Penn   *1670*

---

*William Penn was born in London in 1644, the son of
Admiral William Penn. He originally had been an Anglican
but had been converted by George Fox, the founder of the
Society of Friends, or Quakers. Penn, like hundreds of other
Quakers, was sent to jail for his beliefs and spent two years
there. He wrote extensively on religious freedom, and this essay
was written during one of his imprisonments. King Charles II
owed Penn's father a large debt, and decided to repay it by
giving the family a grant of territory in North America, called
Pennsilvania in honor of the admiral. In 1682 William Penn
arrived in America and established one of the most liberal
colonies, with its Quaker emphasis on religious and civil liberty.
Penn returned to England to work for the persecuted Quakers,
and in 1686, through his influence, all persons imprisoned on
account of their religious beliefs were released.*

THE great case of Liberty of Conscience, so often debated and defended
(however dissatisfactorily to such as have so little conscience as to persecute for
it) is once more brought to public view, by a late act against Dissenters, and Bill,
or an additional one, that we all hoped the wisdom of our rulers had long since
laid aside, as what was fitter to be passed into an act of perpetual oblivion. The
kingdoms are alarmed at this procedure, and thousands greatly at a stand,
wondering what should be the meaning of such hasty resolutions, that seem as
fatal as they were unexpected. Some ask what wrong they have done? Others,
what peace they have broken? and all, what plots they have formed to prejudice
the present government, or occasions given to hatch new jealousies of them and
their proceedings? being not conscious to themselves of guilt in any such respect.

For mine own part, I publicly confess myself to be a very hearty Dissenter
from the established worship of these nations, as believing Protestants to have
much degenerated from their first principles, and as owning the poor despised
Quakers, in life and doctrine, to have espoused the cause of God, and to be the
undoubted followers of Jesus Christ, in his most holy, strait, and narrow way, that
leads to the eternal rest. In all which I know no treason, nor any principle that

would urge me to a thought injurious to the civil peace. If any be defective in this particular, it is equal both individuals and whole societies should answer for their own defaults; but we are clear . . .

First, By Liberty of Conscience, we understand not only a mere Liberty of the Mind, in believing or disbelieving this or that principle or doctrine; but "the exercise of ourselves in a visible way of worship, upon our believing it to be indispensably required at our hands, that if we neglect it for fear or favor of any mortal man, we sin, and incur divine wrath." Yet we would be so understood to extend and justify the lawfulness of our so meeting to worship God, as not to contrive, or abet any contrivance destructive of the government and laws of the land, tending to matters of an external nature, directly or indirectly; but so far only as it may refer to religious matters, and a life to come, and consequently wholly independent of the secular affairs of this, wherein we are supposed to transgress.

Secondly, By imposition, restraint, and persecution, we do not only mean the strict requiring of us to believe this to be true, or that to be false; and upon refusal, to incur the penalties enacted in such cases; but by those terms we mean thus much, "any coercive let or hindrance to us, from meeting together to perform those religious exercises which are according to our faith and persuasion."

The question stated.

For proof of the aforesaid terms thus given, we singly state the question thus:

Whether imposition, restraint, and persecution, upon persons for exercising such a liberty of conscience as is before expressed, and so circumstantiated, be not to impeach the honor of God, the meekness of the Christian religion, the authority of Scripture, the privilege of nature, the principles of common reason, the well being of government, and apprehensions of the greatest personages of former and latter ages?

First, Then we say, that Imposition, Restraint, and Persecution, for matters relating to conscience, directly invade the divine prerogative, and divest the Almighty of a due, proper to none besides himself. And this we prove by these five particulars:

First, If we do allow the honor of our creation due to God only, and that no other besides himself has endowed us with those excellent gifts of Understanding, Reason, Judgment, and Faith, and consequently that he only is the object, as well as the author, both of our Faith, Worship, and Service; then whosoever shall interpose their authority to enact faith and worship in a way that seems not to us congruous with what he has discovered to us to be faith and worship (whose alone property it is to do it) or to restrain us from what we are persuaded is our indispensable duty, they evidently usurp this authority, and invade his incommunicable right of government over conscience: "For the Inspiration of the Almighty gives understanding: and faith is the gift of God," says the divine writ.

Secondly, Such magisterial determinations carry an evident claim to that infallibility, which Protestants have been hitherto so jealous of owning, that, to avoid the Papists, they have denied it to all but God himself.

Either they have forsook their old plea; or if not, we desire to know when, and where, they were invested with that divine excellency; and whether imposition, restraint, and persecution, were ever deemed by God the fruits of his Spirit. However, that itself was not sufficient; for unless it appears as well to us that they have it, as to them who have it, we cannot believe it upon any convincing evidence, but by tradition only, an anti-protestant way of believing.

Thirdly, It enthrones man as king over conscience, the alone just claim and privilege of his Creator; whose thoughts are not as men's thoughts, but has reserved to himself that empire from all the Caesars on earth: For if men, in reference to souls and bodies, things appertaining to this and the other world, shall be subject to their fellow-creatures, what follows, but that Caesar (however he got it) has all, God's share, and his own too? And being Lord of both, both are Caesar's, and not God's.

Fourthly, It defeats God's work of Grace, and the invisible operation of his eternal Spirit, (which can alone beget faith, and is only to be obeyed, in and about religion and worship) and attributes men's conformity to outward force and corporal punishments. A faith subject to as many revolutions as the powers that enact it.

Fifthly and lastly, Such persons assume the judgment of the great tribunal unto themselves; for to whomsoever men are imposedly or restrictively subject and accountable in matters of faith, worship and conscience; in them alone must the power of judgment reside; but it is equally true that God shall judge all by Jesus Christ, and that no man is so accountable to his fellow-creatures, as to be imposed upon, restrained, or persecuted for any matter of conscience whatever.

Thus, and in many more particulars, are men accustomed to intrench upon Divine Property, to gratify particular interests in the world; and (at best) through a misguided apprehension to imagine "they do God good service," that where they cannot give faith, they will use force; which kind of sacrifice is nothing less unreasonable that the other is abominable: God will not give his honor to another; and to him only, that searches the heart and tries the reins, it is our duty to ascribe the gifts of understanding and faith, without which none can please God.

RESOLUTION OF THE
GERMANTOWN MENNONITES

February 18, 1688

The first slaves had been brought to Jamestown, Virginia, in 1619, and slavery quickly spread in both the North and the South. Among the first to protest the institution of slavery were the Mennonites in Germantown, Pennsylvania, who on February 18, 1688, adopted the following resolution. The Mennonites were members of an evangelical Protestant sect, originating in Switzerland, Holland, and Germany during the sixteenth and seventeenth centuries. Because of religious persecution and economic problems at home, the Mennonites, Moravians, and other German minorities had migrated to Pennsylvania, known for its religious tolerance. They established the prosperous farms that are still part of the Pennsylvania landscape.

THESE are the reasons why we are against the traffic of men-body, as followeth: Is there any that would be done or handled at this manner? *viz.*, to be sold or made a slave for all the time of his life? How fearful and faint-hearted are many at sea, when they see a strange vessel, being afraid it should be a Turk, and they should be taken, and sold for slaves into Turkey. Now, what is this better done, than Turks do? Yea, rather is it worse for them, which they say are Christians; for we do hear that the most part of such negers are brought are brought hither against their will and consent, and that many of them are stolen. Now, though they be black, we cannot conceive there is more liberty to have them slaves, as it is to have other white ones. There is a saying, that we should do all men like as we will be done ourselves; making no difference of what generation, descent, or colour they are. And those who steal or rob men, and those who bury or purchase them, are they not all alike? Here is liberty of conscience, which is right and reasonable; here ought to be likewise liberty of the body, except of evil-doers, which is another case. But to bring men hither, or to rob or sell them against their will, we stand against. . . . Ah, do consider according to Christianity! . . . Pray, what thing in the world can be done worse towards us, than if men should rob or steal us away, and sell us for slaves to strange countries; separating husbands from wives and children. Being now this is not done in the manner we would be done at; therefore, we contradict, and are against this traffic of men-body. And we who profess that it is not lawful to steal, must likewise, avoid to purchase such things as are stolen, but rather help to stop this robbing and stealing. . . .

Now consider well this thing, if it is good or bad. And in case you find it to be good to handle these blacks in that manner, we desire and require you hereby lovingly, that you may inform us herein, which at this time was never done, *viz.*, that Christians have such a liberty to do so. To the end we shall be satisfied on this point and satisfy likewise our good friends and acquaintances in our native country, to whom it is a terror, or fearful thing, that men should be handled so in Pennsylvania.

This is from our meeting at Germantown, held ye 18th of the 2nd month, 1688, to be delivered to the monthly meeting at Richard Worrell's.

Garret Henderich, Derick Op De Graeff,
Francis Daniel Pastorius, Abram Op De Graeff.

PENN'S PLAN OF UNION

William Penn   *1697*

This is perhaps the earliest plan for union of the colonies; it was written by William Penn in 1697 and presented to the London Board of Trade. In 1699 Penn paid a second trip to Pennsylvania and, in his Charter of Liberties, surrendered to a single elected assembly the right to make laws for the colony. He returned to England in 1701. His last years were difficult ones involved in legal disputes about boundaries, and he even spent nine months in a debtor's prison.

A brief and plain scheme how the English colonies in the North parts of America,—*viz.*, Boston, Connecticut, Rhode Island, New York, New Jerseys, Pennsylvania, Maryland, Virginia, and Carolina,—may be made more useful to the crown and one another's peace and safety with an universal concurrence.

1. That the several colonies before mentioned do meet once a year, and

oftener if need be during the war, and at least once in two years in times of peace, by their stated and appointed deputies, to debate and resolve of such measures as are most advisable for their better understanding and the public tranquility and safety.

2. That, in order to it, two persons, well qualified for sense, sobriety, and substance, be appointed by each province as their representatives or deputies, which in the whole make the congress to consist of twenty persons.

3. That the king's commissioner, for that purpose specially appointed, shall have the chair and preside in the said congress.

4. That they shall meet as near as conveniently may be to the most central colony for ease of the deputies.

5. Since that may in all probability be New York, both because it is near the centre of the colonies and for that it is a frontier and in the king's nomination, the governor of that colony may therefore also be the king's high commissioner during the session, after the manner of Scotland.

6. That their business shall be to hear and adjust all matters of complaint or difference between province and province. As, 1st, where persons quit their own province and go to another, that they may avoid their just debts, though they be able to pay them; 2d, where offenders fly justice, or justice cannot well be had upon such offenders in the provinces that entertain them; 3d, to prevent or cure injuries in point of commerce; 4th, to consider the ways and means to support the union and safety of these provinces against the public enemies. In which congress the quotas of men and charges will be much easier and more equally set than it is possible for any establishment made here to do; for the provinces, knowing their own condition and one another's, can debate that matter with more freedom and satisfaction, and better adjust and balance their affairs in all respects for their common safety.

7. That, in times of war, the king's high commissioner shall be general or chief commander of the several quotas upon service against the common enemy, as he shall be advised, for the good and benefit of the whole.

THE ALBANY PLAN OF UNION

Benjamin Franklin   *1754*

The French and Indian War started in 1754, and for
nine years England and France fought for control of the North

American continent. In his autobiography, Benjamin Franklin described the preparation of a plan of union of the colonies as follows: "In 1754, War with France being again apprehended, a Congress of Commissioners from the different Colonies, was by an Order of the Lords of Trade, to be assembled at Albany, there to confer with the Chiefs of the Six Nations, concerning the Means of defending both their country and ours. . . . In our way thither, I projected and drew up a plan for the Union of all the colonies, under one government so far as might be necessary for Defense and other important general purposes. . . . A previous Question was first taken whether a Union should be established, which pass'd in the Affirmative unanimously. A Committee was then appointed one Member from each Colony, to consider the several Plans and report. Mine happen'd to be prefer'd, and with a few Amendments was accordingly reported. . . . The Plan was unanimously agreed to, and copies ordered to be transmitted to the Board of Trade and to the Assemblies of the several Provinces. Its fate was singular. The Assemblies did not adopt it as they all thought there were too much Prerogative in it; and in England it was judg'd to have too much of the Democratic. The Board of Trade therefore did not approve it."

———

IT is proposed that humble application be made for an act of Parliament of Great Britain by virtue of which one general government may be formed in America, including all the said colonies, within and under which government each colony may retain its present constitution, except in the particulars wherein a change may be directed by the said act, as hereafter follows.

1. That the said general government be administered by a president general, to be appointed and supported by the Crown; and a Grand Council, to be chosen by the representatives of the people of the several colonies met in their respective assemblies.

2. That within———months after the passing such act, the House of Representatives that happen to be sitting within that time, or that shall be especially for that purpose convened, may and shall choose members for the Grand Council, in the following proportion, that is to say:

Massachusetts Bay	7
New Hampshire	2
Connecticut	5
Rhode Island	2

New York	4
New Jerseys	3
Pennsylvania	6
Maryland	4
Virginia	7
North Carolina	4
South Carolina	4
	48

3.————who shall meet for the first time at the city of Philadelphia, being called by the president general as soon as conveniently may be after his appointment.

4. That there shall be a new election of the members of the Grand Council every three years; and, on the death or resignation of any member, his place shall be supplied by a new choice at the next sitting of the Assembly of the colony he represented.

5. That after the first three years, when the proportion of money arising out of each colony to the general treasury can be known, the number of members to be chosen for each colony shall, from time to time, in all ensuing elections, be regulated by that proportion, yet so as that the number to be chosen by any one province be not more than seven nor less than two.

6. That the Grand Council shall meet once in every year, and oftener if occasion require, at such time and place as they shall adjourn to at the last preceding meeting, or as they shall be called to meet at by the president general on any emergency; he having first obtained in writing the consent of seven of the members to such call and sent duly and timely notice to the whole.

7. That the Grand Council have power to choose their speaker; and shall neither be dissolved, prorogued, nor continued sitting longer than six weeks at one time, without their own consent or the special command of the Crown.

8. That the members of the Grand Council shall be allowed for their service ten shillings sterling per diem, during their session and journey to and from the place of meeting; twenty miles to be reckoned a day's journey.

9. That the assent of the president general be requisite to all acts of the Grand Council, and that it be his office and duty to cause them to be carried into execution.

10. That the president general, with the advice of the Grand Council, hold or direct all Indian treaties in which the general interest of the colonies may be concerned; and make peace or declare war with Indian nations.

11. That they make such laws as they judge necessary for regulating all Indian trade.

12. That they make all purchases from Indians, for the Crown, of lands not now within the bounds of particular colonies, or that shall not be within their bounds when some of them are reduced to more convenient dimensions.

13. That they make new settlements on such purchases by granting lands in the King's name, reserving a quitrent to the Crown for the use of the general treasury.

14. That they make laws for regulating and governing such new settlements, till the Crown shall think fit to form them into particular governments.

15. That they raise and pay soldiers and build forts for the defense of any of the colonies and equip vessels of force to guard the coasts and protect the trade on the ocean, lakes, or great rivers; but they shall not impress men in any colony without the consent of the legislature.

16. That for these purposes they have power to make laws and lay and levy such general duties, imposts, or taxes as to them shall appear most equal and just (considering the ability and other circumstances of the inhabitants in the several colonies), and such as may be collected with the least inconvenience to the people; rather discouraging luxury than loading industry with unnecessary burdens.

17. That they may appoint a general treasurer and particular treasurer in each government when necessary; and, from time to time, may order the sums in the treasuries of each government into the general treasury; or draw on them for special payments, as they find most convenient.

18. Yet no money to issue but by joint orders of the president general and Grand Council; except where sums have been appropriated to particular purposes and the president general is previously empowered by an act to draw for such sums.

19. That the general accounts shall be yearly settled and reported to the several assemblies.

20. That a quorum of the Grand Council, empowered to act with the president general, do consist of twenty-five members, among whom shall be one or more from a majority of the colonies.

21. That the laws made by them for the purposes aforesaid shall not be repugnant but, as near as may be, agreeable to the laws of England and shall be transmitted to the King in Council for approbation as soon as may be after their passing; and if not disapproved within three years after presentation, to remain in force.

22. That in case of the death of the president general, the speaker of the Grand Council for the time being shall succeed and be vested with the same powers and authorities, to continue till the King's pleasure be known.

23. That all military commission officers, whether for land or sea service, to act under this general constitution, shall be nominated by the president general; but the approbation of the Grand Council is to be obtained before they receive their commissions. And all civil officers are to be nominated by the Grand Council and to receive the president general's approbation before they officiate.

Benjamin Franklin, plaster bust, circa 1779-84, by Jean Jacques Caffiéri.

24. But in case of vacancy by death or removal of any officer, civil or military, under this constitution, the Governor of the province in which such vacancy happens may appoint, till the pleasure of the president general and Grand Council can be known.

25. That the particular military as well as civil establishments in each colony remain in their present state, the general constitution notwithstanding; and that on sudden emergencies any colony may defend itself and lay the accounts of expense thence arising before the president general and General Council, who may allow and order payment of the same, as far as they judge such accounts just and reasonable.

JOIN, or DIE.

II

THE AMERICAN REVOLUTION

RESOLUTIONS OF THE STAMP ACT CONGRESS

John Dickinson   *October 19, 1765*

On March 22, 1765, the British Parliament passed the Stamp Act, the first direct tax levied on the colonies. Every kind of legal document was required to have a tax stamp on it, and the cost of the stamps had to be paid in pounds sterling. All offenses against the Stamp Act were to be tried in an admiralty court, where the defendant would have no trial by jury. The Massachusetts House of Representatives sent a letter to the other colonies requesting a meeting in New York City to consult on the present state of the colonies, and nine colonies attended. John Dickinson of Pennsylvania is credited with drafting the following declaration, which was approved on October 19, 1765, and sent to the House of Commons. Parliament repealed the Stamp Act in March 1766. A major political figure and theorist, Dickinson was president of both Pennsylvania and Delaware at different times. His Letters from a Farmer in Pennsylvania to the Inhabitants of the British Colonies *were influential in England and America.*

THE members of this Congress, sincerely devoted with the warmest sentiments of affection and duty to His Majesty's person and Government, inviolably attached to the present happy establishment of the Protestant succession, and with minds deeply impressed by a sense of the present and impending misfortunes of the British colonies on this continent; having considered as maturely as time will permit the circumstances of the said colonies, esteem it our indispensable duty to make the following declarations of our humble opinion respecting the most essential rights and liberties of the colonists, and of the grievances under which they labour, by reason of several late Acts of Parliament.

I. That His Majesty's subjects in these colonies owe the same allegiance to the Crown of Great Britain that is owing from his subjects born within the realm, and all due subordination to that august body the Parliament of Great Britain.

II. That His Majesty's liege subjects in these colonies are intitled to all the inherent rights and liberties of his natural born subjects within the kingdom of Great Britain.

III. That it is inseparably essential to the freedom of a people, and the undoubted right of Englishmen, that no taxes be imposed on them but with their own consent, given personally or by their representatives.

IV. That the people of these colonies are not, and from their local circumstances cannot be, represented in the House of Commons in Great Britain.

V. That the only representatives of the people of these colonies are persons chosen therein by themselves, and that no taxes ever have been, or can be constitutionally imposed on them, but by their respective legislatures.

VI. That all supplies to the Crown being free gifts of the people, it is unreasonable and inconsistent with the principles and spirit of the British Constitution, for the people of Great Britain to grant to His Majesty the property of the colonists.

VII. That trial by jury is the inherent and invaluable right of every British subject in these colonies.

VIII. That the late Act of Parliament, entitled "An Act for granting and applying certain stamp duties, and other duties, in the British colonies and plantations in America, etc.," by imposing taxes on the inhabitants of these colonies; and the said Act, and several other Acts, by extending the jurisdiction of the courts of Admiralty beyond its ancient limits, have a manifest tendency to subvert the rights and liberties of the colonists.

IX. That the duties imposed by several late Acts of Parliament, from the peculiar circumstances of these colonies, will be extremely burthensome and grievous; and from the scarcity of specie, the payment of them absolutely impracticable.

X. That as the profits of the trade of these colonies ultimately center in Great Britain, to pay for the manufactures which they are obliged to take from thence, they eventually contribute very largely to all supplies granted there to the Crown.

XI. That the restrictions imposed by several late Acts of Parliament on the trade of these colonies will render them unable to purchase the manufactures of Great Britain.

XII. That the increase, prosperity, and happiness of these colonies depend on the full and free enjoyments of their rights and liberties, and an intercourse with Great Britain mutually affectionate and advantageous.

XIII. That it is the right of the British subjects in these colonies to petition the King or either House of Parliament.

Lastly, That it is the indispensable duty of these colonies to the best of sovereigns, to the mother country, and to themselves, to endeavour by a loyal and dutiful address to His Majesty, and humble applications to both Houses of Parliament, to procure the repeal of the Act for granting and applying certain stamp duties, of all clauses of any other Acts of Parliament, whereby the jurisdiction of the Admiralty is extended as aforesaid, and of the other late Acts for the restriction of American commerce.

THE ASSOCIATION

October 20, 1774

Most members of the first Continental Congress thought that a commercial boycott would cause the British government to listen to the demands of the colonies. On October 20, 1774, the Congress voted to not import or consume goods from, or export goods to, Great Britain, virtually cutting off trade with Britain.

WE, his majesty's most loyal subjects, the delegates of the several colonies of New-Hampshire, Massachusetts-Bay, Rhode-Island, Connecticut, New-York, New-Jersey, Pennsylvania, the three lower counties of Newcastle, Kent and Sussex on Delaware, Maryland, Virginia, North-Carolina, and South-Carolina, deputed to represent them in a continental Congress, held in the city of Philadelphia, on the 5th day of September, 1774, avowing our allegiance to his majesty, our affection and regard for our fellow-subjects in Great-Britain and elsewhere, affected with the deepest anxiety, and most alarming apprehensions, at those grievances and distresses, with which his Majesty's American subjects are oppressed; and having taken under our most serious deliberation, the state of the whole continent, find, that the present unhappy situation of our affairs is occasioned by a ruinous system of colony administration, adopted by the British ministry about the year 1763, evidently calculated for enslaving these colonies, and, with them, the British Empire. In prosecution of which system, various acts of parliament have been passed, for raising a revenue in America, for depriving the American subjects, in many instances, of the constitutional trial by jury, exposing their lives to danger, by directing a new and illegal trial beyond the seas, for crimes alleged to have been committed in America. And in prosecution of the same system, several late, cruel, and oppressive acts have been passed, respecting the town of Boston and the Massachusetts-Bay, and also an act for extending the province of Quebec, so as to border on the western frontiers of these colonies, establishing an arbitrary government therein, and discouraging the settlement of British subjects in that wide extended country; thus, by the influence of civil principles and ancient prejudices, to dispose the inhabitants to act with hostility against the free Protestant colonies, whenever a wicked ministry shall chuse so to direct them.

To obtain redress of these grievances, which threaten destruction to the lives, liberty, and property of his majesty's subjects, in North-America, we are of opinion, that a non-importation, non-consumption, and non-exportation agreement, faithfully adhered to, will prove the most speedy, effectual, and peaceable measure. And, therefore, we do, for ourselves, and the inhabitants of the several colonies, whom we represent, firmly agree and associate, under the sacred ties of virtue, honour and love of our country, as follows:

1. That from and after the first day of December next, we will not import, into British America, from Great-Britain or Ireland, any goods, wares, or merchandize whatsoever, or from any other place, any such goods, wares, or merchandize, as shall have been exported from Great-Britain or Ireland; nor will we, after that day, import any East-India tea from any part of the world; nor any molasses, syrups, paneles, coffee, or pimento, from the British plantations or from Dominica; nor wines from Madeira, or the Western Islands; nor foreign indigo.

2. We will neither import nor purchase, any slave imported after the first day of December next; after which time, we will wholly discontinue the slave trade, and will neither be concerned in it ourselves, nor will we hire our vessels,

nor sell our commodities or manufactures to those who are concerned in it.

3. As a non-consumption agreement, strictly adhered to, will be an effectual security for the observation of the non-importation, we, as above, solemnly agree and associate, that from this day, we will not purchase or use any tea, imported on account of the East-India company, or any on which a duty hath been or shall be paid; and from and after the first day of March next, we will not purchase or use any East-India tea whatever; nor will we, nor shall any person for or under us, purchase or use any of those goods, wares, or merchandize, we have agreed not to import, which we shall know, or have cause to suspect, were imported after the first day of December, except such as come under the rules and directions of the tenth article hereafter mentioned.

4. The earnest desire we have not to injure our fellow-subjects in Great-Britain, Ireland, or the West-Indies, induces us to suspect a non-exportation, until the tenth day of September, 1775; at which time, if the said acts and parts of acts of the British parliament herein after mentioned, are not repealed, we will not directly or indirectly, export any merchandize or commodity whatsoever to Great-Britain, Ireland, or the West-Indies, except rice to Europe.

5. Such as are merchants, and use the the British and Irish trade, will give orders, as soon as possible, to their factors, agents and correspondents, in Great-Britain and Ireland, not to ship any goods to them, on any pretence whatsoever, as they cannot be received in America; and if any merchant, residing in Great-Britain or Ireland, shall directly or indirectly ship any goods, wares or merchandize, for America, in order to break the said non-importation agreement, or in any manner contravene the same, on such unworthy conduct being well attested, it ought to be made public; and, on the same being so done, we will not, from thenceforth, have any commercial connexion with such merchant.

6. That such as are owners of vessels will give positive orders to their captains, or masters, not to receive on board their vessels any goods prohibited by the said non-importation agreement, on pain of immediate dismission from their service.

7. We will use our utmost endeavors to improve the breed of sheep, and increase their number to the greatest extent; and to that end, we will kill them as seldom as may be, especially those of the most profitable kind; nor will we export any to the West-Indies or elsewhere; and those of us, who are or may become overstocked with, or can conveniently spare any sheep, will dispose of them to our neighbours, especially to the poorer sort, on moderate terms.

8. We will, in our several stations, encourage frugality, economy, and industry, and promote agriculture, arts and the manufactures of this country, especially that of wool; and will discountenance and discourage every species of extravagance and dissipation, especially all horse-racing, and all kinds of

gaming, cock fighting, exhibitions of shews, plays, and other expensive diversions and entertainments; and on the death of any relation or friend, none of us, or any of our families will go into any further mourning-dress, than a black crape or ribbon on the arm or hat, for gentlemen, and a black ribbon and necklace for ladies, and we will discontinue the giving of gloves and scarves at funerals.

9. Such as are venders of goods or merchandize will not take advantage of the scarcity of goods, that may be occasioned by this association, but will sell the same at the rates we have been respectively accustomed to do, for twelve months last past. —And if any vendor of goods or merchandize shall sell such goods on higher terms, or shall, in any manner, or by any device whatsoever, violate or depart from this agreement, no person ought, nor will any of us deal with any such person, or his or her factor or agent, at any time thereafter, for any commodity whatever.

10. In case any merchant, trader, or other person, shall import any goods or merchandize, after the first day of December, and before the first day of February next, the same ought forthwith, at the election of the owner, to be either re-shipped or delivered up to the committee of the country or town, wherein they shall be imported, to be stored at the risque of the importer, until the non-importation agreement shall cease, or be sold under the direction of the committee aforesaid; and in the last-mentioned case, the owner or owners of such goods shall be reimbursed out of the sales, the first cost and charges, the profit, if any, to be applied towards relieving and employing such poor inhabitants of the town of Boston, as are immediate sufferers by the Boston port-bill; and a particular account of all goods so returned, stored, or sold, to be inserted in the public papers; and if any goods or merchandizes shall be imported after the said first day of February, the same ought forthwith to be sent back again, without breaking any of the packages thereof.

11. That a committee be chosen in every county, city, and town, by those who are qualified to vote for representatives in the legislature, whose business it shall be attentively to observe the conduct of all persons touching this association; and when it shall be made to appear, to the satisfaction of a majority of any such committee, that any person within the limits of their appointment has violated this association, that such majority do forthwith cause the truth of the case to be published in the gazette; to the end, that all such foes to the rights of British-America may be publicly known, and universally condemned as the enemies of American liberty; and thenceforth we respectively will break off all dealings with him or her.

12. That the committee of correspondence, in the respective colonies, do frequently inspect the entries of their customhouses, and inform each other, from

time to time, of the true state thereof, and of every other material circumstance that may occur relative to this association.

13. That all manufactures of this country be sold at reasonable prices, so that no undue advantage be taken of a future scarcity of goods.

14. And we do further agree and resolve, that we will have no trade, commerce, dealings or intercourse whatsoever, with any colony or province, in North-America, which shall not accede to, or which shall hereafter violate this association, but will hold them as unworthy of the rights of freemen, and as inimical to the liberties of their country.

And we do solemnly bind ourselves and our constituents, under the ties aforesaid, to adhere to this association, until such parts of the several acts of parliament passed since the close of the last war, as impose or continue duties on tea, wine, molasses, syrups, paneles, coffee, sugar, pimento, indigo, foreign paper, glass, and painters' colours, imported into America, and extend the powers of the admiralty courts beyond their ancient limits, deprive the American subject of trial by jury, authorize the judge's certificate to indemnify the prosecutor from damages, that he might otherwise be liable to from a trial by his peers, require oppressive security from a claimant of ships or goods seized, before he shall be allowed to defend his property, are repealed. —And until that part of the act . . . entitled, "An act for the better securing his majesty's dock-yards, magazines, ships, ammunition, and stores," by which any persons charged with committing any of the offences therein described, in America, may be tried in any shire or county within the realm, is repealed—and until the four acts, passed the last session of parliament, *viz.* that for stopping the port and blocking up the harbour of Boston—that for altering the charter and government of the Massachusetts-Bay—and that which is entitled "An act for the better administration of justice, etc."—and that "for extending the limits of Quebec, etc." are repealed. And we recommend it to the provincial conventions, and to the committees in the respective colonies, to establish such farther regulations as they may think proper, for carrying into execution this association.

The foregoing association being determined upon by the Congress, was ordered to be subscribed by the several members thereof; and thereupon, we have hereunto set our respective names accordingly.

In Congress, Philadelphia, October 20, 1774.

Signed, Peyton Randolph, President.

SPEECH IN VIRGINIA CONVENTION

Patrick Henry   *March 23, 1775*

Perhaps the most famous speech in the eighteenth century was Patrick Henry's speech in the Virginia Convention of Delegates on March 23, 1775. Henry, a brilliant lawyer as well as an outstanding orator, was a Member of the House of Burgesses and a spokesman for the frontier communities. Ten years earlier, in reaction to the Stamp Act, he had introduced seven resolutions, one of which claimed that Virginia had complete legislative autonomy. Later Patrick Henry was a delegate to the first Continental Congress and was twice elected governor of Virginia. Henry opposed the Constitution on the grounds of states' rights, and was probably as responsible as anyone for the adoption of the first ten amendments to the Constitution, the Bill of Rights.

[MR. PRESIDENT:] No man thinks more highly than I do of the patriotism, as well as abilities, of the very worthy gentlemen who have just addressed the house. But different men often see the same subjects in different lights; and, therefore, I hope it will not be thought disrespectful to those gentlemen, if, entertaining as I do, opinions of a character very opposite to theirs, I shall speak forth my sentiments freely, and without reserve. This is no time for ceremony. The question before the house is one of awful moment to this country. For my own part, I consider it as nothing less than a question of freedom or slavery. And in proportion to the magnitude of the subject, ought to be the freedom of the debate. It is only in this way that we can hope to arrive at truth, and fulfill the great responsibility which we hold to God and our country. Should I keep back my opinions at such a time, through fear of giving offense, I should consider myself as guilty of treason towards my country, and of an act of disloyalty towards the majesty of Heaven, which I revere above all earthly kings.

Mr. President, it is natural to man to indulge in the illusions of hope. We are apt to shut our eyes against a painful truth and listen to the song of that siren, till she transforms us into beasts. Is this the part of wise men, engaged in a great and arduous struggle for liberty? Are we disposed to be of the number of those who, having eyes, see not, and having ears, hear not, the things which so nearly concern their temporal salvation? For my part, whatever anguish of spirit it may cost, I am willing to know the whole truth; to know the worst, and to provide for it.

I have but one lamp by which my feet are guided; and that is the lamp of experience. I know of no way of judging of the future but by the past. And judging by the past, I wish to know what there has been in the conduct of the British ministry for the last ten years, to justify those hopes with which gentlemen have been pleased to solace themselves and the house? Is it that insidious smile with which our petition has been lately received? Trust it not, sir; it will prove a snare to your feet. Suffer not yourselves to be betrayed with a kiss. Ask yourselves how this gracious reception of our petition comports with those warlike preparations which cover our waters and darken our land. Are fleets and armies necessary to a work of love and reconciliation? Have we shown ourselves so unwilling to be reconciled, that force must be called in to win back our love? Let us not deceive ourselves, sir. These are the implements of war and subjugation, the last arguments to which kings resort.

I ask gentlemen, sir, what means this martial array, if its purpose be not to force us to submission? Can gentlemen assign any other possible motive for it? Has Great Britain any enemy in this quarter of the world, to call for all this accumulation of navies and armies? No, sir, she has none. They are meant for us; they can be meant for no other. They are sent over to bind and rivet upon us those chains, which the British ministry have been so long forging. And what have we to oppose to them? Shall we try argument? Sir, we have been trying that for the last ten years. Have we anything new to offer upon the subject? Nothing. We have held the subject up in every light of which it is capable; but it has been all in vain. Shall we resort to entreaty and humble supplication? What terms shall we find, which have not been already exhausted? Let us not, I beseech you, sir, deceive ourselves longer. Sir, we have done every thing that could be done, to avert the storm which is now coming on. We have petitioned, we have remonstrated, we have supplicated, we have prostrated ourselves before the throne, and have implored its interposition to arrest the tyrannical hands of the ministry and parliament. Our petitions have been slighted; our remonstrances have produced additional violence and insult; our supplications have been disregarded; and we have been spurned, with contempt, from the foot of the throne. In vain, after these things, may we indulge the fond hope of peace and reconciliation. There is no longer any room for hope. If we wish to be free, if we mean to preserve inviolate those inestimable privileges for which we have been so long contending, if we mean not basely to abandon the noble struggle in which we have been so long engaged, and which we have pledged ourselves never to abandon, until the glorious object of our contest shall be obtained, we must fight!—I repeat it, sir, we must fight!! An appeal to arms and to the God of Hosts is all that is left us!

They tell us, sir, that we are weak, unable to cope with so formidable an adversary. But when shall we be stronger? Will it be the next week or the next year? Will it be when we are totally disarmed, and when a British guard shall be stationed in every house? Shall we gather strength by irresolution and inaction? Shall we acquire the means of effectual resistance by lying supinely on our backs, and hugging the delusive phantom of hope, until our enemies shall have bound us hand and foot? Sir, we are not weak, if we make a proper use of the means which the God of nature hath placed in our power. Three millions of people, armed in the holy cause of liberty, and in such a country as that which we possess, are invincible by any force which our enemy can send against us. Besides, sir, we shall not fight our battles alone. There is a just God who presides over the destinies of nations, and who will raise up friends to fight our battles for us. The battle, sir, is not to the strong alone; it is to the vigilant, the active, the brave. Besides, sir, we have no election. If we were base enough to desire it, it is now too late to retire from the contest. There is no retreat, but in submission and slavery! Our chains are forged! Their clanking may be heard on the plains of Boston! The war is inevitable—and let it come!! I repeat it, sir, let it come!!!

It is in vain, sir, to extenuate the matter. Gentlemen may cry, peace, peace—but there is no peace. The war is actually begun! The next gale that sweeps from the north will bring to our ears the clash of resounding arms! Our brethren are already in the field! Why stand we here idle? What is it that gentlemen wish? What would they have? Is life so dear, or peace so sweet, as to be purchased at the price of chains and slavery? Forbid it, Almighty God! I know not what course others may take; but as for me, give me liberty, or give me death!

THE BATTLES OF LEXINGTON AND CONCORD

Joseph Warren   *April 26, 1775*

> *This account of the battles of Lexington and Concord*
> *was written by Joseph Warren, president of the Massachusetts*
> *Provincial Congress. A successful doctor, he was also a gifted*
> *orator and political writer. Warren succeeded Samuel Adams as*
> *the head of the committee of safety and sent his friend Paul*
> *Revere to warn the countryside of the British approach. Warren*

*was head of the committee to organize the army in Massachu-
setts and was elected major general of the militia. Volunteering
to serve at Bunker Hill where a battle was about to start, he was
killed on Breed's Hill on June 17, 1775, at age thirty-four, one
of the first casualties of the war.*

FRIENDS and Fellow Subjects:

Hostilities are at length commenced in this colony by the troops under the command of General Gage, and it being of the greatest importance, that an early, true, and authentic account of this inhuman proceeding should be known to you, the Congress of this colony have transmitted the same, and from want of a session of the honorable Continental Congress, think it proper to address you on the alarming occasion.

By the clearest depositions relative to this transaction, it will appear that on the night preceding the 19th of April instant, a body of the King's troops, under the command of Colonel Smith, were secretly landed at Cambridge, with an apparent design to take or destroy the military and other stores provided for the defense of this colony, and deposited at Concord; that some inhabitants of the colony, on the night aforesaid, whilst traveling peaceably on the road between Boston and Concord were seized and greatly abused by armed men, who appeared to be officers of General Gage's army; that the town of Lexington, by these means, was alarmed, and a company of the inhabitants mustered on the occasion; that the regular troops on their way to Concord marched into the said town of Lexington, and the said company, on their approach, began to disperse; that, notwithstanding this, the regulars rushed on with great violence and first began hostilities by firing on said Lexington company, where they killed eight, and wounded several others; that the regulars continued their fire, until those of said company, who were neither killed nor wounded, had made their escape; that Colonel Smith, with the detachment, then marched to Concord, where a number of provincials were again fired on by the troops, two of them killed and several wounded before the provincials fired on them, and that these hostile measures of the troops, produced an engagement that lasted through the day, in which many of the provincials and more of the regular troops were killed and wounded.

To give a particular account of the ravages of the troops as they retreated from Concord to Charlestown would be very difficult, if not impracticable. Let it suffice to say that a great number of the houses on the road were plundered and rendered unfit for use, several were burned, women in childbed were driven by the soldiery naked into the streets, old men peaceably in their houses were shot dead, and such scenes exhibited as would disgrace the annals of the most uncivilized nation.

These, brethren, are marks of ministerial vengeance against this colony for refusing, with her sister colonies, a submission to slavery; but they have not yet detached us from our royal sovereign. We profess to be his loyal and dutiful subjects, and, so hardly dealt with as we have been, are still ready, with our lives and fortunes, to defend his person, family, Crown, and dignity. Nevertheless, to the persecution and tyranny of his cruel Ministry we will not tamely submit— appealing to Heaven for the justice of our cause, we determine to die or be free.

We cannot think that the honor, wisdom, and valor of Britons will suffer them to be largely inactive spectators of measures in which they themselves are so deeply interested—measures pursued in opposition to the solemn protests of many noble lords and expressed sense of conspicuous commoners whose knowledge and virtue have long characterized them as some of the greatest men in the nation; measures executed contrary to the interest, petitions, and resolves of many large, respectable, and opulent counties, cities, and boroughs in Great Britain; measures highly incompatible with justice, but still pursued with a specious pretense of easing the nation of its burdens; measures which, if successful, must end in the ruin and slavery of Britain, as well as the persecuted American colonies.

We sincerely hope that the Great Sovereign of the universe, who has so often appeared for the English nation, will support you in every rational and manly exertion with these colonies for saving it from ruin, and that, in a constitutional connection with the mother country, we shall soon be together a free and happy people.

By order,

Joseph Warren, President

LETTER TO JOHN ADAMS AND RESPONSE

Abigail Smith Adams was the wife of John Adams, the second president of the United States. Although she lacked formal education, she was an avid reader of the classics and history. From 1774, when John attended the first Continental Congress in Philadelphia, throughout the next decade, Abigail raised the children and cared for the family's farm and house-

hold. After the Revolutionary War, the family spent five years in Europe, where John held various diplomatic posts. Abigail ran many of the family's business affairs during the twelve years when her husband was vice-president under Washington and then president. Abigail Adams wrote often to her husband and "dear friend" during their frequent separations.

Abigail Adams to John Adams
March 31, 1776

I wish you would ever write me a Letter half as long as I write you; and tell me if you may where your Fleet are gone? What sort of Defence Virginia can make against our common Enemy? Whether it is so situated as to make an able Defence? Are not the Gentry Lords and the common people vassals, are they not like the uncivilized Natives Brittain represents us to be? I hope their Riffel Men who have shewen themselves very savage and even Blood thirsty; are not a specimen of the Generality of the people.

I am willing to allow the Colony great merrit for having produced a Washington but they have been shamefully duped by a Dunmore.

I have sometimes been ready to think that the passion for Liberty cannot be Equally Strong in the Breasts of those who have been accustomed to deprive their fellow Creatures of theirs. Of this I am certain that it is not founded upon that generous and christian principal of doing to others as we would that others should do unto us.

Do not you want to see Boston; I am fearfull of the small pox, or I should have been in before this time. I got Mr. Crane to go to our House and see what state it was in. I find it has been occupied by one of the Doctors of a Regiment, very dirty, but no other damage has been done to it. The few things which were left in it are all gone. Cranch has the key which he never deliverd up. I have wrote to him for it and am determined to get it cleand as soon as possible and shut it up. I look upon it a new acquisition of property, a property which one month ago I did not value at a single Shilling, and could with pleasure have seen it in flames.

The Town in General is left in a better state than we expected, more oweing to a percipitate flight than any Regard to the inhabitants, tho some individuals discoverd a sense of honour and justice and have left the rent of the Houses in which they were, for the owners and the furniture unhurt, or if damaged sufficent to make it good.

Others have committed abominable Ravages. The Mansion House of your

President is safe and the furniture unhurt whilst both the House and Furniture of the Solisiter General have fallen a prey to their own merciless party. Surely the very Fiends feel a Reverential awe for Virtue and patriotism, whilst they Detest the paricide and traitor.

I feel very differently at the approach of spring to what I did a month ago. We knew not then whether we could plant or sow with safety, whether when we had toiled we could reap the fruits of our own industry, whether we could rest in our own Cottages, or whether we should not be driven from the sea coasts to seek shelter in the wilderness, but now we feel as if we might sit under our own vine and eat the good of the land.

I feel *a gaieti de Coar* to which before I was a stranger. I think the Sun looks brighter, the Birds sing more melodiously, and Nature puts on a more chearfull countanance. We feel a temporary peace, and the poor fugitives are returning to their deserted habitations.

Tho we felicitate ourselves, we sympathize with those who are trembling least the Lot of Boston should be theirs. But they cannot be in similar circumstances unless pusilanimity and cowardise should take possession of them. They have time and warning given them to see the Evil and shun it.—I long to hear that you have declared an independancy—and by the way in the new Code of Laws which I suppose it will be necessary for you to make, I desire you would Remember the Ladies, and be more generous and favourable to them than your ancestors. Do not put such unlimited power into the hands of the Husbands. Remember all Men would be tyrants if they could. If perticuliar care and attention is not paid to the Ladies we are determined to foment a Rebelion, and will not hold ourselves bound by any Laws in which we have no voice, or Representation.

That your Sex are Naturally Tyrannical is a Truth so thoroughly established as to admit of no dispute, but such of you as wish to be happy willingly give up the harsh title of Master for the more tender and endearing one of Friend. Why then, not put it out of the power of the vicious and the Lawless to use us with cruelty and indignity with impunity. Men of Sense in all Ages abhor those customs which treat us only as the vassals of your Sex. Regard us then as Beings placed by providence under your protection and in imitation of the Supreem Being make use of that power only for our happiness.

John Adams to Abigail Adams
April 14, 1776

You justly complain of my short Letters, but the critical State of Things and the Multiplicity of Avocations must plead my Excuse.—You ask where the Fleet is. The inclosed Papers will inform you. You ask what Sort of Defence Virginia can make. I believe they will make an able Defence. Their Militia and minute Men have been some time employed in training themselves, and they have Nine Battallions of regulars as they call them, maintained among them, under good Officers, at the Continental Expence. They have set up a Number of Manufactories of Fire Arms, which are busily employed. They are tolerably supplied with Powder, and are successfull and assiduous, in making Salt Petre. Their neighbouring Sister or rather Daughter Colony of North Carolina, which is a warlike Colony, and has several Battallions at the Continental Expence, as well as a pretty good Militia, are ready to assist them, and they are in very good Spirits, and seem determined to make a brave Resistance.—The Gentry are very rich, and the common People very poor. This Inequality of Property, gives an Aristocratical Turn to all their Proceedings, and occasions a strong Aversion in their Patricians, to Common Sense. But the Spirit of these Barons, is coming down, and it must submit.

John Adams, portrait by John Trumbull, 1793.

It is very true, as you observe they have duped by Dunmore. But this is a Common Case. All the Colonies are duped, more or less, at one Time and another. A more egregious Bubble was never blown up, than the Story of Commissioners coming to treat with the Congress. Yet it has gained Credit like a Charm, not only without but against the clearest Evidence. I never shall forget the Delusion, which seized our best and most sagacious Friends the dear Inhabitants of Boston, the Winter before last. Credulity and the Want of Foresight, are Imperfections in the human Character, that no Politician can sufficiently guard against.

You have given me some Pleasure, by your Account of a certain House in Queen Street. I had burned it, long ago, in Imagination. It rises now to my View like a Phoenix.—What shall I say of the Solicitor General? I pity his pretty Children, I pity his Father, and his sisters. I wish I could be clear that it is no moral Evil to pity him and his Lady. Upon Repentance they will certainly have a large Share in the Compassions of many. But let Us take Warning and give it to our Children. Whenever Vanity, and Gaiety, a Love of Pomp and Dress, Furniture, Equipage, Buildings, great Company, expensive Diversions, and elegant Entertainments get the better of the Principles and Judgments of Men or Women there is no knowing where they will stop, nor into what Evils, natural, moral, or political, they will lead us.

Your Description of your own *Gaiety de Coeur*, charms me. Thanks be to God you have just Cause to rejoice—and may the bright Prospect be obscured by no Cloud.

As to Declarations of Independency, be patient. Read our Privateering Laws, and our Commercial Laws. What signifies a Word.

As to your extraordinary Code of Laws, I cannot but laugh. We have been told that our Struggle has loosened the bands of Government every where. That Children and Apprentices were disobedient—that schools and Colledges were grown turbulent—that Indians slighted their Guardians and Negroes grew insolent to their Masters. But your Letter was the first Intimation that another Tribe more numerous and powerfull than all the rest were grown discontented.—This is rather too coarse a Compliment but you are so saucy, I wont blot it out.

Depend upon it, We know better than to repeal our Masculine systems. Altho they are in full Force, you know they are little more than Theory. We dare not exert our Power in its full Latitude. We are obliged to go fair, and softly, and in Practice you know We are the subjects. We have only the Name of Masters, and rather than give up this, which would compleatly subject Us to the Despotism of the Peticoat, I hope General Washington, and all our brave Heroes would fight. I am sure every good Politician would plot, as long as he would against Despotism, Empire, Monarchy, Aristocracy, Oligarchy, or Ochlocracy.—A fine Story indeed. I begin to think the Ministry as deep as they are wicked. After stirring up Tories, Landjobbers, Trimmers, Bigots, Canadians, Indians, Negroes, Hanoverians, Hessians, Russians, Irish Roman Catholicks, Scotch Renegadoes, at last they have stimulated them to demand new Priviledges and threaten to rebell.

THE VIRGINIA BILL OF RIGHTS

George Mason   *June 12, 1776*

George Mason was a neighbor of George Washington, and like Jefferson, a believer in the rights of the common man. A signer of the Declaration of Independence, he also attended the Constitutional Convention and was an active participant. Mason drafted a Virginia Bill of Rights on June 12, 1776, and it was adopted with slight changes by the Virginia Convention. This document was very important; it influenced Jefferson in the writing of the Declaration of Independence and was the basis of the Bill of Rights.

A declaration of rights made by the representatives of the good people of Virginia, assembled in full and free convention; which rights do pertain to them and their posterity, as the basis and foundation of government.

1. That all men are by nature equally free and independent, and have certain inherent rights, of which, when they enter into a state of society, they cannot by any compact deprive or divest their posterity; namely, the enjoyment of life and liberty, with the means of acquiring and possessing property, and pursuing and obtaining happiness and safety.

2. That all power is vested in, and consequently derived from, the people; that magistrates are their trustees and servants, and at all times amenable to them.

3. That government is, or ought to be instituted for the common benefit, protection, and security of the people, nation, or community; of all the various modes and forms of government, that is best which is capable of producing the greatest degree of happiness and safety, and is most effectually secured against the danger of maladministration; and that when any government shall be found inadequate or contrary to these purposes, a majority of the community hath an indubitable, unalienable and indefeasible right to reform, alter or abolish it, in such manner as shall be judged most conducive to the public weal.

4. That no man, or set of men, are entitled to exclusive or separate emoluments or privileges from the community, but in consideration of publick services; which, not being descendible, neither ought the offices of magistrate, legislator or judge to be hereditary.

5. That the legislative and executive powers of the state should be separate and distinct from the judiciary; and that the members of the two first may be restrained from oppression, by feeling and participating the burthens of the people, they should, at fixed periods, be reduced to a private station, return into that body from which they were originally taken, and the vacancies be supplied by frequent, certain, and regular elections, in which all, or any part of the former members to be again eligible or ineligible, as the laws shall direct.

6. That elections of members to serve as representatives of the people in assembly, ought to be free; and that all men having sufficient evidence of permanent common interest with, and attachment to the community, have the right of suffrage, and cannot be taxed or deprived of their property for publick uses, without their own consent, or that of their representatives so elected, nor bound by any law to which they have not, in like manner, assented for the public good.

7. That all power of suspending laws, or the execution of laws, by any authority without consent of the representatives of the people, is injurious to their rights, and ought not to be exercised.

8. That in all capital or criminal prosecutions a man hath a right to demand the cause and nature of his accusation, to be confronted with the accusers and witnesses, to call for evidence in his favour, and to a speedy trial by an impartial jury of his vicinage, without whose unanimous consent he cannot be found guilty; nor can he be compelled to give evidence against himself; that no man be deprived of his liberty, except by the law of the land or the judgment of his peers.

9. That excessive bail ought not to be required, nor excessive fines imposed, nor cruel and unusual punishments inflicted.

10. That general warrants, whereby an officer or messenger may be commanded to search suspected places without evidence of a fact committed, or to seize any person or persons not named, or whose offense is not particularly described and supported by evidence, are grievous and oppressive, and ought not to be granted.

11. That in controversies respecting property, and in suits between man and man, the ancient trial by jury is preferable to any other, and ought to be held sacred.

12. That the freedom of the press is one of the great bulwarks of liberty, and can never be restrained but by despotick governments.

13. That a well-regulated militia, composed of the body of the people trained to arms, is the proper, natural and safe defence of a free state; that standing armies in time of peace should be avoided as dangerous to liberty; and that in all cases the military should be under strict subordination to, and governed by, the civil power.

14. That the people have a right to uniform government; and, therefore, that no government separate from, or independent of the government of Virginia, ought to be erected or established within the limits thereof.

15. That no free government, or the blessings of liberty, can be preserved to any people, but by a firm adherence to justice, moderation, temperance, frugality and virtue and by frequent recurrence to fundamental principles.

16. That religion, or the duty which we owe to our Creator, and the manner of discharging it, can be directed only by reason and conviction, not by force or violence; and therefore all men are equally entitled to the free exercise of religion, according to the dictates of conscience; and that it is the mutual duty of all to practice Christian forbearance, love, and charity towards each other.

THE DECLARATION OF INDEPENDENCE

Thomas Jefferson   *July 4, 1776*

At the second Continental Congress, Richard Henry Lee of Virginia moved a resolution for independence which was seconded by John Adams and passed. On June 11, 1776, a committee was appointed by the Congress to draft a statement on the reasons for separation from England. The committee included John Adams, Benjamin Franklin, Thomas Jefferson, Robert Livingston, and Roger Sherman, but it was Jefferson who prepared a first draft and submitted it to the others for review. Minor changes were made by the other members of the committee, and further changes were made after it was presented to the Congress on June 28. The words remain largely those of Jefferson. The Declaration was adopted by the Continental Congress on July 4 and four days later read to the city of Philadelphia. Copies were made and sent to the legislatures of the colonies and the army, and were published widely.

THE UNANIMOUS DECLARATION OF THE
THIRTEEN UNITED STATES OF AMERICA

WHEN in the Course of human events, it becomes necessary for one people to dissolve the political bands which have connected them with another, and to assume among the Powers of the earth, the separate and equal nation to which the Laws of Nature and of Nature's God entitle them, a decent respect to the opinions of mankind requires that they should declare the causes which impel them to the separation.

We hold these truths to be self-evident, that all men are created equal, that they are endowed by their Creator with certain unalienable Rights, that among these are Life, Liberty and the pursuit of Happiness. That to secure these rights, Governments are instituted among Men, deriving their just powers from the consent of the governed, That whenever any Form of Government becomes destructive of these ends, it is the Right of the People to alter or to abolish it, and to institute new Government, laying its foundation on such principles and organizing its powers in such form, as to them shall seem most likely to effect their Safety and Happiness. Prudence, indeed, will dictate that Governments long established should not be changed for light and transient causes; and accordingly all experience hath shown, that mankind are more disposed to suffer, while evils are sufferable, than to right themselves by abolishing the forms to which they are accustomed. But when a long train of abuses and usurpations, pursuing invariably the same Object evinces a design to reduce them under absolute Despotism, it is their right, it is their duty, to throw off such Government, and to provide new Guards for their future security. —Such has been the patient sufferance of these Colonies; and such is now the necessity which constrains them to alter their former Systems of Government. The history of the present King of Great Britain is a history of repeated injuries and usurpations, all having in direct object the establishment of an absolute Tyranny over these States. To prove this, let Facts be submitted to a candid world.

He has refused his Assent to Laws, the most wholesome and necessary for the public good.

He has forbidden his Governors to pass Laws of immediate and pressing importance, unless suspended in their operation till his Assent should be obtained; and when so suspended, he has utterly neglected to attend to them.

He has refused to pass other Laws for the accommodation of large districts of people, unless those people would relinquish the right of Representation in the Legislature, a right inestimable to them and formidable to tyrants only.

He has called together legislative bodies at places unusual, uncomfortable, and distant from the depository of their Public Records, for the sole purpose of fatiguing them into compliance with his measures.

He has dissolved Representative Houses repeatedly, for opposing with manly firmness his invasions on the rights of the people.

He has refused for a long time, after such dissolutions, to cause others to be elected; whereby the Legislative Powers, incapable of Annihilation, have returned to the People at large for their exercise; the State remaining in the mean time exposed to all the dangers of invasion from without, and convulsions within.

He has endeavored to prevent the population of these States; for that purpose obstructing the Laws of Naturalization of Foreigners; refusing to pass others to encourage their migration hither, and raising the conditions of new Appropriations of Lands.

He has obstructed the Administration of Justice, by refusing his Assent to Laws for establishing Judiciary Powers.

He has made Judges dependent on his Will alone, for the tenure of their offices, and the amount and payment of their salaries.

He has erected a multitude of New Offices, and sent hither swarms of

Officers to harass our People, and eat out their substance.

He has kept among us, in times of peace, Standing Armies without the Consent of our legislature.

He has affected to render the Military independent of and superior to the Civil Power.

He has combined with others to subject us to a jurisdiction foreign to our constitution, and unacknowledged by our laws; giving his Assent to their acts of pretended legislation:

For quartering large bodies of armed troops among us:

For protecting them, by a mock Trial, from Punishment for any Murders which they should commit on the Inhabitants of these States:

For cutting off our Trade with all parts of the world:

For imposing taxes on us without our Consent:

For depriving us in many cases, of the benefits of Trial by Jury:

For transporting us beyond Seas to be tried for pretended offences:

For abolishing the free System of English Laws in a neighboring Province, establishing therein an Arbitrary government, and enlarging its Boundaries so as to render it at once an example and fit instrument for introducing the same absolute rule into these Colonies:

For taking away our Charters, abolishing our most valuable Laws, and altering fundamentally the Forms of our Governments:

For suspending our own Legislature, and declaring themselves invested with Power to legislate for us in all cases whatsoever.

He has abdicated Government here, by declaring us out of his Protection and waging War against us.

He has plundered our seas, ravaged our Coasts, burnt our towns, and destroyed the lives of our people.

He is at this time transporting large armies of foreign mercenaries to compleat the works of death, desolation and tyranny, already begun with circumstances of Cruelty and perfidy scarcely paralleled in the most barbarous ages, and totally unworthy the Head of a civilized nation.

He has constrained our fellow Citizens taken Captive on the high Seas to bear Arms against their Country, to become the executioners of their friends and Brethren, or to fall themselves by their Hands.

He has excited domestic insurrections amongst us, and has endeavored to bring on the inhabitants of our frontiers, the merciless Indian Savages, whose known rule of warfare, is an undistinguished destruction of all ages, sexes and conditions.

In every stage of these Oppressions We have Petitioned for Redress in the most humble terms: Our repeated Petitions have been answered only by repeated injury. A Prince, whose character is thus marked by every act which may define a Tyrant, is unfit to be the ruler of a free People.

Nor have We been wanting in attention to our Brittish brethren. We have warned them from time to time of attempts by their legislature to extend an unwarrantable jurisdiction over us. We have reminded them of the circumstances of our emigration and settlement here. We have appealed to their native justice and magnanimity, and we have conjured them by the ties of our common kindred to disavow these usurpations, which, would inevitably interrupt our connections and correspondence. They too have been deaf to the voice of justice and of consanguinity. We must, therefore, acquiesce in the necessity, which denounces our Separation, and hold them, as we hold the rest of mankind, Enemies in War, in Peace Friends.

We, therefore, the Representatives of the United States of America, in General Congress, Assembled, appealing to the Supreme Judge of the world for the rectitude of our intentions, do, in the Name, and by Authority of the good People of these colonies, solemnly publish and declare, That these United Colonies are, and of Right ought to be Free and Independent States; that they are absolved from all Allegiance to the British Crown, and that all political connection between them and the State of Great Britain, is and ought to be totally dissolved; and that as Free and Independent States, they have full Power to levy War, conclude Peace, contract Alliances, establish Commerce, and to do all other Acts and Things which Independent States may of right do. And for the support of this Declaration, with a firm reliance on the Protection of Divine Providence, we mutually pledge to each other our Lives, our Fortunes and our sacred Honor.

JOHN HANCOCK, President

New Hampshire
    Josiah Bartlett,
    Wm. Whipple,
    Matthew Thornton.

Massachusetts-Bay
    Saml. Adams,
    John Adams,
    Robt. Treat Paine,
    Elbridge Gerry.

Rhode Island
    Step. Hopkins,
    William Ellery.

New York
    Wm. Floyd,
    Phil. Livingston,
    Frans. Lewis,
    Lewis Morris.

Pennsylvania
    Robt. Morris,
    Benjamin Rush,
    Benja. Franklin,
    John Morton,
    Geo. Clymer,
    Jas. Smith,
    Geo. Taylor,
    James Wilson,
    Geo. Ross.

Connecticut
> Roger Sherman,
> Sam'el Huntington,
> Wm. Williams,
> Oliver Wolcott.

Georgia
> Button Gwinnett,
> Lyman Hall,
> Geo. Walton.

Maryland
> Samuel Chase,
> Wm. Paca,
> Thos. Stone,
> Charles Carroll of Carrollton.

Virginia
> George Wythe,
> Richard Henry Lee,
> Th. Jefferson,
> Benja. Harrison,
> Ths. Nelson, Jr.,
> Francis Lightfoot Lee,
> Carter Braxton.

Delaware
> Caesar Rodney,
> Geo. Read,
> Tho. M'Kean.

North Carolina
> Wm. Hooper,
> Joseph Hewes,
> John Penn.

South Carolina
> Edward Rutledge,
> Thos. Heyward, Junr.,
> Thomas Lynch, Junr.,
> Arthur Middleton.

New Jersey
> Richd. Stockton,
> Jno. Witherspoon,
> Fras. Hopkinson,
> John Hart,
> Abra. Clark.

SPEECH ON AMERICAN INDEPENDENCE

Samuel Adams   *August 1, 1776*

> *Samuel Adams was a brewer by occupation who became*
> *active in Boston politics in 1756 at the age of thirty-four. A*
> *brilliant publicist, a major influence on others, and a leader in*
> *the movement for independence, Adams took the leading role in*
> *events that led to the Boston Tea Party. He was a delegate to the*

Continental Congress, a signer of the Declaration of Independence, and on August 1, 1776, gave this speech in the State House in Philadelphia. In 1793, upon the death of John Hancock, Samuel Adams became governor of Massachusetts.

WE are now on this continent, to the astonishment of the world, three millions of souls united in one cause. We have large armies, well disciplined and appointed, with commanders inferior to none in military skill, and superior in activity and zeal. We are furnished with arsenals and stores beyond our most sanguine expectations, and foreign nations are waiting to crown our success by their alliances. There are instances of, I would say, an almost astonishing Providence in our favor; our success has staggered our enemies, and almost given faith to infidels; so we may truly say it is not our own arm which has saved us.

The hand of Heaven appears to have led us on to be, perhaps, humble instruments and means in the great providential dispensation which is completing. We have fled from the political Sodom; let us not look back, lest we perish and become a monument of infamy and derision to the world. For can we ever expect more unanimity and a better preparation for defense; more infatuation of counsel among our enemies, and more valor and zeal among ourselves? The same force and resistance which are sufficient to procure us our liberties will secure us a glorious independence and support us in the dignity of free, imperial states. We cannot suppose that our opposition has made a corrupt and dissipated nation more friendly to America, or created in them a greater respect for the rights of mankind. We can therefore expect a restoration and establishment of our privileges, and a compensation for the injuries we have received, from their want of power, from their fears, and not from their virtues. The unanimity and valor which will effect an honorable peace can render a future contest for our liberties unnecessary. He who has strength to chain down the wolf is a madman if he let him loose without drawing his teeth and paring his nails.

We have no other alternative than independence, or the most ignominious and galling servitude. The legions of our enemies thicken on our plains; desolation and death mark their bloody career; whilst the mangled corpses of our countrymen seem to cry out to us as a voice from Heaven.

Our union is now complete; our constitution composed, established, and approved. You are now the guardians of your own liberties. We may justly address you, as the *decemviri* did the Romans, and say: "Nothing that we propose can pass into a law without your consent. Be yourselves, O Americans, the authors of those laws on which your happiness depends."

You have now in the field armies sufficient to repel the whole force of your enemies and their base and mercenary auxiliaries. The hearts of your soldiers beat high with the spirit of freedom; they are animated with the justice of their cause, and while they grasp their swords can look up to Heaven for assistance. Your adversaries are composed of wretches who laugh at the rights of humanity, who turn religion into derision, and would, for higher wages, direct their swords against their leaders or their country. Go on, then, in your generous enterprise, with gratitude to Heaven for past success, and confidence of it in the future. For my own part, I ask no greater blessing than to share with you the common danger and common glory. If I have a wish dearer to my soul than that my ashes may be mingled with those of a Warren and a Montgomery, it is that these American States may never cease to be free and independent.

FROM *COMMON SENSE*—AMERICAN AFFAIRS

Thomas Paine   *1776*

Thomas Paine was born in Thetford, Norfolk, England, in 1737. In 1774 in London, Paine met Benjamin Franklin, who gave him some letters of introduction to take to America. Arriving penniless in Philadelphia, Thomas Paine began to write. In late 1775 and 1776, many Americans were beginning to think about the relationship between the colonies and England. Paine's pamphlet, Common Sense, *pointed out the reasons for complete independence and was widely read throughout the colonies. In July 1776, Paine joined the revolutionary army. In December, in* The Crisis, *he wrote: "These are the times that try men's souls: The summer soldier and the sunshine patriot will in this crisis, shrink from the service of his country; but he that stands it now, deserves the love and thanks of man and woman." Paine continued as a revolutionary after the war and returned to England, where he wrote* The Rights of Man, *and then spent the next ten years in France during its revolution.*

IN the following pages I offer nothing more than simple facts, plain arguments, and common sense; and have no other preliminaries to settle with the reader, than that he will divest himself of prejudice and prepossession, and suffer his reason and his feelings to determine for themselves; that he will put on, or rather that he will not put off, the true character of a man, and generously enlarge his views beyond the present day.

Volumes have been written on the subject of the struggle between England and America. Men of all ranks have embarked in the controversy, from different motives, and with various designs; but all have been ineffectual, and the period of debate is closed. Arms, as the last resource, decide the contest; the appeal was the choice of the king, and the continent hath accepted the challenge. . . .

The sun never shined on a cause of greater worth. 'Tis not the affair of a city, a country, a province, or a kingdom, but of a continent—of at least one eighth part of the habitable globe. 'Tis not the concern of a day, a year, or an age; posterity are virtually involved in the contest, and will be more or less affected, even to the end of time, by the proceedings now. Now is the seed time of continental union, faith and honor. The least fracture now will be like a name engraved with the point of a pin on the tender rind of a young oak; the wound would enlarge with the tree, and posterity read it in full grown characters.

By referring the matter from argument to arms, a new era for politics is struck; a new method of thinking hath arisen. All plans, proposals, etc. prior to the nineteenth of April, *i.e.* to the commencement of hostilities, are like the almanacks of the last year; which, though proper then, are superceded and useless now. Whatever was advanced by the advocates on either side of the question then, terminated in one and the same point, *viz.* a union with Great Britain; the only difference between the parties was the method of effecting it; the one proposing force, the other friendship; but it hath so far happened that the first hath failed, and the second hath withdrawn her influence.

As much hath been said of the advantages of reconciliation, which, like an agreeable dream, hath passed away and left us as we were, it is but right, that we should examine the contrary side of the argument, and inquire into some of the many material injuries which these colonies sustain, and always will sustain, by being connected with, and dependant on Great Britain. To examine that connexion and dependance, on the principles of nature and common sense, to see what we have to trust to, if separated, and what we are to expect, if dependant.

I have heard it asserted by some, that as America hath flourished under her former connexion with Great-Britain, that the same connexion is necessary towards her future happiness, and will always have the same effect. Nothing can be more fallacious than this kind of argument. We may as well assert, that because a child has thrived upon milk, that it is never to have meat; or that the first twenty years of our lives is to become a precedent for the next twenty. But even this is admitting more than is true, for I answer roundly, that America would have flourished as much, and probably much more, had no European power had any thing to do with her. The commerce by which she hath enriched herself are the necessaries of life, and will always have a market while eating is the custom of Europe.

But she has protected us, say some. That she hath engrossed us is true, and defended the continent at our expence as well as her own is admitted, and she would have defended Turkey from the same motive, *viz.* the sake of trade and dominion.

Alas, we have been long led away by ancient prejudices, and made large sacrifices to superstition. We have boasted the protection of Great-Britain, without considering, that her motive was interest not attachment; that she did not protect us from our enemies on our account, but from her enemies on her own account, from those who had no quarrel with us on any other account, and who will always be our enemies on the same account. Let Britain wave her pretensions to the continent, or the continent throw off the dependance, and we should be at peace with France and Spain were they at war with Britain. The miseries of Hanover['s] last war ought to warn us against connexions.

It hath lately been asserted in parliament, that the colonies have no relation to each other but through the parent country, *i.e.* that Pensylvania and the Jerseys, and so on for the rest, are sister colonies by the way of England; this is certainly a very round-about way of proving relationship, but it is the nearest and only true way of proving enemyship, if I may so call it. France and Spain never were, nor perhaps ever will be our enemies as Americans, but as our being the subjects of Great Britain.

But Britain is the parent country, say some. Then the more shame upon her conduct. Even brutes do not devour their young, nor savages make war upon their families; wherefore the assertion, if true, turns to her reproach; but it happens not to be true, or only partly so, and the phrase parent or mother country hath been jesuitically adopted by the [King] and his parasites, with a low papistical design of gaining an unfair bias on the credulous weakness of our minds. Europe, and not England, is the parent country of America. This new world hath been the asylum for the persecuted lovers of civil and religious liberty from every part of Europe. Hither have they fled, not from the tender embraces of the mother, but from the cruelty of the monster; and it is so far true of England, that the same tyranny which drove the first emigrants from home, pursues their descendants still.

In this extensive quarter of the globe, we forget the narrow limits of three hundred and sixty miles (the extent of England) and carry our friendship on a larger scale; we claim brotherhood with eve[ry] European christian, and triumph in the generosity of the sentiment.

It is pleasant to observe by what regular gradations we surmount the force of local prejudice, as we enlarge our acquaintance with the world. A man born in any town in England divided into parishes, will naturally associate most with his fellow parishioners (because their interests in many cases will be common) and distinguish him by the name of neighbour; if he meet him but a few miles from home, he drops the narrow idea of a street, and salutes him by the name of townsman; if he travels out of the county, and meet him in any other, he forgets the minor divisions of street and town, and calls him countryman, i.e. countyman; but if in their foreign excursions they should associate in France or any other part of Europe, their local remembrance would be enlarged into that of Englishmen. And by a just parity of reasoning, all Europeans meeting in America, or any other quarter of the globe, are countrymen; for England, Holland, Germany, or Sweden, when compared with the whole, stand in the same places on the larger scale, which the divisions of street, town, and county do on the smaller ones; distinctions too limited for continental minds. Not one third of the inhabitants, even of this province, are of English descent. Wherefore I reprobate the phrase of parent or mother country applied to England only, as being false, selfish, narrow and ungenerous.

But admitting that we were all of English descent, what does it amount to? Nothing. Britain, being now an open enemy, extinguishes every other name and title: And to say that reconciliation is our duty, is truly farcical. The first king of England, of the present line (William the Conqueror) was a Frenchman, and half the peers of England are descendants from the same country; wherefore by the same method of reasoning, England ought to be governed by France.

Much hath been said of the united strength of Britain and the colonies, that in conjunction they might bid defiance to the world. But this is mere presumption; the fate of war is uncertain, neither do the expressions mean any thing; for this continent would never suffer itself to be drained of inhabitants to support the British arms in either Asia, Africa, or Europe.

Besides, what have we to do with setting the world at defiance? Our plan is commerce, and that, well attended to, will secure us the peace and friendship of all Europe; because it is the interest of all Europe to have America a free port. Her trade will always be a protection, and her barrenness of gold and silver secure her from invaders.

I challenge the warmest advocate for reconciliation, to shew, a single advantage that this continent can reap, by being connected with Great Britain. I repeat the challenge, not a single advantage is derived. Our corn will fetch its price in any market in Europe, and our imported goods must be paid for buy them where we will.

But the injuries and disadvantages we sustain by that connection, are without number; and our duty to mankind at large, as well as to ourselves, instruct us to renounce the alliance: Because, any submission to, or dependance on Great Britain, tends directly to involve this continent in European wars and quarrels; and sets us at variance with nations, who would otherwise seek our friendship, and against whom, we have neither anger nor complaint. As Europe is our market for trade, we ought to form no partial connection with any part of it. It is the true interest of America to steer clear of European contentions, which she never can do, while by her dependance on Britain, she is made the make-weight in the scale of British politics.

Europe is too thickly planted with kingdoms to be long at peace, and whenever a war breaks out between England and any foreign power, the trade of America goes to ruin, because of her connection with Britain. The next war may not turn out like the last, and should it not, the advocates for reconciliation now will be wishing for separation then, because, neutrality in that case, would be a safer convoy than a man of war. Every thing that is right or natural pleads for separation. The blood of the slain, the weeping voice of nature cries, 'Tis Time To Part. Even the distance at which the Almighty hath placed England and America, is a strong and natural proof, that the authority of the one, over the other, was never the design of Heaven. The time likewise at which the continent was discovered, adds weight to the argument, and the manner in which it was peopled encreases the force of it. The reformation was preceded by the discovery of America, as if the Almighty graciously meant to open a sanctuary to the persecuted in future years, when home should afford neither friendship nor safety. . . .

A government of our own is our natural right: And when a man seriously reflects on the precariousness of human affairs, he will become convinced, that it is infinitely wiser and safer, to form a constitution of our own in a cool deliberate manner, while we have it in our power, than to trust such an interesting event to time and chance. If we omit it now, some Massenello may hereafter arise, who laying hold of popular disquietudes, may collect together the desperate and the discontented, and by assuming to themselves the powers of government, may sweep away the liberties of the continent like a deluge. Should the government of America return again into the hands of Britain, the tottering situation of things, will be a temptation for some desperate adventurer to try his fortune; and in such a case, what relief can Britain give? Ere she could hear the news the fatal business might be done, and ourselves suffering like the wretched Britons under the oppression of the Conqueror. Ye that oppose independance now, ye know not what ye do; ye are opening a door to eternal tyranny, by keeping vacant the seat of government. There are thousands and tens of thousands, who would think it glorious to expel from the continent, that barbarous and hellish power, which hath stirred up the Indians and Negroes to destroy us; the cruelty hath a double guilt, it is dealing brutally by us, and treacherously by them.

To talk of friendship with those in whom our reason forbids us to have faith, and our affections wounded through a thousand pores instruct us to detest, is madness and folly. Every day wears out the little remains of kindred between us and them, and can there be any reason to hope, that as the relationship expires, the affection will increase, or that we shall agree better, when we have ten times more and greater concerns to quarrel over than ever?

Ye that tell us of harmony and reconciliation, can ye restore to us the time that is past? Can ye give to prostitution its former innocence? Neither can ye reconcile Britain and America. The last cord now is broken, the people of England are presenting addresses against us. There are injuries which nature cannot forgive; she would cease to be nature if she did. As well can the lover forgive the ravisher of his mistress, as the continent forgive the murders of Britain. The Almighty hath implanted in us these unextinguishable feelings for good and wise purposes. They are the guardians of his image in our hearts. They distinguish us from the herd of common animals. The social compact would dissolve, and justice be extirpated [from] the earth, or have only a casual existence were we callous to the touches of affection. The robber and the murderer, would often escape unpunished, did not the injuries which our tempers sustain, provoke us into justice.

O ye that love mankind! Ye that dare oppose, not only the tyranny, but the tyrant, stand forth! Every spot of the old world is over-run with oppression. Freedom hath been hunted round the globe. Asia, and Africa, have long expelled her. —Europe regards her like a stranger, and England hath given her warning to depart. O! receive the fugitive, and prepare in time an asylum for mankind.

RESOLUTION OF
CONGRESS ON PUBLIC LANDS

October 10, 1780

---

*On October 10, 1780, the Continental Congress passed
the following resolution relative to the ownership and control of*

the western lands. Many of the colonies had claims to lands west of the Appalachian Mountains. What should happen to this territory?

RESOLVED, that the unappropriated lands that may be ceded or relinquished to the United States, by any particular States, pursuant to the recommendation of Congress on the 6 day of September last, shall be disposed of for the common benefit of the United States, and be settled and formed into distinct republican States, which shall become members of the Federal Union, and shall have the same rights of sovereignty, freedom and independence, as the other States; that each State which shall be so formed shall contain a suitable extent of territory, not less than one hundred nor more than one hundred and fifty miles square, or as near thereto as circumstances will admit;

That the necessary and reasonable expences which any particular State shall have incurred since the commencement of the present war, in subduing any of the British posts, or in maintaining forts or garrisons within and for the defence, or in acquiring any part of the territory that may be ceded or relinquished to the United States, shall be reimbursed;

That the said lands shall be granted and settled at such times and under such regulations as shall hereafter be agreed on by the United States in Congress assembled, or any nine or more of them.

THE ARTICLES OF CONFEDERATION

John Dickinson   *March 1, 1781*

On June 7, 1776, Richard Henry Lee moved that the Continental Congress appoint a committee to draw up articles of confederation among the several states. One member of each state was chosen for this committee, and on July 12 it presented a plan of union drafted by John Dickinson of Pennsylvania. The plan was debated, and in November 1777, was adopted in greatly revised form. All states had to ratify the Articles of Confederation, and they were not adopted until March 1781. The resulting government was weak and was superseded by that set up under the Constitution.

TO ALL TO WHOM these Presents shall come, we the undersigned Delegates of the States affixed to our Names send greeting. Whereas the Delegates of the United States of America in Congress assembled did on the fifteenth day of November in the Year of our Lord One Thousand Seven Hundred and Seventy seven, and in the Second Year of the Independence of America agree to certain articles of Confederation and perpetual Union between the States of Newhampshire, Massachusetts-bay, Rhodeisland and Providence Plantations, Connecticut, New York, New Jersey, Pennsylvania, Delaware, Maryland, Virginia, North-Carolina, South-Carolina and Georgia in the Words following, *viz.* "Articles of Confederation and perpetual Union between the states of Newhampshire, Massachusetts-bay, Rhodeisland and Providence Plantations, Connecticut, New-York, New-Jersey, Pennsylvania, Delaware, Maryland, Virginia, North-Carolina, South-Carolina and Georgia.

ART. I. The Stile of this confederacy shall be "The United States of America."

ART. II. Each state retains its sovereignty, freedom and independence, and every Power, Jurisdiction and right, which is not by this confederation expressly delegated to the united states, in Congress assembled.

ART. III. The said states hereby severally enter into a firm league of friendship with each other, for their common defence, the security of their Liberties, and their mutual and general welfare, binding themselves to assist each other, against all force offered to, or attacks made upon them, or any of them, on account of religion, sovereignty, trade, or any other pretence whatever.

ART. IV. The better to secure and perpetuate mutual friendship and intercourse among the people of the different states in this union, the free inhabitants of each of these states, paupers, vagabonds and fugitives from Justice excepted, shall be entitled to all privileges and immunities of free citizens in the several states; and the people of each state shall have free ingress and regress to and from any other state, and shall enjoy therein all the privileges of trade and commerce, subject to the same duties, impositions and restrictions as the inhabitants thereof respectively, provided that such restriction shall not extend so far as to prevent the removal of property imported into any state, to any other state of which the Owner is an inhabitant; provided also that no imposition, duties or restriction shall be laid by any state, on the property of the united states, or either of them.

If any Person guilty of, or charged with treason, felony, or other high misdemeanor in any state, shall flee from Justice, and be found in any of the united states, he shall upon demand of the Governor or executive power, of the state from which he fled, be delivered up and removed to the state having jurisdiction of his offence.

Full faith and credit shall be given in each of these states to the records, acts and judicial proceedings of the courts and magistrates of every other state.

ART. V. For the more convenient management of the general interests of the united states, delegates shall be annually appointed in such manner as the legislature of each state shall direct, to meet in Congress on the first Monday in November, in every year, with a power reserved to each state, to recal its delegates, or any of them, at any time within the year, and to send others in their stead, for the remainder of the Year.

No state shall be represented in Congress by less than two, nor by more than seven Members; and no person shall be capable of being a delegate for more than three years in any term of six years; nor shall any person, being a delegate, be capable of holding any office under the united states, for which he, or another for his benefit receives any salary, fees or emolument of any kind.

Each state shall maintain its own delegates in a meeting of the states, and while they act as members of the committee of the states.

In determining questions in the united states, in Congress assembled, each state shall have one vote.

Freedom of speech and debate in Congress shall not be impeached or questioned in any Court, or place out of Congress, and the members of congress shall be protected in their persons from arrests and imprisonments, during the time of their going to and from, and attendance on congress, except for treason, felony, or breach of the peace.

ART. VI. No state without the Consent of the united states in congress assembled, shall send any embassy to, or receive any embassy from, or enter into any conference, agreement, or alliance or treaty with any King, prince or state; nor shall any person holding any office of profit or trust under the united states, or any of them, accept of any present, emolument, office or title of any kind whatever from any king, prince or foreign state; nor shall the united states in congress assembled, or any of them, grant any title of nobility.

No two or more states shall enter into any treaty, confederation or alliance whatever between them, without the consent of the united states in congress assembled, specifying accurately the purposes for which the same is to be entered into, and how long it shall continue.

No state shall lay any imposts or duties, which may interfere with any stipulations in treaties, entered into by the united states in congress assembled, with any king, prince or state, in pursuance of any treaties already proposed by congress, to the courts of France and Spain.

No vessels of war shall be kept up in time of peace by any state, except such number only, as shall be deemed necessary by the united states in congress assembled, for the defence of such state, or its trade; nor shall any body of forces be kept up by any state, in time of peace, except such number only, as in the judgment of the united states, in congress assembled, shall be deemed requisite to garrison the forts necessary for the defence of such state; but every state shall always keep up a well regulated and disciplined militia, sufficiently armed and accoutred, and shall provide and constantly have ready for use, in public stores, a due number of field pieces and tents, and a proper quantity of arms, ammunition and camp equipage.

No state shall engage in any war without the consent of the united states in congress assembled, unless such state be actually invaded by enemies, or shall have received certain advice of a resolution being formed by some nation of Indians to invade such state, and the danger is so imminent as not to admit of a delay, till the united states in congress assembled can be consulted: nor shall any state grant commissions to any ships or vessels of war, nor letters of marque or reprisal, except it be after a declaration of war by the united states in congress assembled, and then only against the kingdom or state and the subjects thereof, against which war has been so declared, and under such regulations as shall be established by the united states in congress assembled, unless such state be infested by pirates, in which case vessels of war may be fitted out for that occasion, and kept so long as the danger shall continue, or until the united states in congress assembled shall determine otherwise.

ART. VII. When land-forces are raised by any state for the common defence, all officers of or under the rank of colonel, shall be appointed by the legislature of each state respectively by whom such forces shall be raised, or in such manner as such state shall direct, and all vacancies shall be filled up by the state which first made the appointment.

ART. VIII. All charges of war, and all other expences that shall be incurred for the common defence or general welfare, and allowed by the united states in congress assembled, shall be defrayed out of a common treasury, which shall be supplied by the several states, in proportion to the value of all land within each state, granted to or surveyed for any Person, as such land and the buildings and improvements thereon shall be estimated according to such mode as the united states in congress assembled, shall from time to time direct and appoint. The taxes for paying that proportion shall be laid and levied by the authority and direction of the legislatures of the several states within the time agreed upon by the united states in congress assembled.

ART. IX. The united states in congress assembled, shall have the sole and exclusive right and power of determing on peace and war, except in the cases mentioned in the sixth article—of sending and receiving ambassadors—entering into treaties and alliances, provided that no treaty of commerce shall be made whereby the legislative power of the respective states shall be restrained from imposing such imposts and duties on foreigners, as their own people are subjected to, or from prohibiting the exportation or importation of any species of goods or commodities whatsoever—of establishing rules for deciding in all cases, what captures on land or water shall be legal, and in what manner prizes taken by land or naval forces in the service of the united states shall be divided or appropriated.—of granting letters of marque and reprisal in times of peace— appointing courts for the trial of piracies and felonies committed on the high seas and establishing courts for receiving and determining finally appeals in all cases of captures, provided that no member of congress shall be appointed a judge of any of the said courts.

The united states in congress assembled shall also be the last resort on appeal in all disputes and differences now subsisting or that hereafter may arise between two or more states concerning boundary, jurisdiction or any other cause whatever; which authority shall always be exercised in the manner following. Whenever the legislative or executive authority or lawful agent of any state in controversy with another shall present a petition to congress, stating the matter in question and praying for a hearing, notice thereof shall be given by order of congress to the legislative or executive authority of the other state in controversy, and a day assigned for the appearance of the parties by their lawful agents, who shall then be directed to appoint by joint consent, commissioners or judges to constitute a court for hearing and determing the matter in question: but if they cannot agree, congress shall name three persons out of each of the united states, and from the list of such persons each party shall alternately strike out one, the petitioners beginning, until the number shall be reduced to thirteen; and from that number not less than seven, nor more than nine names as congress shall direct, shall in the presence of congress be drawn out by lot, and the persons whose names shall be so drawn or any five of them, shall be commissioners or judges, to hear and finally determine the controversy, so always as a major part of the judges who shall hear the cause shall agree in the determination: and if either party shall neglect to attend at the day appointed, without shewing reasons, which congress shall judge sufficient, or being present shall refuse to strike, the congress shall proceed to nominate three persons out of each state, and the secretary of congress shall strike in behalf of such party absent or refusing; and the judgment and sentence of the court to be appointed, in the manner before prescribed, shall be final and conclusive; and if any of the parties shall refuse to submit to the authority of such court, or to appear to defend their claim or cause, the court shall nevertheless proceed to pronounce sentence, or judgment, which shall in like manner be final and decisive, the judgment or sentence and other proceedings being in either case transmitted to congress, and lodged among the acts of congress for the security of the parties concerned:

provided that every commissioner, before he sits in judgment, shall take an oath to be administered by one of the judges of the supreme or superior court of the state, where the cause shall be tried, "well and truly to hear and determine the matter in question, according to the best of his judgment, without favour, affection or hope of reward:" provided also that no state shall be deprived of territory for the benefit of the united states.

All controversies concerning the private right of soil claimed under different grants of two or more states, whose jurisdictions as they may respect such lands, and the states which passed such grants are adjusted, the said grants or either of them being at the same time claimed to have originated antecedent to such settlement of jurisdiction, shall on the petition of either party to the congress of the united states, be finally determined as near as may be in the same manner as is before prescribed for deciding disputes respecting territorial jurisdiction between different states.

The united states in congress assembled shall also have the sole and exclusive right and power of regulating the alloy and value of coin struck by their own authority, or by that of the respective states—fixing the standard of weights and measures throughout the united states.—regulating the trade and managing all affairs with the Indians, not members of any of the states, provided that the legislative right of any state within its own limits be not infringed or violated—establishing and regulating post-offices from one state to another, throughout all the united states, and exacting such postage on the papers passing thro' the same as may be requisite to defray the expences of the said office—appointing all officers of the land forces, in the service of the united states, excepting regimental officers.—appointing all the officers of the naval forces, and commissioning all officers whatever in the service of the united states—making rules for the government and regulation of the said land and naval forces, and directing their operations.

The united states in congress assembled shall have authority to appoint a committee, to sit in the recess of congress, to be denominated "A Committee of the States," and to consist of one delegate from each state; and to appoint such other committees and civil officers as may be necessary for managing the general affairs of the united states under their direction—to appoint one of their number to preside, provided that no person be allowed to serve in the office of president more than one year in any term of three years; to ascertain the necessary sums of Money to be raised for the service of the united states, and to appropriate and apply the same for defraying the public expences—to borrow money, or emit bills on the credit of the united states, transmitting every half year to the respective states an account of the sums of money so borrowed or emitted,—to build and equip a navy—to agree upon the number of land forces, and to make requisitions from each state for its quota, in proportion to the number of white inhabitants in such state; which requisition shall be binding, and thereupon the legislature of each state shall appoint the regimental officers, raise the men and cloath, arm and equip them in a soldier like manner, at the expence of the united states, and the officers and men so cloathed, armed and equipped shall march to the place appointed, and within the time agreed on by the united states in congress assembled: But if the united states in congress assembled shall, on consideration of circumstances judge proper that any state should not raise men, or should raise a smaller number than its quota, and that any other state should raise a greater number of men that the quota thereof, such extra number shall be raised, officered, cloathed, armed and equipped in the same manner as the quota of such state, unless the legislature of such state shall judge that such extra number cannot be safely spared out of the same, in which case they shall raise officer, cloath, arm and equip as many of such extra number as they judge can be safely spared. And the officers and men so cloathed, armed and equipped, shall march to the place appointed, and within the time agreed on by the united states in congress assembled.

The united states in congress assembled shall never engage in a war, nor grant letters of marque and reprisal in time of peace, nor enter into any treaties or alliances, nor coin money, nor regulate the value thereof, nor ascertain the sums and expences necessary for the defence and welfare of the united states, or any of them, nor emit bills, nor borrow money on the credit of the united states, nor appropriate money, nor agree upon the number of vessels of war, to be built or purchased, or the number of land or sea forces to be raised, nor appoint a commander in chief of the army or navy, unless nine states assent to the same: nor shall a question on any other point, except for adjourning from day to day be determined, unless by the votes of a majority of the united states in congress assembled.

The congress of the united states shall have power to adjourn to any time within the year, and to any place within the united states, so that no period of adjournment be for a longer duration than the space of six Months, and shall publish the Journal of their proceedings monthly, except such parts thereof relating to treaties, alliances or military operations as in their judgment require secresy; and the yeas and nays of the delegates of each state on any question shall be entered on the Journal, when it is desired by any delegate; and the delegates of a state, or any of them, at his or their request shall be furnished with a transcript of the said Journal, except such parts as are above excepted, to lay before the legislatures of the several states.

ART. X. The committee of the states, or any nine of them, shall be authorised to execute, in the recess of congress, such of the powers of congress as the united states in congress assembled, by the consent of nine states, shall from time to time think expedient to vest them with; provided that no power be delegated to the said committee, for the exercise of which, by the articles of confederation, the voice of nine states in the congress of the united states assembled is requisite.

ART. XI. Canada acceding to this confederation, and joining in the measures of the united states, shall be admitted into, and entitled to all the advantages of this union: but no other colony shall be admitted into the same, unless such admission be agreed to by nine states.

ART. XII. All bills of credit emitted, monies borrowed and debts contracted by, or under the authority of congress, before the assembling of the united states, in pursuance of the present confederation, shall be deemed and considered as a charge against the united states, for payment and satisfaction whereof the said united states, and the public faith are hereby solemnly pledged.

ART. XIII. Every state shall abide by the determinations of the united states in congress assembled, on all questions which by this confederation are submitted to them. And the Articles of this confederation shall be inviolably observed by every state, and the union shall be perpetual; nor shall any alteration at any time hereafter be made in any of them; unless such alteration be agreed to in a congress of the united states, and be afterwards confirmed by the legislatures of every state.

AND WHEREAS it hath pleased the Great Governor of the World to incline the hearts of the legislatures we respectively represent in congress, to approve of, and to authorize us to ratify the said articles of confederation and perpetual union. Know ye that we the under-signed delegates, by virtue of the power and authority to us given for that purpose, do by these presents, in the name and in behalf of our respective constituents, fully and entirely ratify and confirm each and every of the said articles of confederation and perpetual union, and all and singular the matters and things therein contained: And we do further solemnly plight and engage the faith of our respective constituents, that they shall abide by the determinations of the united states in congress assembled, on all questions, which by the said confederation are submitted to them. And that the articles thereof shall be inviolably observed by the states we respectively represent, and that the union shall be perpetual. In Witness whereof we have hereunto set our hands in Congress. Done at Philadelphia in the state of Pennsylvania the ninth Day of July in the Year of our Lord one Thousand seven Hundred and Seventy-eight, and in the third year of the independence of America.

Josiah Bartlett
John Wentworth Jun[r]
August 8th 1778

On the part and
behalf of the State
of New Hamp-
shire

John Hancock
Samuel Adams
Elbridge Gerry
Francis Dana
James Lovell
Samuel Holten

On the part and
behalf of The State
of Massachusetts
Bay

William Ellery
Henry Marchant
John Collins

On the part and
behalf of the State
of Rhode-Island
and Providence
Plantations

Roger Sherman
Samuel Huntington
Oliver Wolcott
Titus Hosmer
Andrew Adams

On the part and
behalf of the State
of Connecticut

Ja[s] Duane
Fra[s] Lewis
W[m] Duer
Gouv Morris

On the Part and
Behalf of the
State of New
York

Jno Witherspoon
Nath[l] Scudder

On the Part and in
Behalf of the
State of New
Jersey. Nov[r] 26,
1778.—

Rob[t] Morris
Daniel Roberdeau
Jon[a] Bayard Smith.
William Clingan
Joseph Reed
  22d July 1778

On the part and be-
half of the State
of Pennsylvania

Tho M:Kean
  Feby 12 1779
John Dickinson
  May 5th 1779
Nicholas Van Dyke,

On the part and be-
half of the State
of Delaware

John Hanson
  March 1 1781
Daniel Carroll d°

On the part and be-
half of the State
of Maryland

Richard Henry Lee
John Banister
Thomas Adams
Jn° Harvie
Francis Lightfoot Lee

On the Part and
Behalf of the
State of Virginia

John Penn
  July 21st 1778
Corn[s] Harnett
Jn° Williams

On the part and
Behalf of the
State of N°
Carolina

Henry Laurens
William Henry
  Drayton
Jn° Mathews
Rich[d] Hutson
Tho[s] Heyward Jun[r]

On the part and
behalf of the State
of South-Carolina

Jn° Walton
  24th July 1778
Edw[d] Telfair
Edw[d] Langworthy

On the part and be-
half of the State
of Georgia

Notes on the
State of Virginia—Religion

Thomas Jefferson   *1782*

In 1780, François Marbois, the secretary of the French legation at Philadelphia, circulated a questionnaire among the states to various members of the Continental Congress. One such questionnaire was given to Thomas Jefferson, then governor of Virginia. Over the next few years, Jefferson worked on the answers, which he called Notes on Virginia. *In 1785, with the encouragement of Benjamin Franklin, the notes were privately published in Paris. Two years later, an edition was published by the English publisher, John Stockdale.* The Notes on the State of Virginia *is one of the major literary works written by an American in the eighteenth century. Jefferson's comments on religion are particularly pertinent in view of his work in the establishment of religious freedom in America.*

THE first settlers in this country were emigrants from England, of the English church, just at a point of time when it was flushed with complete victory over the religious of all other persuasions. Possessed, as they became, of the powers of making, administering, and executing the laws, they shewed equal intolerance in this country with their Presbyterian brethren, who had emigrated to the northern government. The poor Quakers were flying from persecution in England. They cast their eyes on these new countries as asylums of civil and religious freedom; but they found them free only for the reigning sect. Several acts of the Virginia assembly of 1659, 1662, and 1693, had made it penal in parents to refuse to have their children baptized; had prohibited the unlawful assembling of Quakers; had made it penal for any master of a vessel to bring a Quaker into the state; had ordered those already here, and such as should come thereafter, to be imprisoned till they should abjure the country; provided a milder punishment for their first and second return, but death for their third; had inhibited all persons from suffering their meetings in or near their houses, entertaining them individually, or disposing of books which supported their tenets. If no capital execution took place here, as did in New-England, it was not owing to the moderation of the church, or spirit of the legislature, as may be inferred from the law itself; but to historical circumstances which have not been handed down to us. The Anglicans retained full possession of the country about a century. Other opinions began then to creep in, and the great care of the government to support their own church, having begotten an equal degree of indolence in its clergy, two-thirds of the people had become dissenters at the commencement of the present revolution. The laws indeed were still oppressive on them, but the spirit of the one party had subsided into moderation, and of the other had risen to a degree of determination which commanded respect.

The present state of our laws on the subject of religion is this. The convention of May 1776, in their declaration of rights, declared it to be a truth, and a natural right, that the exercise of religion should be free; but when they proceeded to form on that declaration the ordinance of government, instead of taking up every principle declared in the bill of rights, and guarding it by legislative sanction, they passed over that which asserted our religious rights, leaving them as they found them. The same convention, however, when they met as a member of the general assembly in October 1776, repealed all acts of parliament which had rendered criminal the maintaining any opinions in matters of religion, the forbearing to repair to church, and the exercising any mode of worship; and suspended the laws giving salaries to the clergy, which suspension was made perpetual in October 1779. Statutory oppressions in religion being thus wiped away, we remain at present under those only imposed by the common law, or by our own acts of assembly. At the common law, heresy was a capital offence, punishable by burning. Its definition was left to the ecclesiastical judges, before whom the conviction was, till the statute of the first year of the reign of Elizabeth circumscribed it, by declaring, that nothing should be deemed heresy, but what had been so determined by authority of the canonical scriptures, or by one of the four first general councils, or by some other council having for the grounds of their declaration the express and plain words of the scriptures. Heresy, thus circumscribed, being an offence at the common law, our act of assembly of October 1777, c. 17. gives cognizance of it to the general court, by declaring, that the jurisdiction of that court shall be general in all matters at the common law. The execution is by the writ *De haeretico comburendo*. By our own act of assembly of 1705, c. 30, if a person brought up in the Christian religion denies the being of a God, or the Trinity, or asserts there are more Gods than one, or denies the Christian religion to be true, or the scriptures to be of divine authority, he is punishable on the first offence by incapacity to hold any office or employment ecclesiastical, civil, or military; on the second by disability to sue, to take any gift or legacy, to be guardian, executor, or administrator, and by three years imprisonment, without bail. A father's right to the custody of his own children being founded in law on his right of guardianship, this being taken away, they may of course be severed from him, and put, by the authority of a court, into more orthodox hands. This is a summary view of that religious slavery, under which a people have been willing to remain, who have lavished their lives and fortunes for the establishment of their civil freedom.

The error seems not sufficiently eradicated, that the operations of the mind, as well as the acts of the body, are subject to the coercion of the laws. But our rulers can have authority over such natural rights only as we have submitted to them. The rights of conscience we never submitted, we could not submit. We are answerable for them to our God. The legitimate powers of government extend to such acts only as are injurious to others. But it does me no injury for my neighbour to say there are twenty gods, or no god. It neither picks my pocket nor breaks my leg. If it be said, his testimony in a court of justice cannot be relied on, reject it then, and be the stigma on him. Constraint may make him worse by making him a hypocrite, but it will never make him a truer man. It may fix obstinately in his errors, but will not cure them. Reason and free enquiry are the only effectual agents against error. Give a loose to them, they will support the true religion, by bringing every false one to their tribunal, to the test of their investigation. They are the natural enemies of error, and of error only. Had not the Roman government permitted free enquiry, Christianity could never have been introduced. Had not free enquiry been indulged, at the aera of the reformation, the corruptions of Christianity could not have been purged away. If it be restrained now, the present corruptions will be protected, and new ones encouraged. Was the government to prescribe to us our medicine and diet, our bodies would be in such keeping as our souls are now. Thus in France the emetic was once forbidden as a medicine, and the potatoe as an article of food. Government is just as infallible too when it fixes systems in physics. Galileo was sent to the inquisition for affirming that the earth was a sphere: the government had declared it to be as flat as a trencher, and Galileo was obliged to abjure his error. This error however at length prevailed, the earth became a globe, a Descartes declared it was whirled round its axis by a vortex. The government in which he lived was wise enough to see that this was no question of civil jurisdiction, or we should all have been involved by authority in vortices. In fact, the vortices have been exploded, and the Newtonian principle of gravitation is now more firmly established, on the basis of reason, than it would be were the government to step in, and to make it an article of necessary faith. Reason and experiment have been indulged, and error has fled before them. It is error alone which needs the support of government. Truth can stand by itself. Subject opinion to coercion: whom will you make your inquisitors? Fallible men; men governed by bad passions, by private as well as public reasons. And why subject it to coercion? To produce uniformity. But is uniformity of opinion desireable? No more than of face and stature. Introduce the bed of Procrustes then, and as there is danger that the large men may beat the small, make us all of a size, by lopping the former and stretching the latter. Difference of opinion is advantageous in religion. The several sects perform the office of a *Censor morum* over each other. Is uniformity attainable? Millions of innocent men, women, and children, since the introduction of Christianity, have been burnt, tortured, fined, imprisoned; yet we have not advanced one inch towards uniformity. What has been the effect of coercion? To make one half the world fools, and the other half hypocrites. To support roguery and error all over the earth. Let us reflect that it is inhabited by a thousand millions of people. That these profess probably a thousand different systems of religion. That ours is but one of that thousand. That if there be but one right, and ours that one, we should wish to see the 999 wandering sects gathered into the fold of truth. But against such a majority we cannot effect this by force. Reason and persuasion are the only practicable instruments. To make way for these, free enquiry must be indulged; and how can we wish others to indulge it while we refuse it ourselves. But every state, says an inquisitor, has established some religion. No two, say I, have established the same. Is this a proof of the infallibility of establishments? Our sister states of Pennsylvania and New York, however, have long subsisted without any establishment at all. The experiment was new and doubtful when they made it. It has answered beyond conception. They flourish infinitely. Religion is well supported; of various kinds, indeed, but all good enough; all sufficient to preserve peace and order: or if a sect arises, whose tenets would subvert morals, good sense has fair play, and reasons and laughs it out of doors, without suffering the state to be troubled with it. They do not hang more malefactors than we do. They are not more disturbed with religious dissensions. On the contrary, their harmony is unparalleled, and can be ascribed to nothing but their unbounded tolerance, because there is no other circumstance in which they differ from every nation on earth. They have made the happy discovery, that the way to silence religious disputes, is to take no notice of them. Let us too give this experiment fair play, and get rid, while we may, of those tyrannical laws. It is true, we are as yet secured against them by the spirit of the times. I doubt whether the people of this country would suffer an execution for heresy, or a three years imprisonment for not comprehending the mysteries of the Trinity. But is the spirit of the people an infallible, a permanent reliance? Is it government? Is this the kind of protection we receive in return for the rights we give up? Besides, the spirit of the times may alter, will alter. Our rulers will become corrupt, our people careless. A single zealot may commence persecutor, and better men be his victims. It can never be too often repeated, that the time for fixing every essential right on a legal basis is while our rulers are honest, and ourselves united. From the conclusion of this war we shall be going down hill. It will not then be necessary to resort every moment to the people for support. They will be forgotten, therefore, and their rights disregarded. They will forget themselves, but in the sole faculty of making money, and will never think of uniting to effect a due respect for their rights. The shackles, therefore, which shall not be knocked off at the conclusion of this war, will remain on us long, will be made heavier and heavier, till our rights shall revive or expire in a convulsion.

To Those Who Would
Remove to America

Benjamin Franklin   *1782*

Benjamin Franklin was a printer, a publisher, a scientist, a philosopher, a member of the state and federal assemblies, a statesman and diplomat, and one of the leading figures of the eighteenth century. Franklin was sent to England in 1757 and again in 1764 to represent the views of the colonies. In 1775, Franklin returned to America, where he participated actively in the discussions leading to the Declaration of Independence. He served as ambassador to France from 1776 to 1785, and while in Paris wrote the following article, which was published in London and Dublin and translated into French, German, and Italian.

MANY persons in Europe having by letters expressed to the writer of this, who is well acquainted with North America, their desire of transporting and establishing themselves in that country, but who appear to have formed, through ignorance, mistaken ideas and expectations of what is to be obtained there; he thinks it may be useful, and prevent inconvenient, expensive, and fruitless removals and voyages of improper persons, if he gives some clearer and truer notions of that part of the world than appear to have hitherto prevailed.

He finds it is imagined by numbers that the inhabitants of North America are rich, capable of rewarding, and disposed to reward, all sorts of ingenuity; that they are at the same time ignorant of all the sciences, and consequently, that strangers possessing talents in the *belles-lettres*, fine arts, etc., must be highly esteemed, and so well paid as to become easily rich themselves; that there are also abundance of profitable offices to be disposed of, which the natives are not qualified to fill; and that, having few persons of family among them, strangers of birth must be greatly respected, and of course easily obtain the best of those offices, which will make all their fortunes; that the governments too, to encourage emigration from Europe, not only pay the expense of personal transportation, but give lands gratis to strangers, with Negroes to work for them, utensils of husbandry, and stocks of cattle. These are all wild imaginations; and those who go to America with expectations founded upon them will surely find themselves disappointed.

The truth is that though there are in that country few people so miserable as the poor of Europe, there are also very few that in Europe would be called rich; it is rather a general happy mediocrity that prevails. There are few great proprietors of the soil, and few tenants; most people cultivate their own lands, or follow some handicraft or merchandise; very few rich enough to live idly upon their rents or incomes, or to pay the high prices given in Europe for paintings, statues, architecture, and the other works of art that are more curious than useful. Hence the natural geniuses that have arisen in America with such talents have uniformly quitted that country for Europe, where they can be more suitably rewarded. It is true that letters and mathematical knowledge are in esteem there, but they are at the same time more common than is apprehended; there being already existing nine colleges or universities: *viz.*, four in New England, and one in each of the provinces of New York, New Jersey, Pennsylvania, Maryland, and Virginia, all furnished with learned professors; besides a number of smaller academies. These educate many of their youth in the languages, and those sciences that qualify men for the professions of divinity, law, or physic. Strangers indeed are by no means excluded from exercising those professions; and the quick increase of inhabitants everywhere gives them a chance of employ, which they have in common with the natives. Of civil offices, or employments, there are few; no superfluous ones, as in Europe; and it is a rule established in some of the states that no office should be so profitable as to make it desirable. The thirty-sixth article of the Constitution of Pennsylvania runs expressly in these words: "As every freeman, to preserve his independence (if he has not a sufficient estate), ought to have some profession, calling, trade, or farm, whereby he may honestly subsist there can be no necessity for, nor use in, establishing offices of profit, the usual effects of which are dependence and servility unbecoming freemen, in the possessors and expectants; faction, contention, corruption, and disorder among the people. Wherefore, whenever an office, through increase of fees or otherwise, becomes so profitable as to occasion many to apply for it, the profits ought to be lessened by the legislature."

These ideas prevailing more or less in all the United States, it cannot be worth any man's while, who has a means of living at home, to expatriate himself in hopes of obtaining a profitable civil office in America; and, as to military offices, they are at an end with the war, the armies being disbanded. Much less is it advisable for a person to go thither who has no other quality to recommend him but his birth. In Europe it has indeed its value; but it is a commodity that cannot be carried to a worse market than that of America, where people do not inquire concerning a stranger: "What is he?" but: "What can he do?" If he has any useful art, he is welcome; and if he exercises it, and behaves well, he will be respected by all that know him; but a mere man of quality, who on that account wants to live upon the public, by some office or salary, will be despised and disregarded. The husbandman is in honor there, and even the mechanic, because their employments are useful. The people have a saying, that God Almighty is himself a mechanic, the greatest in the universe; and he is respected and admired more for the variety, ingenuity, and utility of his handiwork, than for the antiquity of his family. . . .

Who then are the kind of persons to whom an emigration to America may be advantageous? And what are the advantages they may reasonably expect?

Land being cheap in that country, from the vast forests still void of inhabitants, and not likely to be occupied in an age to come, insomuch that the propriety of an hundred acres of fertile soil full of wood may be obtained near the frontiers, in many places, for eight or ten Guineas, hearty young labouring men, who understand the husbandry of corn and cattle, which is nearly the same in that country as in Europe, may easily establish themselves there. A little money saved of the good wages they receive there, while they work for others, enables them to buy the land and begin their plantation, in which they are assisted by the good-will of their neighbours, and some credit. Multitudes of poor people from England, Ireland, Scotland, and Germany, have by this means in a few years become wealthy farmers, who, in their own countries, where all the lands are fully occupied, and the wages of labour low, could never have emerged from the poor condition wherein they were born.

From the salubrity of the air, the healthiness of the climate, the plenty of good provisions, and the encouragement to early marriages by the certainty of subsistence in cultivating the earth, the increase of inhabitants by natural generation is very rapid in America, and becomes still more so by the accession of strangers; hence there is a continual demand for more artisans of all the necessary and useful kinds, to supply those cultivators of the earth with houses, and with furniture and utensils of the grosser sorts, which cannot so well be brought from Europe. Tolerably good workmen in any of those mechanic arts are sure to find employ, and to be well paid for their work, there being no restraints preventing strangers from exercising any art they understand, nor any permission necessary. If they are poor, they begin first as servants or journeymen; and if they are sober, industrious, and frugal, they soon become masters, establish themselves in business, marry, raise families, and become respectable citizens. . . .

What Is an American?

Michel Guillaume St. Jean de Crèvecoeur   *1782*

Michel Guillaume St. Jean de Crèvecoeur was a French-man who migrated to Canada and served with Montcalm in the French and Indian War. In the 1760s he traveled in America, and from 1769 to 1780, farmed in Orange County, New York. A royalist during the Revolutionary War, he returned to France in 1790. In his Letters from an American Farmer, *which was written in 1782 and from which the following is taken, he gives an interesting and philosophical picture of the country and its citizens.*

I wish I could be acquainted with the feelings and thoughts which must agitate the heart and present themselves to the mind of an enlightened Englishman when he first lands on this continent. He must greatly rejoice that he lived at a time to see this fair country discovered and settled. He must necessarily feel a share of national pride when he views the chain of settlements which embellish these extended shores. Here he sees the industry of his native country displayed in a new manner, and traces, in their works, the embryos of all the arts, sciences, and ingenuity which flourish in Europe. Here he beholds fair cities, substantial villages, extensive fields, an immense country filled with decent houses, good roads, orchards, meadows, and bridges, where, a hundred years ago, all was wild, wooded, and uncultivated! What a train of pleasing ideas this fair spectacle must suggest! It is a prospect which must inspire a good citizen with the most heart-felt pleasure!

The difficulty consists in the manner of viewing so extensive a scene. He is arrived on a new continent; a modern society offers itself to his contemplation, different from what he had hitherto seen. It is not composed, as in Europe, of great lords who possess everything and of a herd of people who have nothing. Here are no aristocratical families, no courts, no kings, no bishops, no ecclesiastical dominion, no invisible power giving to a few a very visible one, no great manufactures employing thousands, no great refinements of luxury. The rich and the poor are not so far removed from each other as they are in Europe. Some few towns excepted, we are all tillers of the earth, from Nova Scotia to West Florida. We are a people of cultivators, scattered over an immense territory, communicating with each other by means of good roads and navigable rivers, united by the silken bands of mild government, all respecting the laws without dreading their power, because they are equitable. We are all animated with the spirit of an industry which is unfettered and unrestrained, because each person works for himself. If he travels through our rural districts, he views not the hostile castle and the haughty mansion contrasted with the clay-built hut and the miserable cabin where cattle and men help to keep each other warm and dwell in meanness, smoke, and indigence. A pleasing uniformity of decent competence appears throughout our habitations. The meanest of our log houses is a dry and comfortable habitation. Lawyer or merchant are the fairest titles our towns afford; that of a farmer is the only appellation of the rural inhabitants of our country. It must take some time ere he can reconcile himself to our dictionary, which is but short in words of dignity and names of honor. There, on a Sunday, he sees a congregation of respectable farmers and their wives, all clad in neat homespun, well mounted, or riding in their own humble wagons. There is not among them an esquire, saving the unlettered magistrate. There he sees a parson as simple as his flock, a farmer who does not riot on the labor of others. We have no princes for whom we toil, starve, and bleed. We are the most perfect society now existing in the world. Here man is free as he ought to be; nor is this pleasing equality so transitory as many others are. Many ages will not see the shores of our great lakes replenished with inland nations, nor the unknown bounds of North America entirely peopled. Who can tell how far it extends? Who can tell the millions of men whom it will feed and contain, for no European foot has, as yet, traveled half the extent of this mighty continent?

The next wish of this traveler will be to know whence came all these people. They are a mixture of English, Scotch, Irish, French, Dutch, Germans, and Swedes. From this promiscuous breed, that race now called Americans have arisen. The eastern provinces must indeed be excepted, as being the unmixed descendants of English men. I have heard many wish that they had been more intermixed also; for my part, I am no wisher, and think it much better as it has happened. They exhibit a most conspicuous figure in this great and variegated picture. They too enter for a great share in the pleasing perspective displayed in these thirteen provinces. I know it is fashionable to reflect on them, but I respect them for what they have done, for the activity and wisdom with which they have settled their territory, for the decency of their manners, for their early love of letters, their ancient college, the first in this hemisphere, for their industry, which to me, who am but a farmer, is the criterion of everything. There never was a people, situated as they are, who with so ungrateful a soil have done more in so short a time. Do you think that the monarchical ingredients which are more prevalent in other governments have purged them from all foul stains? Their histories assert the contrary.

In this great American asylum the poor of Europe have by some means met together, and in consequence of various causes. To what purpose should they ask one another what countrymen they are? Alas, two-thirds of them had no country. Urged by a variety of motives, here they came. Everything has tended to regenerate them. New laws, a new mode of living, a new social system. Here they are become men. In Europe they were as so many useless plants, wanting vegetative mold and refreshing showers. They withered and were mowed down by want, hunger, and war; but now, by the power of transplantation, like all other plants, they have taken root and flourished! Formerly they were not numbered in any civil lists of their country except in those of the poor; here they rank as citizens. By what invisible power has this surprising metamorphosis been performed? By that of the laws and that of their industry. The laws, the indulgent laws, protect them as they arrive, stamping on them the symbol of adoption; they receive ample rewards for their labors; these accumulated rewards procure them land; those lands confer on them the title of freemen, and to that title every benefit is affixed which men can possibly require. This is the great operation daily performed by our laws.

What attachment can a poor European emigrant have for a country where he had nothing? The knowledge of the language, the love of a few kindred as poor as himself, were the only cords that tied him. His country is now that which gives him his land, bread, protection, and consequence. . . .What then is the American, this new man? He is neither a European nor the descendant of a European; thence that strange mixture of blood which you will find in no other country. I could point out to you a family whose grandfather was an Englishman, whose wife was Dutch, whose son married a French woman, and whose present four sons have now four wives of different nations. He is an American who, leaving behind him all his ancient prejudices and manners, receives new ones from the new mode of life he has embraced, the new government he obeys, and the new rank he holds. He becomes an American by being received in the broad lap of our great alma mater. Here individuals of all nations are melted into a new race of men whose labors and posterity will one day cause great changes in the world. Americans are the western pilgrims, who are carrying along with them the great mass of arts, sciences, vigor, and industry which began long since in the East. They will finish the great circle. The Americans were once scattered all over Europe. Here they are incorporated into one of the finest systems of population which has ever appeared and which will hereafter become distinct by the power of the different climates they inhabit. The American ought therefore to love this country much better than that in which either he or his forefathers were born. Here the rewards of his industry follow with equal steps the progress of his labor. His labor is founded on the basis of nature, self-interest: can it want a stronger allurement? Wives and children, who before in vain demanded of him a morsel of bread, now, fat and frolicsome, gladly help their father to clear those fields whence exuberant crops are to rise, to feed and to clothe them all, without any part being claimed either by a despotic prince, a rich abbot, or a mighty lord. Here religion demands but little of him—a small voluntary salary to the minister, and gratitude to God—can he refuse these? The American is a new man who acts on new principles; he must therefore entertain new ideas and form new opinions. From involuntary idleness, servile dependence, penury, and useful labor, he has passed to toils of a very different nature, rewarded by ample subsistence.

This is an American.

III

FORGING A
NEW NATION

REPORT OF GOVERNMENT
FOR THE WESTERN TERRITORY

Thomas Jefferson   *April 23, 1784*

---

*One of the major issues facing the Continental Congress
was the extent of the territories owned by each of the states and
what to do with the remaining land. In 1783 Virginia ceded its
western lands to the United States. On April 23, 1784, Thomas
Jefferson introduced in Congress a plan relative to the western
states and their organization into new states. A part of his
recommended legislation included forbidding slavery in the
new states, but this clause was defeated by a vote of seven to six.*

THE Committee to whom was recommitted the report of a plan for a temporary government of the western territory have agreed to the following resolutions.

Resolved, that so much of the territory ceded or to be ceded by individual states to the United States as is already purchased or shall be purchased of the

Indian inhabitants and offered for sale by Congress, shall be divided into distinct states, in the following manner, as nearly as such cessions will admit; that is to say, by parallels of latitude, so that each state shall comprehend from north to south two degrees of latitude beginning to count from the completion of forty-five degrees north of the equator; and by meridians of longitude, one of which shall pass thro' the lowest point of the rapids of Ohio, and the other through the Western Cape of the mouth of the Great Kanhaway, . . . But the territory eastward of this last meridian, between the Ohio, Lake Erie, and Pennsylvania shall be one state whatsoever may be its comprehension of latitude. . . .

That the settlers on any territory so purchased, and offered for sale, shall, either on their own petition, or on the order of Congress, receive authority from them with appointments of time and place for their free males of full age, within the limits of their state to meet together for the purpose of establishing a temporary government, to adopt the constitution and laws of any one of the original states, so that such laws nevertheless shall be subject to alteration by their ordinary legislature; and to erect, subject to a like alteration, counties or townships for the election of members for their legislature.

That when any such State shall have acquired twenty thousand inhabitants, on giving due proof thereof to Congress, they shall receive from them authority with appointment of time and place to call a convention of representatives to establish a permanent Constitution and Government for themselves, Provided that both the temporary and permanent governments be established on these principles as their basis.

First. That they shall forever remain a part of this confederacy of the United States of America. Second. That they shall be subject to the articles of Confederation in all those cases in which the original states shall be so subject and to all the acts and ordinances of the United States in Congress assembled, conformable thereto. Third. That they shall in no case interfere with the primary disposal of the soil by the United States . . . nor with the ordinances and regulations which Congress may find necessary for securing the title to such soil to the bona fide purchasers. Fourth. That they shall be subject to pay a part of the federal debts contracted or to be contracted, to be apportioned on them by Congress, according to the same common rule and measure, by which apportionments thereof shall be made on the other states. Fifth. That no tax shall be imposed on lands, the property of the United States. Sixth. That their respective governments shall be republican. Seventh. That the lands of non-resident proprietors shall in no case, be taxed higher than those of residents . . . before the admission thereof to a vote by its delegates in Congress.

That whensoever any of the said states shall have, of free inhabitants, as many as shall then be in any one the least numerous of the thirteen Original states, such State shall be admitted by its delegates into the Congress of the United States on an equal footing with the said original states: provided the consent of so many states in Congress is first obtained as may at the time be competent to such admission. And in order to adopt the said Articles of Confederation to the state of Congress when its numbers shall be thus increased, it shall be proposed to the legislatures of the states originally parties thereto, to require the assent of two thirds of the United States in Congress assembled in all those cases wherein by the said articles the assent of nine states is now required; which being agreed to by them shall be binding on the new states. Until such admission by their delegates into Congress, any of the said states after the establishment of their temporary government shall have authority to keep a sitting member in Congress, with a right of debating, but not of voting.

That measures not inconsistent with the principles of the Confederation and necessary for the preservation of peace and good order among the settlers in any of the said new states until they shall assume a temporary Government as aforesaid, may from time to time be taken by the United States in Congress assembled.

That the preceding articles shall be formed into a charter of compact, shall be duly executed by the President of the United States in Congress assembled, under his hand and the seal of the United States, shall be promulgated and shall stand as fundamental constitutions between the thirteen original states and each of the several states now newly described, unalterable . . . but by the joint consent of the United States in Congress assembled, and of the particular state within which such alteration is proposed to be made.

VIRGINIA STATUTE OF RELIGIOUS FREEDOM

Thomas Jefferson   *January 16, 1786*

> *The Virginia Statute of Religious Freedom was drawn up by Thomas Jefferson in 1777 and introduced into the General Assembly when Jefferson was governor in 1779. There was a long struggle for its enactment, but it was finally passed by the Virginia Senate on January 16, 1786. The act made religious taxes illegal and allowed for liberty of religious opinion. The separation of church and state and freedom of religion became law for the entire country with the passage of the First Amend-*

*ment to the Constitution, almost two centuries after the found-
ing of Jamestown. Thomas Jefferson specified for his tombstone
the following inscription, and not one word more: "Here was
buried Thomas Jefferson, Author of the Declaration of Independence, of the Statute of Virginia for Religious Freedom, and
Father of the University of Virginia, because by these, as testimo-
nials that I have lived, I wish most to be remembered."*

I. WHEREAS Almighty God hath created the mind free; that all attempts
to influence it by temporal punishments or burthens, or by civil incapacitations,
tend only to beget habits of hypocrisy and meanness, and are a departure from
the plan of the Holy author of our religion, who being Lord both of body and
mind, yet chose not to propagate it by coercions on either, as was in his Almighty
power to do; that the impious presumption of legislators and rulers, civil as well
as ecclesiastical, who being themselves but fallible and uninspired men, have
assumed dominion over the faith of others, setting up their own opinions and
modes of thinking as the only true and infallible, and as such endeavouring to
impose them on others, hath established and maintained false religions over the
greatest part of the world, and through all time; that to compel a man to furnish
contributions of money for the propagation of opinions which he disbelieves,
is sinful and tyrannical; that even the forcing him to support this or that teacher
of his own religious persuasion, is depriving him of the comfortable liberty of
giving his contributions to the particular pastor whose morals he would make
his pattern, and whose powers he feels most persuasive to righteousness, and
is withdrawing from the ministry those temporary rewards, which proceeding
from an approbation of their personal conduct, are an additional incitement to
earnest and unremitting labours for the instruction of mankind; that our civil
rights have no dependence on our religious opinions, any more than our
opinions in physics or geometry; that therefore the proscribing any citizen as
unworthy the public confidence by laying upon him an incapacity of being called
to offices of trust and emolument, unless he profess or renounce this or that religious opinion, is depriving him injuriously of those privileges and advantages to
which in common with his fellow-citizens he has a natural right, that it tends only
to corrupt the principles of that religion it is meant to encourage, by bribing with
a monopoly of worldly honours and emoluments, those who will externally
profess and conform to it; that though indeed these are criminal who do not
withstand such temptation, yet neither are those innocent who lay the bait in their
way; that to suffer the civil magistrate to intrude his powers into the field of
opinion, and to restrain the profession or propagation of principles on

supposition of their ill tendency, is a dangerous fallacy, which at once destroys all religious liberty, because he being of course judge of that tendency will make his opinions the rule of judgment, and approve or condemn the sentiments of others only as they shall square with or differ from his own; that it is time enough for the rightful purposes of civil government, for its officers to interfere when principles break out into overt acts against peace and good order; and finally, that truth is great and will prevail if left to herself, that she is the proper and sufficient antagonist to error, and has nothing to fear from the conflict, unless by human interposition disarmed of her natural weapons, free argument and debate, errors ceasing to be dangerous when it is permitted freely to contradict them.

II. Be it enacted by the General Assembly, that no man shall be compelled to frequent or support any religious worship, place or ministry whatsoever, nor shall be enforced, restrained, molested, or burthened in his body or goods, nor shall otherwise suffer on account of his religious opinions or belief; but that all men shall be free to profess, and by argument to maintain, their opinion in matters of religion, and that the same shall in no wise diminish, enlarge or affect their civil capacities.

III. And though we well know that this assembly, elected by the people for the ordinary purposes of legislation only, have no power to restrain the acts of succeeding assemblies, constituted with powers equal to our own, and that therefore to declare this act to be irrevocable would be of no effect in law; yet as we are free to declare, and do declare, that the rights hereby asserted are of the natural rights of mankind, and that if any act shall hereafter be passed to repeal the present, or to narrow its operation, such act will be an infringement of natural right.

THE NORTHWEST ORDINANCE

July 13, 1787

The land west of the Alleghenies attracted a number of settlers. At one time several states claimed land to the west, but Virginia and other states ceded their holdings to the Confederation. Congress passed the Northwest Ordinance on July 13, 1787. This important act provided for the formation of new states and their entry into the Union on equal terms with the

*original states, as well as provisions for education, civil liberties,
and the exclusion of slavery. Eventually five states—Ohio,
Indiana, Illinois, Michigan and Wisconsin—were formed from
this territory and admitted to the Union.*

BE it ordained by the United States in Congress assembled, That the said territory, for the purposes of temporary government, be one district, subject, however, to be divided into two districts, as future circumstances may, in the opinion of Congress, make it expedient.

Be it ordained by the authority aforesaid, That the estates, both of resident and non-resident proprietors in the said territory, dying intestate, shall descend to, and be distributed among their children, and the descendants of a deceased child, in equal parts; the descendants of a deceased child or grandchild to take the share of their deceased parent in equal parts among them: And where there shall be no children or descendants, then in equal parts to the next of kin in equal degree; and among collaterals, the children of a deceased brother or sister of the intestate shall have, in equal parts among them, their deceased parents' share; and there shall in no case be a distinction between kindred of the whole and half-blood; saving, in all cases, to the widow of the intestate her third part of the real estate for life, and one-third part of the personal estate; and this law relative to descents and dower, shall remain in full force until altered by the legislature of the district. And until the governor and judges shall adopt laws as hereinafter mentioned, estates in the said territory may be devised or bequeathed by wills in writing, signed and sealed by him or her in whom the estate may be (being of full age), and attested by three witnesses; and real estates may be conveyed by lease and release, or bargain and sale, signed sealed and delivered by the person, being of full age, in whom the estate may be, and attested by two witnesses, provided such wills be duly proved, and such conveyances be acknowledged, or the execution thereof duly proved, and be recorded within one year after proper magistrates, courts, and registers shall be appointed for that purpose; and personal property may be transferred by delivery; saving, however to the French and Canadian inhabitants, and other settlers of the Kaskaskies, St. Vincents and the neighboring villages who have heretofore professed themselves citizens of Virginia, their laws and customs now in force among them, relative to the descent and conveyance, of property.

Be it ordained by the authority aforesaid, That there shall be appointed from time to time by Congress, a governor, whose commission shall continue in force for the term of three years, unless sooner revoked by Congress; he shall reside in the district, and have a freehold estate therein in 1,000 acres of land, while in the exercise of his office.

There shall be appointed from time to time by Congress, a secretary, whose commission shall continue in force for four years unless sooner revoked; he shall reside in the district, and have a freehold estate therein in 500 acres of land, while in the exercise of his office. It shall be his duty to keep and preserve the acts and laws passed by the legislature, and the public records of the district, and the proceedings of the governor in his executive department, and transmit authentic copies of such acts and proceedings, every six months, to the Secretary of Congress: There shall also be appointed a court to consist of three judges, any two of whom to form a court, who shall have a common law jurisdiction, and reside in the district, and have each therein a freehold estate in 500 acres of land while in the exercise of their offices; and their commissions shall continue in force during good behavior.

The governor and judges, or a majority of them, shall adopt and publish in the district such laws of the original States, criminal and civil, as may be necessary and best suited to the circumstances of the district, and report them to Congress from time to time: which laws shall be in force in the district until the organization of the General Assembly therein, unless disapproved of by Congress; but afterwards the Legislature shall have authority to alter them as they shall think fit.

The governor, for the time being, shall be commander-in-chief of the militia, appoint and commission all officers in the same below the rank of general officers; all general officers shall be appointed and commissioned by Congress.

Previous to the organization of the general assembly, the governor shall appoint such magistrates and other civil officers in each county or township, as he shall find necessary for the preservations of the peace and good order in the same: After the general assembly shall be organized, the powers and duties of the magistrates and other civil officers shall be regulated and defined by the said assembly; but all magistrates and other civil officers not herein otherwise directed, shall, during the continuance of this temporary government, be appointed by the governor.

For the prevention of crimes and injuries, the laws to be adopted or made shall have force in all parts of the district, and for the execution of process, criminal and civil, the governor shall make proper divisions thereof; and he shall proceed from time to time as circumstances may require, to lay out the parts of the district in which the Indian titles shall have been extinguished, into counties and townships, subject however to such alterations as may thereafter be made by the legislature.

So soon as there shall be five thousand free male inhabitants of full age in the district, upon giving proof thereof to the governor, they shall receive authority, with time and place, to elect representatives from their counties or townships to represent them in the general assembly: Provided, That, for every five hundred free male inhabitants, there shall be one representative, and so on progressively with the number of free male inhabitants shall the right of representation increase, until the number of representatives shall amount to twenty-five; after which, the number and proportion of representatives shall be regulated by the legislature: Provided, That no person be eligible or qualified to act as a representative unless he shall have been a citizen of one of the United States three years, and be a resident in the district, or unless he shall have resided in the district three years; and, in either case, shall likewise hold in his own right, in fee simple, two hundred acres of land within the same: Provided, also, That a freehold in fifty acres of land in the district, having been a citizen of one of the states, and being resident in the district, or the like freehold and two years residence in the district, shall be necessary to qualify a man as an elector of a representative.

The representatives thus elected, shall serve for the term of two years; and, in case of the death of a representative, or removal from office, the governor shall issue a writ to the county or township for which he was a member, to elect another in his stead, to serve for the residue of the term.

The general assembly or legislature shall consist of the governor, legislative council, and a house of representatives. The Legislative Council shall consist of five members, to continue in office five years, unless sooner removed by Congress; any three of whom to be a quorum: and the members of the Council shall be nominated and appointed in the following manner, to wit: As soon as representatives shall be elected, the Governor shall appoint a time and place for them to meet together; and, when met, they shall nominate ten persons, residents in the district, and each possessed of a freehold in five hundred acres of land, and return their names to Congress; five of whom Congress shall appoint and commission to serve as aforesaid; and, whenever a vacancy shall happen in the council, by death or removal from office, the house of representatives shall nominate two persons, qualified as aforesaid, for each vacancy, and return their names to Congress; one of whom Congress shall appoint and commission for the residue of the term. And every five years, four months at least before the expiration of the time of service of the members of council, the said house shall nominate ten persons, qualified as aforesaid, and return their names to Congress; five of whom Congress shall appoint and commission to serve as members of the council five years, unless sooner removed. And the governor, legislative council, and house of representatives, shall have authority to make laws in all cases, for the good government of the district, not repugnant to the principles and articles in this ordinance established and declared. And all bills, having passed by a majority in the house, and by a majority in the council, shall be referred to the governor for his assent; but no bill, or legislative act whatever, shall be of any force without his assent. The governor shall have power to convene, prorogue, and dissolve the general assembly, when, in his opinion, it shall be expedient.

The governor, judges, legislative council, secretary, and such other officers as Congress shall appoint in the district, shall take an oath or affirmation of fidelity and of office; the governor before the president of congress, and all other officers before the Governor. As soon as a legislature shall be formed in the district, the council and house assembled in one room, shall have authority, by joint ballot, to elect a delegate to Congress, who shall have a seat in Congress, with a right of debating but not of voting during this temporary government.

And, for extending the fundamental principles of civil and religious liberty, which form the basis whereon these republics, their laws and constitutions are erected; to fix and establish those principles as the basis of all laws, constitutions, and governments, which forever hereafter shall be formed in the said territory: to provide also for the establishment of States, and permanent government therein, and for their admission to a share in the federal councils on an equal footing with the original States, at as early periods as may be consistent with the general interest:

It is hereby ordained and declared by the authority aforesaid, That the following articles shall be considered as articles of compact between the original States and the people and States in the said territory and forever remain unalterable, unless by common consent, to wit:

ART. 1. No person, demeaning himself in a peaceable and orderly manner, shall ever be molested on account of his mode of worship or religious sentiments, in the said territory.

ART. 2. The inhabitants of the said territory shall always be entitled to the benefits of the writ of *habeas corpus*, and of the trial by jury; of a proportionate representation of the people in the legislature; and of judicial proceedings according to the course of the common law. All persons shall be bailable, unless for capital offences, where the proof shall be evident or the presumption great. All fines shall be moderate; and no cruel or unusual punishments shall be inflicted. No man shall be deprived of his liberty or property, but by the judgment of his peers or the law of the land; and, should the public exigencies make it necessary, for the common preservation, to take any person's property, or to demand his particular services, full compensation shall be made for the same. And, in the just preservation of rights and property, it is understood and declared, that no law ought ever to be made, or have force in the said territory, that shall, in any manner whatever, interfere with or affect private contracts or engagements, *bona fide*, and without fraud, previously formed.

ART. 3. Religion, morality, and knowledge, being necessary to good government and the happiness of mankind, schools and the means of education shall forever be encouraged. The utmost good faith shall always be observed towards the Indians; their lands and property shall never be taken from them without their consent; and, in their property, rights, and liberty, they shall never be invaded or disturbed, unless in just and lawful wars authorized by Congress; but laws founded in justice and humanity, shall from time to time be made for preventing wrongs being done to them, and for preserving peace and friendship with them.

ART. 4. The said territory, and the States which may be formed therein, shall forever remain a part of this Confederacy of the United States of America, subject to the Articles of Confederation, and to such alterations therein as shall be constitutionally made; and to all the acts and ordinances of the United States in Congress assembled, conformable thereto. The inhabitants and settlers in the said territory shall be subject to pay a part of the federal debts contracted or to be contracted, and a proportional part of the expenses of government, to be apportioned on them by Congress according to the same common rule and measure by which apportionments thereof shall be made on the other States; and the taxes for paying their proportion shall be laid and levied by the authority and direction of the legislatures of the district or districts, or new States, as in the original States, within the time agreed upon by the United States in Congress assembled. The legislatures of those districts or new States, shall never interfere with the primary disposal of the soil by the United States in Congress assembled, nor with any regulations Congress may find necessary for securing the title in such soil to the *bona fide* purchasers. No tax shall be imposed on lands the property of the United States; and, in no case, shall non-resident proprietors be taxed higher than residents. The navigable waters leading into the Mississippi and St. Lawrence, and the carrying places between the same, shall be common highways and forever free, as well to the inhabitants of the said territory as to the citizens of the United States, and those of any other States that may be admitted into the confederacy, without any tax, impost, or duty therefor.

ART. 5. There shall be formed in the said territory, not less than three nor more than five States; and the boundaries of the States, as soon as Virginia shall alter her act of cession, and consent to the same, shall become fixed and established as follows, to wit: The western State in the said territory, shall be bounded by the Mississippi, the Ohio and Wabash Rivers; a direct line drawn from the Wabash and Post Vincents, due North, to the territorial line between the United States and Canada; and, by the said territorial line, to the Lake of the Woods and Mississippi. The middle State shall be bounded by the said direct line, the Wabash from Post Vincents to the Ohio, by the Ohio, by a direct line, drawn due north from the mouth of the Great Miami, to the said territorial line, and by the said territorial line. The eastern State shall be bounded by the last mentioned direct line, the Ohio, Pennsylvania, and the said territorial line: Provided, however, and it is further understood and declared, that the boundaries of these three States shall be subject so far to be altered, that, if Congress shall hereafter find it expedient, they shall have authority to form one or two States in that part of the said territory which lies north of an east and west line drawn through the southerly bend or extreme of lake Michigan. And, whenever any of the said States shall have sixty thousand free inhabitants therein, such State shall be admitted, by its delegates, into the Congress of the United States, on an equal footing with the original States in all respects whatever, and shall be at liberty to form a permanent constitution and State government: Provided, the constitution and government so to be formed, shall be republican, and in conformity to the principles contained in these articles; and, so far as it can be consistent with the general interest of the confederacy, such admission shall be allowed at an earlier period, and where there may be a less number of free inhabitants in the State than sixty thousand.

ART. 6. There shall be neither slavery nor involuntary servitude in the said territory, otherwise than in the punishment of crimes whereof the party shall have been duly convicted: Provided, always, That any person escaping into the same, from whom labor or service is lawfully claimed in any one of the original States, such fugitive may be lawfully reclaimed and conveyed to the person claiming his or her labor or service as aforesaid.

Be it ordained by the authority aforesaid, That the resolutions of the 23rd of April 1784, relative to the subject of this ordinance, be, and the same are hereby repealed and declared null and void.

THE CONSTITUTION
OF THE UNITED STATES

September 17, 1787

In September 1786 Alexander Hamilton introduced a motion at a meeting of five states in Annapolis, Maryland, that all the states should send delegates to meet in Philadelphia the following year to "devise such provisions as shall seem to them necessary to render the Constitution of the Federal government adequate to the exigencies of the union." Fifty-five delegates from twelve states—Rhode Island deciding not to attend—made their way to Philadelphia for a federal or constitutional convention. Many of the delegates may have intended to follow their instructions of meeting "for the sole purpose of revising the Articles of the Confederation." The convention was scheduled to open on May 14, 1787, but it was eleven days before a quorum arrived. George Washington was unanimously elected the convention's president. On May 29, Edmund Randolph introduced a plan prepared by James Madison and the Virginia delegation, known as the Virginia Resolves. For two months the convention debated various ideas. Finally, on July 26, a committee of five was selected to prepare a tentative constitution; they prepared a first draft which was then debated for five more weeks. The final agreements were then presented to a style committee: James Madison, Alexander Hamilton, Gouverneur Morris, Rufus King and William Samuel Johnson. Morris did most of the writing of the final draft. Thirty-nine delegates were present on the final day, September 17, 1787, when the Constitution of the United States was finally approved and signed and sent to the states for ratification. The United States Constitution is the oldest written constitution still in effect today. Written for thirteen states and four million people, it now covers fifty states and over 230 million people. Perhaps the convention's genius was the ability to draft a single document that men of different political principles could agree to accept.

WE THE PEOPLE of the United States, in Order to form a more perfect Union, establish Justice, insure domestic Tranquility, provide for the common defence, promote the general Welfare, and secure the Blessings of Liberty to ourselves and our Posterity, do ordain and establish this Constitution for the United States of America.

ART. I

SEC. 1. All legislative Powers herein granted shall be vested in a Congress of the United States, which shall consist of a Senate and House of Representatives.

SEC. 2. The House of Representatives shall be composed of Members chosen every second Year by the People of the several States, and the Electors in each State shall have the Qualifications requisite for Electors of the most numerous Branch of the State Legislature.

No Person shall be a Representative who shall not have attained to the Age of twenty five Years, and been seven Years a Citizen of the United States, and who shall not, when elected, be an Inhabitant of that State in which he shall be chosen.

Representatives and direct Taxes shall be apportioned among the several States which may be included within this Union, according to their respective Numbers, which shall be determined by adding to the whole Number of free Persons, including those bound to Service for a Term of Years, and excluding Indians not taxed, three fifths of all other Persons. The actual Enumeration shall be made within three Years after the first Meeting of the Congress of the United States, and within every subsequent Term of ten Years, in such Manner as they shall by Law direct. The Number of Representatives shall not exceed one for every thirty Thousand, but each State shall have at Least one Representative; and until such enumeration shall be made, the State of New Hampshire shall be entitled to chuse three, Massachusetts eight, Rhode-Island and Providence Plantations one, Connecticut five, New-York six, New Jersey four, Pennsylvania eight, Delaware one, Maryland six, Virginia ten, North Carolina five, South Carolina five, and Georgia three.

When vacancies happen in the Representation from any State, the Executive Authority thereof shall issue Writs of Election to fill such Vacancies.

The House of Representatives shall chuse their Speaker and other Officers; and shall have the sole Power of Impeachment.

SEC. 3. The Senate of the United States shall be composed of two Senators from each State, chosen by the Legislature thereof, for six Years; and each Senator shall have one Vote.

Immediately after they shall be assembled in Consequence of the first Election, they shall be divided as equally as may be into three Classes. The Seats of the Senators of the first Class shall be vacated at the Expiration of the second Year, of the second Class at the Expiration of the fourth Year, and of the third Class at the Expiration of the sixth Year, so that one third may be chosen every second Year; and if Vacancies happen by Resignation, or otherwise, during the Recess of the Legislature of any State, the Executive thereof may make temporary Appointments until the next Meeting of the Legislature, which shall then fill such Vacancies.

No Person shall be a Senator who shall not have attained to the Age of thirty Years, and been nine Years a Citizens of the United States, and who shall not, when elected, be an Inhabitant of that State for which he shall be chosen.

The Vice President of the United States shall be President of the Senate, but shall have no Vote, unless they be equally divided.

The Senate shall chuse their other Officers, and also a President *pro tempore*, in the Absence of the Vice President, or when he shall exercise the Office of President of the United States.

The Senate shall have the sole Power to try all Impeachments. When sitting for that Purpose, they shall be on Oath or Affirmation. When the President of the United States is tried, the Chief Justice shall preside: And no Person shall be convicted without the Concurrence of two thirds of the Members present.

Judgment in Cases of Impeachment shall not extend further than to removal from Office, and disqualification to hold and enjoy any Office of honor, Trust or Profit under the United States: but the Party convicted shall nevertheless be liable and subject to Indictment, Trial, Judgment and Punishment, according to Law.

SEC. 4. The Times, Places and Manner of holding Elections for Senators and Representatives, shall be prescribed in each State by the Legislature thereof; but the Congress may at any time by Law make or alter such Regulations, except as to the Places of chusing Senators.

The Congress shall assemble at least once in every Year, and such Meeting shall be on the first Monday in December, unless they shall by Law appoint a different Day.

SEC. 5. Each House shall be the Judge of the Elections, Returns and Qualifications of its own Members, and a Majority of each shall constitute a Quorum to do Business; but a smaller Number may adjourn from day to day, and may be authorized to compel the Attendance of absent Members, in such Manner, and under such Penalties as each House may provide.

Each House may determine the Rules of its Proceedings, punish its Members for disorderly Behaviour, and with the Concurrence of two thirds, expel a Member.

Each House shall keep a Journal of its Proceedings, and from time to time publish the same, excepting such Parts as may in their Judgment require Secrecy; and the Yeas and Nays of the Members of either House on any question shall, at the Desire of one fifth of those Present, be entered on the Journal.

Neither House, during the Session of Congress, shall, without the Consent of the other, adjourn for more than three days, nor to any other Place than that in which the two Houses shall be sitting.

SEC. 6. The Senators and Representatives shall receive a Compensation for their Services, to be ascertained by Law, and paid out of the Treasury of the United States. They shall in all Cases, except Treason, Felony and Breach of the Peace, be privileged from Arrest during their Attendance at the Session of their respective Houses, and in going to and returning from the same; and for any

Speech or Debate in either House, they shall not be questioned in any other Place.

No Senator or Representative shall, during the Time for which he was elected, be appointed to any civil Office under the Authority of the United States which shall have been created, or the Emoluments whereof shall have been increased during such time; and no Person holding any Office under the United States, shall be a Member of either House during his Continuance in Office.

SEC. 7. All Bills for raising Revenue shall originate in the House of Representatives; but the Senate may propose or concur with Amendments as on other Bills.

Every Bill which shall have passed the House of Representatives and the Senate, shall, before it become a Law, be presented to the President of the United States; If he approve he shall sign it, but if not he shall return it, with his Objections to that House in which it shall have originated, who shall enter the Objections at large on their Journal, and proceed to reconsider it. If after such Reconsideration two thirds of that House shall agree to pass the Bill, it shall be sent, together with the Objections, to the other House, by which it shall likewise be reconsidered, and if approved by two thirds of that House, it shall become a Law. But in all such Cases the Votes of both Houses shall be determined by yeas and Nays, and the Names of the Persons voting for and against the Bill shall be entered on the Journal of each House respectively. If any Bill shall not be returned by the President within ten Days (Sundays excepted) after it shall have been presented to him, the Same shall be a Law, in like Manner as if he had signed it, unless the Congress by their Adjournment prevent its Return, in which Case it shall not be a Law.

Every Order, Resolution, or Vote to which the Concurrence of the Senate and House of Representatives may be necessary (except on a question of Adjournment) shall be presented to the President of the United States; and before the Same shall take Effect, shall be approved by him, or being disapproved by him, shall be repassed by two thirds of the Senate and House of Representatives, according to the Rules and Limitations prescribed in the Case of a Bill.

SEC. 8. The Congress shall have Power To lay and collect Taxes, Duties, Imposts and Excises, to pay the Debts and provide for the common Defence and general Welfare of the United States; but all Duties, Imposts and Excises shall be uniform throughout the United States;

To borrow Money on the credit of the United States;

To regulate Commerce with foreign Nations, and among the several States, and with the Indian Tribes;

To establish an uniform Rule of Naturalization, and uniform Laws on the subject of Bankruptcies throughout the United States;

To coin Money, regulate the Value thereof, and of foreign Coin, and fix the Standard of Weights and Measures;

To provide for the Punishment of counterfeiting the Securities and current Coin of the United States;

To establish Post Offices and post Roads;

To promote the Progress of Science and useful Arts, by securing for limited Times to Authors and Inventors the exclusive Right to their respective Writings and Discoveries;

To constitute Tribunals inferior to the supreme Court;

To define and punish Piracies and Felonies committed on the high Seas, and Offences against the Law of Nations;

To declare War, grant Letters of Marque and Reprisal, and make Rules concerning Captures on Land and Water;

To raise and support Armies; but no Appropriation of Money to that Use shall be for a longer Term than two Years;

To provide and maintain a Navy;

To make Rules for the Government and Regulation of the land and naval Forces;

To provide for calling forth the Militia to execute the Laws of the Union, suppress Insurrections and repel Invasions;

To provide for organizing, arming, and disciplining, the Militia, and for governing such Part of them as may be employed in the Service of the United States, reserving to the States respectively, the Appointment of the Officers, and the Authority of training the Militia according to the discipline prescribed by Congress;

To exercise exclusive Legislation in all Cases whatsoever, over such District (not exceeding ten Miles square) as may, by Cession of particular States, and the Acceptance of Congress, become the Seat of the Government of the United States, and to exercise like Authority over all Places purchased by the Consent of the Legislature of the State in which the Same shall be, for the Erection of Forts, Magazines, Arsenals, dock-Yards, and other needful Buildings;—And

To make all Laws which shall be necessary and proper for carrying into Execution the foregoing Powers, and all other Powers vested by this Constitution in the Government of the United States, or in any Department or Officer thereof.

SEC. 9. The Migration or Importation of such Persons as any of the States now existing shall think proper to admit, shall not be prohibited by the Congress prior to the Year one thousand eight hundred and eight, but a Tax or duty may be imposed on such Importation, not exceeding ten dollars for each Person.

The Privilege of the Writ of *Habeas Corpus* shall not be suspended, unless when in Cases of Rebellion or Invasion the public Safety may require it.

No Bill of Attainder or *ex post facto* Law shall be passed.

No Capitation, or other direct, Tax shall be laid, unless in Proportion to the Census or Enumeration herein before directed to be taken.

No Tax or Duty shall be laid on Articles exported from any State.

No Preference shall be given by any Regulation of Commerce or Revenue to the Ports of one State over those of another; nor shall Vessels bound to, or from, one State, be obliged to enter, clear, or pay Duties in another.

No Money shall be drawn from the Treasury, but in Consequence of Appropriations made by Law; and a regular Statement and Account of the Receipts and Expenditures of all public Money shall be published from time to time.

No Title of Nobility shall be granted by the United States: And no Person holding any Office of Profit or Trust under them, shall, without the Consent of Congress, accept of any present, Emolument, Office, or Title, of any kind whatever, from any King, Prince or foreign State.

SEC. 10. No State shall enter into any Treaty, Alliance, or Confederation; grant Letters of Marque and Reprisal; coin Money; emit Bills of Credit; make any Thing but gold and silver Coin a Tender in Payment of Debts; pass any Bill of Attainder, *ex post facto* Law, or Law impairing the Obligation of Contracts, or grant any Title of Nobility.

No State shall, without the Consent of the Congress, lay any Imposts or Duties on Imports or Exports, except what may be absolutely necessary for executing it's inspection Laws: and the net Produce of all Duties and Imposts, laid by any State on Imports or Exports, shall be for the Use of the Treasury of the United States; and all such laws shall be subject to the Revision and Controul of the Congress.

No State shall, without the Consent of Congress, lay any Duty of Tonnage, keep Troops, or Ships of War in time of Peace, enter into any Agreement or Compact with another State, or with a foreign Power, or engage in War, unless actually invaded, or in such imminent Danger as will not admit of delay.

ART. II

SEC. 1. The executive Power shall be vested in a President of the United States of America. He shall hold his Office during the Term of four Years, and, together with the Vice President, chosen for the same Term, be elected, as follows:

Each State shall appoint, in such Manner as the Legislature thereof may direct, a Number of Electors, equal to the whole Number of Senators and Representatives to which the State may be entitled in the congress: but no Senator or Representative, or Person holding an Office of Trust or Profit under the United States, shall be appointed an Elector.

The Electors shall meet in their respective States, and vote by Ballot for two Persons, of whom one at least shall not be an Inhabitant of the same State with themselves. And they shall make a List of all the Persons voted for, and of the Number of Votes for each; which List they shall sign and certify, and transmit sealed to the Seat of the Government of the United States, directed to the President of the Senate. The President of the Senate shall, in the Presence of the Senate and House of Representatives, open all the Certificates, and the Votes shall then be counted. The Person having the greatest Number of Votes shall be the President, if such Number be a Majority of the whole Number of Electors appointed; and if there be more than one who have such Majority, and have an equal Number of Votes, then the House of Representatives shall immediately chuse by Ballot one of them for President; and if no person have a Majority, then from the five highest on the list the said House shall in like Manner chuse the President. But in chusing the President, the Votes shall be taken by States, the Representation from each State having one Vote; A quorum for this Purpose shall consist of a Member or Members from two thirds of the States, and a Majority of all the States shall be necessary to a Choice. In every Case, after the Choice of the President, the Person having the greatest Number of Votes of the Electors shall be the Vice President. But if there should remain two or more who have equal Votes, the Senate shall chuse from them by Ballot the Vice President.

The Congress may determine the Time of chusing the Electors, and the Day on which they shall give their Votes; which Day shall be the same throughout the United States.

No Person except a natural born Citizen, or a Citizen of the United States, at the time of the Adoption of this Constitution, shall be eligible to the Office of President; neither shall any Person be eligible to that Office who shall not have attained to the Age of thirty five Years, and been fourteen Years a Resident within the United States.

In Case of the Removal of the President from Office, or of his Death, Resignation, or Inability to discharge the Powers and Duties of the said Office, the Same shall devolve on the Vice President, and the Congress may by Law provide for the Case of Removal, Death, Resignation or Inability, both of the President and Vice President, declaring what Officer shall then act as President, and such Officer shall act accordingly, until the Disability be removed, or a President shall be elected.

The President shall, at stated Times, receive for his Services, a Compensation, which shall neither be encreased nor diminished during the Period for which he shall have been elected, and he shall not receive within that Period any other Emolument from the United States, or any of them.

Before he enter on the Execution of his Office, he shall take the following

Oath or Affirmation:—"I do solemnly swear (or affirm) that I will faithfully execute the Office of President of the United States, and will to the best of my Ability, preserve, protect and defend the Constitution of the United States."

SEC. 2. The President shall be Commander in Chief of the Army and Navy of the United States, and of the Militia of the several States, when called into the actual Service of the United States; he may require the Opinion, in writing, of the principal Officer in each of the executive Departments, upon any Subject relating to the Duties of their respective Offices, and he shall have Power to grant Reprieves and Pardons for Offences against the United States, except in Case of Impeachment.

He shall have Power, by and with the Advice and Consent of the Senate, to make Treaties, provided two thirds of the Senators present concur; and he shall nominate, and by and with the Advice and Consent of the Senate, shall appoint Ambassadors, other public Ministers and Consuls, Judges of the supreme Court, and all other Officers of the United States, whose Appointments are not herein otherwise provided for, and which shall be established by Law: but the Congress may by Law vest the Appointment of such inferior Officers, as they think proper, in the President alone, in the Courts of Law, or in the Heads of Departments.

The President shall have Power to fill up all Vacancies that may happen during the Recess of the Senate, by granting Commissions which shall expire at the End of their next Session.

SEC. 3. He shall from time to time give to the Congress Information of the State of the Union, and recommend to their Consideration such Measures as he shall judge necessary and expedient; he may, on extraordinary Occasions, convene both Houses, or either of them, and in Case of Disagreement between them, with Respect to the Time of Adjournment, he may adjourn them to such Time as he shall think proper; he shall receive Ambassadors and other public Ministers; he shall take Care that the Laws be faithfully executed, and shall Commission all the Officers of the United States.

SEC. 4. The President, Vice President and all civil Officers of the United States, shall be removed from Office on Impeachment for, and Conviction of, Treason, Bribery, or other high Crimes and Misdemeanors.

ART. III

SEC. 1. The Judicial Power of the United States, shall be vested in one supreme Court, and in such inferior Courts as the Congress may from time to time ordain and establish. The Judges, both of the supreme and inferior Courts, shall hold their Offices during good Behaviour, and shall, at stated Times, receive for their Services, a Compensation, which shall not be diminished during their Continuance in Office.

SEC. 2. The judicial Power shall extend to all Cases, in Law and Equity, arising under this Constitution, the Laws of the United States, and Treaties made, or which shall be made, under their Authority;—to all Cases affecting Ambassadors, other public Ministers and Consuls;—to all Cases of admiralty and maritime Jurisdiction;—to Controversies to which the United States shall be a Party;—to Controversies between two or more States;—between a State and Citizens of another State;—between Citizens of different States,—between Citizens of the same State claiming Lands under Grants of different States, and between a State, or the Citizen thereof, and foreign States, Citizens or Subjects.

In all Cases affecting Ambassadors, other public Ministers and Consuls, and those in which a State shall be Party, the supreme Court shall have original Jurisdiction. In all the other Cases before mentioned, the supreme Court shall have appellate Jurisdiction, both as to Law and Fact, with such Exceptions, and under such Regulations as the Congress shall make.

The Trial of all Crimes, except in Cases of Impeachment, shall be by Jury; and such Trial shall be held in the State where the said Crimes shall have been committed; but when not committed within any State, the Trial shall be at such Place or Places as the Congress may by Law have directed.

SEC. 3. Treason against the United States, shall consist only in levying War against them, or in adhering to their Enemies, giving them Aid and Comfort. No Person shall be convicted of Treason unless on the Testimony of two Witnesses to the same overt Act, or on Confession in open Court.

The Congress shall have Power to declare the Punishment of Treason, but no Attainder of Treason shall work Corruption of Blood, or Forfeiture except during the Life of the Person attainted.

ART. IV

SEC. 1. Full Faith and Credit shall be given in each State to the Public Acts, Records, and judicial Proceedings of every other State. And the Congress may by general Laws prescribe the Manner in which such Acts, Records and Proceedings shall be proved, and the Effect thereof.

SEC. 2. The Citizens of each State shall be entitled to all Privileges and Immunities of Citizens in the several States.

A Person charged in any State with Treason, Felony, or other Crime, who shall flee from Justice, and be found in another State, shall on Demand of the executive Authority of the State from which he fled, be delivered up, to be removed to the State having Jurisdiction of the Crime.

No Person held to Service or Labour in one State, under the Laws thereof, escaping into another, shall, in Consequence of any Law or Regulation therein, be discharged from such Service or Labour, but shall be delivered up on Claim of the Party to whom such Service or Labour may be due.

SEC. 3. New States may be admitted by the Congress into this Union; but no new States shall be formed or erected within the Jurisdiction of any other State; nor any State be formed by the Junction of two or more States, or Parts of States, without the Consent of the Legislatures of the States concerned as well as of the Congress.

The Congress shall have Power to dispose of and make all needful Rules and Regulations respecting the Territory or other Property belonging to the United States; and nothing in this Constitution shall be so construed as to Prejudice any Claims of the United States, or of any particular State.

SEC. 4. The United States shall guarantee to every State in this Union a Republican Form of Government, and shall protect each of them against Invasion; and on Application of the Legislature, or of the Executive (when the Legislature cannot be convened) against domestic Violence.

ART. V

The Congress, whenever two thirds of both Houses shall deem it necessary, shall propose Amendments to this Constitution, or, on the Application of the Legislatures of two thirds of the several States, shall call a Convention for proposing Amendments, which, in either Case, shall be valid to all Intents and Purposes, as Part of this Constitution, when ratified by the Legislatures of three fourths of the several States, or by Conventions in three fourths thereof, as the one or the other Mode of Ratification may be proposed by the Congress; Provided that no Amendment which may be made prior to the Year One thousand eight hundred and eight shall in any Manner affect the first and fourth Clauses in the Ninth Section of the first Article; and that no State, without its Consent, shall be deprived of it's equal Suffrage in the Senate.

ART. VI

All Debts contracted and Engagements entered into, before the Adoption of this Constitution, shall be as valid against the United States under this Constitution, as under the Confederation.

This Constitution, and the Laws of the United States which shall be made in Pursuance thereof; and all Treaties made, or which shall be made, under the Authority of the United States, shall be the supreme Law of the Land; and the Judges in every State shall be bound thereby, any Thing in the Constitution or Laws of any State to the Contrary notwithstanding.

The Senators and Representatives before mentioned, and the Members of the several State Legislatures, and all executive and judicial Officers, both of the United States and of the several States, shall be bound by Oath or Affirmation, to support this Constitution; but no religious Test shall ever be required as a Qualification to any Office or public Trust under the United States.

ART. VII

The Ratification of the Conventions of nine States, shall be sufficient for the Establishment of this Constitution between the States so ratifying the Same.

Done in Convention by the Unanimous Consent of the States present the Seventeenth Day of September in the Year of our Lord one thousand seven hundred and Eighty seven and of the Independence of the United States of America the Twelfth. In witness whereof We have hereunto subscribed our Names.

G° WASHINGTON—Presid^t
and deputy from Virginia

New Hampshire	John Langdon Nicholas Gilman
Massachusetts	Nathaniel Gorham Rufus King
Connecticut	Wm Saml Johnson Roger Sherman
New York	Alexander Hamilton
New Jersey	Wil: Livingston David Brearley Wm Paterson Jona: Dayton
Pennsylvania	B Franklin Thomas Mifflin Robt Morris Geo. Clymer Thos FitzSimons Jared Ingersoll James Wilson Gouv Morris

Delaware	Geo: Read Gunning Bedford jun John Dickinson Richard Bassett Jaco: Broom
Maryland	James McHenry Dan of St Thos Jenifer Danl Carroll
Virginia	John Blair— James Madison Jr.
North Carolina	Wm Blount Richd Dobbs Spaight Hu Williamson
South Carolina	J. Rutledge Charles Cotes- worth Pinckney Charles Pinckney Pierce Butler
Georgia	William Few Abr Baldwin

SPEECH BEFORE FEDERAL CONVENTION

Benjamin Franklin   *September 17, 1787*

> *Benjamin Franklin was eighty-one years of age when the*
> *Constitutional Convention was held. Upon his return as United*
> *States minister to Paris in 1785, he was elected president of*
> *Pennsylvania. For more than forty years, he had been working*
> *on the national scene for unity. Perhaps that is why his com-*
> *ments are so poignant.*

"MR. President: I confess that there are several parts of this Constitution which I do not at present approve, but I am not sure I shall never approve them. For, having lived long, I have experienced many instances of being obliged, by better information or fuller consideration, to change opinions, even on important subjects, which I once thought right, but found to be otherwise. It is therefore that, the older I grow, the more apt I am to doubt my own judgment, and to pay more respect to the judgment of others. Most men, indeed, as well as most sects in religion, think themselves in possession of all truth, and that wherever others differ from them, it is so far error. Steele, a Protestant, in a dedication, tells the Pope, that the only difference between our churches, in their opinions of the certainty of their doctrines, is, 'the Church of Rome is infallible, and the Church of England is never in the wrong.' But though many private persons think almost as highly of their own infallibility as of that of their sect, few express it so naturally as a certain French lady, who, in a dispute with her sister, said, 'I don't know how it happens, sister, but I meet with nobody but myself that is always in the right— *il n'y a que moi qui a toujours raison.*'

"In these sentiments, sir, I agree to this Constitution, with all its faults, if they are such; because I think a general government necessary for us, and there is no form of government, but what may be a blessing to the people if well administered; and believe further, that this is likely to be well administered for a course of years, and can only end in despotism, as other forms have done before it, when the people shall become so corrupted as to need despotic government, being incapable of any other. I doubt, too, whether any other convention we can obtain may be able to make a better constitution. For, when you assemble a number of men to have the advantage of their joint wisdom, you inevitably assemble with those men all their prejudices, their passions, their errors of opinion, their local interests, and their selfish views. From such an assembly can a perfect production be expected? It therefore astonishes me, sir, to find this system approaching so near to perfection as it does; and I think it will astonish our enemies, who are waiting with confidence to hear that our councils are confounded, like those of the builders of Babel, and that our States are on the point of separation, only to meet hereafter for the purpose of cutting one another's throats. Thus I consent, sir, to this Constitution, because I expect no better, and because I am not sure that it is not the best. The opinions I have had of its errors I sacrifice to the public good. I have never whispered a syllable of them abroad. Within these walls they were born, and here they shall die. If every one of us, in returning to our constituents, were to report the objections he has had to it, and endeavor to gain partisans in support of them, we might prevent its being generally received, and thereby lose all the salutary effects and great advantages resulting naturally in our favor among foreign nations, as well as among ourselves, from our real or apparent unanimity. Much of the strength and efficiency of any government, in procuring and securing happiness to the people, depends on opinion—on the general opinion of the goodness of the government, as well as of the wisdom and integrity of its governors. I hope, therefore, that for our own sakes, as a part of the people, and for the sake of posterity, we shall act heartily and unanimously in recommending this Constitution (if approved by Congress and confirmed by the conventions) wherever our influence may extend, and turn our future thoughts and endeavors to the means of having it well administered.

"On the whole, sir, I cannot help expressing a wish that every member of the Convention, who may still have objections to it, would with me, on this occasion, doubt a little of his own infallibility, and, to make manifest our unanimity, put his name to this instrument." He then moved that the Constitution be signed by the members, and offered the following as a convenient form, *viz.*: "Done in Convention by the unanimous consent of the States present, the 17th of September, etc. In witness whereof, we have hereunto subscribed our names." . . .

Whilst the last members were signing, Dr. Franklin, looking towards the president's chair, at the back of which a rising sun happened to be painted, observed to a few members near him, that painters had found it difficult to distinguish, in their art, a rising from a setting sun. "I have," said he, "often and often, in the course of the session, and the vicissitudes of my hopes and fears as to its issue, looked at that behind the president, without being able to tell whether it was rising or setting; but now, at length, I have the happiness to know that it is a rising, and not a setting sun."

THE FEDERALIST PAPERS

The Constitution had to be submitted to thirteen states, and in each state the same issues fought over in Philadelphia had to be argued openly. Nine states had to approve the Constitution before it would become effective, but if any of the large states—Virginia, Pennsylvania, Massachusetts or New York—turned it down, it could mean the end of the Union. American newspapers devoted much space to the new Constitution. Elbridge Gerry, Samuel Adams, Patrick Henry, George Mason and others printed and voiced their objections. Alexander Hamilton, John Jay and James Madison came to the defense of the Constitution in The Federalist Papers, *a series of eighty-five separate essays published in New York's newspapers from October 1787 until August 1788. Hamilton wrote the majority of the essays, while Madison wrote twenty-six and Jay five. It is important to realize that these documents were aimed not at the leading politicians but at all of the citizens of New York. These essays received wide publicity and were reprinted in the press of several states. The first thirty-six essays were printed in book form in March 1788 and a second volume followed in May.*

Each of these men had distinguished careers both before and after writing these essays. Alexander Hamilton was a captain of artillery in the war, a prominent New York lawyer, and became secretary of the treasury under George Washington. John Jay was an American statesman, diplomat and jurist, a delegate from New York to the Continental Congress, minister to Spain, first chief justice of the Supreme Court and governor of New York. James Madison served in the Continental and United States Congresses, was "the Father of the Constitution," became secretary of state under Jefferson for eight years, and succeeded Jefferson as president for another eight years.

The Federalist No. 1

Alexander Hamilton   *October 27, 1787*

TO the People of the State of New York:

After an unequivocal experience of the inefficiency of the subsisting federal government, you are called upon to deliberate on a new Constitution for the United States of America. The subject speaks its own importance; comprehending in its consequences nothing less than the existence of the Union, the safety and welfare of the parts of which it is composed, the fate of an empire in many respects, the most interesting in the world. It has been frequently remarked that it seems to have been reserved to the people of this country, by their conduct and example, to decide the important question, whether societies of men are really capable or not of establishing good government from reflection and choice, or whether they are forever destined to depend for their political constitutions on accident and force. If there be any truth in the remark, the crisis at which we are arrived may with propriety be regarded as the era in which that decision is to be made; and a wrong election of the part we shall act may, in this view, deserve to be considered as the general misfortune of mankind.

This idea will add the inducements of philanthropy to those of patriotism, to heighten the solicitude which all considerate and good men must feel for the event. Happy will it be if our choice should be directed by a judicious estimate of our true interests, unperplexed and unbiased by considerations not connected with the public good. But this is a thing more ardently to be wished than seriously to be expected. The plan offered to our deliberations affects too many particular interests, innovates upon too many local institutions, not to involve in its discussion a variety of objects foreign to its merits, and of views, passions, and prejudices little favorable to the discovery of truth.

Among the most formidable of the obstacles which the new Constitution will have to encounter may readily be distinguished the obvious interest of a certain class of men in every State to resist all changes which may hazard a diminution of the power, emolument, and consequence of the offices they hold under the state establishments; and the perverted ambition of another class of men who will either hope to aggrandize themselves by the confusions of their country or will flatter themselves with fairer prospects of elevation from the subdivision of the empire into several partial confederacies than from its union under one government.

It is not, however, my design to dwell upon observations of this nature.

I am well aware that it would be disingenuous to resolve indiscriminately the opposition of any set of men (merely because their situations might subject them to suspicion) into interested or ambitious views. Candor will oblige us to admit that even such men may be actuated by upright intentions; and it cannot be doubted that much of the opposition which has made its appearance, or may hereafter make its appearance, will spring from sources, blameless at least, if not respectable—the honest errors of minds led astray by preconceived jealousies and fears.

So numerous, indeed, and so powerful are the causes which serve to give a false bias to the judgment that we, upon many occasions, see wise and good men on the wrong as well as on the right side of questions of the first magnitude to society. This circumstance, if duly attended to, would furnish a lesson of moderation to those who are ever so much persuaded of their being in the right in any controversy. And a further reason for caution, in this respect, might be drawn from the reflection that we are not always sure that those who advocate the truth are influenced by purer principles than their antagonists. Ambition, avarice, personal animosity, party opposition, and many other motives not more laudable than these, are apt to operate as well upon those who support as those who oppose the right side of a question. Were there not even these inducements to moderation, nothing could be more ill judged than that intolerant spirit which has, at all times, characterized political parties. For in politics, as in religion, it is equally absurd to aim at making proselytes by fire and sword. Heresies in either can rarely be cured by persecution.

And yet, however just these sentiments will be allowed to be, we have already sufficient indications that it will happen in this as in all former cases of great national discussion. A torrent of angry and malignant passions will be let loose. To judge from the conduct of the opposite parties, we shall be led to conclude that they will mutually hope to evince the justness of their opinions, and to increase the number of their converts by the loudness of their declamations and the bitterness of their invectives. An enlightened zeal for the energy and efficiency of government will be stigmatized as the offspring of a temper fond of despotic power and hostile to the principles of liberty.

An overscrupulous jealousy of danger to the rights of the people, which is more commonly the fault of the head than of the heart, will be represented as mere pretense and artifice, the stale bait for popularity at the expense of public good. It will be forgotten, on the one hand, that jealousy is the usual concomitant of love, and that the noble enthusiasm of liberty is apt to be infected with a spirit of narrow and illiberal distrust. On the other hand, it will be equally forgotten that the vigor of government is essential to the security of liberty; that, in the contemplation of a sound and well-informed judgment, their interest can never be separated; and that a dangerous ambition more often lurks behind the specious mask of zeal for the rights of the people than under the forbidding appearance of zeal for the firmness and efficiency of government. History will teach us that the former has been found a much more certain road to the introduction of despotism than the latter, and that of those men who have overturned the liberties of republics, the greatest number have begun their career by paying an obsequious court to the people, commencing demagogues and ending tyrants.

In the course of the preceding observations, I have had an eye, my fellow citizens, to putting you upon your guard against all attempts, from whatever quarter, to influence your decision in a matter of the utmost moment to your welfare, by any impressions other than those which may result from the evidence of truth. You will, no doubt, at the same time, have collected from the general scope of them that they proceed from a source not unfriendly to the new Constitution. Yes, my countrymen, I own to you that, after having given it an attentive consideration, I am clearly of opinion it is your interest to adopt it. I am convinced that this is the safest course for your liberty, your dignity, and your happiness. I affect not reserves which I do not feel. I will not amuse you with an appearance of deliberation when I have decided. I frankly acknowledge to you my convictions, and I will freely lay before you the reasons on which they are founded. The consciousness of good intentions disdains ambiguity. I shall not, however, multiply professions on this head. My motives must remain in the depository of my own breast. My arguments will be open to all, and may be judged of by all. They shall at least be offered in a spirit which will not disgrace the cause of truth.

I propose, in a series of papers, to discuss the following interesting particulars: the utility of the Union to your political prosperity; the insufficiency of the present Confederation to preserve that Union; the necessity of a government at least equally energetic with the one proposed, to the attainment of this object; the conformity of the proposed Constitution to the true principles of republican government; its analogy to your own state constitution; and, lastly, the additional security which its adoption will afford to the preservation of that species of government, to liberty, and to property.

In the progress of this discussion I shall endeavor to give a satisfactory answer to all the objections, which shall have made their appearance, that may seem to have any claim to your attention.

It may perhaps be thought superfluous to offer arguments to prove the utility of the Union, a point, no doubt, deeply engraved on the hearts of the great body of the people in every state, and one which, it may be imagined, has no adversaries. But the fact is that we already hear it whispered in the private circles of those who oppose the new Constitution that the thirteen states are of too great extent for any general system, and that we must of necessity resort to separate confederacies of distinct portions of the whole. This doctrine will, in all probability, be gradually propagated, till it has votaries enough to countenance an open avowal of it. For nothing can be more evident, to those who are able to take an enlarged view of the subject, than the alternative of an adoption of the new Constitution or a dismemberment of the Union.

THE FEDERALIST NO. 2

John Jay   *October 1787*

TO the People of the State of New York:

When the people of America reflect that they are now called upon to decide a question, which, in its consequences, must prove one of the most important that ever engaged their attention, the propriety of their taking a very comprehensive, as well as a very serious, view of it, will be evident.

Nothing is more certain than the indispensable necessity of government, and it is equally undeniable, that whenever and however it is instituted, the people must cede to it some of their natural rights, in order to vest it with requisite powers. It is well worthy of consideration therefore, whether it would conduce more to the interest of the people of America that they should, to all general purposes, be one nation, under one federal government, or that they should divide themselves into separate confederacies, and give to the head of each the same kind of powers which they are advised to place in one national government.

It has until lately been a received and uncontradicted opinion, that the prosperity of the people of America depended on their continuing firmly united, and the wishes, prayers, and efforts of our best and wisest citizens have been constantly directed to that object. But politicians now appear, who insist that this opinion is erroneous, and that instead of looking for safety and happiness in union, we ought to seek it in a division of the States into distinct confederacies or sovereignties. However extraordinary this new doctrine may appear, it nevertheless has its advocates; and certain characters who were much opposed to it formerly, are at present of the number. Whatever may be the arguments or inducements which have wrought this change in the sentiments and declarations of these gentlemen, it certainly would not be wise in the people at large to adopt these new political tenets without being fully convinced that they are founded in truth and sound policy.

It has often given me pleasure to observe, that independent America was not composed of detached and distant territories, but that one connected, fertile, wide-spreading country was the portion of our western sons of liberty. Providence has in a particular manner blessed it with a variety of soils and productions, and watered it with innumerable streams, for the delight and accommodation of its inhabitants. A succession of navigable waters forms a kind of chain round its borders, as if to bind it together; while the most noble rivers in the world, running at convenient distances, present them with highways for the easy communication of friendly aids, and the mutual transportation and exchange of their various commodities.

With equal pleasure I have as often taken notice, that Providence has been pleased to give this one connected country to one united people—a people descended from the same ancestors, speaking the same language, professing the same religion, attached to the same principles of government, very similar in their manners and customs and who, by their joint counsels, arms, and efforts, fighting side by side throughout a long and bloody war, have nobly established general liberty and independence.

This country and this people seem to have been made for each other, and it appears as if it was the design of Providence, that an inheritance so proper and convenient for a band of brethren, united to each other by the strongest ties, should never be split into a number of unsocial, jealous, and alien sovereignties.

Similar sentiments have hitherto prevailed among all orders and denominations of men among us. To all general purposes we have uniformly been one people; each individual citizen everywhere enjoying the same national rights, privileges, and protection. As a nation we have made peace and war; as a nation we have vanquished our common enemies; as a nation we have formed alliances, and made treaties, and entered into various compacts and conventions with foreign states.

A strong sense of the value and blessings of union induced the people, at a very early period, to institute a federal government to preserve and perpetuate it. They formed it almost as soon as they had a political existence; nay, at a time when their habitations were in flames, when many of their citizens were bleeding, and when the progress of hostility and desolation left little room for those calm and mature inquiries and reflections which must ever precede the formation of a wise and well-balanced government for a free people. It is not to be wondered at, that a government instituted in times so inauspicious, should on experiment be found greatly deficient and inadequate to the purpose it was intended to answer.

This intelligent people perceived and regretted these defects. Still continuing no less attached to union than enamored of liberty, they observed the danger which immediately threatened the former and more remotely the latter; and being persuaded that ample security for both could only be found in a national government more wisely framed, they, as with one voice, convened the late convention at Philadelphia, to take that important subject under consideration.

This convention, composed of men who possessed the confidence of the people, and many of whom had become highly distinguished by their patriotism, virtue, and wisdom, in times which tried the minds and hearts of men, undertook the arduous task. In the mild season of peace, with minds unoccupied by other subjects, they passed many months in cool, uninterrupted, and daily consultation; and finally, without having been awed by power, or influenced by any passions except love for their country, they presented and recommended to the people the plan produced by their joint and very unanimous councils.

Admit, for so is the fact, that this plan is only recommended, not imposed, yet let it be remembered that it is neither recommended to blind approbation, nor to blind reprobation; but to that sedate and candid consideration which the magnitude and importance of the subject demand, and which it certainly ought to receive. But this (as was remarked in the foregoing number of this paper) is more to be wished than expected, that it may be so considered and examined. Experience on a former occasion teaches us not to be too sanguine in such hopes. It is not yet forgotten that well-grounded apprehensions of imminent danger induced the people of America to form the memorable Congress of 1774. That body recommended certain measures to their constituents, and the event proved their wisdom; yet it is fresh in our memories how soon the press began to team with pamphlets and weekly papers against those very measures. Not only many of the officers of government, who obeyed the dictates of personal interest, but others, from a mistaken estimate of consequences, or the undue influence of former attachments or whose ambition aimed at objects which did not correspond with the public good, were indefatigable in their efforts to persuade the people to reject the advice of that patriotic Congress. Many, indeed, were deceived and deluded, but the great majority of the people reasoned and decided judiciously; and happy they are in reflecting that they did so.

They considered that the Congress was composed of many wise and experienced men. That, being convened from different parts of the country, they brought with them and communicated to each other a variety of useful information. That, in the course of the time they passed together in inquiring into and discussing the true interests of their country, they must have acquired very accurate knowledge on that head. That they were individually interested in the public liberty and prosperity, and therefore that it was not less their inclination than their duty to recommend only such measures as, after the most mature deliberation, they really thought prudent and advisable.

These and similar considerations then induced the people to rely greatly on the judgment and integrity of the Congress; and they took their advice, notwithstanding the various arts and endeavors used to deter them from it. But if the people at large had reason to confide in the men of that Congress, few of whom had been fully tried or generally known, still greater reason have they now to respect the judgment and advice of the convention, for it is well known that some of the most distinguished members of that Congress, who have been since tried and justly approved for patriotism and abilities, and who have grown old in acquiring political information, were also members of this convention, and carried into it their accumulated knowledge and experience.

It is worthy of remark that not only the first, but every succeeding Congress, as well as the late convention, have invariably joined with the people in thinking that the prosperity of America depended on its Union. To preserve and perpetuate it was the great object of the people in forming that convention, and it is also the great object of the plan which the convention has advised them to adopt. With what propriety, therefore, or for what good purposes, are attempts at this particular period made by some men to depreciate the importance of the Union? Or why is it suggested that three or four confederacies would be better than one? I am persuaded in my own mind that the people have always thought right on this subject, and that their universal and uniform attachment to the cause of the Union rests on great and weighty reasons, which I shall endeavor to develop and explain in some ensuing papers. They who promote the idea of substituting a number of distinct confederacies in the room of the plan of the convention, seem clearly to foresee that the rejection of it would put the continuance of the Union in the utmost jeopardy. That certainly would be the case, and I sincerely wish that it may be as clearly foreseen by every good citizen, that whenever the dissolution of the Union arrives, America will have reason to exclaim, in the words of the poet: "Farewell! A long farewell to all my greatness."

THE FEDERALIST NO. 51

James Madison   *February 19, 1788*

TO the People of the State of New York:
To what expedient, then, shall we finally resort, for maintaining in

practice the necessary partition of power among the several departments, as laid down in the Constitution? The only answer that can be given is, that as all these exterior provisions are found to be inadequate, the defect must be supplied, by so contriving the interior structure of the government as that its several constituent parts may, by their mutual relations, be the means of keeping each other in their proper places. Without presuming to undertake a full development of this important idea, I will hazard a few general observations, which may perhaps place it in a clearer light, and enable us to form a more correct judgment of the principles and structure of the government planned by the convention.

In order to lay a due foundation for that separate and distinct exercise of the different powers of government, which to a certain extent is admitted on all hands to be essential to the preservation of liberty, it is evident that each department should have a will of its own; and consequently should be so constituted that the members of each should have as little agency as possible in the appointment of the members of the others. Were this principle rigorously adhered to, it would require that all the appointments for the supreme executive, legislative, and judiciary magistracies should be drawn from the same fountain of authority, the people, through channels having no communication whatever with one another. Perhaps such a plan of constructing the several departments would be less difficult in practice than it may in contemplation appear. Some difficulties, however, and some additional expense would attend the execution of it. Some deviations, therefore, from the principle must be admitted. In the constitution of the judiciary department in particular, it might be inexpedient to insist rigorously on the principle: first, because peculiar qualifications being essential in the members, the primary consideration ought to be to select that mode of choice which best secures these qualifications; secondly, because the permanent tenure by which the appointments are held in that department, must soon destroy all sense of dependence on the authority conferring them.

James Madison

It is equally evident, that the members of each department should be as little dependent as possible on those of the others, for the emoluments annexed to their offices. Were the executive magistrate, or the judges, not independent of the legislature in this particular, their independence in every other would be merely nominal.

But the great security against a gradual concentration of the several powers in the same department, consists in giving to those who administer each department the necessary constitutional means and personal motives to resist encroachments of the others. The provision for defence must in this, as in all other cases, be made commensurate to the danger of attack. Ambition must be made to counteract ambition. The interest of the man must be connected with the constitutional rights of the place. It may be a reflection on human nature, that such devices should be necessary to control the abuses of government. But what is government itself, but the greatest of all reflections on human nature? If men were angels, no government would be necessary. If angels were to govern men, neither external nor internal controls on government would be necessary. In framing a government which is to be administered by men over men, the great difficulty lies in this: you must first enable the government to control the governed; and in the next place oblige it to control itself. A dependence on the people is, no doubt, the primary control on the government; but experience has taught mankind the necessity of auxiliary precautions.

This policy of supplying, by opposite and rival interests, the defect of better motives, might be traced through the whole system of human affairs, private as well as public. We see it particularly displayed in all the subordinate distributions of power, where the constant aim is to divide and arrange the several offices in such a manner as that each may be a check on the other—that the private interest of every individual may be a sentinel over the public rights. These inventions of prudence cannot be less requisite in the distribution of the supreme powers of the State.

But it is not possible to give to each department an equal power of self-defence. In republican government, the legislative authority necessarily pre-dominates. The remedy for this inconveniency is to divide the legislature into different branches; and to render them, by different modes of election and different principles of action, as little connected with each other as the nature of their common functions and their common dependence on the society will admit. It may even be necessary to guard against dangerous encroachments by still further precautions. As the weight of the legislative authority requires that it should be thus divided, the weakness of the executive may require, on the other hand, that it should be fortified. An absolute negative on the legislature appears, at first view, to be the natural defence with which the executive magistrate should be armed. But perhaps it would be neither altogether safe nor alone sufficient. On ordinary occasions it might not be exerted with the requisite firmness, and on extraordinary occasions it might be perfidiously abused. May not this defect of an absolute negative be supplied by some qualified connection between this weaker department and the weaker branch of the stronger department, by which the latter may be led to support the constitutional rights of the former, without being too much detached from the rights of its own department?

If the principles on which these observations are founded be just, as I persuade myself they are, and they be applied as a criterion to the several State constitutions, and to the federal Constitution, it will be found that if the latter does not perfectly correspond with them, the former are infinitely less able to bear such a test.

There are, moreover, two considerations particularly applicable to the federal system of America, which place that system in a very interesting point of view.

First. In a single republic, all the power surrendered by the people is submitted to the administration of a single government; and the usurpations are guarded against by a division of the government into distinct and separate departments. In the compound republic of America, the power surrendered by the people is first divided between two distinct governments, and then the portion allotted to each subdivided among distinct and separate departments. Hence a double security arises to the rights of the people. The different governments will control each other, at the same time that each will be controlled by itself.

Second. It is of great importance in a republic not only to guard the society against the oppression of its rulers, but to guard one part of the society against the injustice of the other part. Different interests necessarily exist in different classes of citizens. If a majority be united by a common interest, the rights of the minority will be insecure. There are but two methods of providing against this evil: the one by creating a will in the community independent of the majority— that is, of the society itself; the other, by comprehending in the society so many separate descriptions of citizens as will render an unjust combination of a majority of the whole very improbable, if not impracticable. The first method prevails in all governments possessing an hereditary or self-appointed authority. This, at best, is but a precarious security; because a power independent of the society may as well espouse the unjust views of the major, as the rightful interests of the minor party, and may possibly be turned against both parties. The second method will be exemplified in the federal republic of the United States. Whilst all authority in it will be derived from and dependent on the society, the society itself will be broken into so many parts, interests, and classes of citizens, that the rights of individuals, or of the minority, will be in little danger from interested combinations of the majority. In a free government the security for civil rights must be the same as that for religious rights. It consists in the one case in the multiplicity of interests, and in the other in the multiplicity of sects. The degree of security in both cases will depend on the number of interests and sects; and this may be presumed to depend on the extent of country and number of people comprehended under the same government. This view of the subject must particularly recommend a proper federal system to all the sincere and considerate friends of republican government, since it shows that in exact proportion as the territory of the Union may be formed into more circumscribed Confederacies, or States, oppressive combinations of a majority will be facilitated; the best security, under the republic forms, for the rights of every class of citizens, will be diminished; and consequently the stability and independence of some member of the government, the only other security, must be proportionally increased. Justice is the end of government. It is the end of civil society. It ever has been and ever will be pursued until it be obtained, or until liberty be lost in the pursuit. In a society under the forms of which the stronger faction can readily unite and oppress the weaker, anarchy may as truly be said to reign as in a state of nature, where the weaker individual is not secured against the violence of the stronger; and as, in the latter state, even the stronger individuals are prompted, by the uncertainty of their condition, to submit to a government which may protect the weak as well as themselves; so, in the former state, will the more powerful factions or parties be gradually induced, by a like motive, to wish for a government which will protect all parties, the weaker as well as the more powerful. It can be little doubted that if the State of Rhode Island was separated from the Confederacy and left to itself, the insecurity of rights under the popular form of government within such narrow limits would be displayed by such reiterated oppressions of factious majorities that some power altogether independent of the people would soon be called for by the voice of the very factions whose misrule had proved the necessity of it. In the extended republic of the United States, and among the great variety of interests, parties, and sects which it embraces, a coalition of a majority of the whole society could seldom take place on any other principles than those of justice and the general good; whilst there being thus less danger to a minor from the will of a major party, there must be less pretext, also, to provide for the security of the former, by introducing into the government a will not dependent on the latter, or, in other words, a will independent of the society itself. It is no less certain that it is important, notwithstanding the contrary opinions which have been entertained, that the larger the society, provided it lie within a practical sphere, the more duly capable it will be of self-government. And happily for the republican cause, the practicable sphere may be carried to a very great extent, by a judicious modification and mixture of the federal principle.

ON THE CONSTITUTIONALITY
OF A NATIONAL BANK

Alexander Hamilton   *February 23, 1791*

---

*Alexander Hamilton, as secretary of the treasury, was the
key member of Washington's cabinet since financing was the
most critical problem facing the new government. In December
1790 Hamilton presented a plan to Congress for the adoption of
a national bank. The bank could provide the government with
short-term borrowings and increase the amount of capital
available to business. Congress passed the bill in February 1791.
Before signing the bill, George Washington asked the advice of
his cabinet on the constitutionality of the plan. Thomas Jefferson
wrote an opinion against the bill. Alexander Hamilton wrote an
opinion in favor of the bill, and convinced Washington to sign
the bill into law, thereby chartering the first Bank of the
United States.*

. . . IN entering upon the argument it ought to be premised that the
objections of the secretary of state and the attorney general are founded on a
general denial of the authority of the United States to erect corporations. The
latter, indeed, expressly admits that if there be anything in the bill which is not
warranted by the Constitution, it is the clause of incorporation.

Now it appears to the secretary of the treasury that this general principle
is inherent in the very definition of government and essential to every step of the
progress to be made by that of the United States, namely: that every power vested
in a government is in its nature sovereign and includes, by force of the term, a
right to employ all the means requisite and fairly applicable to the attainment of
the ends of such power, and which are not precluded by restrictions and
exceptions specified in the Constitution, or not immoral, or contrary to the
essential ends of political society. . . .

If it would be necessary to bring proof to a proposition so clear as that
which affirms that the powers of the federal government, as to its objects, were
sovereign, there is a clause of its Constitution which would be decisive. It is that
which declares that the Constitution, and the laws of the United States made in

pursuance of it, and all treaties made, or which shall be made, under their authority, shall be the supreme law of the land. The power which can create a supreme law of the land in any case is doubtless sovereign as to such case.

This general and indisputable principle puts at once an end to the abstract question whether the United States have power to erect a corporation; that is to say, to give a legal or artificial capacity to one or more persons, distinct from the natural. For it is unquestionably incident to sovereign power to erect corporations, and consequently to that of the United States, in relation to the objects entrusted to the management of the government. The difference is this: where the authority of the government is general, it can create corporations in all cases; where it is confined to certain branches of legislation, it can create corporations only in those cases. . . .

It is not denied that there are implied as well as express powers and that the former are as effectually delegated as the latter. And for the sake of accuracy it shall be mentioned, that there is another class of powers, which may be properly denominated resulting powers. It will not be doubted, that if the United States should make a conquest of any of the territories of its neighbours, they would possess sovereign jurisdiction over the conquered territory. This would be rather a result, from the whole mass of the powers of the government, and from the nature of political society, than a consequence of either of the powers specially enumerated. . . .

It is conceded that implied powers are to be considered as delegated equally with express ones. Then it follows that as a power of erecting a corporation may as well be implied as any other thing, it may as well be employed as an instrument or mean of carrying into execution any of the specified powers as any other instrument or mean whatever.

The only question must be, in this, as in every other case, whether the mean to be employed or, in this instance, the corporation to be erected, has a natural relation to any of the acknowledged objects or lawful ends of the government. Thus a corporation may not be erected by Congress for superintending the police of the city of Philadelphia, because they are not authorized to regulate the police of that city. But one may be erected in relation to the collection of taxes, or to the trade with foreign countries, or to the trade between the states, or with the Indian tribes; because it is the province of the federal government to regulate those objects, and because it is incident to a general sovereign or legislative power to regulate a thing, to employ all the means which relate to its regulation to the best and greatest advantage. . . .

Through this mode of reasoning respecting the right of employing all the means requisite to the execution of the specified powers of the government, it is objected that none but necessary and proper means are to be employed; and the secretary of state maintains that no means are to be considered as necessary but those without which the grant of the power would be nugatory. . . .

It is essential to the being of the national government that so erroneous a conception of the meaning of the word "necessary" should be exploded.

It is certain that neither the grammatical nor popular sense of the term requires that construction. According to both, "necessary" often means no more than needful, requisite, incidental, useful, or conducive to. It is a common mode of expression to say that it is necessary for a government or a person to do this or that thing, when nothing more is intended or understood than that the interests of the government or person require, or will be promoted by, the doing of this or that thing. The imagination can be at no loss for exemplifications of the use of the word in this sense. And it is the true one in which it is to be understood as used in the Constitution.

The whole turn of the clause containing it indicates that it was the intent of the Convention, by that clause, to give a liberal latitude to the exercise of the specified powers. The expressions have peculiar comprehensiveness. They are, "to make all laws necessary and proper for carrying into execution the foregoing powers, and all other powers vested by the Constitution in the government of the United States, or in any department or officer thereof."

To understand the word as the secretary of state does would be to depart from its obvious and popular sense and to give it a restrictive operation, an idea never before entertained. It would be to give it the same force as if the word "absolutely" or "indispensably" had been prefixed to it. . . .

This restrictive interpretation of the word "necessary" is also contrary to this sound maxim of construction; namely, that the powers contained in a constitution of government, especially those which concern the general administration of the affairs of a country, its finances, trade, defense, etc., ought to be construed liberally in advancement of the public good. This rule does not depend on the particular form of a government, or on the particular demarcation of the boundaries of its powers, but on the nature and objects of government itself. The means by which national exigencies are to be provided for, national inconveniences obviated, national prosperity promoted, are of such infinite variety, extent, and complexity that there must of necessity be great latitude of discretion in the selection and application of those means. Hence, consequently, the necessity and propriety of exercising the authorities entrusted to a government on principles of liberal construction. . . .

The truth is that difficulties on this point are inherent in the nature of the federal Constitution; they result inevitably from a division of the legislative power. The consequence of this division is that there will be cases clearly within the power of the national government; others clearly without its powers; and a third class which will leave room for controversy and difference of opinion, and concerning which a reasonable latitude of judgment must be allowed.

But the doctrine which is contended for is not chargeable with the consequences imputed to it. It does not affirm that the national government is sovereign in all respects but that it is sovereign to a certain extent; that is, to the extent of the objects of its specified powers.

It leaves, therefore, a criterion of what is constitutional and of what is not so. This criterion is the end to which the measure relates as a mean. If the end be clearly comprehended within any of the specified powers, and if the measure have an obvious relation to that end, and is not forbidden by a particular provision of the Constitution, it may safely be deemed to come within the compass of the national authority.

There is also this further criterion, which may materially assist the decision: Does the proposed measure abridge a preexisting right of any state or of any individual? If it does not, there is a strong presumption in favor of its constitutionality, and slighter relations to any declared object of the Constitution may be permitted to turn the scale. . . .

It is presumed to have been satisfactorily shown in the court of the preceding observations:

1. That the power of the government, as to the objects entrusted to its management, is, in its nature, sovereign.

2. That the right of erecting corporations is one inherent in, and inseparable from, the idea of sovereign power.

3. That the position that the government of the United States can exercise no power but such as is delegated to it by its Constitution does not militate against this principle.

4. That the word "necessary," in the general clause, can have no restrictive operation derogating from the force of this principle; indeed, that the degree in which a measure is or is not "necessary" cannot be a test of constitutional right but of expediency only.

5. That the power to erect corporations is not to be considered as an independent or substantive power but as an incidental and auxiliary one and was therefore more properly left to implication than expressly granted.

6. That the principle in question does not extend the power of the government beyond the prescribed limits, because it only affirms a power to incorporate for purposes within the sphere of the specified powers.

And lastly, that the right to exercise such a power in certain cases is unequivocally granted in the most positive and comprehensive terms. . . .

A hope is entertained that it has, by this time, been made to appear, to the satisfaction of the President, that a bank has a natural relation to the power of collecting taxes—to that of regulating trade—to that of providing for the common defense—and that, as the bill under consideration contemplates the government in the light of a joint proprietor of the stock of the bank, it brings the case within the provision of the clause of the Constitution which immediately respects the property of the United States.

Under a conviction that such a relation subsists, the secretary of the treasury, with all deference, conceives that it will result as a necessary consequence from the position that all the specified powers of government are sovereign, as to the proper objects; that the incorporation of a bank is a constitutional measure; and that the objections taken to the bill, in this respect, are ill-founded. . . .

AMENDMENTS I–X: THE BILL OF RIGHTS

December 15, 1791

As soon as the Constitution had been signed in 1787, pressures developed to amend it in order to define individual liberties and rights. Without such amendments, it is possible that the Constitution would never have received the necessary support in the states for its ratification. In 1789, James Madison sponsored certain constitutional amendments. Twelve amendments were eventually approved by Congress on September 25, 1789, and ten were ratified by the states. On December 15, 1791, these ten amendments, the Bill of Rights, were ratified by Virginia, the eleventh state, and became part of the law of the land.

AMENDMENTS I —X

Articles in addition to, and Amendment of the Constitution of the United States of America, proposed by Congress, and ratified by the Legislatures of the several States, pursuant to the fifth Article of the original Constitution.

ART. I

Congress shall make no law respecting an establishment of religion, or prohibiting the free exercise thereof; or abridging the freeom of speech, or of the press; or the right of the people peaceably to assemble, and to petition the government for a redress of grievances.

ART. II

A well regulated Militia, being necessary to the security of a free State, the right of the people to keep and bear Arms, shall not be infringed.

ART. III

No Soldier shall, in time of peace be quartered in any house, without the consent of the Owner, nor in time of war, but in a manner to be prescribed by law.

ART. IV

The right of the people to be secure in their persons, houses, papers, and effects, against unreasonable searches and seizures, shall not be violated, and no Warrants shall issue, but upon probable cause, supported by Oath or affirmation, and particularly describing the place to be searched, and the persons or things to be seized.

ART. V

No person shall be held to answer for a capital, or otherwise infamous crime, unless on a presentment or indictment of a Grand Jury, except in cases arising in the land or naval forces, or in the Militia, when in actual service in time of War or public danger; nor shall any person be subject for the same offence to be twice put in jeopardy of life or limb; nor shall be compelled in any criminal case to be a witness against himself, nor be deprived of life, liberty, or property, without due process of law; nor shall private property be taken for public use, without just compensation.

ART. VI

In all criminal prosecutions, the accused shall enjoy the right to a speedy and public trial, by an impartial jury of the State and district wherein the crime shall have been committed, which district shall have been previously ascertained by law, and to be informed of the nature and cause of the accusation; to be confronted with the witnesses against him; to have compulsory process for obtaining witnesses in his favor, and to have the Assistance of Counsel for his defence.

ART. VII

In Suits at common law, where the value in controversy shall exceed twenty dollars, the right of trial by jury shall be preserved, and no fact tried by a jury, shall be otherwise re-examined in any Court of the United States, than according to the rules of the common law.

ART. VIII

Excessive bail shall not be required, nor excessive fines imposed, nor cruel and unusual punishments inflicted.

ART. IX

The enumeration in the Constitution, of certain rights, shall not be construed to deny or disparage others retained by the people.

ART. X

The powers not delegated to the United States by the Constitution, nor prohibited by it to the States, are reserved to the States respectively, or to the people.

AMENDMENT XI
JUDICIAL POWERS CONSTRUED

February 7, 1795

Proposed by the third Congress on March 5, 1794, this amendment was ratified by the twelfth state, North Carolina, on February 7, 1795. It was declared to have been ratified in a message from the president to Congress on January 8, 1798.

THE Judicial power of the United States shall not be construed to extend to any suit in law or equity, commenced or prosecuted against one of the United States by Citizens of another State, or by Citizens or Subjects of any Foreign State.

FAREWELL ADDRESS

George Washington   *September 17, 1796*

---

*George Washington was a skilled surveyor and soldier,
and from 1753 to 1759, was a British officer in the French and
Indian War. Washington was elected to the Virginia House of
Burgesses in 1758 and was reelected until the House was
dissolved by the colonial governor in 1774. He was one of
Virginia's delegates to the first and second Continental Congresses in 1774 and 1775 and was elected commander of the
Continental Army in June 1775. An excellent strategist and a
strong leader of men, he led the colonists to victory against a
better equipped and thoroughly disciplined British army.
Washington favored a strong federal government and was
elected president of the Constitutional Convention in 1787.
George Washington was unanimously elected president by the
first electoral college in 1789 and reelected president in 1793.*

*George Washington's Farewell Address was not presented
by him. It was first published in a newspaper in Philadelphia,
the* American Daily Advertiser, *on September 17, 1796, and was
subsequently printed in other papers throughout the country.
Washington wanted to remove his name from consideration as
a candidate for a third term as president as well as give his
advice on the future of the nation.*

FRIENDS and Fellow Citizens:

The period for a new election of a citizen to administer the executive government of the United States being not far distant, and the time actually arrived when your thoughts must be employed in designating the person who is to be clothed with that important trust, it appears to me proper, especially as it may conduce to a more distinct expression of the public voice, that I should now apprise you of the resolution I have formed to decline being considered among the number of those out of whom a choice is to be made.

I beg you, at the same time, to do me the justice to be assured that this resolution has not been taken without a strict regard to all the considerations appertaining to the relation which binds a dutiful citizen to his country; and that, in withdrawing the tender of service which silence in my situation might imply, I am influenced by no diminution of zeal for your future interest, no deficiency of grateful respect for your past kindness, but act under. . . a full conviction that the step is compatible with both.

The acceptance of and continuance hitherto in the office to which your suffrages have twice called me have been a uniform sacrifice of inclination to the opinion of duty and to a deference for what appeared to be your desire. I constantly hoped that it would have been much earlier in my power, consistently with motives which I was not at liberty to disregard, to return to that retirement from which I had been reluctantly drawn. The strength of my inclination to do this, previous to the last election, had even led to the preparation of an address to declare it to you; but mature reflection on the then perplexed and critical posture of our affairs with foreign nations, and the unanimous advice of persons entitled to my confidence, impelled me to abandon the idea.

George Washington, portrait by Gilbert Stuart, 1797

I rejoice that the state of your concerns, external as well as internal, no longer renders the pursuit of inclination incompatible with the sentiment of duty or propriety; and am persuaded, whatever partiality may be retained for my services, that, in the present circumstances of our country, you will not disapprove of my determination to retire.

The impressions with which I first undertook the arduous trust were explained on the proper occasion. In the discharge of this trust, I will only say that I have, with good intentions, contributed toward the organization and administration of the government the best exertions of which a very fallible judgment was capable. Not unconscious, in the outset, of the inferiority of my qualifications, experience in my own eyes, perhaps still more in the eyes of others, has strengthened the motives to diffidence of myself; and every day the increasing weight of years admonishes me more and more that the shade of retirement is as necessary to me as it will be welcome. Satisfied that, if any circumstances have given peculiar value to my services, they were temporary, I have the consolation to believe that, while choice and prudence invite me to quit the political scene, patriotism does not forbid it. . . .

In looking forward to the moment which is intended to terminate the career of my public life, my feelings do not permit me to suspend the deep acknowledgment of that debt of gratitude which I owe to my beloved country for the many honors it has conferred upon me; still more for the steadfast confidence with which it has supported me; and for the opportunities I have thence enjoyed of manifesting my inviolable attachment, by services, faithful and persevering, though in usefulness unequal to my zeal.

If benefits have resulted to our country from these services, let it always be remembered to your praise, and as an instructive example in our annals, that, under circumstances in which the passions agitated in every direction were liable to mislead, amidst appearances sometimes dubious, vicissitudes of fortune often discouraging, in situations in which not unfrequently want of success has countenanced the spirit of criticism, the constancy of your support was the essential prop of the efforts and a guarantee of the plans by which they were effected.

Profoundly penetrated with this idea, I shall carry it with me to my grave as a strong incitement to unceasing vows that Heaven may continue to you the choicest tokens of its beneficence; that your Union and brotherly affection may be perpetual; that the free Constitution, which is the work of your hands, may be sacredly maintained; that its administration in every department may be stamped with wisdom and virtue; that, in fine, the happiness of the people of these States, under the auspices of liberty, may be made complete by so careful a preservation and so prudent a use of this blessing as will acquire to them the glory of recommending it to the applause, the affection, and adoption of every nation which is yet a stranger to it.

Here, perhaps, I ought to stop. But a solicitude for your welfare, which cannot end but with my life, and the apprehension of danger natural to that solicitude, urge me, on an occasion like the present, to offer to your solemn contemplation, and to recommend to your frequent review, some sentiments which are the result of much reflection, of no inconsiderable observation, and which appear to me all-important to the permanency of your felicity as a people. These will be offered to you with the more freedom as you can only see in them the disinterested warnings of a parting friend who can possibly have no personal motive to bias his counsel. Nor can I forget, as an encouragement to it, your indulgent reception of my sentiments on a former and not dissimilar occasion.

Interwoven as is the love of liberty with every ligament of your hearts, no recommendation of mine is necessary to fortify or confirm the attachment.

The unity of government which constitutes you one people is also now dear to you. It is justly so, for it is a main pillar in the edifice of your real independence; the support of your tranquillity at home, your peace abroad; of your safety; of your prosperity in every shape; of that very liberty which you so highly prize. But as it is easy to foresee that, from different causes and from different quarters, much pains will be taken, many artifices employed to weaken in your minds the conviction of this truth; as this is the point in your political fortress against which the batteries of internal and external enemies will be most constantly and actively (though often covertly and insidiously) directed, it is of infinite moment that you should properly estimate the immense value of your national Union to your collective and individual happiness; that you should cherish a cordial, habitual, and immovable attachment to it, accustoming yourselves to think and speak of it as of the palladium of your political safety and prosperity, watching for its preservation with jealous anxiety, discountenancing whatever may suggest even a suspicion that it can in any event be abandoned, and indignantly frowning upon the first dawning of every attempt to alienate any portion of our country from the rest or to enfeeble the sacred ties which now link together the various parts.

For this you have every inducement of sympathy and interest. Citizens by birth or choice of a common country, that country has a right to concentrate your affections. The name of American, which belongs to you, in your national capacity, must always exalt the just pride of patriotism more than any appellation derived from local discriminations. With slight shades of difference, you have the same religion, manners, habits, and political principles. You have in a common cause fought and triumphed together. The independence and liberty you possess are the work of joint councils and joint efforts, of common dangers, sufferings, and successes.

But these considerations, however powerfully they address themselves to your sensibility, are greatly outweighed by those which apply more immediately to your interest. Here every portion of our country finds the most commanding motives for carefully guarding and preserving the Union of the whole.

The North, in an unrestrained intercourse with the South, protected by the equal laws of a common government, finds in the productions of the latter great additional resources of maritime and commercial enterprise and precious materials of manufacturing industry. The South, in the same intercourse, benefiting by the agency of the North, sees its agriculture grow and its commerce expand. Turning partly into its own channels the seamen of the North, it finds its particular navigation invigorated; and while it contributes, in different ways, to nourish and increase the general mass of the national navigation, it looks forward to the protection of a maritime strength, to which itself is unequally adapted.

The East, in a like intercourse with the West, already finds, and in the progressive improvement of interior communications by land and water will more and more find, a valuable vent for the commodities which it brings from abroad or manufactures at home. The West derives from the East supplies requisite to its growth and comfort, and, what is perhaps of still greater consequence, it must of necessity owe the secure enjoyment of indispensable outlets for its own productions to the weight, influence, and the future maritime strength of the Atlantic side of the Union, directed by an indissoluble community of interest, as one nation. Any other tenure by which the West can hold this essential advantage, whether derived from its own separate strength or from an apostate and unnatural connection with any foreign power, must be intrinsically precarious.

While then every part of our country thus feels an immediate and particular interest in Union, all the parts combined in the united mass of means and efforts cannot fail to find greater strength, greater resource, proportionably greater security from external danger, a less frequent interruption of their peace by foreign nations; and—what is of inestimable value!—they must derive from Union an exemption from those broils and wars between themselves which so frequently afflict neighboring countries not tied together by the same government, which their own rivalships alone would be sufficient to produce but which opposite foreign alliances, attachments, and intrigues would stimulate and embitter. Hence, likewise, they will avoid the necessity of those overgrown military establishments which under any form of government are inauspicious to liberty and which are to be regarded as particularly hostile to republican liberty. In this sense it is that your Union ought to be considered as a main prop of your liberty and that the love of the one ought to endear to you the preservation of the other.

These considerations speak a persuasive language to every reflecting and virtuous mind and exhibit the continuance of the Union as a primary object of patriotic desire. Is there a doubt whether a common government can embrace so large a sphere? Let experience solve it. To listen to mere speculation in such a case were criminal. We are authorized to hope that a proper organization of the whole, with the auxiliary agency of governments for the respective subdivisions, will afford a happy issue to the experiment. It is well worth a fair and full experiment. With such powerful and obvious motives to Union affecting all parts of our country, while experience shall not have demonstrated its impracticability, there will always be reason to distrust the patriotism of those who in any quarter may endeavor to weaken its bands.

In contemplating the causes which may disturb our Union, it occurs as a matter of serious concern that any ground should have been furnished for characterizing parties by geographical discriminations: Northern and Southern; Atlantic and Western; whence designing men may endeavor to excite a belief that there is a real difference of local interests and views. One of the expedients of party to acquire influence, within particular districts, is to misrepresent the opinions and aims of other districts. You cannot shield yourselves too much against the jealousies and heartburnings which spring from these misrepresentations. They tend to render alien to each other those who ought to be bound together by fraternal affection.

The inhabitants of our Western country have lately had a useful lesson on this head. They have seen, in the negotiation by the executive, and in the unanimous ratification by the Senate of the treaty with Spain, and in the universal satisfaction of that event throughout the United States, a decisive proof how unfounded were the suspicions propagated among them of a policy in the general government and in the Atlantic states unfriendly to their interests in regard to the Mississippi. They have been witnesses to the formation of two treaties, that with Great Britain and that with Spain, which secure to them everything they could desire, in respect to our foreign relations, towards confirming their prosperity. Will it not be their wisdom to rely for the preservation of these advantages on the Union by which they were procured? Will they not henceforth be deaf to those advisers, if such there are, who would sever them from their brethren and connect them with aliens?

To the efficacy and permanency of your Union, a government for the whole is indispensable. No alliances, however strict between the parts, can be an adequate substitute. They must inevitably experience the infractions and interruptions which all alliances in all times have experienced. Sensible of this momentous truth, you have improved upon your first essay by the adoption of a Constitution of government better calculated than your former for an intimate Union and for the efficacious management of your common concerns. This government, the offspring of our own choice uninfluenced and unawed, adopted upon full investigation and mature deliberation, completely free in its principles, in the distribution of its powers, uniting security with energy, and containing within itself a provision for its own amendment, has a just claim to your confidence and your support.

Respect for its authority, compliance with its laws, acquiescence in its measures are duties enjoined by the fundamental maxims of true liberty. The basis of our political systems is the right of the people to make and to alter their constitutions of government. But the constitution which at any time exists, till changed by an explicit and authentic act of the whole people, is sacredly obligatory upon all. The very idea of the power and right of the people to establish government presupposes the duty of every individual to obey the established government.

All obstructions to the execution of the laws, all combinations and associations, under whatever plausible character, with the real design to direct, control, counteract, or awe the regular deliberation and action of the constituted authorities, are destructive of this fundamental principle, and of fatal tendency. They serve to organize faction, to give it an artificial and extraordinary force, to put in the place of the delegated will of the nation the will of a party, often a small but artful and enterprising minority of the community; and, according to the alternate triumphs of different parties, to make the public administration the mirror of the ill-concerted and incongruous projects of faction rather than the organ of consistent and wholesome plans digested by common councils and modified by mutual interests.

However combinations or associations of the above description may now and then answer popular ends, they are likely, in the course of time and things, to become potent engines by which cunning, ambitious, and unprincipled men will be enabled to subvert the power of the people and to usurp for themselves the reins of government, destroying afterward the very engines which have lifted them to unjust dominion.

Toward the preservation of your government and the permanency of your present happy state, it is requisite not only that you speedily discountenance irregular oppositions to its acknowledged authority but also that you resist with care the spirit of innovation upon its principles, however specious the pretexts. One method of assault may be to effect, in the forms of the Constitution, alterations which will impair the energy of the system and thus to undermine what cannot be directly overthrown. In all the changes to which you may be invited, remember that time and habit are at least as necessary to fix the true character of governments as of other human institutions; that experience is the surest standard by which to test the real tendency of the existing constitution of a country; that facility in changes upon the credit of mere hypothesis and opinion exposes to perpetual change, from the endless variety of hypothesis and opinion; and remember, especially, that for the efficient management of your common interests, in a country so extensive as ours, a government of as much vigor as is consistent with the perfect security of liberty is indispensable.

Liberty itself will find in such a government, with powers properly distributed and adjusted, its surest guardian. It is, indeed, little else than a name where the government is too feeble to withstand the enterprises of faction, to confine each member of society within the limits prescribed by the laws and to maintain all in the secure and tranquil enjoyment of the rights of person and property.

I have already intimated to you the danger of parties in the state, with particular reference to the founding of them on geographical discriminations. Let me now take a more comprehensive view and warn you in the most solemn manner against the baneful effects of the spirit of party generally.

This spirit, unfortunately, is inseparable from our nature, having its root in the strongest passions of the human mind. It exists under different shapes in all governments, more or less stifled, controlled, or repressed; but, in those of the popular form, it is seen in its greatest rankness and is truly their worst enemy.

The alternate domination of one faction over another, sharpened by the spirit of revenge natural to party dissension, which in different ages and countries has perpetrated the most horrid enormities, is itself a frightful despotism. But this leads at length to a more formal and permanent despotism. The disorders and miseries which result gradually incline the minds of men to seek security and repose in the absolute power of an individual; and sooner or later the chief of some prevailing faction, more able or more fortunate than his competitors, turns this disposition to the purposes of his own elevation on the ruins of public liberty.

Without looking forward to an extremity of this kind (which nevertheless ought not to be entirely out of sight), the common and continual mischiefs of the spirit of party are sufficient to make it the interest and duty of a wise people to discourage and restrain it.

It serves always to distract the public councils and enfeeble the public administration. It agitates the community with ill-founded jealousies and false alarms, kindles the animosity of one part against another, foments occasionally riot and insurrection. It opens the door to foreign influence and corruption, which find a facilitated access to the government itself through the channels of party passions. Thus the policy and the will of one country are subjected to the policy and will of another.

There is an opinion that parties in free countries are useful checks upon the administration of the government and serve to keep alive the spirit of liberty. This within certain limits is probably true, and, in governments of a monarchical cast, patriotism may look with indulgence, if not with favor, upon the spirit of party. But in those of the popular character, in governments purely elective, it is a spirit not to be encouraged. From their natural tendency, it is certain there will always be enough of that spirit for every salutary purpose. And there being constant danger of excess, the effort ought to be, by force of public opinion, to mitigate and assuage it. A fire not to be quenched, it demands a uniform vigilance to prevent its bursting into a flame, lest instead of warming it should consume.

It is important, likewise, that the habits of thinking in a free country should inspire caution in those entrusted with its administration to confine themselves within their respective constitutional spheres, avoiding in the exercise of the powers of one department to encroach upon another. The spirit of encroachment tends to consolidate the powers of all the departments in one and thus to create, wherever the form of government, a real despotism. A just estimate of that love of power and proneness to abuse it which predominates in the human heart is sufficient to satisfy us of the truth of this position.

The necessity of reciprocal checks in the exercise of political power, by dividing and distributing it into different depositories, and constituting each the guardian of the public weal against invasions by the others, has been evinced by experiments ancient and modern, some of them in our country and under our own eyes. To preserve them must be as necessary as to institute them. If, in the opinion of the people, the distribution or modification of the constitutional powers be in any particular wrong, let it be corrected by an amendment in the way which the Constitution designates. But let there be no change by usurpation; for, though this, in one instance, may be the instrument of good, it is the customary weapon by which free governments are destroyed. The precedent must always greatly overbalance in permanent evil any partial or transient benefit which the use can at any time yield.

Of all the dispositions and habits which lead to political prosperity, religion and morality are indispensable supports. In vain would that man claim the tribute of patriotism who should labor to subvert these great pillars of human happiness, these firmest props of the duties of men and citizens. The mere politician, equally with the pious man, ought to respect and to cherish them. A volume could not trace all their connections with private and public felicity.

Let it simply be asked—Where is the security for property, for reputation, for life, if the sense of religious obligation desert the oaths, which are the instruments of investigation in courts of justice? And let us with caution indulge the supposition that morality can be maintained without religion. Whatever may be conceded to the influence of refined education on minds of peculiar structure, reason and experience both forbid us to expect that national morality can prevail in exclusion of religious principle.

It is substantially true that virtue or morality is a necessary spring of popular government. The rule indeed extends with more or less force to every species of free government. Who that is a sincere friend to it can look with indifference upon attempts to shake the foundation of the fabric?

Promote, then, as an object of primary importance, institutions for the general diffusion of knowledge. In proportion as the structure of a government gives force to public opinion, it is essential that public opinion should be enlightened.

As a very important source of strength and security, cherish public credit. One method of preserving it is to use it as sparingly as possible, avoiding occasions of expense by cultivating peace, but remembering also that timely disbursements to prepare for danger frequently prevent much greater disbursements to repel it; avoiding likewise the accumulation of debt, not only by shunning occasions of expense but by vigorous exertions in time of peace to discharge the debts which unavoidable wars may have occasioned, not ungenerously throwing upon posterity the burden which we ourselves ought to bear. The execution of these maxims belongs to your representatives, but it is necessary that public opinion should cooperate.

To facilitate to them the performance of their duty, it is essential that you should practically bear in mind that toward the payment of debts there must be revenue; that no taxes can be devised which are not more or less inconvenient and unpleasant; that the intrinsic embarrassment inseparable from the selection of the proper objects (which is always the choice of difficulties) ought to be a decisive motive for a candid construction of the conduct of the government in making it, and for a spirit of acquiescence in the measures for obtaining revenue which the public exigencies may at any time dictate.

Observe good faith and justice towards all nations. Cultivate peace and harmony with all. Religion and morality enjoin this conduct; and can it be that good policy does not equally enjoin it? It will be worthy of a free, enlightened, and, at no distant period, a great nation to give to mankind the magnanimous and too novel example of a people always guided by an exalted justice and benevolence. Who can doubt that in the course of time and things the fruits of such a plan would richly repay any temporary advantages that might be lost by a steady adherence to it? Can it be that Providence has not connected the permanent felicity of a nation with its virtue? The experiment, at least, is recommended by every sentiment which ennobles human nature. Alas! is it rendered impossible by its vices?

In the execution of such a plan nothing is more essential than that permanent, inveterate antipathies against particular nations and passionate attachments for others should be excluded and that in place of them just and amicable feelings toward all should be cultivated. The nation which indulges toward another an habitual hatred or an habitual fondness is in some degree a slave. It is a slave to its animosity or to its affection, either of which is sufficient to lead it astray from its duty and its interest. Antipathy in one nation against another disposes each more readily to offer insult and injury, to lay hold of slight causes of umbrage, and to be haughty and intractable when accidental or trifling occasions of dispute occur.

Hence, frequent collisions, obstinate, envenomed, and bloody contests. The nation prompted by ill will and resentment sometimes impels to war the government, contrary to the best calculations of policy. The government sometimes participates in the national propensity, and adopts, through passion, what reason would reject; at other times, it makes the animosity of the nation subservient to projects of hostility instigated by pride, ambition, and other sinister and pernicious motives. The peace often, and sometimes perhaps the liberty, of nations has been the victim.

So, likewise, a passionate attachment of one nation for another produces a variety of evils. Sympathy for the favorite nation, facilitating the illusion of an imaginary common interest in cases where no real common interest exists, and infusing into one the enmities of the other, betrays the former into a participation in the quarrels and wars of the latter without adequate inducement or justification. It leads also to concessions to the favorite nation of privileges denied to others, which is apt doubly to injure the nation making the concessions, by unnecessarily parting with what ought to have been retained, and by exciting jealousy, ill will, and disposition to retaliate in the parties from whom equal privileges are withheld.

And it gives to ambitious, corrupted, or deluded citizens (who devote themselves to the favorite nation) facility to betray or sacrifice the interests of their own country, without odium, sometimes even with popularity, gilding with the appearances of a virtuous sense of obligation, a commendable deference for public opinion, or laudable zeal for public good, the base or foolish compliances of ambition, corruption, or infatuation. As avenues to foreign influence in innumerable ways, such attachments are particularly alarming to the truly enlightened and independent patriot. How many opportunities do they afford to tamper with domestic factions, to practise the arts of seduction, to mislead public opinion, to influence or awe the public councils! Such an attachment of a small or weak toward a great and powerful nation dooms the former to be the satellite of the latter.

Against the insidious wiles of foreign influence, I conjure you to believe me, fellow-citizens, the jealousy of a free people ought to be constantly awake, since history and experience prove that foreign influence is one of the most baneful foes of republican government. But that jealousy, to be useful, must be impartial, else it becomes the instrument of the very influence to be avoided instead of a defense against it. Excessive partiality for one foreign nation and excessive dislike of another cause those whom they actuate to see danger only on one side and serve to veil and even second the arts of influence on the other. Real patriots, who may resist the intrigues of the favorite, are liable to become suspected and odious, while its tools and dupes usurp the applause and confidence of the people to surrender their interests.

The great rule of conduct for us, in regard to foreign nations, is in extending our commercial relations to have with them as little political connection as possible. So far as we have already formed engagements, let them be fulfilled with perfect good faith. Here let us stop.

Europe has a set of primary interests which to us have none, or a very remote relation. Hence she must be engaged in frequent controversies, the causes of which are essentially foreign to our concerns. Hence, therefore, it must be unwise in us to implicate ourselves, by artificial ties, in the ordinary vicissitudes of her politics or the ordinary combinations and collisions of her friendships or enmities.

Our detached and distant situation invites and enables us to pursue a different course. If we remain one people, under an efficient government, the period is not far off when we may defy material injury from external annoyance; when we may take such an attitude as will cause the neutrality we may at any time resolve upon to be scrupulously respected; when belligerent nations, under the impossibility of making acquisitions upon us, will not lightly hazard the giving us provocation; when we may choose peace or war, as our interest guided by our justice shall counsel.

Why forgo the advantages of so peculiar a situation? Why quit our own to stand upon foreign ground? Why, by interweaving our destiny with that of any part of Europe, entangle our peace and prosperity in the toils of European ambition, rivalship, interest, humor, or caprice?

It is our true policy to steer clear of permanent alliances with any portion of the foreign world. So far, I mean, as we are now at liberty to do it; for let me not be understood as capable of patronizing infidelity to existing engagements (I hold the maxim no less applicable to public than to private affairs that honesty is always the best policy). I repeat it, therefore: let those engagements be observed in their genuine sense. But, in my opinion, it is unnecessary and would be unwise to extend them.

Taking care always to keep ourselves, by suitable establishments, on a respectable defensive posture, we may safely trust to temporary alliances for extraordinary emergencies.

Harmony, and a liberal intercourse with all nations are recommended by policy, humanity, and interest. But even our commercial policy should hold an equal and impartial hand, neither seeking nor granting exclusive favors or preferences; consulting the natural course of things; diffusing and diversifying by gentle means the streams of commerce but forcing nothing; establishing with powers so disposed, in order to give to trade a stable course, to define the rights of our merchants, and to enable the government to support them, conventional rules of intercourse, the best that present circumstances and mutual opinion will permit, but temporary and liable to be from time to time abandoned or varied, as experience and circumstances shall dictate; constantly keeping in view that it is folly in one nation to look for disinterested favors from another; that it must pay with a portion of its independence for whatever it may accept under that character; that, by such acceptance, it may place itself in the condition of having given equivalents for nominal favors and yet of being reproached with ingratitude for not giving more. There can be no greater error than to expect, or calculate upon, real favors from nation to nation. It is an illusion which experience must cure, which a just pride ought to discard.

In offering to you, my countrymen, these counsels of an old and affectionate friend, I dare not hope they will make the strong and lasting impression I could wish; that they will control the usual current of the passions or prevent our nation from running the course which has hitherto marked the destiny of nations. But if I may even flatter myself that they may be productive of some partial benefit, some occasional good; that they may now and then recur to moderate the fury of party-spirit, to warn against the mischiefs of foreign intrigue, to guard against the impostures of pretended patriotism, this hope will be a full recompense for the solicitude for your welfare by which they have been dictated. . . .

The inducements of interest for observing that conduct will best be referred to your own reflections and experience. With me, a predominant motive has been to endeavor to gain time to our country to settle and mature its yet recent institutions, and to progress without interruption to that degree of strength and consistency which is necessary to give it, humanly speaking, the command of its own fortune.

Though, in reviewing the incidents of my administration, I am unconscious of intentional error, I am nevertheless too sensible of my defects not to think it probable that I may have committed many errors. Whatever they may be, I fervently beseech the Almighty to avert or mitigate the evils to which they may tend. I shall also carry with me the hope that my country will never cease to view them with indulgence, and that after forty-five years of my life dedicated to its service, with an upright zeal, the faults of incompetent abilities will be consigned to oblivion as myself must soon be to the mansions of rest.

Relying on its kindness in this as in other things, and actuated by that fervent love toward it which is so natural to a man who views in it the native soil of himself and his progenitors for several generations, I anticipate with pleasing expectations that retreat in which I promise myself to realize, without alloy, the sweet enjoyment of partaking, in the midst of my fellow citizens, the benign influence of good laws under a free government, the ever favorite object of my heart, and the happy reward, as I trust, of our mutual cares, labors, and dangers.

IV

THE YOUNG REPUBLIC

INAUGURAL ADDRESS

John Adams   *March 4, 1797*

*John Adams spent over thirty years in the service of his
state and his country. He was a delegate to the first Continental
Congress, led the debates on the Declaration of Independence,
was an American minister for a decade and signed the Treaty
of Paris, served as vice-president under Washington for two
terms and was elected president in 1796. Defeated by Jefferson
in his reelection bid, Adams retired to his home in Quincy,
Massachusetts, where he died on July 4, 1826, the fiftieth
anniversary of the Declaration of Independence, and the same
day that Thomas Jefferson died.*

WHEN it was first perceived, in early times, that no middle course for
America remained between unlimited submission to a foreign legislature and a
total independence of its claims, men of reflection were less apprehensive of
danger from the formidable power of fleets and armies they must determine to
resist than from those contests and dissensions which would certainly arise

concerning the forms of government to be instituted over the whole and over the parts of this extensive country. Relying, however, on the purity of their intentions, the justice of their cause, and the integrity and intelligence of the people, under an overruling Providence which had so signally protected this country from the first, the representatives of this nation, then consisting of little more than half its present number, not only broke to pieces the chains which were forging and the rod of iron that was lifted up, but frankly cut asunder the ties which had bound them, and launched into an ocean of uncertainty.

The zeal and ardor of the people during the Revolutionary war, supplying the place of government, commanded a degree of order sufficient at least for the temporary preservation of society. The Confederation which was early felt to be necessary was prepared from the models of the Batavian and Helvetic confederacies, the only examples which remain with any detail and precision in history, and certainly the only ones which the people at large had ever considered. But reflecting on the striking difference in so many particulars between this country and those where a courier may go from the seat of government to the frontier in a single day, it was then certainly foreseen by some who assisted in Congress at the formation of it that it could not be durable.

Negligence of its regulations, inattention to its recommendations, if not disobedience to its authority, not only in individuals but in States, soon appeared with their melancholy consequences—universal languor, jealousies and rivalries of States, decline of navigation and commerce, discouragement of necessary manufactures, universal fall in the value of lands and their produce, contempt of public and private faith, loss of consideration and credit with foreign nations, and at length in discontents, animosities, combinations, partial conventions, and insurrection, threatening some great national calamity.

In this dangerous crisis the people of America were not abandoned by their usual good sense, presence of mind, resolution, or integrity. Measures were pursued to concert a plan to form a more perfect union, establish justice, insure domestic tranquillity, provide for the common defense, promote the general welfare, and secure the blessings of liberty. The public disquisitions, discussions, and deliberations issued in the present happy Constitution of Government.

Employed in the service of my country abroad during the whole course of these transactions, I first saw the Constitution of the United States in a foreign country. Irritated by no literary altercation, animated by no public debate, heated by no party animosity, I read it with great satisfaction, as the result of good heads prompted by good hearts, as an experiment better adapted to the genius, character, situation, and relations of this nation and country than any which had ever been proposed or suggested. In its general principles and great outlines, it was conformable to such a system of government as I had ever most esteemed, and in some States, my own native State in particular, had contributed to establish. Claiming a right of suffrage in common with my fellow-citizens, in the adoption or rejection of a constitution which was to rule me and my posterity, as well as them and theirs, I did not hesitate to express my approbation of it on all occasions, in public and in private. It was not then, nor has been since, any objection to it in my mind that the Executive and Senate were not more permanent. Nor have I ever entertained a thought of promoting any alteration in it but such as the people themselves, in the course of their experience, should see and feel to be necessary or expedient, and by their representatives in Congress and the State legislatures, according to the Constitution itself, adopt and ordain.

Returning to the bosom of my country after a painful separation from it for ten years, I had the honor to be elected to a station under the new order of things, and I have repeatedly laid myself under the most serious obligations to support the Constitution. The operation of it has equaled the most sanguine expectations of its friends, and from an habitual attention to it, satisfaction in its administration, and delight in its effects upon the peace, order, prosperity, and happiness of the nation I have acquired an habitual attachment to it and veneration for it.

What other form of government, indeed, can so well deserve our esteem and love?

There may be little solidity in an ancient idea that congregations of men into cities and nations are the most pleasing objects in the sight of superior intelligences, but this is very certain, that, to a benevolent human mind, there can be no spectacle presented by any nation more pleasing, more noble, majestic, or august, than an assembly like that which has so often been seen in this and the other Chamber of Congress, of a Government in which the Executive authority, as well as that of all the branches of the Legislature, are exercised by citizens selected at regular periods by their neighbors to make and execute laws for the general good. Can anything essential, anything more than mere ornament and decoration, be added to this by robes and diamonds? Can authority be more amiable and respectable when it descends from accidents or institutions established in remote antiquity than when it springs fresh from the hearts and judgments of an honest and enlightened people? For it is the people only that are represented. It is their power and majesty that is reflected, and only for their good, in every legitimate government, under whatever form it may appear. The existence of such a government as ours for any length of time is a full proof of a general dissemination of knowledge and virtue throughout the whole body of the people. And what object or consideration more pleasing than this can be presented to the human mind? If national pride is ever justifiable or excusable it is when it springs, not from power or riches, grandeur or glory, but from conviction of national innocence, information, and benevolence.

In the midst of these pleasing ideas we should be unfaithful to ourselves if we should ever lose sight of the danger to our liberties if anything partial or extraneous should infect the purity of our free, fair, virtuous, and independent elections. If an election is to be determined by a majority of a single vote, and that can be procured by a party through artifice or corruption, the Government may be the choice of a party for its own ends, not of the nation for the national good. If that solitary suffrage can be obtained by foreign nations by flattery or menaces, by fraud or violence, by terror, intrigue, or venality, the Government may not be the choice of the American people, but of foreign nations. It may be foreign nations who govern us, and not we, the people, who govern ourselves, and candid men will acknowledge that in such cases choice would have little advantage to boast of over lot or chance.

Such is the amiable and interesting system of government (and such are some of the abuses to which it may be exposed) which the people of America have exhibited to the admiration and anxiety of the wise and virtuous of all nations for eight years under the administration of a citizen who, by a long course of great actions, regulated by prudence, justice, temperance, and fortitude, conducting a people inspired with the same virtues and animated with the same ardent patriotism and love of liberty to independence and peace, to increasing wealth and unexampled prosperity, has merited the gratitude of his fellow-citizens, commanded the highest praises of foreign nations, and secured immortal glory with posterity.

In that retirement which is his voluntary choice may he long live to enjoy the delicious recollection of his services, the gratitude of mankind, the happy fruits of them to himself and the world, which are daily increasing, and that splendid prospect of the future fortunes of his country which is opening from year to year. His name may be still a rampart, and the knowledge that he lives a bulwark, against all open or secret enemies of his country's peace. This example has been recommended to the imitation of his successors by both Houses of Congress and by the voice of the legislatures and the people throughout the nation.

On this subject it might become me better to be silent or to speak with diffidence; but as something may be expected, the occasion, I hope, will be admitted as an apology if I venture to say that if a preference, upon principle, of a free republican government, formed upon long and serious reflection, after a diligent and impartial inquiry after truth; if an attachment to the Constitution of the United States and a conscientious determination to support it until it shall be altered by the judgments and the wishes of the people, expressed in the mode prescribed in it; if a respectful attention to the constitutions of the individual States and a constant caution and delicacy toward the State governments; if an equal and impartial regard to the rights, interests, honor, and happiness of all the States in the Union, without preference or regard to a northern or southern, eastern or western, position, their various political opinions on unessential points or their personal attachments; if a love of virtuous men of all parties and denominations; if a love of science and letters and a wish to patronize every rational effort to encourage schools, colleges, universities, academies, and every institution for propagating knowledge, virtue, and religion among all classes of the people, not only for their benign influence on the happiness of life in all its stages and classes, and of society in all its forms, but as the only means of preserving our Constitution from its natural enemies, the spirit of sophistry, the spirit of party, the spirit of intrigue, the profligacy of corruption, and the pestilence of foreign influence, which is the angel of destruction to elective governments; if a love of equal laws, of justice, and humanity in the interior administration; if an inclination to improve agriculture, commerce, and manufactures for necessity, convenience, and defense; if a spirit of equity and humanity toward the aboriginal nations of America, and a disposition to meliorate their condition by inclining them to be more friendly to us, and our citizens to be more friendly to them; if an inflexible determination to maintain peace and inviolable faith with all nations, and that system of neutrality and impartiality among the belligerent powers of Europe which has been adopted by this Government and so solemnly sanctioned by both Houses of Congress and applauded by the legislatures of the States and the public opinion, until it shall be otherwise ordained by Congress; if a personal esteem for the French nation, formed in a residence of several years chiefly among them, and a sincere desire to preserve the friendship which has been so much for the honor and interest of both nations; if, while the conscious honor and integrity of the people of America and the internal sentiment of their power and energies must be preserved, an earnest endeavor to investigate every just cause and remove every colorable pretense of complaint; if an intention to pursue by amicable negotiation a reparation for the injuries that have been committed on the commerce of our fellow-citizens by whatever nation, and if success can not be obtained, to lay the facts before the Legislature, that they may consider what further measures the honor and interest of the Government and its constituents demand; if a resolution to do justice as far as may depend upon me, at all times and to all nations, and maintain peace, friendship, and benevolence with all the world; if an unshaken confidence in the honor, spirit, and resources of the American people, on which I have so often hazarded my all and never been deceived; if elevated ideas of the high destinies of this country and of my own duties toward it, founded on a knowledge of the moral principles and intellectual improvements of the people deeply engraven on my mind in early life, and not obscured but exalted by experience and age; and with humble reverence, I feel it my duty to add, if a veneration for the religion of a people who profess and call themselves Christians, and a fixed resolution to consider a decent respect for Christianity among the best recommendations for the public service, can enable me in any degree to comply with your wishes, it shall be my strenuous endeavor that this sagacious injunction of the two Houses shall not be without effect.

With this great example before me, with the sense and spirit, the faith and honor, the duty and interest, of the same American people pledged to support the Constitution of the United States, I entertain no doubt of its continuance in all its energy, and my mind is prepared without hesitation to lay myself under the most solemn obligations to support it to the utmost of my power.

And may that Being who is supreme over all, the Patron of Order, the Fountain of Justice, and the Protector in all ages of the world of virtuous liberty, continue His blessing upon this nation and its Government and give it all possible success and duration consistent with the ends of His providence.

THE VIRGINIA RESOLUTIONS

James Madison   *December 24, 1798*

In 1798, Congress had passed the Alien and Sedition acts. The former allowed the president to deport any potentially dangerous alien and the latter made writing or speaking out against the government punishable by imprisonment. These laws seemed to Jefferson and Madison an infringement of personal liberties and also placed excessive power in the hands of the federal government. Both men wrote resolutions in opposition to these acts. Jefferson's were adopted by the Kentucky legislature and Madison's by the Virginia legislature. These resolutions declared that a state might take steps to veto an unconstitutional act. Both the Alien and Sedition acts lapsed in 1800.

RESOLVED, that the General Assembly of Virginia doth unequivocally express a firm resolution to maintain and defend the Constitution of the United

States, and the constitution of this state against every aggression, either foreign or domestic; and that they will support the government of the United States in all measures warranted by the former.

That this Assembly most solemnly declares a warm attachment to the union of the states, to maintain which it pledges its powers; and that, for this end, it is their duty to watch over and oppose every infraction of those principles which constitute the only basis of that union, because a faithful observance of them can alone secure its existence and the public happiness.

That this Assembly does explicitly and peremptorily declare that it views the powers of the federal government as resulting from the compact to which the states are parties, as limited by the plain sense and intention of the instrument constituting that compact, as no further valid than they are authorized by the grants enumerated in that compact; and that, in case of a deliberate, palpable, and dangerous exercise of other powers, not granted by the said compact, the states who are parties thereto, have the right, and are in duty bound to interpose for arresting the progress of the evil, and for maintaining, within their respective limits, the authorities, rights, and liberties appertaining to them. . . .

That the General Assembly does particularly protest against the palpable and alarming infractions of the Constitution in the two late cases of the Alien and Sedition Acts, passed at the last session of Congress; the first of which exercises a power nowhere delegated to the federal government, and which, by uniting legislative and judicial powers to those of executive, subverts the general principles of free government, as well as the particular organization and positive provisions of the federal Constitution; and the other of which acts exercises, in like manner, a power not delegated by the Constitution, but, on the contrary, expressly and positively forbidden by one of the amendments thereto, a power which, more than any other, ought to produce universal alarm, because it is leveled against the right of freely examining public characters and measures, and of free communication among the people thereon, which has ever been justly deemed the only effectual guardian of every other right.

That this state having, by its Convention, which ratified the federal Constitution, expressly declared that, among other essential rights, "the liberty of conscience and the press cannot be canceled, abridged, restrained, or modified, by any authority of the United States," and from its extreme anxiety to guard these rights from every possible attack of sophistry and ambition, having, with other states, recommended an amendment for that purpose, which amendment was, in due time, annexed to the Constitution, it would mark a reproachful inconsistency and criminal degeneracy if an indifference were now to be shown to the most palpable violation of one of the rights thus declared and secured, and to the establishment of a precedent which may be fatal to the other.

That the good people of the commonwealth, having ever felt, and continuing to feel, the most sincere affection for their brethren of the other states; the truest anxiety for establishing and perpetuating the union of all; and the most scrupulous fidelity to the Constitution, which is the pledge of mutual friendship and the instrument of mutual happiness; the General Assembly does solemnly appeal to the like dispositions in other states, in confidence that they will concur with this commonwealth in declaring, as it does hereby declare, that the acts aforesaid are unconstitutional. . . .

FIRST INAUGURAL ADDRESS

Thomas Jefferson   *March 4, 1801*

Ranking among the best and most important of the presidential addresses was Thomas Jefferson's first Inaugural Address, presented on March 4, 1801, in Washington, D.C. He made a plea for conciliation and spoke of unity, of tolerance, of hope in the future and in a philosophy of government.

FRIENDS and Fellow-Citizens:

Called upon to undertake the duties of the first executive office of our country, I avail myself of the presence of that portion of my fellow-citizens which is here assembled to express my grateful thanks for the favor with which they have been pleased to look toward me, to declare a sincere consciousness that the task is above my talents, and that I approach it with those anxious and awful presentiments which the greatness of the charge and the weakness of my powers so justly inspire. A rising nation, spread over a wide and fruitful land, traversing all the seas with the rich productions of their industry, engaged in commerce with nations who feel power and forget right, advancing rapidly to destinies beyond the reach of mortal eye—when I contemplate these transcendent objects, and see the honor, the happiness, and the hopes of this beloved country committed to the issue and the auspices of this day, I shrink from the contemplation, and humble myself before the magnitude of the undertaking. Utterly, indeed, should I despair did not the presence of many whom I here see remind me that in the other high authorities provided by our Constitution I shall find resources of wisdom, of virtue, and of zeal on which to rely under all difficulties. To you, then, gentlemen, who are charged with the sovereign functions of legislation, and to those associated with you, I look with encouragement for that guidance and support which may enable us to steer with safety the vessel in which we are all embarked amidst the conflicting elements of a troubled world.

During the contest of opinion through which we have passed the animation of discussions and of exertions has sometimes worn an aspect which might impose on strangers unused to think freely and to speak and to write what they think; but this being now decided by the voice of the nation, announced according to the rules of the Constitution, all will, of course, arrange themselves under the will of the law, and unite in common efforts for the common good.

All, too, will bear in mind this sacred principle, that though the will of the majority is in all cases to prevail, that will to be rightful must be reasonable; that the minority possess their equal rights, which equal law must protect, and to violate would be oppression. Let us, then, fellow-citizens, unite with one heart and one mind. Let us restore to social intercourse that harmony and affection without which liberty and even life itself are but dreary things. And let us reflect that, having banished from our land that religious intolerance under which mankind so long bled and suffered, we have yet gained little if we countenance a political intolerance as despotic, as wicked, and capable of as bitter and bloody persecutions. During the throes and convulsions of the ancient world, during the agonizing spasms of infuriated man, seeking through blood and slaughter his long-lost liberty, it was not wonderful that the agitation of the billows should reach even this distant and peaceful shore; that this should be more felt and feared by some and less by others, and should divide opinions as to measures of safety. But every difference of opinion is not a difference of principle. We have called by different names brethren of the same principle. We are all Republicans, we are all Federalists. If there be any among us who would wish to dissolve this Union or to change its republican form, let them stand undisturbed as monuments of the safety with which error of opinion may be tolerated where reason is left free to combat it. I know, indeed, that some honest men fear that a republican government can not be strong, that this Government is not strong enough; but would the honest patriot, in the full tide of successful experiment, abandon a government which has so far kept us free and firm on the theoretic and visionary fear that this

Government, the world's best hope, may by possibility want energy to preserve itself? I trust not. I believe this, on the contrary, the strongest Government on earth. I believe it the only one where every man, at the call of the law, would fly to the standard of the law, and would meet invasions of the public order as his own personal concern. Sometimes it is said that man can not be trusted with the government of himself. Can he, then, be trusted with the government of others? Or have we found angels in the forms of kings to govern him? Let history answer this question.

Let us, then, with courage and confidence pursue our own Federal and Republican principles, our attachment to union and representative government. Kindly separated by nature and a wide ocean from the exterminating havoc of one quarter of the globe; too high-minded to endure the degradations of the others; possessing a chosen country, with room enough for our descendants to the thousandth and thousandth generation; entertaining a due sense of our equal right to the use of our own faculties, to the acquisitions of our own industry, to honor and confidence from our fellow-citizens, resulting not from birth, but from our actions and their sense of them; enlightened by a benign religion, professed, indeed, and practiced in various forms, yet all of them inculcating honesty, truth, temperance, gratitude, and the love of man; acknowledging and adoring an overruling Providence, which by all its dispensations proves that it delights in the happiness of man here and his greater happiness hereafter—with all these blessings, what more is necessary to make us a happy and a prosperous people? Still one thing more, fellow-citizens—a wise and frugal Government, which shall restrain men from injuring one another, shall leave them otherwise free to regulate their own pursuits of industry and improvement, and shall not take from the mouth of labor the bread it has earned. This is the sum of good government, and this is necessary to close the circle of our felicities.

About to enter, fellow-citizens, on the exercise of duties which comprehend everything dear and valuable to you, it is proper you should understand what I deem the essential principles of our Government, and consequently those which ought to shape its Administration. I will compress them within the narrowest compass they will bear, stating the general principle, but not all its limitations. Equal and exact justice to all men, of whatever state or persuasion, religious or political; peace, commerce, and honest friendship with all nations, entangling alliances with none; the support of the State governments in all their rights, as the most competent administrations for our domestic concerns and the surest bulwarks against antirepublican tendencies; the preservation of the General Government in its whole constitutional vigor, as the sheet anchor of our peace at home and safety abroad; a jealous care of the right of election by the people—a mild and safe corrective of abuses which are lopped by the sword of revolution where peaceable remedies are unprovided; absolute acquiescence in the decisions of the majority, the vital principle of republics, from which is no appeal but to force, the vital principle and immediate parent of despotism; a well-disciplined militia, our best reliance in peace and for the first moments of war, till regulars may relieve them; the supremacy of the civil over the military authority; economy in the public expense, that labor may be lightly burthened; the honest payment of our debts and sacred preservation of the public faith; encouragement of agriculture, and of commerce as its handmaid; the diffusion of information and arraignment of all abuses at the bar of the public reason; freedom of religion; freedom of the press, and freedom of person under the protection of the *habeas corpus*, and trial by juries impartially selected. These principles form the bright constellation which has gone before us and guided our steps through an age of revolution and reformation. The wisdom of our sages and blood of our heroes have been devoted to their attainment. They should be the creed of our political faith, the text of civic instruction, the touchstone by which to try the services of those we trust; and should we wander from them in moments of error or of alarm, let us hasten to retrace our steps and to regain the road which alone leads to peace, liberty, and safety.

I repair, then, fellow-citizens, to the post you have assigned me. With experience enough in subordinate offices to have seen the difficulties of this the greatest of all, I have learned to expect that it will rarely fall to the lot of imperfect man to retire from this station with the reputation and the favor which bring him into it. Without pretensions to that high confidence you reposed in our first and greatest revolutionary character, whose preëminent services had entitled him to the first place in his country's love and destined for him the fairest page in the volume of faithful history, I ask so much confidence only as may give firmness and effect to the legal administration of your affairs. I shall often go wrong through defect of judgment. When right, I shall often be thought wrong by those whose positions will not command a view of the whole ground. I ask your indulgence for my own errors, which will never be intentional, and your support against the errors of others, who may condemn what they would not if seen in all its parts. The approbation implied by your suffrage is a great consolation to me for the past, and my future solicitude will be to retain the good opinion of those who have bestowed it in advance, to conciliate that of others by doing them all the good in my power, and to be instrumental to the happiness and freedom of all.

Relying, then, on the patronage of your good will, I advance with obedience to the work, ready to retire from it whenever you become sensible how much better choice it is in your power to make. And may that Infinite Power which rules the destinies of the universe lead our councils to what is best, and give them a favorable issue for your peace and prosperity.

THE LOUISIANA PURCHASE

April 30, 1803

At the end of the French and Indian War, France ceded Louisiana to Spain. In 1800, Spain, by the secret Treaty of San Idelfonso, exchanged the territory to France for a part of the Italian peninsula. When news of the cession of Louisiana became public knowledge, it roused the Americans, particularly those in the West, for whoever controlled New Orleans controlled the Mississippi. The river was vital to the settlers of Tennessee, Kentucky and Ohio as their one highway to the outside world. Jefferson sent Robert Livingston and James Monroe to France to see if Napoleon would consider selling New Orleans and Florida. Because France was on the brink of war with England, Talleyrand, Napoleon's minister, offered to sell all of Louisiana to the Americans for sixty million francs, about fifteen million dollars. Jefferson had no constitutional authority to purchase the territory and no one knew how far west the territory extended. When questioned about the boundaries, Talleyrand said: "I can give you no direction. You have made a noble bargain for yourselves and I suppose you will make the most of it." With the purchase of 827,000 square miles, the area of the United States was doubled, and the country extended to the Rocky Mountains.

ART. I. Whereas, by the article the third of the treaty concluded at St. Idelfonso, the 1st October, 1800 between the First Consul of the French Republic and his Catholic Majesty, it was agreed as follows: "His Catholic Majesty promises and engages on his part, to cede to the French Republic, six months after the full and entire execution of the conditions and stipulations herein relative to his royal highness the duke of Parma, the colony or province of Louisiana, with the same extent that it now has in the hands of Spain, and that it had when France possessed it; and such as it should be after the treaties subsequently entered into between Spain and other states." And whereas, in pursuance of the Treaty, and particularly of the third article, the French Republic has an incontestible title to the domain and to the possession of the said territory:—The First Consul of the

French Republic desiring to give to the United States a strong proof of his friendship, doth hereby cede to the said United States, in the name of the French Republic, forever and in full sovereignty, the said territory with all its rights and appurtenances, as fully and in the same manner as they have been acquired by the French Republic, in virtue of the above-mentioned Treaty, concluded with his Catholic Majesty.

ART. II. In the cession made by the preceding article are included in the adjacent islands belonging to Louisiana, all public lots and squares, vacant lands, and all public buildings, fortifications, barracks, and other edifices which are not private property.—The Archives, papers, and documents, relative to the domain and sovereignty of Louisiana, and its dependencies, will be left in the possession of the Commissaries of the United States, and copies will be afterwards given in due form to the Magistrates and Municipal officers, of such of the said papers and documents as may be necessary to them.

ART. III. The inhabitants of the ceded territory shall be incorporated in the Union of the United States, and admitted as soon as possible, according to the principles of the Federal Constitution, to the enjoyment of all the rights, advantages and immunities of citizens of the United States; and in the mean time they shall be maintained and protected in the free enjoyment of their liberty, property, and the Religion which they profess. . . .

INSTRUCTIONS TO MERIWETHER LEWIS

Thomas Jefferson   *June 20, 1803*

Jefferson was interested in the West long before the Louisiana Purchase, on both political and scientific grounds. While Louisiana was still French, he had obtained $2,500 from Congress for an expedition to explore the source of the Missouri River and the regions west to the Pacific Coast. His secretary, Meriwether Lewis, was chosen to lead the expedition, with William Clark as second in command. The following instructions to Meriwether Lewis were written by Thomas Jefferson on June 20, 1803. The expedition left St. Louis on May 14, 1804, and returned September 23, 1806.

YOUR situation as secretary of the president of the United States has made you acquainted with the objects of my confidential message of Jan. 18, 1803, to the legislature. You have seen the act they passed, which, though expressed in general terms, was meant to sanction those objects, and you are appointed to carry them into execution.

Instruments for ascertaining by celestial observations the geography of the country through which you will pass, have already been provided. Light

Lewis and Clark mural, artist unknown.

articles for barter, and presents among the Indians, arms for your attendants, say for from ten to twelve men, boats, tents, and other traveling apparatus, with ammunition, medicine, surgical instruments, and provision you will have prepared with such aids as the secretary of war can yield in his department. And from him also you will receive authority to engage among our troops, by voluntary agreement, the number of attendants above mentioned, over whom you, as their commanding officer, are invested with all the powers the laws give in such a case.

As your movements while within the limits of the United States will be better directed by occasional communications, adapted to circumstances as they arise, they will not be noticed here. What follows will respect your proceedings after your departure from the United States.

Your mission has been communicated to the ministers here from France, Spain, and Great Britain, and through them to their governments; and such assurances given them as to its objects as we trust will satisfy them. The country of Louisiana having been ceded by Spain to France, the passport you have from the minister of France, the representative of the present sovereign of the country, will be a protection with all its subjects. And that from the minister of England will entitle you to the friendly aid of any traders of that allegiance with whom you may happen to meet.

The object of your mission is to explore the Missouri River, and such principal stream of it, as, by its course and communication with the waters of the Pacific Ocean may offer the most direct and practicable water communication across this continent, for the purposes of commerce.

Beginning at the mouth of the Missouri, you will take observations of latitude and longitude at all remarkable points on the river, and especially at the mouths of rivers, at rapids, at islands and other places and objects distinguished by such natural marks and characters of a durable kind, as that they may with certainty be recognized hereafter. The courses of the river between these points of observation may be supplied by the compass, the logline, and by time, corrected by the observations themselves. The variations of the compass, too, in different places, should be noticed.

The interesting points of the portage between the heads of the Missouri and the water offering the best communication with the Pacific Ocean should be fixed by observation, and the course of that water to the ocean, in the same manner as that of the Missouri.

Your observations are to be taken with great pains and accuracy, to be entered distinctly, and intelligibly for others as well as yourself to comprehend all the elements necessary, with the aid of the usual tables to fix the latitude and longitude of the places at which they were taken, and are to be rendered to the war office for the purpose of having the calculations made concurrently by proper persons within the United States. Several copies of these, as well as your other notes, should be made at leisure times and put into the care of the most trustworthy of your attendants, to guard by multiplying them against the accidental losses to which they will be exposed. A further guard would be that one of these copies be written on the paper of the birch, as less liable to injury from damp than common paper.

The commerce which may be carried on with the people inhabiting the line you will pursue renders a knowledge of these people important. You will therefore endeavor to make yourself acquainted, as far as a diligent pursuit of your journey shall admit, with the names of the nations and their numbers; the extent and limits of their possessions; their relations with other tribes or nations; their language, traditions, monuments; their ordinary occupations in agriculture, fishing, hunting, war, arts, and the implements for these; their food, clothing, and domestic accommodations; the diseases prevalent among them, and the remedies they use; moral and physical circumstance which distinguish them from the tribes they know; peculiarities in their laws, customs and dispositions; and articles of commerce they may need or furnish, and to what extent.

And considering the interest which every nation has in extending and strengthening the authority of reason and justice among the people around them, it will be useful to acquire what knowledge you can of the state of morality, religion, and information among them, as it may better enable those who endeavor to civilize and instruct them to adapt their measures to the existing notions and practices of those on whom they are to operate.

Other objects worthy of notice will be: the soil and face of the country, its growth and vegetable productions, especially those not of the United States; the animals of the country generally, and especially those not known in the United States; the remains and accounts of any which may be deemed rare or extinct; the mineral productions of every kind; but more particularly metals, limestone, pit coal, and saltpeter; salines and mineral waters, noting the temperature of the last and such circumstances as may indicate their character; volcanic appearances; climate as characterized by the thermometer, by the proportion of rainy, cloudy, and clear days, by lightning, hail, snow, ice, by the access and recess of frost, by the winds, prevailing at different seasons, the dates at which particular plants put forth or lose their flowers, or leaf, times of appearance of particular birds, reptiles, or insects.

Although your route will be along the channel of the Missouri, yet you will endeavor to inform yourself, by inquiry, of the character and extent of the country watered by its branches, and especially on its southern side. The North River, or Rio Bravo, which runs into the Gulf of Mexico, and the North River, or Rio Colorado, which runs into the Gulf of California, are understood to be the principal streams heading opposite to the waters of the Missouri, and running southwardly. Whether the dividing grounds between the Missouri and them are mountains or flatlands, what are their distance from the Missouri, the character of the intermediate country, and the people inhabiting it are worthy of particular inquiry.

The northern waters of the Missouri are less to be inquired after, because they have been ascertained to a considerable degree, and are still in a course of ascertainment by English traders and travelers. But if you can learn anything certain of the most northern source of the Mississippi, and of its position relative to the Lake of the Woods, it will be interesting to us. Some account, too, of the path of the Canadian traders from the Mississippi, at the mouth of the Ouisconsin [Wisconsin] River, to where it strikes the Missouri and of the soil and rivers in its course, is desirable.

In all your intercourse with the natives, treat them in the most friendly and conciliatory manner which their own conduct will admit; allay all jealousies as to the object of your journey, satisfy them of its innocence; make them acquainted with the position, extent, character, peaceable and commercial dispositions of the United States, of our wish to be neighborly, friendly, and useful to them, and of our dispositions to a commercial intercourse with them; confer with them on the points most convenient, as mutual emporiums and the articles of most desirable interchange for them and us. If a few of their influential chiefs, within practicable distance, wish to visit us, arrange such a visit with them, and furnish them with authority to call on our officers, on their entering the

United States, to have them conveyed to this place at public expense. If any of them should wish to have some of their young people brought up with us and taught such arts as may be useful to them, we will receive, instruct, and take care of them. Such a mission, whether of influential chiefs or of young people, would give some security to your own party.

Carry with you some matter of the kinepox [cowpox], inform those of them with whom you may be of its efficacy as a preservative from the small pox; and instruct and encourage them in the use of it. This may be especially done wherever you may winter.

As it is impossible for us to foresee in what manner you will be received by those people, whether with hospitality or hostility, so is it impossible to prescribe the exact degree of perseverance with which you are to pursue your journey. We value too much the lives of citizens to offer them to probable destruction. Your numbers will be sufficient to secure you against the unauthorized opposition of individuals, or of small parties; but if a superior force, authorized or not authorized, by a nation should be arrayed against your further passage, and inflexibly determined to arrest it, you must decline its further pursuit, and return. In the loss of yourselves, we should lose also the information you will have acquired. By returning safely with that, you may enable us to renew the essay with better calculated means. To your own discretion, therefore, must be left the degree of danger you may risk, and the point at which you should decline, only saying we wish you to err on the side of your safety, and bring back your party safe, even if it be with less information.

As far up the Missouri as the white settlements extend, an intercourse will probably be found to exist, between them and the Spanish posts at St. Louis, opposite Cahokia, or St. Genevieve opposite Kaskaskia. From still further up the river, the traders may furnish a conveyance for letters. Beyond that you may perhaps be able to engage Indians to bring letters for the government to Cahokia or Kaskaskia on promising that they shall there receive such special compensation as you shall have stipulated with them. Avail yourself of these means to communicate to us at seasonable intervals a copy of your journal, notes, and observations of every kind, putting into cipher whatever might do injury if betrayed.

Should you reach the Pacific Ocean, inform yourself of the circumstances which may decide whether the furs of those parts may not be collected as advantageously at the head of the Missouri (convenient as is supposed to the waters of the Colorado and Oregon or Columbia) as at Nootka Sound or any other point of that coast; and that trade be consequently conducted through the Missouri and United States more beneficially than by the circumnavigation now practised.

On your arrival on that coast, endeavor to learn if there be any port within your reach frequented by the sea vessels of any nation, and to send two of your trusted people back by sea, in such way as shall appear practicable, with a copy of your notes. And should you be of opinion that the return of your party by the way they went will be eminently dangerous, then ship the whole, and return by sea by way of Cape Horn or the Cape of Good Hope, as you shall be able.

As you will be without money, clothes, or provisions, you must endeavor to use the credit of the United States to obtain them; for which purpose open letters of credit shall be furnished you authorizing you to draw on the executive of the United States or any of its officers in any part of the world, in which drafts can be disposed of, and to apply with our recommendations to the consuls, agents, merchants, or citizens of any nation with which we have intercourse, assuring them in our name that any aids they may furnish you shall be honorably repaid and on demand. Our consuls, Thomas Howes at Batavia in Java, William Buchanan of the Isles of France and Bourbon, and John Elmslie at the Cape of Good Hope will be able to supply your necessities by drafts on us.

Should you find it safe to return by the way you go, after sending two of your party round by sea, or with your whole party if no conveyance by sea can be found, do so; making such observations on your return as may serve to supply, correct, or confirm those made on your outward journey.

In reentering the United States and reaching a place of safety, discharge any of your attendants who may desire and deserve it, procuring for them immediate payment of all arrears of pay and clothing which may have incurred since their departure; and assure them that they shall be recommended to the liberality of the legislature for the grant of a soldier's portion of land each, as proposed in my message to Congress; and repair yourself with your papers to the seat of government.

To provide, on the accident of your death, against anarchy, dispersion, and the consequent danger to your party, and total failure of the enterprise, you are hereby authorized, by any instrument signed and written in your hand, to name the person among them who shall succeed to the command on your decease; and, by like instruments, to change the nomination from time to time, as further experience of the characters accompanying you shall point out superior fitness. And all the powers and authorities given to yourself are, in the event of your death, transferred to and vested in the successor so named, with further power to him, and his successors, in like manner, to name each his successor, who, on the death of his predecessor shall be invested with all the powers and authorities given to yourself.

Given under my hand at the city of Washington, this 20th day of June 1803.

Th. Jefferson, Pr. United States of America

MARBURY V. MADISON

John Marshall *1803*

---

*John Marshall was a lawyer, an officer in the Rev-
olutionary War, a congressman, secretary of state and the
author of a five-volume biography of George Washington. In
1801 he was appointed chief justice of the Supreme Court, a
position he held for thirty-five years. Marshall was the principal
founder of the concept of judicial review and of constitutional
law.*

*Marbury had been appointed justice of the peace by
President Adams, but his commission, signed and sealed, had
not been delivered before Jefferson became president. Marbury
sued James Madison, the secretary of state, to obtain his commission. In this, one of the most famous of his decisions,
Marshall and the Supreme Court declared that a law of Congress was void because it was contrary to the Constitution.
Marshall established the right of the Supreme Court to review
any law of Congress or of a state legislature.*

MARSHALL, C.J. . . . It is therefore decidedly the opinion of the court, that
when a commission has been signed by the President, the appointment is made;
and that the commission is complete, when the seal of the United States has been
affixed to it by the secretary of state. . . .

Mr. Marbury, then, since his commission was signed by the President, and
sealed by the secretary of state, was appointed; and as the law creating the office,
gave the officer a right to hold for five years, independent of the executive, the
appointment was not revocable; but vested in the officer legal rights, which are
protected by the laws of his country.

To withhold his commission, therefore, is an act deemed by the court not
warranted by law, but violative of a vested legal right. . . .

The government of the United States has been emphatically termed a
government of laws, and not of men. It will certainly cease to deserve this high
appellation, if the laws furnish no remedy for the violation of a vested
legal right. . . .

It is, then, the opinion of the Court,

1st. That by signing the commission of Mr. Marbury, the president of the United States appointed him a justice of peace for the county of Washington in the district of Columbia; and that the seal of the United States, affixed thereto by the secretary of state, is conclusive testimony of the verity of the signature, and of the completion of the appointment; and that the appointment conferred on him a legal right to the office for the space of five years.

2dly. That, having this legal title to the office, he has a consequent right to the commission, a refusal to deliver which, is a plain violation of that right, for which the laws of his country afford him a remedy. . . .

This, then, is a plain case for a *mandamus*, either to deliver the commission, or a copy of it from the record; and it only remains to be enquired,

Whether it can issue from this court.

The act to establish the judical courts of the United States authorizes the Supreme Court "to issue writs of *mandamus*, in cases warranted by the principles and usages of law, to any courts appointed, or persons holding office, under the authority of the United States."

The secretary of state, being a person holding an office under the authority of the United States, is precisely within the letter of the description; and if this court is not authorized to issue a writ of *mandamus* to such an officer, it must be because the law is unconstitutional, and therefore absolutely incapable of conferring the authority and assigning the duties which its words purport to confer and assign.

The Constitution vests the whole judical power of the United States in one supreme court, and such inferior courts as congress shall, from time to time, ordain and establish. This power is expressly extended to all cases arising under the laws of the United States; and consequently, in some form, may be exercised over the present case; because the right claimed is given by a law of the United States.

In the distribution of this power it is declared, that "the supreme court shall have original jurisdiction in all cases affecting ambassadors, other public ministers and consuls, and those in which a state shall be a party. In all other cases, the supreme court shall have appellate jurisdiction." . . .

If it had been intended to leave it in the discretion of the legislature to apportion the judical power between the supreme and inferior courts according to the will of that body, it would certainly have been useless to have proceeded further than to have defined the judical power, and the tribunals in which it should be vested. The subsequent part of the section is mere surplusage, is entirely without meaning, if such is to be the construction. If Congress remains at liberty to give this court appellate jurisdiction, where the constitution has declared their jurisdiction shall be original; and original jurisdiction where the constitution has declared it shall be appellate; the distribution of jurisdiction, made in the constitution, is form without substance.

Affirmative words are often, in their operation, negative of other objects than those affirmed; and in this case, a negative or exclusive sense must be given to them or they have no operation at all.

It cannot be presumed, that any clause in the constitution is intended to be without effect; and therefore such a construction is inadmissable, unless the words require it. . . .

The authority, therefore, given to the supreme court, by the act establishing the judical courts of the United States, to issue writs of *mandamus* to public officers, appears not to be warranted by the constitution; and it becomes necessary to inquire whether a jurisdiction so conferred can be exercised.

The question whether an act repugnant to the constitution can become the law of the land, is a question deeply interesting to the United States; but, happily not of an intricacy proportioned to its interest. It seems only necessary to recognize certain principles, supposed to have been long and well established, to decide it.

That the people have an original right to establish, for their future government such principles as, in their opinion, shall most conduce to their own happiness, is the basis on which the whole American fabric has been erected. The exercise of this original right is a very great exertion, nor can it nor ought it to be frequently repeated. The principles therefore so established are deemed fundamental. And as the authority from which they proceed is supreme and can seldom act, they are designed to be permanent.

This original and supreme will organizes the government, and assigns to different departments their respective powers. It may either stop here or establish certain limits not to be transcended by those departments.

The government of the United States is of the latter description. The powers of the legislature are defined and limited; and that those limits may not be mistaken or forgotten, the constitution is written. To what purpose are powers limited, and to what purpose is that limitation committed to writing, if these limits may, at any time, be passed by those intended to be restrained? The distinction between a government with limited and unlimited powers is abolished if those limits do not confine the persons on whom they are imposed and if acts prohibited and acts allowed are of equal obligation. It is a proposition too plain to be contested, that the constitution controls any legislative act repugnant to it; or, that the legislature may alter the constitution by an ordinary act.

Between these alternatives there is no middle ground. The constitution is either a superior paramount law, unchangeable by ordinary means, or it is on a level with ordinary legislative acts, and, like other acts, is alterable when the legislature shall please to alter it.

If the former part of the alternative be true, then a legislative act contrary to the constitution is not law; if the latter part be true, then written constitutions are absurd attempts, on the part of the people, to limit a power in its own nature illimitable.

Certainly all those who have framed written constitutions contemplate them as forming the fundamental and paramount law of the nation, and consequently the theory of every such government must be that an act of the legislature repugnant to the Constitution is void.

This theory is essentially attached to a written constitution, and is consequently to be considered, by this court as one of the fundamental principles of our society. It is not, therefore, to be lost sight of in the further consideration of this subject.

If an act of the legislature repugnant to the constitution is void, does it, notwithstanding its invalidity, bind the courts and oblige them to give it effect? Or, in other words, though it be not law, does it constitute a rule as operative as if it was a law? This would be to overthrow in fact what was established in theory, and would seem, at first view, an absurdity too gross to be insisted on. It shall, however, receive a more attentive consideration.

It is emphatically the province and duty of the judicial department to say what the law is. Those who apply the rule to particular cases must of necessity expound and interpret that rule. If two laws conflict with each other, the courts must decide on the operation of each.

So if a law be in opposition to the constitution; if both the law and the constitution apply to a particular case, so that the court must either decide that case conformably to the law, disregarding the constitution, or conformably to the constitution, disregarding the law, the court must determine which of these conflicting rules governs the case. This is of the very essence of judicial duty.

If, then, the courts are to regard the constitution, and the constitution is superior to any ordinary act of the legislature, the constitution, and not such ordinary act, must govern the case to which they both apply.

Those, then, who controvert the principle that the constitution is to be considered in court as a paramount law, are reduced to the necessity of maintaining that courts must close their eyes on the constitution and see only the law.

This doctrine would subvert the very foundation of all written constitutions. It would declare that an act which, according to the principles and theory of our government, is entirely void, is yet, in practice, completely obligatory. It would declare that if the legislature shall do what is expressly forbidden, such act, notwithstanding the express prohibition, is in reality effectual. It would be giving to the legislature a practical and real omnipotence with the same breath which professes to restrict their powers within narrow limits. It is prescribing limits and declaring that those limits may be passed at pleasure.

That it thus reduces to nothing what we have deemed the greatest improvement on political institutions, a written constitution, would of itself be sufficient, in America, where written constitutions have been viewed with so much reverence, for rejecting the construction. But the peculiar expressions of the constitution of the United States furnish additional arguments in favor of its rejection.

The judicial power of the United States is extended to all cases arising under the constitution.

Could it be the intention of those who gave this power to say that, in using it, the constitution should not be looked into? That a case arising under the constitution should be decided without examining the instrument under which it arises?

This is too extravagant to be maintained. In some cases, then, the constitution must be looked into by the judges. And if they can open it at all, what part of it are the forbidden to read or to obey?

There are many other parts of the constitution which serve to illustrate this subject.

It is declared that "no tax or duty shall be laid on articles exported from any state." Suppose a duty on the export of cotton, of tobacco, or of flour, and a suit instituted to recover it, ought judgment to be rendered in such a case? Ought the judges to close their eyes on the constitution, and only see the law?

The constitution declares "that no bill of attainder or *ex post facto* law shall be passed." If, however, such a bill should be passed, and a person should be prosecuted under it, must the court condemn to death those victims whom the constitution endeavors to preserve?

"No person," says the constitution, "shall be convicted of treason unless on the testimony of two witnesses to the same overt act, or on confession in open court."

Here the language of the constitution is addressed especially to the courts. It prescribes, directly for them, a rule of evidence not to be departed from. If the legislature should change that rule, and declare one witness, or a confession out of court, sufficient for conviction, must the constitutional principle yield to the legislative act?

From these, and many other selections which might be made, it is apparent that the framers of the constitution contemplated that instrument as a rule for the government of courts, as well as of the legislature. Why otherwise does it direct the judges to take an oath to support it? This oath certainly applies in an especial manner to their conduct in their official character. How immoral to impose it on them if they were to be used as the instruments, and the knowing instruments, for violating what they swear to support!

The oath of office, too, imposed by the legislature, is completely demonstrative of the legislative opinion on this subject. It is in these words: "I do solemnly swear that I will administer justice without respect to persons, and do equal right to the poor and to the rich; and that I will faithfully and impartially discharge all the duties incumbent on me as———, according to the best of my abilities and understanding, agreeably to the constitution and laws of the United States." Why does a judge swear to discharge his duties agreeably to the constitution of the United States, if that constitution forms no rule for his government?— if it is closed upon him, and cannot be inspected by him?

If such be the real state of things, this is worse than solemn mockery. To prescribe, or to take this oath, becomes equally a crime.

It is also not entirely unworthy of observation, that in declaring what shall be the supreme law of the land, the constitution itself is first mentioned, and not the laws of the United States generally, but those only which shall be made in pursuance of the constitution, have that rank.

Thus, the particular phraseology of the constitution of the United States confirms and strengthens the principle, supposed to be essential to all written constitutions, that a law repugnant to the constitution is void, and that courts, as well as other departments, are bound by that instrument.

[*Mandamus* denied.]

AMENDMENT XII
CHOOSING PRESIDENT AND VICE-PRESIDENT

June 15, 1804

Proposed by Congress December 9, 1803, its ratification was completed June 15, 1804.

THE Electors shall meet in their respective states, and vote by ballot for President and Vice-President, one of whom, at least shall not be an inhabitant of the same state with themselves; they shall name in their ballots the person voted for as President, and in distinct ballots the person voted for as Vice-

President, and they shall make distinct lists of all persons voted for as President, and of all persons voted for as Vice-President, and of the number of votes for each, which lists they shall sign and certify, and transmit sealed to the seat of the government of the United States, directed to the President of the Senate;—The President of the Senate shall, in the presence of the Senate and House of Representatives, open all the certificates and the votes shall then be counted;—The person having the greatest number of votes for President, shall be the President, if such number be a majority of the whole number of Electors appointed; and if no person have such majority, then from the persons having the highest numbers not exceeding three on the list of those voted for as President, the House of Representatives shall choose immediately, by ballot, the President. But in choosing the President, the votes shall be taken by states, the representation from each state having one vote; a quorum for this purpose shall consist of a member or members from two-thirds of the states, and a majority of all the states shall be necessary to a choice. And if the House of Representatives shall not choose a President whenever the right of choice shall devolve upon them, before the fourth day of March next following, then the Vice-President shall act as President, as in the case of the death or other constitutional disability of the President.—The person having the greatest number of votes as Vice-President, shall be the Vice-President, if such number be a majority of the whole number of Electors appointed, and if no person have a majority, then from the two highest numbers on the list, the Senate shall choose the Vice-President; a quorum for the purpose shall consist of two-thirds of the whole number of Senators, and a majority of the whole number shall be necessary to a choice. But no person constitutionally ineligible to the office of President shall be eligible to that of Vice-President of the United States.

SPEECH TO THE
IROQUOIS SIX NATIONS

Red Jacket   *Summer 1805*

From the earliest days of the Pilgrims, whites tried to convert the Indians to the Christian religion. In 1805, a number of Indian chiefs and warriors gathered at Buffalo Grove in New York at the request of a member of the Boston

Missionary Society. The Seneca chief, Red Jacket, made this speech regarding the way white customs were being forced on the Indians.

———————————

FRIEND AND BROTHER, it was the will of the Great Spirit that we should meet together this day. He orders all things and has given us a fine day for our council. He has taken His garment from before the sun and caused it to shine with brightness upon us. Our eyes are opened, that we see clearly; our ears are unstopped, that we have been able to hear distinctly the words you have spoken. For all these favors we thank the Great Spirit, and Him only.

Brother, this council fire was kindled by you. It was at your request that we came together at this time. We have listened with attention to what you have said. You requested us to speak our minds freely. This gives us great joy, for we now consider that we stand upright before you and can speak what we think. All have heard your voice, and all speak to you now as one man. Our minds are agreed.

Brother, you say you want an answer to your talk before you leave this place. It is right you should have one as you are a great distance from home and we do not wish to detain you. But we will first look back a little and tell you what our fathers have told us and what we have heard from the white people.

Brother, listen to what we say.

There was a time when our forefathers owned this great island. Their seats extended from the rising to the setting sun. The Great Spirit had made it for the use of Indians. He had created the buffalo, the deer, and other animals for food. He has made the bear and the beaver. Their skins served us for clothing. He had scattered them over the country and taught us how to take them. He had caused the earth to produce corn for bread. All this He had done for his red children because He loved them. If we had some disputes about our hunting ground they were generally settled without the shedding of much blood.

But an evil day came upon us. Your forefathers crossed the great water and landed on this island. Their numbers were small. They found friends and not enemies. They told us they had fled from their own country for fear of wicked men and had come here to enjoy their religion. They asked for a small seat. We took pity on them, granted their request; and they sat down amongst us. We gave them corn and meat; they gave us poison in return.

The white people, brother, had now found our country. Tidings were carried back and more came amongst us. Yet we did not fear them. We took them to be friends. They called us brothers. We believed them and gave them a larger seat. At length their numbers had greatly increased. They wanted more land; they wanted our country. Our eyes were opened and our minds became uneasy. Wars took place. Indians were hired to fight against Indians, and many of our people were destroyed. They also brought strong liquor amongst us. It was strong and powerful and has slain thousands.

Brother, our seats were once large and yours were small. You have now become a great people, and we have scarcely a place left to spread our blankets. You have got our country but are not satisfied; you want to force your religion upon us.

Brother, continue to listen.

You say that you are sent to instruct us how to worship the Great Spirit aggreeably to His mind, and, if we do not take hold of the religion which you white people teach, we shall be unhappy hereafter. You say that you are right and we are lost. How do we know this to be true? We understand that your religion is written in a book. If it was intended for us as well as you, why has not the Great Spirit given to us, and not only to us, but why did He not give to our forefathers the knowledge of that book, with the means of understanding it rightly? We only know what you tell us about it. How shall we know when to believe, being so often deceived by the white people?

Brother, you say there is but one way to worship and serve the Great Spirit. If there is but one religion, why do you white people differ so much about it? Why not all agreed, as you can all read the book?

Brother, we do not understand these things. We are told that your religion was given to your forefathers and has been handed down from father to son. We also have a religion which was given to our forefathers and has been handed down to us, their children. We worship in that way. It teaches us to be thankful for all the favors we receive, to love each other, and to be united. We never quarrel about religion.

Brother, the Great Spirit has made us all, but He has made a great difference between His white and red children. He has given us different complexions and different customs. To you He has given the arts. To these He has not opened our eyes. We know these things to be true. Since He has made so great a difference between us in other things, why may we not conclude that He has given us a different religion according to our understanding? The Great Spirit does right. He knows what is best for His children; we are satisfied.

Brother, we do not wish to destroy your religion or take it from you. We only want to enjoy our own.

Brother, you say you have not come to get our land or our money but to enlighten our minds. I will now tell you that I have been at your meetings and saw you collect money from the meeting. I cannot tell what this money was intended for, but suppose that it was for your minister, and if we should conform to your way of thinking, perhaps you may want some from us.

Brother, we are told that you have been preaching to the white people in this place. These people are our neighbors. We are acquainted with them. We will wait a little while and see what effect your preaching has upon them. If we find it does them good, makes them honest and less disposed to cheat Indians, we will then consider again of what you have said.

Brother, you have now heard our answer to your talk, and this is all we have to say at present. As we are going to part, we will come and take you by the hand and hope the Great Spirit will protect you on your journey and return you safe to your friends.

LETTER TO JEFFERSON
ON THE EXPEDITION

Meriwether Lewis   *September 23, 1806*

Lewis and Clark in their two-year journey had traveled from the East, ascended the Missouri, crossed the Rocky Mountains, and descended the Columbia to the Pacific. They described and mapped the country. In September 1806, upon completion of their historic exploration of the West, Meriwether Lewis sent the following report to Thomas Jefferson from St. Louis.

SIR,

It is with pleasure that I announce to you the safe arrival of myself and party at 12 OClk. today at this place with our papers and baggage. In obedience to your orders we have penitrated the Continent of North America to the Pacific Ocean, and sufficiently explored the interior of the country to affirm with confidence that we have discovered the most practicable rout which dose exist across the continent by means of the navigable branches of the Missouri and Columbia Rivers. Such is that by way of the Missouri to the foot of the rapids five miles below the great falls of that river a distance of 2575 miles, thence by land passing the Rocky Mountains to a navigable part of the Kooskooske 340; with the Kooskooske 73 mls. a South Easterly branch of the Columbia 154 miles and the latter river 413 mls. to the Pacific Ocean; making the total distance from the confluence of the Missouri and Mississippi to the discharge of the Columbia into the Pacific Ocean 3555 miles. The navigation of the Missouri may be deemed safe and good; it's difficulties arrise from it's falling banks, timber imbeded in the mud of it's channel, it's sand bars and steady rapidity of it's current, all which may be overcome with a great degree of certainty by taking the necessary precautions. The passage by land of 340 miles from the Missouri to the Kooskooske is the most formidable part of the tract proposed across the Continent; of this distance 200 miles is along a good road, and 140 over tremendious mountains which for 60 mls. are covered with eternal snows; however a passage over these mountains is practicable from the latter part of June to the last of September, and the cheep rate at which horses are to be obtained from the Indians of the Rocky Mountains and West of them, reduces the expences of transportation over this portage to a mere trifle. The navigation of the Kooskooske, the South East branch of the Columbia itself is safe and good from the 1st of April to the middle of August, by making three portages on the latter; the first of which in decending is that of 1200 paces at the great falls of the Columbia, 261 mls. from the Ocean, the second of two miles at the long narrows six miles below the falls, and the 3rd also of 2 miles at the great rapids 65 miles still lower down. The tides flow up the Columbia 183 miles, or within seven miles of the great rapids, thus far large sloops might ascend in safety, and vessels of 300 tons burthen could with equal safety reach the entrance of the river Multnomah, a large Southern branch of the Columbia, which taking it's rise on the confines of Mexico with the Callarado and Apostles river, discharges itself into the Columbia 125 miles from it's mouth. From the head of tide water to the foot of the long narrows the Columbia could be most advantageously navigated with large batteauxs, and from thence upwards by perogues. The Missouri possesses sufficient debth of water as far as is specifyed for boats of 15 tons burthen, but those of smaller capacity are to be preferred.

We view this passage across the Continent as affording immence advantages to the fur trade, but fear that the advantages which it offers as a communication for the productions of the East Indies to the United States and thence to Europe will never be found equal on an extensive scale to that by way of the Cape of Good hope; still we believe that many articles not bulky brittle nor of a very perishable nature may be conveyed to the United States by this rout with more facility and at less expence than by that at present practiced.

The Missouri and all it's branches from the Chyenne upwards abound more in beaver and Common Otter, than any other streams on earth, particularly that proportion of them lying within the Rocky Mountains. The furs of all this immence tract of country including such as may be collected on the upper portion of the River St. Peters, Red river and the Assinniboin with the immence country watered by the Columbia, may be conveyed to the mouth of the Columbia by the 1st of August in each year and from thence be shiped to, and arrive in Canton earlier than the furs at present shiped from Montreal annually arrive in London. The British N. West Company of Canada were they permitted by the United States might also convey their furs collected in the Athabaske, on the Saskashawan, and South and West of Lake Winnipic by that rout within the period before mentioned. Thus the productions [of] nine tenths of the most valuable fur country of America could be conveyed by the rout proposed to the East Indies.

In the infancy of the trade across the continent, or during the period that the trading establishments shall be confined to the Missouri and it's branches, the men employed in this trade will be compelled to convey the furs collected in that quarter as low on the Columbia as tide water, in which case they could not return to the falls of the Missouri until about the 1st of October, which would be so late in the season that there would be considerable danger of the river being obstructed by ice before they could reach this place and consequently that the comodites brought from the East indies would be detained untill the following spring; but this difficulty will at once vanish when establishments are also made on the Columbia, and a sufficient number of men employed at them to convey annually the productions of the East indies to the upper establishment on the Kooskooske, and there exchange them with the men of the Missouri for their furs, in the begining of July. By this means the furs not only of the Missouri but those also of the Columbia may be shiped to the East indies by the season before mentioned, and the comodities of the East indies arrive at St. Louis or the mouth of the Ohio by the last of September in each year.

Although the Columbia dose not as much as the Missouri abound in beaver and Otter, yet it is by means despicable in this rispect, and would furnish a valuable fur trade distinct from any other consideration in addition to the otter and beaver which it could furnish. There might be collected considerable quantities of the skins of three speceis of bear affording a great variety of colours and of superior delicacy, those also of the tyger cat, several species of fox, martin and several others of an inferior class of furs, besides the valuable Sea Otter of the coast.

If the government will only aid, even in a very limited manner, the enterprize of her Citizens I am fully convinced that we shal shortly derive the benifits of a most lucrative trade from this source, and that in the course of ten or twelve years a tour across the Continent by the rout mentioned will be undertaken by individuals with as little concern as a voyage across the Atlantic is at present.

The British N. West Company of Canada has for several years, carried on a partial trade with the Minnetares Ahwayhaways and Mandans on the Missouri from the establishments on the Assinniboin at the entrance of Mouse river; at present I have good reason for beleiving that they intend shortly to form an establishment near those nations with a view to engroce the fur trade of the Missouri. The known enterprize and resources of this Company, latterly strengthened by an union with their powerfull rival the X.Y. Company renders them formidable in that distant part of the continent to all other traders; and in my opinion if we are to regard the trade of the Missouri as an object of importance to the United States; the strides of this Company towards the Missouri cannot be too vigilantly watched nor too firmly and speedily opposed by our government. The embarrasments under which the nagivation of the Missouri at present labours from the unfriendly dispositions of the Kancez, the several bands of Tetons, Assinniboins and those tribes that resort to the British establishments on the Saskashawan is also a subject which requires the earliest attention of our government. As I shall shortly be with you I have deemed it unnecessary here to detail the several ideas which have presented themselves to my mind on those subjects, more especially when I consider that a thorough knowledge of the geography of the country is absolutely necessary to their being unde[r]stood, and leasure has not yet permited us to make but one general map of the country which I am unwilling to wrisk by the Mail.

As a sketch of the most prominent features of our perigrination since we left the Mandans may not be uninteresting, I shall indeavour to give it to you by way of letter from this place, where I shall necessarily be detained several days in order to settle with and discharge the men who accompanyed me on the voyage as well as to prepare for my rout to the City of Washington.

We left Fort Clatsop where we wintered near the entrance of the Columbia on the 27th of March last, and arrived at the foot of the Rocky mountains on the 10th of May where we were detained untill the 24th of June in consequence of the snow which rendered a passage over those Mountains impracticable untill that moment; had it not been for this detention I should ere this have joined you at Montichello. In my last communication to you from the Mandans I mentioned my intention of sending back a canoe with a small party from the Rocky Mountains; but on our arrival at the great falls of the Missouri on the 14th of June 1805, in view of that formidable snowey barrier, the discourageing difficulties which we had to encounter in making a portage of eighteen miles of our canoes and baggage around those falls were such that my friend Capt. Clark and myself conceived it inexpedient to reduce the party, lest by doing so we should lessen the ardor of those who remained and thus hazard the fate of the expedition, and therefore declined that measure, thinking it better that the government as well as our friends should for a moment feel some anxiety for our fate than to wrisk so much; experience has since proved the justice of our dicision, for we have more than once owed our lives and the fate of the expedition to our number which consisted of 31 men.

I have brought with me several skins of the Sea Otter, two skins of the native sheep of America, five skins and skelitons complete of the Bighorn or mountain ram, and a skin of the Mule deer beside the skins of several other quadrupeds and birds natives of the countries through which we have passed. I have also preserved a pretty extensive collection of plants, and collected nine other vocabularies.

I have prevailed on the great Cheif of the Mandan nation to accompany me to Washington; he is now with my frind and colligue Capt. Clark at this place, in good health and sperits, and very anxious to proceede.

With rispect to the exertions and services rendered by that esteemable man Capt. William Clark in the course of late voyage I cannot say too much; if sir any credit be due for the success of that arduous enterprize in which we have been mutually engaged, he is equally with myself entitled to your consideration and that of our common country.

The anxiety which I feel in returning once more to the bosom of my friends is a sufficient guarantee that no time will be unnecessarily expended in this quarter.

I have detained the post several hours for the purpose of making you this haisty communication. I hope that while I am pardoned for this detention of the mail, the situation in which I have been compelled to write will sufficiently apologize for having been this laconic.

The rout by which I purpose traveling from hence to Washington is by way of Cahokia, Vincennes, Louisvill Ky., the Crab orchard, Abington, Fincastle, Stanton and Charlottsville. Any letters directed to me at Louisville ten days after the receipt of this will most probably meet me at that place. I am very anxious to learn the state of my friends in Albemarle particularly whether my mother is yet living. I am with every sentiment of esteem Your Obt. and very Humble servent.
MERIWETHER LEWIS CAPT.
1st U.S. Regt. Infty.

N.B. The whole of the party who accompanyed me from the Mandans have returned in good health, which is not, I assure you, to me one of the least pleasing considerations of the Voyage. M.L.

SPEECH TO GOVERNOR HARRISON

Tecumseh   *August 12, 1810*

------

*Tecumseh was a chief of the Shawnee, and William
Henry Harrison was the governor of the Indiana Territory.
Pioneers of the old Northwest coveted the Indians' land, and
Harrison signed treaties with a few Indians to take over their
hunting grounds. Tecumseh formed a confederacy among
many tribes and led the Shawnee in a revolt against white rule
in 1811, which was put down by Harrison in the battle of
Tippecanoe. William Henry Harrison went on to further
military victories in the War of 1812, became a United States
senator, and was elected the ninth president of the United States
in 1840. Tecumseh commanded the Indian allies fighting on
the British side in the War of 1812 and was killed at the
Thames in Canada.*

IT is true I am a Shawanee. My forefathers were warriors. Their son is a
warrior. From them I only take my existence; from my tribe I take nothing. I am
the maker of my own fortune; and oh! that I could make that of my red people,
and of my country, as great as the conceptions of my mind, when I think of the
Spirit that rules the universe. I would not then come to Governor Harrison, to
ask him to tear the treaty, and to obliterate the landmark; but I would say to him,
Sir, you have liberty to return to your own country. The being within, communing
with past ages, tells me, that once, nor until lately, there was no white man on
this continent. That it then all belonged to red men, children of the same parents,
placed on it by the Great Spirit that made them, to keep it, to traverse it, to enjoy
its productions, and to fill it with the same race. Once a happy race. Since made
miserable by the white people, who are never contented, but always encroach-
ing. The way, and the only way to check and to stop this evil, is, for all the red
men to unite in claiming a common and equal right in the land, as it was at first,
and should be yet; for it never was divided, but belongs to all, for the use of each.
That no part has a right to sell, even to each other, much less to strangers; those
who want all, and will not do with less. The white people have no right to take
the land from the Indians, because they had it first; it is theirs. They may sell, but
all must join. Any sale not made by all is not valid. The late sale is bad. It was

made by a part only. Part do not know how to sell. It requires all to make a bargain for all. All red men have equal rights to the unoccupied land. The right of occupancy is as good in one place as in another. There cannot be two occupations in the same place. The first excludes all others. It is not so in hunting or travelling; for there the same ground will serve many, as they may follow each other all day; but the camp is stationary, and that is occupancy. It belongs to the first who sits down on his blanket or skins, which he has thrown upon the ground, and till he leaves it no other has a right.

THE STAR SPANGLED BANNER

Francis Scott Key   *September 14, 1814*

> *During the War of 1812, Francis Scott Key, a lawyer and attorney for the District of Columbia, was sent by President Madison under a flag of truce to negotiate the release of a friend, Dr. William Beanes. On September 13-14, 1814, the British bombarded Fort McHenry, Baltimore, Maryland. Despite a twenty-five-hour shelling in which they fired more than 1,500 rounds, the British were never able to approach the fort. Francis Scott Key wrote a stanza during the bombardment and finished the poem the next day. The poem was published in the* Baltimore Patriot *and set to the old tune "Anacreon in Heaven." "The Star Spangled Banner" was officially designated the national anthem by act of Congress, March 3, 1931.*

Oh, say, can you see, by the dawn's early light,
What so proudly we hailed at the twilight's last gleaming,
Whose broad stripes and bright stars through the perilous fight,
O'er the ramparts we watched were so gallantly streaming?
And the rockets' red glare, the bombs bursting in air,
Gave proof through the night that our flag was still there.
Oh, say, does that star-spangled banner yet wave
O'er the land of the free, and the home of the brave?

On the shore, dimly seen through the mists of the deep,

Where the foe's haughty host in dread silence reposes,
What is that which the breeze, o'er the towering steep,
As it fitfully blows, half conceals, half discloses?
Now it catches the gleam of the morning's first beam,
In fully glory reflected, now shines on the stream.
'Tis the star-spangled banner; oh, long may it wave
O'er the land of the free, and the home of the brave!

And where is that band who so vauntingly swore
That the havoc of war and the battle's confusion,
A home and a country should leave us no more?
Their blood has washed out their foul footsteps' pollution.
No refuge could save the hireling and slave
From the terror of flight, or the gloom of the grave:
And the star-spangled banner in triumph doth wave
O'er the land of the free, and the home of the brave!

Oh! thus be it ever when freemen shall stand
Between their loved homes and the war's desolation!
Blest with victory and peace, may the heaven-rescued land
Praise the Power that hath made and preserved us a nation!
Then conquer we must, for our cause it is just,
And this be our motto: "In God is our trust!"
And the star-spangled banner in triumph shall wave,
O'er the land of the free, and the home of the brave!

LETTER TO SAMUEL KERCHEVAL

Thomas Jefferson   *July 12, 1816*

> *After two terms as president, Thomas Jefferson retired to
> Monticello. There he received a letter asking his opinion on
> whether a state constitutional convention should be called for
> possible legislative reform in Virginia. Jefferson wrote the
> following letter to Samuel Kercheval, a resident of Clarke
> County, Virginia, with his ideas on political institutions and
> reform.*

SOME men look at constitutions with sanctimonious reverence, and deem them like the ark of the covenant, too sacred to be touched. They ascribe to the men of the preceding age a wisdom more than human, and suppose what they did to be beyond amendment. I knew that age well; I belonged to it, and labored with it. It deserved well of its country. It was very like the present, but without the experience of the present; and forty years of experience in government is worth a century of book-reading; and this they would say themselves, were they to rise from the dead. I am certainly not an advocate for frequent and untried changes in laws and constitutions. I think moderate imperfections had better be borne with; because, when once known, we accommodate ourselves to them, and find practical means of correcting their ill effects. But I know also, that laws and institutions must go hand in hand with the progress of the human mind. As that becomes more developed, more enlightened, as new discoveries are made, new truths disclosed, and manners and opinions change with the change of circumstances, institutions must advance also, and keep pace with the times. We might as well require a man to wear still the coat which fitted him when a boy, as civilized society to remain ever under the regimen of their barbarous ancestors. It is this preposterous idea which has lately deluged Europe in blood. Their monarchs, instead of wisely yielding to the gradual change of circumstances, of favoring progressive accommodation to progressive improvements, have clung to old abuses, entrenched themselves behind steady habits, and obliged their subjects to seek through blood and violence rash and ruinous innovations, which, had they been referred to the peaceful deliberations and collected wisdom of the nation, would have been put into acceptable and salutary forms. Let us follow no such examples, nor weakly believe that one generation is not as capable as another of taking care of itself, and of ordering its own affairs. Let us, as our sister States have done, avail ourselves of our reason and experience, to correct the crude essays of our first and unexperienced, although wise, virtuous, and well-meaning councils. And lastly, let us provide in our constitution for its revision as stated periods. What these periods should be, nature herself indicates. By the European tables of mortality, of the adults living at any one moment of time, a majority will be dead in about nineteen years. At the end of that period then, a new majority is come into place; or, in other words, a new generation. Each generation is as independent as the one preceding, as that was of all which had gone before. It has then, like them, a right to choose for itself the form of government it believes most promotive of its own happiness; consequently, to accommodate to the circumstances in which it finds itself, that received from its predecessors; and it is for the peace and good of mankind, that a solemn opportunity of doing this every nineteen or twenty years, should be provided by the constitution; so that it may be handed on, with periodical repairs, from generation to generation, to the end of time, if anything human can so long endure. It is now forty years since the constitution of Virginia was formed. The same tables inform us, that, within that period, two-thirds of the adults then living are now dead. Have then the remaining third, even if they had the wish, the right to hold in obedience to their will, and to laws heretofore made by them, the other two-thirds, who, with themselves, compose the present mass of adults? If they have not, who has? The dead? But the dead have no rights. They are nothing; and nothing cannot own something. Where there is no substance, there can be no accident. This corporeal globe, and everything upon it, belong to its present corporeal inhabitants, during their generation. They alone have a right to direct what is the concern of themselves alone, and to declare the law of that direction; and this declaration can only be made by their majority. That majority, then, has a right to depute representatives to a convention, and to make the constitution what they think will be the best for themselves. But how collect their voice? This is the real difficulty. If invited by private authority, or county or district meetings, these divisions are so large that few will attend; and their voice will be imperfectly, or falsely pronounced. Here, then, would be one of the advantages of the ward divisions I have proposed. The mayor of every ward, on a question like the present, would call his ward together, take the simple yea or nay of its members, convey these to the county court, who would hand on those of all its wards to the proper general authority; and the voice of the whole people would be thus fairly, fully, and peaceably expressed, discussed, and decided by the common reason of the society. If this avenue be shut to the call of sufferance, it will make itself heard through that of force, and we shall go on, as other nations are doing, in the endless circle of oppression, rebellion, reformation; and oppression, rebellion, reformation, again; and so on forever.

These, sir, are my opinions of the governments we see among men, and of the principles by which alone we may prevent our own from falling into the same dreadful track. . . .

McCulloch v. Maryland

John Marshall   *1819*

The charter of the first Bank of the United States expired in 1811. A Second Bank of the United States was chartered in 1816. Several states passed laws taxing this new federal bank.

McCulloch, the cashier of the branch in Baltimore, issued notes without complying with the Maryland laws or paying the state taxes. The questions that had to be addressed by the Supreme Court were whether Congress had the right to incorporate a national bank and whether the states were able to tax such a bank. In one of the most important opinions of his career, John Marshall dealt with the question of implied powers of the government, broadly interpreted the Constitution and ruled that the Constitution by implication gives to the government powers which it does not explicitly state. This decision sustained the doctrine of implied powers of Congress and recognized the limitations on the states which prevented them from interfering with the functioning of federal agencies.

MARSHALL, C.J. . . . The first question made in this cause is—Has Congress power to incorporate a bank?

It has been truly said that this can scarcely be considered as an open question, entirely unprejudiced by the former proceedings of the nation respecting it. The principle now contested was introduced at a very early period of our history, has been recognized by many successive legislatures, and has been acted upon by the Judicial Department, in cases of peculiar delicacy, as a law of undoubted obligation. . . .

In discussing this question, the counsel for the State of Maryland have deemed it of some importance, in the construction of the Constitution, to consider that instrument not as emanating from the people but as the act of sovereign and independent states. The powers of the general government, it has been said, are delegated by the states, who alone are truly sovereign; and must be exercised in subordination to the states, who alone possess supreme dominion.

It would be difficult to sustain this proposition. The Convention which framed the Constitution was indeed elected by the state legislatures. But the instrument, when it came from their hands, was a mere proposal, without obligation or pretensions to it. It was reported to the then existing Congress of the United States with a request that it might "be submitted to a Convention of Delegates, chosen in each state by the people thereof, under the recommendation of its legislature, for their assent and ratification." This mode of proceeding was adopted; and by the Convention, by Congress, and by the state legislatures the instrument was submitted to the people. They acted upon it in the only manner in which they can act safety, effectively, and wisely, on such a subject— by assembling in convention.

It is true, they assembled in their several states; and where else should they have assembled? No political dreamer was ever wild enough to think of breaking down the lines which separate the states, and of compounding the American people into one common mass. Of consequence, when they act, they act in their states. But the measures they adopt do not, on that account, cease to be the measures of the people themselves, or become the measures of the state governments.

From these conventions the Constitution derives its whole authority. The government proceeds directly from the people; is "ordained and established" in the name of the people; and is declared to be ordained "in order to form a more perfect union, establish justice, ensure domestic tranquillity, and secure the blessings of liberty to themselves and to their posterity." The assent of the states, in their sovereign capacity, is implied in calling a convention, and thus submitting that instrument to the people. But the people were at perfect liberty to accept or reject it; and their act was final. It required not the affirmance, and could not be negatived, by the state governments. The Constitution, when thus adopted, was of complete obligation, and bound the state sovereignties. . . .

The government of the Union, then (whatever may be the influence of this fact on the case), is emphatically and truly, a government of the people. In form and in substance it emanates from them. Its powers are granted by them and are to be exercised directly on them and for their benefit.

This government is acknowledged by all to be one of enumerated powers. The principle that it can exercise only the powers granted to it would seem too apparent to have required to be enforced by all those arguments which its enlightened friends, while it was depending before the people, found it necessary to urge. That principle is now universally admitted. But the question respecting the extent of the powers actually granted is perpetually arising, and will probably continue to arise as long as our system shall exist.

In discussing these questions, the conflicting powers of the general and state governments must be brought into view, and the supremacy of their respective laws, when they are in opposition, must be settled.

If any one proposition could command the universal assent of mankind, we might expect it would be this—that the government of the Union though limited in its powers is supreme within its sphere of action. This would seem to result necessarily from its nature. It is the government of all; its powers are delegated by all; it represents all; and acts for all. Though any one state may be willing to control its operations, no state is willing to allow others to control them. The nation, on those subjects on which it can act, must necessarily bind its component parts.

But this question is not left to mere reason: the people have, in express terms, decided it by saying, "this Constitution, and the laws of the United States, which shall be made in pursuance thereof, shall be the supreme law of the land," and by requiring that the members of the state legislatures, and the officers of the Executive and Judicial departments of the states shall take the oath of fidelity to it.

The government of the United States, then, though limited in its powers is supreme; and its laws, when made in pursuance of the Constitution, form the supreme law of the land, "anything in the constitution or laws of any state to the contrary, notwithstanding.". . .

A constitution, to contain an accurate detail of all the subdivisions of which its great powers will admit, and of all the means by which they may be carried into execution, would partake the prolixity of a legal code, and could scarcely be embraced by the human mind. It would probably never be understood by the public. Its nature, therefore, requires that only its great outlines should be marked, its important objects designated, and the minor ingredients which compose those objects be deduced from the nature of the objects themselves. That this idea was entertained by the framers of the American Constitution is not only to be inferred from the nature of the instrument but from the language. Why else were some of the limitations found in the 9th Section of the 1st Article introduced? It is also, in some degree, warranted by their having omitted to use any restrictive term which might prevent its receiving a fair and just interpretation. In considering this question, then, we must never forget that it is a constitution we are expounding.

Although, among the enumerated powers of government, we do not find the word "bank" or "incorporation," we find the great powers to lay and collect taxes; to borrow money; to regulate commerce; to declare and conduct a war; and to raise and support armies and navies. The sword and the purse, all the external relations, and no inconsiderable portion of the industry of the nation are entrusted to its government. It can never be pretended that these vast powers draw after them others of inferior importance, merely because they are inferior. Such an idea can never be advanced. But it may with great reason be contended that a government, entrusted with such ample powers, on the due execution of which the happiness and prosperity of the nation so vitally depends, must also be entrusted with ample means for their execution. The power being given, it is the interest of the nation to facilitate its execution. It can never be their interest, and cannot be presumed to have been their intention, to clog and embarrass its execution by withholding the most appropriate means.

Throughout this vast republic, from the St. Croix to the Gulf of Mexico, from the Atlantic to the Pacific, revenue is to be collected and expended, armies are to be marched and supported. The exigencies of the nation may require that the treasure raised in the North should be transported to the South, that raised in the East conveyed to the West, or that this order should be reversed. Is that construction of the Constitution to be preferred which would render these operations difficult, hazardous, and expensive? Can we adopt that construction (unless the words imperiously require it) which would impute to the framers of that instrument, when granting these powers for the public good, the intention of impeding their exercise by withholding a choice of means? If, indeed, such be the mandate of the Constitution, we have only to obey; but that instrument does not profess to enumerate the means by which the powers it confers may be executed; nor does it prohibit the creation of a corporation if the existence of such a being be essential to the beneficial exercise of those powers. It is then the subject of fair inquiry, how far such means may be employed.

It is not denied that the powers given to the government imply the ordinary means of execution. That, for example, of raising revenue and applying it to national purposes is admitted to imply the power of conveying money from place to place, as the exigencies of the nation may require, and of employing the usual means of conveyance. But it is denied that the government has its choice of means; or, that it may employ the most convenient means, if, to employ them, it be necessary to erect a corporation. . . .

The government which has a right to do an act, and has imposed on it the duty of performing that act, must, according to the dictates of reason, be allowed to select the means; and those who contend that it may not select any appropriate means, that one particular mode of effecting the object is excepted, take upon themselves the burden of establishing that exception.

The creation of a corporation, it is said, appertains to sovereignty. This is admitted. But to what portion of sovereignty does it appertain? Does it belong to one more than to another? In America, the powers of sovereignty are divided between the government of the Union and those of the states. They are each sovereign with respect to the objects committed to it, and neither sovereign with respect to the objects committed to the other. We cannot comprehend that train of reasoning which would maintain that the extent of power granted by the people is to be ascertained, not by the nature and terms of the grant but by its date. Some state constitutions were formed before, some since that of the United States. We cannot believe that their relation to each other is in any degree dependent upon this circumstance. Their respective powers must, we think, be precisely the same as if they had been formed at the same time. Had they been formed at the same time, and had the people conferred on the general government the power contained in the Constitution, and on the states the whole residuum of power, would it have been asserted that the government of the Union was not sovereign with respect to those objects which were entrusted to it, in relation to which its laws were declared to be supreme? If this could not have been asserted, we cannot well comprehend the process of reasoning which maintains that a power appertaining to sovereignty cannot be connected with that vast portion of it which is granted to the general government, so far as it is calculated to subserve the legitimate objects of that government.

The power of creating a corporation, though appertaining to sovereignty, is not, like the power of making war or levying taxes or of regulating commerce, a great substantive and independent power, which cannot be implied as incidental to other powers, or used as a means of executing them. It is never the end for which other powers are exercised, but a means by which other objects are accomplished. No contributions are made to charity for the sake of an incorporation, but a corporation is created to administer the charity; no seminary of learning is instituted in order to be incorporated, but the corporate character is conferred to subserve the purposes of education. No city was ever built with the sole object of being incorporated, but is incorporated as affording the best means of being well governed. The power of creating a corporation is never used for its own sake, but for the purpose of effecting something else. No sufficient reason is, therefore, perceived why it may not pass as incidental to those powers which are expressly given, if it be a direct mode of executing them.

But the Constitution of the United States has not left the right of Congress to employ the necessary means for the execution of the powers conferred on the government to general reasoning. To its enumeration of powers is added that of making "all laws which shall be necessary and proper, for carrying into execution the foregoing powers, and all other powers vested by this Constitution, in the government of the United States, or in any department thereof."

The counsel for the State of Maryland have urged various arguments to prove that this clause, though in terms a grant of power, is not so in effect, but is really restrictive of the general right, which might otherwise be implied, of selecting means for executing the enumerated powers. . . .

But the argument on which most reliance is placed is drawn from the peculiar language of this clause. Congress is not empowered by it to make all laws, which may have relation to the powers conferred on the government, but only such as may be "necessary and proper" for carrying them into execution. The word "necessary" is considered as controlling the whole sentence, and as limited the right to pass laws for the execution of the granted powers, to such as are indispensable and without which the power would be nugatory. That it excludes the choice of means, and leaves to Congress, in each case, that only which is more direct and simple. . . .

We admit, as all must admit, that the powers of the government are limited, and that its limits are not to be transcended. But we think the sound construction of the Constitution must allow to the national legislature that discretion, with respect to the means by which the powers it confers are to be carried into execution, which will enable that body to perform the high duties assigned to it, in the manner most beneficial to the people. Let the end be legitimate, let it be within the scope of the Constitution, and all means which are appropriate, which are plainly adapted to that end, which are not prohibited, but consist with the letter and spirit of the Constitution, are constitutional. . . .

Should Congress, in the execution of its powers, adopt measures which are prohibited by the Constitution; or should Congress, under the pretext of executing its powers, pass laws for the accomplishment of objects not entrusted to the government, it would become the painful duty of this tribunal, should a case requiring such a decision come before it, to say that such an act was not the law of the land. But where the law is not prohibited, and is really calculated to effect any of the objects entrusted to the government, to undertake here to inquire into the degree of its necessity, would be to pass the line which circumscribes the Judicial Department, and to tread on legislative ground. This court disclaims all pretensions to such a power. . . .

After the most deliberate consideration, it is the unanimous and decided opinion of this court that the act to incorporate the Bank of the United States is a law made in pursuance of the Constitution, and is a part of the supreme law of the land. . . .

It being the opinion of the Court that the act incorporating the bank is constitutional; and that the power of establishing a branch in the State of Maryland might be properly exercised by the bank itself, we proceed to inquire whether the State of Maryland may, without violating the Constitution, tax that branch.

That the power of taxation is one of vital importance; that it is retained by the states; that it is not abridged by the grant of a similar power to the government of the Union; that it is to be concurrently exercised by the two governments are truths which have never been denied. But, such is the paramount character of the Constitution that its capacity to withdraw any subject from the action of even this power is admitted. The states are expressly forbidden to lay any duties on imports or exports, except what may be absolutely necessary for executing their inspection laws. If the obligation of this prohibition must be conceded, if it may restrain a state from the exercise of its taxing power on imports and exports, the same paramount character would seem to restrain, as it certainly may restrain, a state from such other exercise of this power as is in its nature incompatible with, and repugnant to, the constitutional laws of the Union. A law, absolutely repugnant to another, as entirely repeals that other as if express terms of repeal were used. . . .

This great principle is that the Constitution and the laws made in pursuance thereof are supreme; that they control the constitution and laws of the respective states, and cannot be controlled by them. From this, which may be almost termed an axiom, other propositions are deduced as corollaries, on the truth or error of which, and on their application to this case, the cause has been supposed to depend. These are (1) that a power to create implies a power to preserve; (2) that a power to destroy, if wielded by a different hand, is hostile to, and incompatible with, these powers to create and preserve; (3) that where this repugnancy exists, that authority which is supreme must control, not yield to, that over which it is supreme. . . .

That the power to tax involves the power to destroy; that the power to destroy may defeat and render useless the power to create; that there is a plain repugnance in conferring on one government a power to control the constitutional measures of another, which other, with respect to those very measures, is declared to be supreme over that which exerts the control, are propositions not to be denied. But all inconsistencies are to be reconciled by the magic of the word "confidence." Taxation, it is said, does not necessarily and unavoidably destroy. To carry it to the excess of destruction would be an abuse, to presume which would banish that confidence which is essential to all government.

But is this a case of confidence? Would the people of any one state trust those of another with a power to control the most insignificant operations of their state government? We know they would not. Why, then, should we suppose that the people of any one state should be willing to trust those of another with a power to control the operations of a government to which they have confided their most important and most valuable interests? In the legislature of the Union alone are all represented. The legislature of the Union alone therefore, can be trusted by the people with the power of controlling measures which concern all, in the confidence that it will not be abused. This, then, is not a case of confidence, and we must consider it as it really is. . . .

If the states may tax one instrument, employed by the government in the execution of its powers, they may tax any and every other instrument. They may tax the mail; they may tax the mint; they may tax patent rights; they may tax the papers of the custom-house; they may tax judicial process; they may tax all the means employed by the government, to an excess which would defeat all the ends of government. This was not intended by the American people. They did not design to make their government dependent on the states. . . .

The question is, in truth, a question of supremacy; and if the right of the states to tax the means employed by the general government be conceded, the declaration that the Constitution, and the laws made in pursuance thereof, shall be the supreme law of the land is empty and unmeaning declamation. . . .

The Court has bestowed on this subject its most deliberate consideration. The result is a conviction that the states have no power, by taxation or otherwise, to retard, impede, burden, or in any manner control the operations of the constitutional laws enacted by Congress to carry into execution the powers vested in the general government. This is, we think, the unavoidable consequence of that supremacy which the Constitution has declared.

We are unanimously of opinion, that the law passed by the legislature of Maryland, imposing a tax on the Bank of the United States, is unconstitutional and void. . . .

MISSOURI COMPROMISE ACTS

Henry Clay   *March 6, 1820–March 2, 1821*

The rapid expansion of American cotton production in the early years of the nineteenth century punctured the hope that slavery would fade away. By the second decade of the century the issue could no longer be ignored. In the North, reformers had begun to demand the abolition of slavery, and businessmen and politicians resented the inordinate political power of the South. Southerners, in turn, feared a strong national government that might restrict slavery in the new territories of the West, as the Northwest Ordinance had done.

Missouri's application for admission as a slave state brought these issues to a head. Lying roughly in the same latitude as the old Northwest Territories, the new state would represent a northward extension of slavery and give the slave states a majority in the United States Senate. On the other hand, denial of admission would realize the worst fears of the South regarding national power. Caught in the middle was Senator Henry Clay of Kentucky, a slaveholder and one of the leading advocates of strong national government.

By isolating the various issues, Clay was able to cobble together a compromise. Separate majorities were secured for the admission of both Missouri and Maine to statehood, maintaining balance in the Senate, and for the creation of a limit to the expansion of slavery in western territories at 36° 30' north latitude, asserting congressional authority to regulate slavery. The crisis was averted, but no true compromise resulted. At best, the issue of "slave power" versus national power was simply put aside for the time being.

MISSOURI ENABLING ACT

March 6, 1820

AN Act to authorize the people of the Missouri territory to form a constitution and state government, and for the admission of such state into the Union on an equal footing with the original states, and to prohibit slavery in certain territories.

Be it enacted That the inhabitants of that portion of the Missouri territory included within the boundaries hereinafter designated, be, and they are hereby, authorized to form for themselves a constitution and state government, and to assume such name as they shall deem proper; and the said state, when formed, shall be admitted into the Union, upon an equal footing with the original states, in all respects whatsoever.

SEC. 2. That the said state shall consist of all the territory included within the following boundaries, to wit: Beginning in the middle of the Mississippi river, on the parallel of thirty-six degrees of north latitude; thence west, along that parallel of latitude, to the St. Francois river; thence up, and following the course of that river, in the middle of the main channel thereof, to the parallel of latitude of thirty-six degrees and thirty minutes; thence west, along the same, to a point where the said parallel is intersected by a meridian line passing through the middle of the mouth of the Kansas river, where the same empties into the Missouri river, thence, from the point aforesaid north, along the said meridian line, to the intersection of the parallel of latitude which passes through the rapids of the river Des Moines, making the said line to correspond with the Indian boundary line; thence east, from the point of intersection last aforesaid, along the said parallel of latitude, to the middle of the channel of the main fork of the said river Des Moines; thence down and along the middle of the main channel of the said river Des Moines, to the mouth of the same, where it empties into the Mississippi river; thence, due east, to the middle of the main channel of the Mississippi river; thence down, and following the course of the Mississippi river, in the middle of the main channel thereof, to the place of beginning: . . .

SEC. 3. That all free white male citizens of the United States, who shall have arrived at the age of twenty-one years, and have resided in said territory three months previous to the day of election, and all other persons qualified to vote for representatives to the general assembly of the said territory, shall be qualified to be elected, and they are hereby qualified and authorized to vote, and choose representatives to form a convention. . . .

SEC. 8. That in all that territory ceded by France to the United States, under the name of Louisiana, which lies north of thirty-six degrees and thirty minutes north latitude, not included within the limits of the state, contemplated by this act, slavery and involuntary servitude, otherwise than in the punishment of crimes, whereof the parties shall have been duly convicted, shall be, and is hereby, forever prohibited: Provided always, That any person escaping into the same, from whom labour or service is lawfully claimed, in any state or territory of the United States, such fugitive may be lawfully reclaimed and conveyed to the person claiming his or her labour or service as aforesaid.

THE CONSTITUTION OF MISSOURI

July 19, 1820

SEC. 26. The general assembly shall not have power to pass laws—

1. For the emancipation of slaves without the consent of their owners; or without paying them, before such emancipation, a full equivalent for such slaves so emancipated, and,

2. To prevent *bona-fide* immigrants to this State, or actual settlers therein, from bringing from any of the United States, or from any of their Territories, such persons as may there be deemed to be slaves, so long as any persons of the same description are allowed to be held as slaves by the laws of this State.

They shall have power to pass laws—

1. To prevent *bona-fide* immigrants to this State of any slaves who may have committed any high crime in any other State or Territory;

2. To prohibit the introduction of any slave for the purpose of speculation, or as an article of trade or merchandise;

3. To prohibit the introduction of any slave, or the offspring of any slave, who heretofore may have been, or who hereafter may be, imported from any foreign country into the United States, or any Territory thereof, in contravention

of any existing statute of the United States; and,

4. To permit the owners of slaves to emancipate them, saving the right of creditors, where the person so emancipating will give security that the slave so emancipated shall not become a public charge.

It shall be their duty, as soon as may be, to pass such laws as may be necessary—

1. To prevent free negroes end [and] mulattoes from coming to and settling in this State, under any pretext whatsoever; and,

2. To oblige the owners of slaves to treat them with humanity, and to abstain from all injuries to them extending to life or limb.

RESOLUTION FOR THE ADMISSION OF MISSOURI

March 2, 1821

Resolved, That Missouri shall be admitted into this union on an equal footing with the original states, in all respects whatever, upon the fundamental condition, that the fourth clause of the twenty-sixth section of the third article of the constitution submitted on the part of said state to Congress, shall never be construed to authorize the passage of any law, and that no law shall be passed in conformity thereto, by which any citizen, of either of the states in this Union, shall be excluded from the enjoyment of any of the privileges and immunities to which such citizen is entitled under the constitution of the United States: Provided, That the legislature of the said state, by a solemn public act, shall declare the assent of the said state to the said fundamental condition, and shall transmit to the President of the United States, on or before the fourth Monday in November next, an authentic copy of the said act; upon the receipt whereof, the President, by proclamation, shall announce the fact; whereupon, and without any further proceeding on the part of Congress, the admission of the said state into this Union shall be considered as complete.

ANNUAL MESSAGE TO CONGRESS—
THE MONROE DOCTRINE

James Monroe   *December 2, 1823*

---

*The Spanish Revolution of 1820 against the restored
Bourbon monarchy inspired a fresh series of revolts, covertly
supported by the United States, in Spain's American empire.
Having upheld the monarchy in Spain, the great powers of
Europe briefly considered intervening to restore Bourbon power
in America as well. Meanwhile, Russia had asserted a claim to
the entire Pacific Coast of North America south to the fifty-first
parallel. This claim was strongly protested by the United States,
and also by Great Britain, which wanted to maintain free trade
in the western hemisphere.*

*In September 1823, Britain suggested a joint declaration
against European intervention in American affairs. Both
President James Monroe and Senator Henry Clay favored the
proposal, but Secretary of State John Quincy Adams could not
accept linkage of United States foreign policy to British power.
Instead, Adams persuaded Monroe to issue a unilateral declaration. This declaration enjoyed the backing of the Royal Navy
nonetheless, since Britain's aims were essentially identical to
those of the United States.*

. . . AT the proposal of the Russian Imperial Government, made through
the minister of the Emperor residing here, a full power and instructions have been
transmitted to the minister of the United States at St. Petersburg to arrange by
amicable negotiation the respective rights and interests of the two nations on the
northwest coast of this continent. A similar proposal had been made by His
Imperial Majesty to the Government of Great Britain, which has likewise been
acceded to. The Government of the United States has been desirous by this
friendly proceeding of manifesting the great value which they have invariably attached to the friendship of the Emperor and their solicitude to cultivate the best
understanding with his Government. In the discussions to which this interest has
given rise and in the arrangements by which they may terminate the occasion

has been judged proper for asserting, as a principle in which the rights and interests of the United States are involved, that the American continents, by the free and independent condition which they have assumed and maintain, are henceforth not to be considered as subjects for future colonization by any European powers. . . .

It was stated at the commencement of the last session that a great effort was then making in Spain and Portugal to improve the condition of the people

James Monroe, portrait by Samuel F.B. Morse, 1819.

of those countries, and that it appeared to be conducted with extraordinary moderation. It need scarcely be remarked that the result has been so far very different from what was then anticipated. Of events in that quarter of the globe, with which we have so much intercourse and from which we derive our origin, we have always been anxious and interested spectators. The citizens of the United States cherish sentiments the most friendly in favor of the liberty and happiness of their fellow-men on that side of the Atlantic. In the wars of the European powers in matters relating to themselves we have never taken any part, nor does it comport with our policy so to do. It is only when our rights are invaded or seriously menaced that we resent injuries or make preparation for our defense. With the movements in this hemisphere we are of necessity more immediately connected, and by causes which must be obvious to all enlightened and impartial observers. The political system of the allied powers is essentially different in this respect from that of America. This difference proceeds from that which exists in their respective Governments; and to the defense of our own, which has been achieved by the loss of so much blood and treasure, and matured by the wisdom of their most enlightened citizens, and under which we have enjoyed unexampled felicty, this whole nation is devoted. We owe it, therefore, to candor and to the amicable relations existing between the United States and those powers to declare that we should consider any attempt on their part to extend their system to any portion of this hemisphere as dangerous to our peace and safety. With the existing colonies or dependencies of any European power we have not interfered and shall not interfere. But with the Governments who have declared their independence and maintained it, and whose independence we have, on great consideration and on just principles acknowledged, we could not view any interposition for the purpose of oppressing them, or controlling in any other manner their destiny, by any European power in any other light than as the manifestation of an unfriendly disposition towards the United States. In the war between those new Governments and Spain we declared our neutrality at the time of their recognition, and to this we have adhered, and shall continue to adhere, provided no change shall occur which, in the judgment of the competent authorities of this Government, shall make a corresponding change on the part of the United States indispensable to their security.

The late events in Spain and Portugal show that Europe is still unsettled. Of this important fact no stronger proof can be adduced than that the allied powers should have thought it proper, on any principle satisfactory to themselves, to have interposed by force in the internal concerns of Spain. To what extent such interposition may be carried, on the same principle, is a question in which all independent powers whose governments differ from theirs are interested, even those most remote, and surely none more so than the United States. Our policy in regard to Europe, which was adopted at an early stage of the wars which have so long agitated that quarter of the globe, nevertheless remains the same, which is, not to interfere in the internal concerns of any of its powers; to consider the government *de facto* as the legitimate government for us; to cultivate friendly relations with it, and to preserve those relations by a frank, firm, and manly policy, meeting in all instances the just claims of every power, submitting to injuries from none. But in regard to those continents circumstances are eminently and conspicuously different. It is impossible that the allied powers should extend their political system to any portion of either continent without endangering our peace and happiness; nor can anyone believe that our southern brethren, if left to themselves, would adopt it of their own accord. It is equally impossible, therefore, that we should behold such interposition in any form with indifference. If we look to the comparative strength and resources of Spain and those new Governments, and their distance from each other, it must be obvious that she can never subdue them. It is still the true policy of the United States to leave the parties to themselves, in the hope that other powers will pursue the same course. . . .

Negro laborers, on the James River or or at Alexandria, Virginia, date unknown, photography by Mathew Brady.

V

A GATHERING
STORM

SOUTH CAROLINA
EXPOSITION AND PROTEST

John C. Calhoun   *December 19, 1828*

---

    *Plantation owners blamed the economic decline of the
eastern seaboard cotton-growing states on tariffs designed to
protect the budding American manufacturing industries. They
argued that these tariffs were unconstitutional since they
favored one section of the country at the expense of another.*
    *Unlike Henry Clay, Vice-President John C. Calhoun
found loyalty to his state more compelling than national
patriotism. In December 1828, he drafted an "exposition [i.e.,
explanation] and protest" for the South Carolina legislature
asserting the prior rights of states over the national government
and demanding repeal of the "Tariff of Abominations." In the
immediate crisis, President-elect Andrew Jackson isolated South
Carolina and Calhoun politically, forcing them to back down,
but the debate on states' rights continued for two decades.*

The South Carolina Protest
against the Tariff of 1828

THE Senate and House of Representatives of South Carolina, now met, and sitting in General Assembly, through the Hon. William Smith and the Hon. Robert Y. Hayne, their representatives in the Senate of the United States, do, in the name and on behalf of the good people of the said commonwealth, solemnly protest against the system of protecting duties, lately adopted by the federal government, for the following reasons:—

1st. Because the good people of this commonwealth believe that the powers of Congress were delegated to it in trust for the accomplishment of certain specified objects which limit and control them, and that every exercise of them for any other purposes, is a violation of the Constitution as unwarrantable as the undisguised assumption of substantive, independent powers not granted or expressly withheld.

2d. Because the power to lay duties on imports is, and in its very nature can be, only a means of effecting objects specified by the Constitution; since no free government, and least of all a government of enumerated powers, can of right impose any tax, any more than a penalty, which is not at once justified by public necessity, and clearly within the scope and purview of the social compact; and since the right of confining appropriations of the public money to such legitimate and constitutional objects is as essential to the liberty of the people as their unquestionable privilege to be taxed only by their consent.

3d. Because they believe that the tariff law passed by Congress at its last session, and all other acts of which the principal object is the protection of manufactures, or any other branch of domestic industry, if they be considered as the exercise of a power in Congress to tax the people at its own good will and pleasure, and to apply the money raised to objects not specified in the Constitution, is a violation of these fundamental principles, a breach of a well-defined trust, and a perversion of the high powers vested in the federal government for federal purposes only.

4th. Because such acts, considered in the light of a regulation of commerce, are equally liable to objection; since, although the power to regulate commerce may, like all other powers, be exercised so as to protect domestic manufactures, yet it is clearly distinguishable from a power to do so *eo nomine,* both in the nature of the thing and in the common acception of the terms; and because the confounding of them would lead to the most extravagant results, since the encouragement of domestic industry implies an absolute control over all the interests, resources, and pursuits of a people, and is consistent with the idea of any other than a simple, consolidated government.

5th. Because, from the contemporaneous exposition of the Constitution in the numbers of the *Federalist*, (which is cited only because the Supreme Court has recognized its authority), it is clear that the power to regulate commerce was considered by the Convention as only incidentally connected with the encouragement of agriculture and manufactures; and because the power of laying imposts and duties on imports was not understood to justify in any case, a prohibition of foreign commodities, except as a means of extending commerce, by coercing foreign nations to a fair reciprocity in their intercourse with us, or for some *bona fide* commercial purpose.

6th. Because, whilst the power to protect manufactures is nowhere expressly granted to Congress, nor can be considered as necessary and proper to carry into effect any specified power, it seems to be expressly reserved to the states, by the 10th section of the 1st article of the Constitution.

7th. Because even admitting Congress to have a constitutional right to protect manufactures by the imposition of duties, or by regulations of commerce, designed principally for that purpose, yet a tariff of which the operation is grossly unequal and oppressive, in such an abuse of power as is incompatible with the principles of a free government and the great ends of civil society, justice, and equality of rights and protection.

8th. Finally, because South Carolina, from her climate, situation, and peculiar institutions, is, and must ever continue to be, wholly dependent upon agriculture and commerce, not only for her prosperity, but for her very existence as a state; because the valuable products of her soil—the blessings by which Divine Providence seems to have designed to compensate for the great disadvantages under which she suffers in other respects—are among the very few that can be cultivated with any profit by slave labor; and if, by the loss of her foreign commerce, these products should be confined to an inadequate market, the fate of this fertile state would be poverty and utter desolation; her citizens, in despair, would emigrate to more fortunate regions, and the whole frame and constitution of her civil policy be impaired and deranged, if not dissolved entirely.

Deeply impressed with these considerations, the representatives of the good people of this commonwealth, anxiously desiring to live in peace with their fellow-citizens, and to do all that in them lies to preserve and perpetuate the union of the states, and liberties of which it is the surest pledge, but feeling it to be their bounden duty to expose and resist all encroachments upon the true spirit of the Constitution, lest any apparent acquiescence in the system of protecting duties should be drawn into precedent—do, in the name of the commonwealth of South Carolina, claim to enter upon the Journal of the Senate their protest against it as unconstitutional, oppressive, and unjust.

SECOND REPLY TO HAYNE

Daniel Webster   *January 26, 1830*

> *In December 1829, Senator Samuel A. Foot of Con-*
> *necticut introduced a resolution limiting sales of federal lands*
> *in the West. Westerners, perceiving northeastern hostility to*
> *westward expansion, and southerners, still smoldering over the*
> *"Tariff of Abominations," joined in opposition to northern*
> *determination to control national economic policy. The ensuing*
> *discussion of Foot's resolution on the floor of the Senate led to a*
> *debate on the very nature of the Union. Speaking for the sec-*
> *tional interests, Senator Robert Hayne of South Carolina*
> *defended the doctrine of states' rights and power to nullify*
> *national policy. Senator Daniel Webster of Massachusetts led the*
> *defense of the resolution, advocating a nationalist view of the*
> *Constitution.*

THIS leads us to inquire into the origin of this government and the source of its power. Whose agent is it? Is it the creature of the State Legislatures, or the creature of the people? If the Government of the United States be the agent of the State governments, then they may control it, provided they can agree in the manner of controlling it; if it be the agent of the people, then the people alone can control it, restrain it, modify it, or reform it. It is observable enough, that the doctrine for which the honorable gentlemen contends leads him to the necessity of maintaining, not only that this General Government is the creature of the States, but that it is the creature of each of the States, severally, so that each may assert the power for itself of determining whether it acts within the limits of its authority. It is the servant of four-and twenty masters, of different wills and different purposes, and yet bound to obey all. This absurdity (for it seems no less) arises from a misconception as to the origin of this government and its true character. It is, sir, the people's Constitution, the people's government, made for the people, made by the people, and answerable to the people. The people of the United States have declared that this Constitution shall be supreme law. We must either admit the proposition, or deny their authority. The States are, unquestionably, sovereign, so far as their sovereignty is not affected by this supreme law. But the State Legislatures, as political bodies, however sovereign, are yet not sovereign over the people. So far as the people have given power to the General Government, so far the grant is unquestionably good, and the Government holds of the people, and not of the State governments. We are all agents of the same supreme power, the people. The General Government and the State governments derive their authority from the same source. Neither can, in relation to the other, be called primary, though one is definite and restricted, and the other general and residuary. The National Government possesses those powers which it can be shown the people have conferred on it, and no more. All the rest belongs to the State Governments, or to the people themselves. So far as the people have restrained State sovereignty by the expression of their will, in the Constitution of the United States, so far, it must be admitted, State sovereignty is effectually controlled. I do not contend that it is, or ought to be, controlled farther. The sentiment to which I have referred propounds that State sovereignty is only to be controlled by its own "feeling of justice"—that is to say, it is not to be controlled at all, for one who is to follow his own feelings is under no legal control. Now, however men may think this ought to be, the fact is that the people of the United States have chosen to impose control on State sovereignties. There are those, doubtless, who wish they had been left without restraint; but the Constitution has ordered the matter differently. To make war, for instance, is an exercise of sovereignty; but the Constitution declares that no State shall make war. To coin money is another exercise of sovereign power; but no State is at liberty to coin money. Again, the Constitution says that no sovereign State shall be so sovereign as to make a treaty. These prohibitions, it must be confessed, are a control on the State sovereignty of South Carolina, as well as of the other States, which does not arise "from her own feelings of honorable justice." The opinion referred to, therefore, is in defiance of the plainest provisions of the Constitution. . . .

But, sir, the people have wisely provided, in the Constitution itself, a proper, suitable mode and tribunal for settling questions of constitutional law. There are in the Constitution grants of powers to Congress, and restrictions on these powers. There are also prohibitions on the States. Some authority must, therefore, necessarily exist, having the ultimate jurisdiction to fix and ascertain the interpretation of these grants, restrictions, and prohibitions. The Constitution has itself pointed out, ordained, and established that authority. How has it accomplished this great and essential end? By declaring, sir, that "the Constitution and the laws of the United States made in pursuance thereof, shall be the supreme law of the land, any thing in the Constitution or laws of any States to the contrary notwithstanding.". . .

I have thus stated the reasons of my dissent to the doctrines which have been advanced and maintained. I am conscious, sir, of having detained you and the Senate much too long. I was drawn into the debate with no previous deliberation such as is suited to the discussion of so grave and important a subject. But it is a subject of which my heart is full, and I have not been willing to suppress the utterance of its spontaneous sentiments. I cannot even now persuade myself to relinquish it without expressing once more my deep conviction that, since it respects nothing less than the Union of the states, it is of most vital and essential importance to the public happiness. I profess, sir, in my career hitherto, to have kept steadily in view the prosperity and honor of the whole country and the preservation of our federal union. It is to that Union we owe our safety at home and our consideration and dignity abroad. It is to that Union that we are chiefly indebted for whatever makes us most proud of our country. That Union we reached only by the discipline of our virtues in the severe school of adversity. It had its origin in the necessities of disordered finance, prostrate commerce, and ruined credit. Under its benign influence, these great interests immediately awoke as from the dead and sprang forth with newness of life. Every year of its duration has teemed with fresh proofs of its utility and its blessings, and although our territory has stretched out wider and wider and our population spread farther and farther, they have not outrun its protection or its benefits. It has been to us all a copious fountain of national, social, and personal happiness. I have not allowed myself, sir, to look beyond the Union, to see what might lie hidden in the dark recess behind. I have not coolly weighed the chances of preserving liberty when the bonds that unite us together shall be broken asunder. I have not accustomed myself to hang over the precipice of disunion, to see whether, with my short sight, I can fathom the depth of the abyss below; nor could I regard him as a safe counselor, in the affairs of this government, whose thoughts should be mainly bent on considering, not how the Union should be best preserved, but how tolerable might be the condition of the people when it shall be broken up and destroyed. While the Union lasts, we have high, exciting, gratifying prospects spread out before us, for us and our children. Beyond that, I seek not to penetrate the veil. God grant that in my day, at least, that curtain may not rise. God grant that, on my vision, never may be opened what lies behind. When my eyes shall be turned to behold for the last times the sun in heaven, may I not see him shining on the broken and dishonored fragments of a once glorious Union; on states dissevered, discordant, belligerent; on a land rent with civil feuds, or drenched, it may be, in fraternal blood! Let their last feeble and lingering glance rather behold the gorgeous ensign of the republic, now known and honored throughout the earth, still full high advanced, its arms and trophies streaming in their original luster, not a stripe erased or polluted, nor a single star obscured, bearing for its motto no such miserable interrogatory as, What is all this worth? nor those other words of delusion and folly, Liberty first, and Union afterward; but everywhere, spread all over in characters of living light, blazing on all its ample folds, as they float over the sea and over the land, and in every wind under the whole heavens, that other sentiment, dear to every true American heart—Liberty and Union, now and forever, one and inseparable!

TO THE PUBLIC

William Lloyd Garrison   *January 1, 1831*

The rapid expansion of America's cotton cultivation in the early 1800s assured the economic survival of slavery. Early proposals to eliminate the institution, including "colonization" of Africa by freed slaves and gradual abolition through "compensated emancipation" failed for lack of financial and moral support. By the 1820s, the religious revival spreading across the northern states inspired increasing demands for the eradication of slavery as a sin against a "higher law." Slavery became not just a political or economic question, but a moral one.

In 1829, Boston journalist William Lloyd Garrison joined the antislavery movement, becoming one of the strongest advocates for the immediate abolition of slavery. In 1831, he founded the Liberator, *a journal that led the abolitionist campaign during its thirty-five years of publication. The following is taken from the first issue of January 1, 1831.*

. . . DURING my recent tour for the purpose of exciting the minds of the people by a series of discourses on the subject of slavery, every place that I visited gave fresh evidence of the fact, that a greater revolution in public sentiment was to be effected in the free states—and particularly in New England—than at the south. I found contempt more bitter, opposition more active, detraction more relentless, prejudice more stubborn, and apathy more frozen, than among slaves owners themselves. Of course, there were individual exceptions to the contrary. This state of things afflicted, but did not dishearten me. I determined, at every hazard, to lift up the standard of emancipation in the eyes of the nation, within sight of Bunker Hill and in the birth place of liberty. That standard is now unfurled; and long may it float, unhurt by the spoliations of time or the missiles of a desperate foe—yea, till every chain be broken, and every bondman be set free! Let Southern oppressors tremble—let their secret abettors tremble—let their Northern apologists tremble—let all the enemies of the persecuted blacks tremble. . . .

I am aware, that many object to the severity of my language; but is there not cause for severity? I will be as harsh as truth, and as uncompromising as justice. On this subject, I do not wish to think, or speak, or write, with moderation. No! No! Tell a man whose house is on fire, to give a moderate alarm; tell him to moderately rescue his wife from the hands of the ravisher; tell the mother to gradually extricate her babe from the fire into which it has fallen;—but urge me not to use moderation in a cause like the present. I am in earnest—I will not equivocate—I will not excuse—I will not retreat a single inch—*AND I WILL BE HEARD*. The apathy of the people is enough to make every statue leap from its pedestal, and to hasten the resurrection of the dead.

It is pretended, that I am retarding the cause of emancipation by the coarseness of my invective, and the precipitancy of my measures. The charge is not true. On this question my influence,—humble as it is,—is felt at this moment to a considerable extent, and shall be felt in the coming years—not perniciously, but beneficially—not as a curse, but as a blessing; and posterity will bear testimony that I was right. I desire to thank God, that he enables me to disregard "the fear of man which bringeth a snare," and to speak his truth in its simplicity and power. . . .

CHEROKEE NATION V. GEORGIA

John Marshall   *1831*

———————

The Cherokee were one of the most numerous tribes of the American Southeast, and, for a time, one of the most successful at assimilating white culture. In the 1820s, some 20,000 Cherokee inhabited prosperous farms in Tennessee, the

*Carolinas and Georgia, employing the methods of their white
neighbors. They had a constitutional government modeled on
the United States, a writing system for their language and the
first newspaper published by native Americans.*

*Unfortunately, assimilation to white culture did not
protect the Cherokee from white acquisitiveness. The discovery of
gold on Cherokee land in Georgia sparked the first great gold
rush in United States history and prompted agitation for
removal of the Cherokee. In 1828, the Georgia legislature
annulled the Cherokee constitution, extended sovereignty over
the tribe and ordered seizure of their lands. The tribe sued for
an injunction upholding their rights. While the Supreme Court
was sympathetic to the Cherokee and recognized their inalienable property rights, it denied the motion. Chief Justice John
Marshall's opinion declared the Cherokee could not sue since
they were not a sovereign nation. Eventually the Cherokee were
evicted from their lands.*

MARSHALL, C. J. This bill is brought by the Cherokee nation, praying an injunction to restrain the state of Georgia from the execution of certain laws of that state, which, as is alleged, go directly to annihilate the Cherokee as a political society, and to seize for the use of Georgia, the lands of the nation which have been assured to them by the United States, in solemn treaties repeatedly made and still in force.

If courts were permitted to indulge their sympathies, a case better calculated to excite them can scarcely be imagined. A people, once numerous, powerful, and truly independent, found by our ancestors in the quiet and uncontrolled possession of an ample domain, gradually sinking beneath our superior policy, our arts and our arms, have yielded their lands, by successive treaties, each of which contains a solemn guarantee of the residue, until they retain no more of their formerly extensive territory than is deemed necessary to their comfortable subsistence. To preserve this remnant, the present application is made.

Before we can look into the merits of the case, a preliminary inquiry presents itself. Has this court jurisdiction of the cause? The third article of the constitution describes the extent of the judicial power. The second section closes an enumeration of the cases to which it is extended, with "controversies between a state or citizens thereof, and foreign states, citizens or subjects." A subsequent clause of the same section gives the supreme court original jurisdiction, in all cases in which a state shall be a party. The party defendant may then unquestionably be sued in this court. May the plaintiff sue in it? Is the Cherokee nation a foreign state, in the sense in which that term is used in the constitution? The counsel for the plaintiffs have maintained the affirmative of this proposition with great earnestness and ability. So much of the argument as was intended to prove the character of the Cherokees as a state, as a distinct political society, separated from others, capable of managing its own affairs and governing itself, has in the opinion of a majority of the judges, been completely successful. They have been uniformly treated as a state, from the settlement of our country. The numerous treaties made with them by the United States, recognise them as a people capable of maintaining the relations of peace and war, of being responsible in their political character for any violation of their engagements, or for any aggression committed on the citizens of the United States, by any individual of their community. Laws have been enacted in the spirit of these treaties. The acts of our government plainly recognize the Cherokee nation as a state, and the courts are bound by those acts.

A question of much more difficulty remains. Do the Cherokees constitute a foreign state in the sense of the constitution? The counsel have shown conclusively, that they are not a state of the Union, and have insisted that, individually, they are aliens, not owing allegiance to the United States. An aggregate of aliens composing a state must, they say, be a foreign state; each individual being foreign, the whole must be foreign.

This argument is imposing, but we must examine it more closely, before we yield to it. The condition of the Indians in relation to the United States is, perhaps, unlike that of any other two people in existence. In general, nations not owing a common allegiance, are foreign to each other. The term foreign nation is, with strict propriety, applicable by either to the other. But the relation of the Indians to the United States is marked by peculiar and cardinal distinctions which exist nowhere else. The Indian territory is admitted to compose a part of the United States. In all our maps, geographical treaties, histories and laws, it is so considered. In all our intercourse with foreign nations, in our commercial regulations, in any attempt at intercourse between Indians and foreign nations, they are considered as within the jurisdictional limits of the United States, subject to many of those restraints which are imposed upon our own citizens. They acknowledge themselves, in their treaties, to be under the protection of the United States; they admit, that the United States shall have the sole and exclusive right of regulating the trade with them, and managing all their affairs as they think proper; and the Cherokees in particular were allowed by the treaty of Hopewell, which preceded the constitution, "to send a deputy of their choice, whenever they think fit, to congress." Treaties were made with some tribes, by the state of

New York, under a then unsettled construction of the confederation, by which they ceded all their lands to that state, taking back a limited grant to themselves, in which they admit their dependence. Though the Indians are acknowledged to have an unquestionable, and heretofore unquestioned, right to the lands they occupy, until that right shall be extinguished by a voluntary cession to our government; yet it may well be doubted, whether those tribes which reside within the acknowledged boundaries of the United States can, with accuracy, be denominated foreign nations. They may, more correctly, perhaps, be denominated domestic dependent nations. They occupy a territory to which we assert a title independent of their will, which must take effect in point of possession, when their right of possession ceases. Meanwhile, they are in a state of pupilage; their relation to the United States resembles that of a ward to his guardian. They look to our government for protection; rely upon its kindness and its power; appeal to it for relief to their wants; and address the president as their great father. They and their country are considered by foreign nations, as well as by ourselves, as being so completely under the sovereignty and dominion of the United States, that any attempt to acquire their lands, or to form a political connection with them would be considered by all as an invasion of our territory and an act of hostility. These considerations go far to support the opinion, that the framers of our constitution had not the Indian tribes in view, when they opened the courts of the Union to controversies between a state or the citizens thereof and foreign states.

In considering this subject, the habits and usages of the Indians, in their intercourse with their white neighbors, ought not to be entirely disregarded. At the time the constitution was framed, the idea of appealing to an American court of justice for an assertion of right or a redress of wrong, had perhaps never entered the mind of an Indian or of his tribe. Their appeal was to the tomahawk, or to the government. This was well understood by the statesmen who framed the constitution of the United States, and might furnish some reason for omitting to enumerate them among the parties who might sue in the courts of the Union. Be this as it may, the peculiar relations between the United States and the Indians occupying our territory are such, that we should feel much difficulty in considering them as designated by the term foreign state, were there no other part of the constitution which might shed light on the meaning of these words. But we think that in construing them, considerable aid is furnished by that clause in the eighth section of the third article, which empowers congress to "regulate commerce with foreign nations, and among the several states, and with the Indian tribes." In this clause, they are as clearly contradistinguished, by a name appropriate to themselves, from foreign nations, as from the several states composing the Union. They are designated by a distinct appellation; and as this appellation can be applied to neither of the others, neither can the application distinguishing either of the others be, in fair construction, applied to them. The objects to which the power of regulating commerce might be directed, are divided into three distinct classes—foreign nations, the several states, and Indian tribes. When forming this article, the convention considered them as entirely distinct. We cannot assume that the distinction was lost, in framing a subsequent article, unless there be something in its language to authorize the assumption.

The counsel for the plaintiffs contend, that the words "Indian tribes" were introduced into the article, empowering congress to regulate commerce, for the purpose of removing those doubts in which the management of Indian affairs was involved by the language of the ninth article of the confederation. Intending to give the whole of managing those affairs to the government about to be instituted, the convention conferred it explicitly; and omitted those qualifications which embarrassed the exercise of it, as granted in the confederation. This may be admitted, without weakening the construction which has been intimated. Had the Indian tribes been foreign nations, in the view of the convention, this exclusive power of regulating intercourse with them might have been, and most probably, would have been, specifically given, in language indicating that idea, not in language contradistinguishing them from foreign nations. Congress might have been empowered "to regulate commerce with foreign nations, including the Indian tribes, and among the several states." This language would have suggested itself to statesmen who considered the Indian tribes as foreign nations, and were yet desirous of mentioning them particularly.

It has been also said, that the same words have not necessarily the same meaning attached to them, when found in different parts of the same instrument; their meaning is controlled by the context. This is undoubtedly true. In common language, the same word has various meanings, and the peculiar sense in which it is used in any sentence, is to be determined by the context. This may not be equally true with respect to proper names. "Foreign nations" is a general term, the application of which to Indian tribes, when used in the American constitution, is, at best, extremely questionable. In one article, in which a power is given to be exercised in regard to foreign nations generally, and to the Indian tribes particularly, they are mentioned as separate, in terms clearly contradistinguishing them from each other. We perceive plainly, that the constitution, in this article, does not comprehend Indian tribes in the general term "foreign nations;" not, we presume, because a tribe may not be a nation, but because it is not foreign to the United States. When, afterwards, the term "foreign state" is introduced, we cannot impute to the convention, the intention to desert its former meaning, and to comprehend Indian tribes within it, unless the context force that construction on us. We find nothing in the context, and nothing in the subject of the article, which leads to it.

The court has bestowed its best attention on this question, and, after mature deliberation, the majority is of opinion, that an Indian tribe or nation within the United States is not a foreign state, in the sense of the constitution, and cannot maintain an action in the courts of the United States.

A serious additional objection exists to the jurisdiction of the court. Is the matter of the bill the proper subject for judicial inquiry and decision? It seeks to restrain a state from the forcible exercise of legislative power over a neighboring people, asserting their independence; their right to which the state denies. On several of the matters alleged in the bill, for example, on the laws making it criminal to exercise the usual powers of self-government in their own country, by the Cherokee nation, this court cannot interpose; at least, in the form in which those matters are presented.

That part of the bill which respects the land occupied by the Indians, and prays the aid of the court to protect their possession, may be more doubtful. The mere question of right might, perhaps, be decided by this court, in a proper case, with proper parties. But the court is asked to do more than decide on the title. The bill requires us to control the legislature of Georgia, and to restrain the exertion of its physical force. The propriety of such an interposition by the court may be well questioned; it savors too much of the exercise of political power, to be within the proper province of the judicial department. But the opinion on the point respecting parties makes it unnecessary to decide this question.

If it be true, that the Cherokee nation have rights, this is not the tribunal in which those rights are to be asserted. If it be true, that wrongs have been inflicted, and that still greater are to be apprehended, this is not the tribunal which can redress the past or prevent the future. The motion for an injunction is denied.

Veto of the Bank Bill

Andrew Jackson   *July 10, 1832*

---

*Andrew Jackson's election as a political outsider in 1828
marked a dramatic shift in American politics. "Old Hickory,"
tough and common, represented the success of the self-made
man, the Jeffersonian ideal of agrarian democracy. Though
widely divergent in background and aims, Jackson's political
coalition united behind opposition to centralized economic
power as represented by the National Bank.*

*By the 1820s the Bank had achieved virtual control of
the national economy. Jackson's pledge to destroy the Bank
posed a real threat since its charter expired in 1836, before the
end of his potential second term. In 1832, Henry Clay, propo-
nent of a strong national economic policy and rival presidential
candidate, made the Bank a campaign issue. Jackson vetoed the
charter renewal bill, depicting the Bank as "The Monster," and
turned the issue against the Whigs. Winning in a landslide,
Jackson used his mandate to justify withdrawal of federal
deposits, bringing about the collapse of the Bank and the Panic
of 1833.*

TO the Senate:

The bill "to modify and continue" the act entitled "An act to incorporate
the subscribers to the Bank of the United States" was presented to me on the 4th
July instant. Having . . . come to the conclusion that it ought not to become a law,
I herewith return it to the Senate, in which it originated, with my objections.

A bank of the United States is in many respects convenient for the
Government and useful to the people. Entertaining this opinion, and deeply
impressed with the belief that some of the powers and privileges possessed by
the existing bank are unauthorized by the Constitution, subversive of the rights
of the States, and dangerous to the liberties of the people, I felt it my duty at an
early period of my Administration to call the attention of Congress to the
practicability of organizing an institution combining all its advantages and
obviating these objections. I sincerely regret that in the act before me I can perceive none of those modifications of the bank charter which are necessary, in
my opinion, to make it compatible with justice, with sound policy, or with the
Constitution of our country.

The present corporate body . . . enjoys an exclusive privilege of banking
under the authority of the General Government, a monopoly of its favor and
support, and, as a necessary consequence, almost a monopoly of the foreign and
domestic exchange. The powers, privileges, and favors bestowed upon it in the
original charter, by increasing the value of the stock far above its par value,
operated as a gratuity of many millions to the stockholders. . . .

The act before me proposes another gratuity to the holders of the same
stock. . . . On all hands it is conceded that its passage will increase at least 20
or 30 per cent more the market price of the stock, subject to the payment of the
annuity of $200,000 per year secured by the act, thus adding in a moment one-
fourth to its par value. It is not our own citizens only who are to receive the

bounty of our Government. More than eight millions of the stock of this bank are held by foreigners. By this act the American Republic proposes virtually to make them a present of some millions of dollars. For these gratuities to foreigners and to some of our own opulent citizens the act secures no equivalent whatever. . . .

Every monopoly and all exclusive privileges are granted at the expense of the public, which ought to receive a fair equivalent. The many millions which this act proposes to bestow on the stockholders of the existing bank must come directly or indirectly out of the earnings of the American people. It is due to them, therefore, if their Government sell monopolies and exclusive privileges, that they should at least exact for them as much as they are worth in open market. The value of the monopoly in this case may be correctly ascertained. The twenty-eight millions of stock would probably be at an advance of 50 per cent, and command in market at least $42,000,000, subject to the payment of the present bonus. The present value of the monopoly, therefore, is $17,000,000, and this the act proposes to sell for three millions, payable in fifteen annual installments of $200,000 each.

It is not conceivable how the present stockholders can have any claim to the special favor of the Government. The present corporation has enjoyed its monopoly during the period stipulated in the original contract. If we must have such a corporation, why should not the Government sell out the whole stock and thus secure to the people the full market value of the privileges granted? Why should not Congress create and sell twenty-eight millions of stock, incorporating the purchasers with all the powers and privileges secured in this act and putting the premium upon the sales into the Treasury?. . .

The modifications of the existing charter proposed by this act are not such, in my view, as make it consistent with the rights of the States or the liberties of the people. The qualification of the right of the bank to hold real estate, the limitation of its power to establish branches, and the power reserved to Congress to forbid the circulation of small notes are restrictions comparatively of little value or importance. All the objectionable principles of the existing corporation, and most of its odious features, are retained without alleviation. . . .

Is there no danger to our liberty and independence in a bank that in its nature has so little to bind it to our country? The president of the bank has told us that most of the State banks exist by its forbearance. Should its influence become concentered, as it may under the operation of such an act as this, in the hands of a self-elected directory whose interests are identified with those of the foreign stockholders, will there not be cause to tremble for the purity of our elections in peace and for the independence of our country in war? Their power would be great whenever they might choose to exert it; but if this monopoly were regularly renewed every fifteen or twenty years on terms proposed by themselves, they might seldom in peace put forth their strength to influence elections or control the affairs of the nation. But if any private citizen or public functionary should interpose to curtail its powers or prevent a renewal of its privileges, it can not be doubted that he would be made to feel its influence. . . .

If we must have a bank with private stockholders, every consideration of sound policy and every impulse of American feeling admonishes that it should be purely American. Its stockholders should be composed exclusively of our own citizens, who at least ought to be friendly to our Government and willing to support it in times of difficulty and danger. . . . To a bank exclusively of American stockholders, possessing the powers and privileges granted by this act, subscriptions for $200,000,000 could be readily obtained. . . .

It is maintained by the advocates of the bank that its constitutionality in all its features ought to be considered as settled by precedent and by the decision of the Supreme Court. To this conclusion I can not assent. Mere precedent is a dangerous source of authority, and should not be regarded as deciding questions of constitutional power except where the acquiescence of the people and the States can be considered as well settled. So far from this being the case on this subject, an argument against the bank might be based on precedent. One Congress, in 1791, decided in favor of a bank; another, in 1811, decided against it. One Congress, in 1815, decided against a bank; another, in 1816, decided in its favor. Prior to the present Congress, therefore, the precedents drawn from that source were equal. If we resort to the States, the expressions of legislative, judicial, and executive opinions against the bank have been probably to those in its favor as 4 to 1. . . .

If the opinion of the Supreme Court covered the whole ground of this act, it ought not to control the coördinate authorities of this Government. The Congress, the Executive, and the Court must each for itself be guided by its own opinion of the Constitution. Each public officer who takes an oath to support the Constitution swears that he will support it as he understands it, and not as it is understood by others. It is as much the duty of the House of Representatives, of the Senate, and of the President to decide upon the constitutionality of any bill or resolution which may be presented to them for passage or approval as it is of the supreme judges when it may be brought before them for judicial decision. The opinion of the judges has no more authority over Congress than the opinion of Congress has over the judges, and on that point the President is independent of both. The authority of the Supreme Court must not, therefore, be permitted to control the Congress or the Executive when acting in their legislative capacities, but to have only such influence as the force of their reasoning may deserve.

But in the case relied upon the Supreme Court have not decided that all the features of this corporation are compatible with the Constitution. It is true that the court have said that the law incorporating the bank is a constitutional exercise of power by Congress; but taking into view the whole opinion of the court and the reasoning by which they have come to that conclusion, I understand them to have decided that inasmuch as a bank is an appropriate means for carrying into effect the enumerated powers of the General Government, therefore the law incorporating it is in accordance with that provision of the Constitution which declares that Congress shall have power "to make all laws which shall be necessary and proper for carrying those powers in execution." Having satisfied themselves that the word "necessary" in the Constitution means "needful," "requisite," "essential," "conducive to," and that "a bank" is a convenient, a useful, and essential instrument in the prosecution of the Government's "fiscal operations," they conclude that to "use one must be within the discretion of Congress" and that "the act to incorporate the Bank of the United States is a law made in pursuance of the Constitution;" "but," say they, "where the law is not prohibited and is really calculated to effect any of the objects intrusted to the Government, to undertake here to inquire into the degree of its necessity would be to pass the line which circumscribes the judicial department and to tread on legislative ground."

The principle here affirmed is that the "degree of its necessity," involving all the details of a banking institution, is a question exclusively for legislative consideration. A bank is constitutional, but it is the province of the Legislature to determine whether this or that particular power, privilege, or exemption is "necessary and proper" to enable the bank to discharge its duties to the Government, and from their decision there is no appeal to the courts of justice. Under the decision of the Supreme Court, therefore, it is the exclusive province of Congress and the President to decide whether the particular features of this act are necessary and proper in order to enable the bank to perform conveniently and efficiently the public duties assigned to it as a fiscal agent, and therefore constitutional, or unnecessary and improper, and therefore unconstitutional. Without commenting on the general principle affirmed by the Supreme Court, let us examine the details of this act in accordance with the rule of legislative action which they have laid down. It will be found that many of the powers and privileges conferred on it can not be supposed necessary for the purpose for which it is proposed to be created, and are not, therefore, means necessary to attain the end in view, and consequently not justified by the Constitution. . . .

If our power over means is so absolute that the Supreme Court will not call in question the constitutionality of an act of Congress the subject of which "is not prohibited, and is really calculated to effect any of the objects entrusted to the Government," although, as in the case before me, it takes away powers expressly granted to Congress and rights scrupulously reserved to the States, it becomes us to proceed in our legislation with the utmost caution. Though not directly, our own powers and the rights of the States may be indirectly legislated away in the use of means to execute substantive powers. We may not enact that Congress shall not have the power of exclusive legislation over the District of Columbia, but we may pledge the faith of the United States that as a means of executing other powers it shall not be exercised for twenty years or forever. We may not pass an act prohibiting the States to tax the banking business carried on within their limits, but we may, as a means of executing our powers over other objects, place that business in the hands of our agents and then declare it exempt from State taxation in their hands. Thus may our own powers and the rights of the States, which we can not directly curtail or invade, be frittered away and extinguished in the use of means employed by us to execute other powers. That a bank of the United States, competent to all the duties which may be required by the Government, might be so organized as not to infringe on our own delegated powers or the reserved rights of the States I do not entertain a doubt. Had the Executive been called upon to furnish the project of such an institution, the duty would have been cheerfully performed. . . .

Under such circumstances the bank comes forward and asks a renewal of its charter for a term of fifteen years upon conditions which not only operate as a gratuity to the stockholders of many millions of collars, but will sanction any abuses and legalize any encroachments. . . .

The bank is professedly established as an agent of the executive branch of the Government, and its constitutionality is maintained on that ground. Neither upon the propriety of present action nor upon the provisions of this act was the Executive consulted. It has had no opportunity to say that it neither needs nor wants an agent clothed with such powers and favored by such exemptions. There is nothing in its legitimate functions which makes it necessary or proper. Whatever interest or influence, whether public or private, has given birth to this act, it can not be found either in the wishes or necessities of the executive department, by which present action is deemed premature, and the powers conferred upon its agent not only unnecessary, but dangerous to the Government and country. . . .

There are no necessary evils in government. Its evils exist only in its abuses. If it would confine itself to equal protection, and, as Heaven does its rains, shower its favors alike on the high and the low, the rich and the poor, it would be an unqualified blessing. In the act before me there seems to be a wide and unnecessary departure from these just principles. . . .

Experience should teach us wisdom. Most of the difficulties our

Government now encounters and most of the dangers which impend over our Union have sprung from an abandonment of the legitimate objects of Government by our national legislation, and the adoption of such principles as are embodied in this act. Many of our rich men have not been content with equal protection and equal benefits, but have besought us to make them richer by act of Congress. By attempting to gratify their desires we have in the results of our legislation arrayed section against section, interest against interest, and man against man, in a fearful commotion which threatens to shake the foundations of our Union. It is time to pause in our career to review our principles, and if possible revive that devoted patriotism and spirit of compromise which distinguished the sages of the Revolution and the fathers of our Union.

MEMORIAL AND PROTEST
OF THE CHEROKEE NATION

Cherokee Tribal Leaders   *March 11, 1836*

Having fought a losing battle for their sovereign rights through the federal courts, the Cherokee became divided and demoralized. In 1835, a minority of tribal leaders conceded defeat, signing away the remnant of Cherokee lands in accord with the Indian Removal Act. In 1836, a delegation representing the majority was sent to Washington, begging the Senate to abrogate the removal agreement. The plea was denied. Two years later, President Martin Van Buren dispatched federal troops to evict the tribe. A few Cherokee fled into the Appalachian Mountains, where their descendants still live, but the majority were rounded up and marched to the Indian Territory. Of the 18,000 Cherokee who commenced the journey, 4,000 died on the "Trail of Tears."

IT cannot be concealed that the situation of the Cherokees is peculiarly distressing. In adverting to that situation it is not done to arouse, at this late day, a useless sympathy, but only as a matter of history, and from necessity in giving a fair and impartial illustration of their difficulties. It is well known to those who have paid any attention to their history for the last five years, that they have been contending for the faithful execution of treaties between their nation and the United States, and that their distresses have not been mitigated; their efforts seem to have increased their difficulties. It remains for them to seek an adjustment by treaty, and an equitable acknowledgement of their rights, and claims, so far as circumstances will permit.

For this purpose, this delegation has been deputed, as the proper organ of the Cherokee people, to settle, by treaty, their difficulties; and they wish, in sincerity, to have them settled, for the good, peace, and harmony of the whole nation. This desired end can only be attained by a contract with the constituted and acknowledged authorities of the Cherokee nation. If the difficulties are attempted to be arranged in any other way, it will not meet the wishes of the Cherokees, and their situation will be miserable beyond description, and their distresses augmented, for they will never agree to a treaty made with unauthorized individuals. Deal with them as friends, and suffer them to be relieved from their sorrows and difficulties by their own act, and whatever may be their situation in time to come, they will console themselves by the reflection, it is the dispensation of an all-wise Providence.

The delegation are sure it cannot be the wish of the Senate of the United States to ratify and have enforced upon the unoffending Cherokee people, a treaty made without their authority, false upon its face, and against the known wishes of the nation. Such is the instrument submitted to your honorable body. For the truth of this statement, should the Senate require further proof, it can be obtained from numerous persons of unimpeachable integrity and veracity. But if it be the fate of the Cherokee people, and the decree has gone forth, that they must leave their homes and native land, and seek a new residence in the wilds of the far west, without their consent, let them be expelled and removed by an act of Congress, when they or their posterity, in after times, may have some claims upon the magnanimity of the American people.

The delegation do solemnly declare, they would consider such an act preferable and more humane than the ratification and enforcement of a fraudulent treaty, false upon its face, and made without the consent of one of the professed contracting parties. The past history of the United States furnishes admonitions against the ratification of treaties made with unauthorized individuals. Resting upon the sacred rights of the Cherokee nation, so often recognized and solemnly guarantied on the faith of treaties, the delegation now appeal to the sympathies, the honor, good faith, and magnanimity of the United States, to preserve and protect their nation from fraud, rapine, plunder, and destruction. They have now discharged their duty to themselves and to their unfortunate people, with that frankness that becomes the occasion. Their case is fairly before your honorable body, and the destiny of the Cherokee people in the hands of the American Senate.

We are all children of the same Great Parent and bound to be kind to each other, without regard to the situation in which we may be placed. If an earthly parent have a child unfortunately weak and poor, how would he feel to see the brothers of that child abusing it for its misfortunes, insulting its feelings, exulting in their own superiority, curling the lip of scorn, with a significant cant of the head, at its earnest supplication for justice? Let every man's own heart give him the answer. You have before you that unfortunate child in the weak and dependent Cherokees. With hands elevated towards the throne of grace and mercy, we all supplicate, saying: Our brothers, is it true you will drive us from the land of our nativity, and from the tombs of our fathers and our mothers? We know you possess the power, but, by the tie that unites us yonder, we implore you to forbear. Our case is with you.

CIVIL DISOBEDIENCE

Henry David Thoreau   *January 1848*

Henry David Thoreau, a practical philosopher who lived by his doctrines, was born in 1817 in Concord, Massachusetts. After graduation from Harvard and a short-lived career as a teacher, Thoreau began to write about his observations on nature and the world. From 1845 to 1847 he lived a spare life in a cottage by Walden Pond, later recording his reflections in Walden; or, A Life in the Woods *(1854). In 1846, he spent a night in jail on a charge of tax evasion, refusing to support a*

*government that upheld slavery and waged war on Mexico. This
incident prompted him to reflect on the nature of civil authority. In January 1848, he presented his views in a lecture on
"Civil Disobedience" at the Concord Lyceum; the lecture was
printed in 1849.*

THE practical reason why, when the power is once in the hands of the
people, a majority are permitted, and for a long period continue, to rule is not
because they are most likely to be in the right, nor because this seems fairest to
the minority, but because they are physically the strongest. But a government in
which the majority rule in all cases cannot be based on justice, even as far as men
understand it. Can there not be a government in which majorities do not virtually
decide right and wrong, but conscience?—in which majorities decide only those
questions to which the rule of expediency is applicable? Must the citizen ever for
a moment, or in the least degree, resign his conscience to the legislator? Why has
every man a conscience, then? I think that we should be men first, and subjects
afterward. It is not desirable to cultivate a respect for the law, so much as for the
right. The only obligation which I have a right to assume is to do at any time what
I think right. It is truly enough said, that a corporation has no conscience; but
a corporation of conscientious men is a corporation with a conscience. Law never
made men a whit more just; and, by means of their respect for it, even the well-
disposed are daily made the agents of injustice. . . .

The mass of men serve the state thus, not as men mainly, but as machines,
with their bodies. They are the standing army, and the militia, jailors, constables,
posse comitatus, etc. In most cases there is no free exercise whatever of the
judgment or of the moral sense; but they put themselves on a level with wood
and earth and stones; and wooden men can perhaps be manufactured that will
serve the purpose as well. Such command no more respect than men of straw
or a lump of dirt. They have the same sort of worth only as horses and dogs. Yet
such as these even are commonly esteemed good citizens. Others—as most
legislators, politicians, lawyers, ministers, and office-holders—serve the state
chiefly with their heads; and, as they rarely make any moral distinctions they are
as likely to serve the Devil, without intending it, as God. A very few, as heroes,
patriots, martyrs, reformers in the great sense, and men, serve the state with their
consciences also, and so necessarily resist it for the most part; and they are
commonly treated as enemies by it.

How does it become a man to behave toward this American government
to-day? I answer, that he cannot without disgrace be associated with it. I cannot

for an instant recognize that political organization as my government which is the slave's government also.

All men recognize the right of revolution; that is, the right to refuse allegiance to, and to resist, the government, when its tyranny or its inefficiency are great and unendurable. But almost all say that such is not the case now. But such was the case, they think, in the Revolution of '75. If one were to tell me that this was a bad government because it taxed certain foreign commodities brought to its ports, it is most probable that I should not make an ado about it, for I can do without them. All machines have their friction; . . . But when the friction comes to have its machine, and oppression and robbery are organized, I say, let us not have such a machine any longer. In other words, when a sixth of the population of a nation which has undertaken to be the refuge of liberty are slaves, and a whole country is unjustly overrun and conquered by a foreign army, and subjected to military law, I think that it is not too soon for honest men to rebel and revolutionize. What makes this duty the more urgent is the fact that the country so overrun is not our own, but ours is the invading army. . . .

Practically speaking, the opponents to a reform in Massachusetts are not a hundred thousand politicians at the South, but a hundred thousand merchants and farmers here, who are more interested in commerce and agriculture than they are in humanity, and are not prepared to do justice to the slave and to Mexico, cost what it may. I quarrel not with far-off foes, but with those who, near at home, cooperate with, and do the bidding of, those far away, and without whom the latter would be harmless. We are accustomed to say, that the mass of men are unprepared; but improvement is slow, because the few are not materially wiser or better than the many. It is not so important that many should be as good as you, so that there be some absolute goodness somewhere; for that will leaven the whole lump. There are thousands who are in opinion opposed to slavery and to the war, who yet in effect do nothing to put an end to them; who, esteeming themselves children of Washington and Franklin, sit down with their hands in their pockets, and say that they know not what to do, and do nothing; who even postpone the question of freedom to the question of free-trade, and quietly read the prices-current along with the latest advices from Mexico, after dinner, and, it may be, fall asleep over them both. What is the price-current of an honest man and patriot to-day? They hesitate, and they regret, and sometimes they petition; but they do nothing in earnest and with effect. They will wait, well disposed, for others to remedy the evil, that they may no longer have it to regret. At most, they give only a cheap vote, and a feeble countenance and God-speed, to the right, as it goes by them. There are nine hundred and ninety-nine patrons of virtue to one virtuous man. But it is easier to deal with the real possessor of a thing than with the temporary guardian of it. . . .

Unjust laws exist: shall we be content to obey them, or shall we endeavor to amend them, and obey them until we have succeeded, or shall we transgress them at once? Men generally, under such a government as this, think that they ought to wait until they have persuaded the majority to alter them. They think that, if they should resist, the remedy would be worse than the evil. But it is the fault of the government itself that the remedy is worse than the evil. It makes it worse. Why is it not more apt to anticipate and provide for reform? Why does it not cherish its wise minority? Why does it cry and resist before it is hurt? Why does it not encourage its citizens to be on the alert to point out its faults, and do better than it would have them? Why does it always crucify Christ, and ex-communicate Copernicus and Luther, and pronounce Washington and Franklin rebels? . . .

I do not hesitate to say, that those who call themselves Abolitionists should at once effectually withdraw their support, both in person and property, from the government of Massachusetts and not wait till they constitute a majority of one, before they suffer the right to prevail through them. I think that it is enough if they have God on their side, without waiting for that other one. Moreover, any man more right than his neighbors constitutes a majority of one already.

I meet this American government, or its representative, the state government, directly, and face to face, once a year—no more—in the person of its tax-gatherer; this is the only mode in which a man situated as I am necessarily meets it; and it then says distinctly, Recognize me; and the simplest, most effectual, and, in the present posture of affairs, the indispensablest mode of treating with it on this head, of expressing your little satisfaction with and love for it, is to deny it then. My civil neighbor, the tax-gatherer, is the very man I have to deal with,—for it is, after all, with men and not with parchment that I quarrel,—and he has voluntarily chosen to be an agent of the government. How shall he ever know well what he is and does as an officer of the government, or as a man, until he is obliged to consider whether he shall treat me, his neighbor, for whom he has respect, as a neighbor and well-disposed man, or as a maniac and disturber of the peace, and see if he can get over this obstruction to his neighborliness without a ruder and more impetuous thought or speech corresponding with his action. I know this well, and if one thousand, if one hundred, if ten men whom I could name,—if ten honest men only,—ay if one honest man, in this State of Massachusetts, ceasing to hold slaves, were actually to withdraw from this copartnership, and be locked up in the county jail therefor, it would be the abolition of slavery in America. For it matters not how small the beginning may seem to be: what is once well done is done forever. . . .

Under a government which imprisons any unjustly, the true place for a just man is also a prison. The proper place to-day, the only place which Massachusetts has provided for her freer and less desponding spirits, is in her prisons, to be put out and locked out of the State by her own act, as they have already put themselves out by their principles. It is there that the fugitive slave, and the Mexican prisoner on parole, and the Indian come to plead the wrongs of his race should find them; on that separate, but more free and honorable ground, where the State places those who are not with her, but against her,—the only house in a slave State in which a free man can abide with honor. If any think that their influence would be lost there, and their voices no longer afflict the ear of the State, that they would not be as an enemy within its walls, they do not know by how much truth is stronger than error, nor how much more eloquently and effectively he can combat injustice who has experienced a little in his own person. Cast your whole vote, not a strip of paper merely, but your whole influence. A minority is powerless while it conforms to the majority; it is not even a minority then; but it is irresistible when it clogs by its whole weight. If the alternative is to keep all just men in prison, or give up war and slavery, the State will not hesitate which to choose. If a thousand men were not to pay their tax-bills this year, that would not be a violent and bloody measure, as it would be to pay them, and enable the State to commit violence and shed innocent blood. This is, in fact, the definition of a peaceable revolution, if any such is possible. If the tax-gatherer, or any other public officer, asks me, as one has done, "But what shall I do?" My answer is, "If you really wish to do anything, resign your office." When the subject has refused allegiance, and the officer has resigned his office, then the revolution is accomplished. But even suppose blood should flow. Is there not a sort of blood shed when the conscience is wounded? Through this wound a man's real manhood and immortality flow out, and he bleeds to an everlasting death. I see this blood flowing now. . . .

The authority of government, even such as I am willing to submit to,— for I will cheerfully obey those who know and can do better than I, and in many things even those who neither know nor can do so well,—is still an impure one: to be strictly just, it must have the sanction and consent of the governed. It can have no pure right over my person and property but what I concede to it. The progress from an absolute to a limited monarchy, from a limited monarchy to a democracy, is a progress toward a true respect for the individual. Even the Chinese philosopher was wise enough to regard the individual as the basis of the empire. Is a democracy, such as we know it, the last improvement possible in government? Is it not possible to take a step further towards recognizing and organizing the rights of man? There will never be a really free and enlightened State until the State comes to recognize the individual as a higher and independent power, from which all its own power and authority are derived, and treats him accordingly. I please myself with imagining a State at last which can afford to be just to all men, and to treat the individual with respect as a neighbor; which even would not think it inconsistent with its own repose if a few were to live aloof from it, not meddling with it, nor embraced by it, who fulfilled all the duties of neighbors and fellow-men. A State which bore this kind of fruit, and suffered it to drop off as fast as it ripened, would prepare the way for a still more perfect and glorious State, which also I have imagined, but not yet anywhere seen.

TREATY OF GUADALUPE HIDALGO

Nicholas Trist   *February 2, 1848*

In the 1820s southerners began settling in the Mexican province of Texas. The American cotton and slavery frontier had temporarily reached beyond the borders of the United States. Achieving independence in 1836, Texas's application for admission to statehood was blocked by northern abolitionists, though southern politicians continued to press for the fulfillment of the nation's "manifest destiny." In the meantime, Antonio Lopez de Santa Anna had returned to the presidency of the Mexican Republic, and was determined to regain the lost province of Texas.

Texas was finally admitted to the union in 1845 and her border dispute with Mexico became a national problem. President James K. Polk's decision to send General Zachary Taylor's army to the Rio Grande in early 1846 provoked the Mexican declaration of war. From the beginning, the war went badly for Mexico, and in April 1847, Nicholas Trist was sent to Mexico to negotiate a treaty. Trist concluded the Treaty of Guadalupe Hidalgo on February 2, 1848. Victory brought the United States a block of land comprising over half of the Mexican nation, stretching to the Pacific. This expansion had dramatic consequences, widening the gulf between the United States and Latin America, and intensifying the internal division over the question of slavery.

ART. I. There shall be firm and universal peace between the United States of America and the Mexican Republic, and between their respective countries, territories, cities, towns, and people, without exception of place or persons. . . .

[Articles II-IV makes the conventional provisions for the cessation of hostilities, restoration of property, exchange of prisoners, and withdrawal of occupation troops.]

ART. V. The boundary line between the two Republics shall commence in the Gulf of Mexico, three leagues from land, opposite the mouth of the Rio Grande, otherwise called Rio Bravo del Norte, or opposite the mouth of its deepest branch, if it should have more than one branch emptying directly into the sea; from thence up the middle of that river, following the deepest channel, where it has more than one, to the point where it strikes the southern boundary of New Mexico; thence, westwardly, along the whole southern boundary of New Mexico (which runs north of the town called *Paso*) to its western termination; thence, northward, along the western line of New Mexico, until it intersects the first branch of the River Gila; (or if it should not intersect any branch of that river, then to the point on the said line nearest to such branch, and thence in a direct line to the same;) thence down the middle of the said branch and of the said river, until it empties into the Rio Colorado; thence across the Rio Colorado, following the division line between Upper and Lower California, to the Pacific Ocean. . . .

ART. VI. The vessels and citizens of the United States shall, in all times, have a free and uninterrupted passage by the Gulf of California, and by the River Colorado below its affluence with the Gila, to and from their possessions north of the boundary line defined in the previous article. . . .

ART. VII. The River Gila, and the part of the Rio Bravo del Norte lying below the southern boundary of New Mexico, being, aggreeably to the fifth article, divided in the middle between the two republics, the navigation of the Gila and of the Bravo below said boundary shall be free and common to the vessels and citizens of both countries; and neither shall, without the consent of the other, construct any work that may impede or interrupt, in whole or in part, the exercise of this right; not even for the purpose of favoring new methods of navigation. . . .

ART. VIII. Mexicans now established in territories previously belonging to Mexico, and which remain for the future within the limits of the United States, as defined by the present treaty, shall be free to continue where they now reside, or to remove at any time to the Mexican republic, retaining the property which they possess in the said territories, or disposing thereof, and removing the proceeds wherever they please, without their being subjected, on this account, to any contribution, tax, or charge whatever. . . .

ART. IX. The Mexicans who, in their territories aforesaid, shall not preserve the character of citizens of the Mexican Republic . . . shall be admitted into the Union of the United States, and be admitted at the proper time (to be judged by the Congress of the United States) to the enjoyment of all the rights of citizens of the United States. . . .

ART. XII. In consideration of the extension acquired by the boundaries of the United States, as defined in the fifth article of the present treaty, the Government of the United States engages to pay to that of the Mexican Republic the sum of fifteen millions of dollars. . . .

ART. XIII. The United States engage, moreover, to assume and pay to the claimants all the amounts now due them, and those hereafter to become due, by reason of the claims already liquidated and decided against the Mexican Republic, under the conventions between the two republics severally concluded on the eleventh day of April, eighteen hundred and thirty-nine, and on the thirtieth day of January, eighteen hundred and forty-three; so that the Mexican Republic shall be absolutely exempt, for the future, from all expense whatever on account of the said claims.

ART. XIV. The United States do furthermore discharge the Mexican Republic from all claims of citizens of the United States, not heretofore decided against the Mexican Government, which may have arisen previously to the date of the signature of this treaty; which discharge shall be final and perpetual, whether the said claims be rejected or be allowed by the board of commissioners provided for in the following article, and whatever shall be the total amount of those allowed. . . .

ART. XV. The United States, exonerating Mexico from all demands on account of the claims of their citizens mentioned in the preceding article, and considering them entirely and forever cancelled, whatever their amount may be, undertake to make satisfaction for the same, to an amount not exceeding three and one quarter millions of dollars. . . .

ART. XXI. If unhappily any disagreement should hereafter arise between the governments of the two republics, whether with respect to the interpretation of any stipulation in this treaty, or with respect to any other particular concerning the political or commercial relations of the two nations, the said governments, in the name of those nations, do promise to each other that they will endeavor, in the most sincere and earnest manner, to settle the differences so arising, and to preserve the state of peace and friendship in which the two countries are now placing themselves; using, for this end, mutual representations and pacific negotiations. And if, by these means, they should not be enabled to come to an agreement, a resort shall not, on this account, be had to reprisals, aggression, or hostility of any kind, by the one republic against the other, until the Government of that which deems itself aggrieved shall have maturely considered, in the spirit of peace and good neighborship, whether it would not be better that such difference should be settled by the arbitration of commissioners appointed on each side, or by that of a friendly nation. And should such course be proposed by either party, it shall be acceded to by the other, unless deemed by it altogether incompatible with the nature of the difference, or circumstances of the case.

SENECA FALLS DECLARATION OF SENTIMENTS AND RESOLUTIONS

Elizabeth C. Stanton   *July 19, 1848*
and Lucretia Mott

The revivalist reform movement of the early nineteenth century spawned a generation of social campaigns. The abolition of slavery was one; the women's suffrage movement was another.

Elizabeth Cady Stanton and Lucretia Mott organized the first national women's rights meeting at Seneca Falls, New York, July 19–20, 1848. The convention opened with the reading of a declaration of rights for women, and the passage of a series of resolutions including a demand for suffrage. The content of the declaration has interesting parallels with the French Revolutionary Declaration of the Rights of Woman, while the style is both a parody of and tribute to the Declaration of Independence.

---

1. DECLARATION OF SENTIMENTS

When, in the course of human events, it becomes necessary for one portion of the family of man to assume among the people of the earth a position different from that which they have hitherto occupied, but one to which the laws of nature and of nature's God entitle them, a decent respect to the opinions of mankind requires that they should declare the causes that impel them to such a course.

We hold these truths to be self-evident: that all men and women are created equal; that they are endowed by their Creator with certain inalienable rights; that among these are life, liberty, and the pursuit of happiness; that to secure these rights governments are instituted, deriving their just powers from the consent of the governed. Whenever any form of government becomes destructive of these ends, it is the right of those who suffer from it to refuse allegiance to it, and to insist upon the institution of a new government, laying its foundation on such principles, and organizing its powers in such form, as to them shall seem most likely to effect their safety and happiness. Prudence, indeed, will dictate that governments long established should not be changed for

Elizabeth Cady Stanton, artist unknown.

light and transient causes; and accordingly all experience hath shown that mankind are more disposed to suffer while evils are sufferable, than to right themselves by abolishing the forms to which they are accustomed. But when a long train of abuses and usurpations, pursuing invariably the same object, evinces a design to reduce them under absolute despotism, it is their duty to throw off such government, and to provide new guards for their future security. Such has been the patient sufferance of the women under this government, and such is now the necessity which constrains them to demand the equal station to which they are entitled.

The history of mankind is a history of repeated injuries and usurpations on the part of man toward woman, having in direct object the establishment of an absolute tyranny over her. To prove this, let facts be submitted to a candid world.

He has never permitted her to exercise her inalienable right to the elective franchise.

He has compelled her to submit to laws, in the formation of which she had no voice.

He has withheld from her rights which are given to the most ignorant and degraded men—both natives and foreigners.

Having deprived her of this first right of a citizen, the elective franchise, thereby leaving her without representation in the halls of legislation, he has oppressed her on all sides.

He has made her, if married, in the eye of the law, civilly dead.

He has taken from her all right in property, even to the wages she earns.

He has made her, morally, an irresponsible being, as she can commit many crimes with impunity, provided they be done in the presence of her husband. In the covenant of marriage, she is compelled to promise obedience to her husband, he becoming, to all intents and purposes, her master—the law giving him power to deprive her of her liberty, and to administer chastisement.

He has so framed the laws of divorce, as to what shall be the proper causes, and in case of separation, to whom the guardianship of the children shall be given, as to be wholly regardless of the happiness of women—the law, in all cases, going upon a false supposition of the supremacy of man, and giving all power into his hands.

After depriving her of all rights as a married woman, if single, and the owner of property, he has taxed her to support a government which recognizes her only when her property can be made profitable to it.

He has monopolized nearly all the profitable employments, and from those she is permitted to follow, she receives but a scanty remuneration. He closes against her all the avenues to wealth and distinction which he considers most honorable to himself. As a teacher of theology, medicine, or law, she is not known.

He has denied her the facilities for obtaining a thorough education, all colleges being closed against her.

He allows her in Church, as well as State, but a subordinate position, claiming Apostolic authority for her exclusion from the ministry, and, with some exceptions, from any public participation in the affairs of the Church.

He has created a false public sentiment by giving to the world a different code of morals for men and women, by which moral delinquencies which exclude women from society, are not only tolerated, but deemed of little account in man.

He has usurped the prerogative of Jehovah himself, claiming it as his right to assign for her a sphere of action, when that belongs to her conscience and to her God.

He has endeavored, in every way that he could, to destroy her confidence in her own powers, to lessen her self-respect and to make her willing to lead a dependent and abject life.

Now, in view of this entire disfranchisment of one-half the people of this country, their social and religious degradation—in view of the unjust laws above mentioned, and because women do feel themselves aggrieved, oppressed, and fraudulently deprived of their most sacred rights, we insist that they have immediate admission to all the rights and privileges which belong to them as citizens of the United States.

In entering upon the great work before us, we anticipate no small amount of misconception, misrepresentation, and ridicule; but we shall use every instrumentality within our power to effect our object. We shall employ agents, circulate tracts, petition the State and National legislatures, and endeavor to enlist the pulpit and the press in our behalf. We hope this Convention will be followed by a series of Conventions embracing every part of the country.

2. RESOLUTIONS

WHEREAS, The great precept of nature is conceded to be, that "man shall pursue his own true and substantial happiness." Blackstone in his Commentaries remarks, that this law of Nature being coeval with mankind, and dictated by God himself, is of course superior in obligation to any other. It is binding over all the globe, in all countries and at all times; no human laws are of any validity if contrary to this, and such of them as are valid, derive all their force, and all their validity, and all their authority, mediately and immediately, from this original; therefore,

Resolved, That all laws which prevent woman from occupying such a station in society as her conscience shall dictate, or which place her in a position inferior to that of man, are contrary to the great precept of nature, and therefore of no force or authority.

Resolved, That woman is man's equal—was intended to be so by the Creator, and the highest good of the race demands that she should be recognized as such.

Resolved, That the women of this country ought to be enlightened in regard to the laws under which they live, that they may no longer publish their degradation by declaring themselves satisfied with their present position, nor their ignorance, by asserting that they have all the rights they want.

Resolved, That inasmuch as man, while claiming for himself intellectual superiority, does accord to woman moral superiority, it is pre-eminently his duty to encourage her to speak and teach, as she has an opportunity, in all religious assemblies.

Resolved, That the same amount of virtue, delicacy, and refinement of behavior that is required of woman in the social state, should also be required of man, and the same transgressions should be visited with equal severity on both man and woman.

Resolved, That the objection of indelicacy and impropriety, which is so often brought against woman when she addresses a public audience, comes with a very ill-grace from those who encourage, by their attendance, her appearance on the stage, in the concert, or in feats of the circus.

Resolved, That woman has too long rested satisfied in the circumscribed limits which corrupt customs and a perverted application of the Scriptures have marked out for her, and that it is time she should move in the enlarged sphere which her great Creator has assigned her.

Resolved, That it is the duty of the women of this country to secure to themselves their sacred right to the elective franchise.

Resolved, That the equality of human rights results necessarily from the fact of the identity of the race in capabilities and responsibilities.

Resolved, That the speedy success of our cause depends upon the zealous and untiring efforts of both men and women, for the overthrow of the monopoly of the pulpit, and for the securing to women an equal participation with men in the various trades, professions, and commerce.

Resolved, therefore, That, being invested by the creator with the same capabilities, and the same consciousness of responsibility for their exercise, it is demonstrably the right and duty of woman, equally with man, to promote every righteous cause by every righteous means; and especially in regard to the great subjects of morals and religion, it is self-evidently her right to participate with her brother in teaching them, both in private and in public, by writing and by speaking, by any instrumentalities proper to be used, and in any assemblies proper to be held; and this being a self-evident truth growing out of the divinely implanted principles of human nature, any custom or authority adverse to it, whether modern or wearing the hoary sanction of antiquity, is to be regarded as a self-evident falsehood, and at war with mankind.

LETTER TO THOMAS AULD,
HIS FORMER MASTER

Frederick Douglass   *September 3, 1848*

———————

Proslavery advocates maintained that blacks were inherently inferior to whites and could not compete equally if emancipated. One of the best rebuttals to this view was Frederick Douglass himself: intelligent, educated and an eloquent spokesman for the abolition of slavery and for black civil rights.

Born on a Maryland plantation in 1817, Douglass was sent to Baltimore at the age of eight to work as a house servant.

*His master's wife taught Douglass to read and write, defying a
state law prohibiting education of slaves. In 1833, his first
escape attempt was thwarted, but five years later, masquerading
as a sailor, he fled to New Bedford, Massachusetts, where he
worked as a laborer for three years. In 1841, he was invited to
speak at an abolitionist meeting in Nantucket. His eloquent
remarks immediately thrust him into the forefront of the
antislavery movement. Until his death in 1895, Douglass
remained a leading advocate of black rights.*

———————————

SIR—The long and intimate, though by no means friendly relation which
unhappily subsisted between you and myself, leads me to hope that you will
easily account for the great liberty which I now take in addressing you in this
open and public manner. The same fact may possibly remove any disagreeable
surprise which you may experience on again finding your name coupled with
mine, in any other way than in an advertisement, accurately describing my
person, and offering a large sum for my arrest. In thus dragging you again before
the public, I am aware that I shall subject myself to no inconsiderable amount
of censure. I shall probably be charged with an unwarrantable, if not a wanton
and reckless disregard of the rights and proprieties of private life. There are those
North as well as South who entertain a much higher respect for rights which are
merely conventional, than they do for rights which are personal and essential.
Not a few there are in our country, who, while they have no scruples against
robbing the laborer of the hard earned results of his patient industry, will be
shocked by the extremely indelicate manner of bringing your name before the
public. Believing this to be the case, and wishing to meet every reasonable or
plausible objection to my conduct, I will frankly state the ground upon which
I justify myself in this instance, as well as on former occasions when I have
thought proper to mention your name in public.

All will agree that a man guilty of theft, robbery, or murder, has forfeited
the right to concealment and private life; that the community have a right to
subject such persons to the most complete exposure. However much they may
desire retirement, and aim to conceal themselves and their movements from the
popular gaze, the public have a right to ferret them out, and bring their conduct
before the proper tribunals of the country for investigation. Sir, you will undoubtedly make the proper application of these generally admitted principles, and will
easily see the light in which you are regarded by me, I will not therefore manifest
ill temper, by calling you hard names. I know you to be a man of some intelligence, and can readily determine the precise estimate which I entertain of your

character. I may therefore indulge in language which may seem to others indirect and ambiguous, and yet be quite well understood by yourself.

I have selected this day on which to address you, because it is the anniversary of my emancipation; and knowing of no better way, I am led to this as the best mode of celebrating that truly important event. Just ten years ago this beautiful September morning, yon bright sun beheld me a slave—a poor, degraded chattel—trembling at the sound of your voice, lamenting that I was a

man, and wishing myself a brute. The hopes which I had treasured up for weeks of a safe and successful escape from your grasp, were powerfully confronted at this late hour by dark clouds of doubt and fear, making my person shake and my bosom to heave with the heavy contest between hope and fear. I have no words to describe to you the deep agony of soul which I experienced on that never to be forgotten morning—(for I left by daylight.) I was making a leap in the dark. The probabilities, so far as I could by reason determine them, were stoutly against the undertaking. The prelimi-

Frederick Douglass, photographer unknown.

naries and precautions I had adopted previously, all worked badly. I was like one going to war without weapons—ten chances of defeat to one of victory. One in whom I had confided, and one who had promised me assistance, appalled by fear at the trial hour, deserted me, thus leaving the responsibility of success or failure solely with myself. You, sir, can never know my feelings. As I look back to them, I can scarcely realize that I have passed through a scene so trying. Trying however as they were, and gloomy as was the prospect, thanks be to the Most High, who is ever the God of the oppressed, at the moment which was to determine my whole earthly career. His grace was sufficient, my mind was made up. I embraced the golden opportunity, took the morning tide at the flood, and a free man, young, active and strong, is the result.

I have often thought I should like to explain to you the grounds upon which I have justified myself in running away from you. I am almost ashamed to do so now, for by this time you may have discovered them yourself. I will, however, glance at them. When yet but a child about six years old, I imbibed the determination to run away. The very first mental effort that I now remember on my part, was an attempt to solve the mystery, Why am I a slave? and with this question my youthful mind was troubled for many days, pressing upon me more heavily at times than others. When I saw the slave-driver whip a slave woman, cut the blood out of her neck, and heard her piteous cries, I went away into the corner of the fence, wept and pondered over the mystery. I had, through some medium, I know not what, got some idea of God, the Creator of all mankind, the black and the white, and that he had made the blacks to serve the whites as slaves. How he could do this and be good, I could not tell. I was not satisfied with this theory, which made God responsible for slavery, for it pained me greatly, and I have wept over it long and often. At one time, your first wife, Mrs. Lucretia, heard me singing and saw me shedding tears, and asked of me the matter, but I was afraid to tell her. I was puzzled with this question, till one night, while sitting in the kitchen, I heard some of the old slaves talking of their parents having been stolen from Africa by white men, and were sold here as slaves. The whole mystery was solved at once. Very soon after this my aunt Jinny and uncle Noah ran away, and the great noise made about it by your father-in-law, made me for the first time acquainted with the fact, that there were free States as well as slave States.

From that time, I resolved that I would some day run away. The morality of the act, I dispose as follows: I am myself; you are yourself; we are two distinct persons, equal persons. What you are, I am. You are a man, and so am I. God created both, and made us separate beings. I am not by nature bound to you, or you to me. Nature does not make your existence depend upon me, or mine to depend upon yours. I cannot walk upon you legs, or you upon mine. I cannot breathe for you, or you for me; I must breathe for myself, and you for yourself. We are distinct persons, and are each equally provided with faculties necessary to our individual existence. In leaving you, I took nothing but what belonged to me, and in no way lessened your means for obtaining an honest living. Your faculties remained yours, and mine became useful to their rightful owner. I therefore see no wrong in any part of the transaction. It is true, I went off secretly, but that was more your fault than mine. Had I let you into the secret, you would have defeated the enterprise entirely; but for this, I should have been really glad to have made you acquainted with my intentions to leave.

You may perhaps want to know how I like my present condition. I am free to say, I greatly prefer it to that which I occupied in Maryland. I am, however, by no means prejudiced against the State as such. Its geography, climate, fertility and products, are such as to make it a very desirable abode for any man; and but for the existence of slavery there, it is not impossible that I might again take up my abode in that State. It is not that I love Maryland less, but freedom more. . . .

. . . After remaining in New Bedford for three years, I met with Wm. Lloyd Garrison, a person of whom you have possibly heard, as he is pretty generally known among slaveholders. He put it into my head that I might make myself serviceable to the cause of the slave by devoting a portion of my time to telling my own sorrows, and those of other slaves which had come under my observation. This was the commencement of a higher state of existence than any to which I had ever aspired. I was thrown into society the most pure, enlightened and benevolent that the country affords. Among these I have never forgotten you, but have invariably made you the topic of conversation—thus giving you all the notoriety I could do. I need not tell you that the opinion formed of you in these circles, is far from being favorable. They have little respect for your honesty, and less for your religion. . . .

So far as my domestic affairs are concerned, I can boast of as comfortable a dwelling as your own. I have an industrious and neat companion, and four dear children—the oldest a girl of nine years, and three fine boys, the oldest eight, the next six, and the youngest four years old. The three oldest are now going regularly to school—two can read and write, and the other can spell with tolerable correctness words of two syllables: Dear fellows! they are all in comfortable beds, and are sound asleep, perfectly secure under my own roof. There are no slaveholders here to rend my heart by snatching them from my arms, or blast a mother's dearest hopes by tearing them from her bosom. These dear children are ours—not to work up into rice, sugar and tobacco, but to watch over, regard, and protect, and to rear them up in the nurture and admonition of the gospel—to train them up in the paths of wisdom and virtue, and, as far as we can to make them useful to the world and to themselves. Oh! sir, a slaveholder never appears to me so completely an agent of hell, as when I think of and look upon my dear children. It is then that my feelings rise above my control.

I meant to have said more with respect to my own prosperity and happiness, but thoughts and feelings which this recital has quickened unfits me to proceed further in that direction. The grim horrors of slavery rise in all their ghastly terror before me, the wails of millions pierce my heart, and chill my blood. I remember the chain, the gag, the bloody whip, the death-like gloom over-shadowing the broken spirit of the fettered bondman, the appalling liability of his being torn away from wife and children, and sold like a beast in the market. Say not that this is a picture of fancy. You well know that I wear stripes on my back inflicted by your direction; and that you, while we were brothers in the same church, caused this right hand, with which I am now penning this letter, to be closely tied to my left, and my person dragged at the pistol's mouth, fifteen miles, from the Bay side to Easton to be sold like a beast in the market, for the alleged crime of intending to escape from your possession. All this and more you remember, and know to be perfectly true, not only of yourself, but of nearly all of the slaveholders around you.

At this moment, you are probably the guilty holder of at least three of my own dear sisters, and my only brother in bondage. These you regard as your property. They are recorded on your ledger, or perhaps have been sold to human flesh mongers, with a view to filling your own ever-hungry purse. Sir, I desire to know how and where these dear sisters are. Have you sold them? or are they still in your possession? What has become of them? are they living or dead? And my dear old grandmother, whom you turned out like an old horse, to die in the woods—is she still alive? Write and let me know all about them. If my grandmother be still alive, she is of no service to you, for by this time she must be nearly eighty years old—too old to be cared for by one to whom she has ceased to be of service, send her to me at Rochester, or bring her to Philadelphia, and it shall be the crowning happiness of my life to take care of her in her old age. Oh! she was to me a mother, and a father, so far as hard toil for my comfort could make her such. Send me my grandmother! that I may watch over and take care of her in her old age. And my sisters, let me know all about them. I would write to them, and learn all I want to know of them, without disturbing you in any way, but that, through your unrighteous conduct, they have been entirely deprived of the power to read and write. You have kept them in utter ignorance, and have therefore robbed them of the sweet enjoyments of writing or receiving letters from absent friends and relatives. Your wickedness and cruelty committed in this respect on your fellow-creatures, are greater than all the stripes you have laid upon my back, or theirs. It is an outrage upon the soul—a war upon the immortal spirit, and one for which you must give account at the bar of our common Father and Creator.

The responsibility which you have assumed in this regard is truly awful—and how you could stagger under it these many years is marvellous. Your mind must have become darkened, your heart hardened, your conscience seared and petrified, or you would have long since thrown off the accursed load and sought relief at the hands of a sin-forgiving God. How, let me ask, would you look upon me, were I some dark night in company with a band of hardened villains, to enter the precincts of your elegant dwelling and seize the person of your own lovely daughter Amanda, and carry her off from your family, friends and all the loved ones of her youth—make her my slave—compel her to work, and I take her wages—place her name on my leger as property—disregard her personal rights—fetter the powers of her immortal soul by denying her the right and privilege of learning to read and write—feed her coarsely—clothe her scantily, and whip her on the naked back occasionally; more and still more horrible, leave her unprotected—a degraded victim to the brutal lust of fiendish overseers, who would pollute, blight, and blast her fair soul—rob her of all dignity—destroy her virtue, and annihilate all in her person the graces that adorn the character of virtuous womanhood? I ask how would you regard me, if such were my conduct? Oh! the vocabulary of the damned would not afford a word sufficiently infernal, to express your idea of my God-provoking wickedness. Yet sir, your treatment of my beloved sisters is in all essential points, precisely like the case I have now supposed. Damning as would be such a deed on my part, it would be no more so than that which you have committed against me and my sisters.

I will now bring this letter to a close, you shall hear from me again unless you let me hear from you. I intend to make use of you as a weapon with which to assail the system of slavery—as a means of concentrating public attention on the system, and deepening their horror of trafficking in the souls and bodies of men. I shall make use of you as a means of exposing the character of the American church and clergy—and as a means of bringing this guilty nation with yourself to repentance. In doing this I entertain no malice towards you personally. There is no roof under which you would be more safe than mine, and there is nothing in my house which you might need for your comfort, which I would not readily grant. Indeed, I should esteem it a privilege, to set you an example as to how mankind ought to treat each other.

I am your fellow man, but not your slave.
Frederick Douglass

Resolutions; The Compromise of 1850

Henry Clay   *January 29–September 20, 1850*

> *The acquisition of vast new territories from Mexico in 1848 once again raised the question of national control over the expansion of slavery. In the presidential election of 1848, the Democratic Party had attempted to address the issue through the doctrine of "popular sovereignty," declaring that the settlers in the new territories, rather than Congress, should decide whether they would be slave or free. The Whig Party candidate, Zachary Taylor, a southerner, a slaveholder and a war hero, decided to avoid the issue altogether, and won the election.*
>
> *Other events helped bring the crisis to a head. The new state of Texas was pressing claims to much of the land ceded by Mexico, implying the continued expansion of the slave frontier.*

*Meanwhile, a one-term representative from Illinois, Abraham
Lincoln, had introduced legislation to emancipate slaves in the
District of Columbia.*

*As the issues lined up in a deadlock, the political system
came to a standstill. For the last time, the "Old Compromiser,"
Henry Clay, stepped forward with an accommodation, which he
proposed on January 29, 1850, and which became law in
September. Northerners were mollified by measures admitting
California as a free state and ending the slave trade in the
District of Columbia; southerners were reassured by the organization of the remaining territories on the basis of popular
sovereignty, national assumption of Texas's debts and the
passage of a fugitive slave bill.*

---

1. CLAY'S RESOLUTIONS
January 29, 1850

IT being desirable, for the peace, concord, and harmony of the Union of
these States, to settle and adjust amicably all existing questions of controversy
between them arising out of the institution of slavery upon a fair, equitable and
just basis: therefore,

1. Resolved, That California, with suitable boundaries, ought, upon her
application to be admitted as one of the States of this Union, without the
imposition by Congress of any restriction in respect to the exclusion or
introduction of slavery within those boundaries.

2. Resolved, That as slavery does not exist by law, and is not likely to be
introduced into any of the territory acquired by the United States from the republic of Mexico, it is inexpedient for Congress to provide by law either for its introduction into, or exclusion from, any part of the said territory; and that appropriate
territorial governments ought to be established by Congress in all of the said
territory, not assigned as the boundaries of the proposed State of California,
without the adoption of any restriction or condition on the subject of slavery.

3. Resolved, That the western boundary of the State of Texas ought to be
fixed on the Rio del Norte, commencing one marine league from its mouth, and
running up that river to the southern line of New Mexico; thence with that line
eastwardly, and so continuing in the same direction to the line as established
between the United States and Spain, excluding any portion of New Mexico,
whether lying on the east or west of that river.

4. Resolved, That it be proposed to the State of Texas, that the United States will provide for the payment of all that portion of the legitimate and *bona fide* public debt of that State contracted prior to its annexation to the United States, and for which the duties on foreign imports were pledged by the said State to its creditors, not exceeding the sum of___dollars, in consideration of the said duties so pledged having been no longer applicable to that object after the said annexation, but having thenceforward become payable to the United States; and upon the condition, also, that the said State of Texas shall, by some solemn and authentic act of her legislature or of a convention, relinquish to the United States any claim which it has to any part of New Mexico.

5. Resolved, That it is inexpedient to abolish slavery in the District of Columbia whilst that institution continues to exist in the State of Maryland, without the consent of that State, without the consent of the people of the District, and without just compensation to the owners of slaves within the District.

6. But, resolved, That it is expedient to prohibit, within the District, the slave trade in slaves brought into it from States or places beyond the limits of the District, either to be sold therein as merchandise, or to be transported to other markets without the District of Columbia.

7. Resolved, That more effectual provision ought to be made by law, according to the requirement of the constitution, for the restitution and delivery of persons bound to service or labor in any State, who may escape into any other State or Territory in the Union. And,

8. Resolved, That Congress has no power to promote or obstruct the trade in slaves between the slaveholding States; but that the admission or exclusion of slaves brought from one into another of them, depends exclusively upon their own particular laws.

2. The Texas and New Mexico Act

September 9, 1850

Be it enacted, That the following propositions shall be, and the same hereby are, offered to the State of Texas, which, when agreed to by the said State, and in an act passed by the general assembly, shall be binding and obligatory, upon the United States, and upon the said State of Texas: Provided, The said agreement by the said general assembly shall be given on or before the first day of December, eighteen hundred and fifty:

FIRST. The State of Texas will agree that her boundary on the north shall commence at the point at which the meridian of one hundred degrees west from

Greenwich is intersected by the parallel of thirty-six degrees thirty minutes north latitude, and shall run from said point due west to the meridian of one hundred and three degrees west from Greenwich; thence her boundary shall run due south to the thirty-second degree of north latitude; thence on the said parallel of thirty-two degrees of north latitude to the Rio Bravo del Norte, and thence with the channel of said river to the Gulf of Mexico.

SECOND. The State of Texas cedes to the United States all her claim to territory exterior to the limits and boundaries which she agrees to establish by the first article of this agreement.

THIRD. The State of Texas relinquishes all claim upon the United States for liability of the debts of Texas, and for compensation or indemnity for the surrender to the United States of her ships, forts, arsenals, custom-houses, custom-house revenue, arms and munitions of war, and public buildings with their sites, which became the property of the United States at the time of the annexation.

FOURTH. The United States, in consideration of said establishment of boundaries, cession of claim to territory, and relinquishment of claims, will pay to the State of Texas the sum of ten millions of dollars in a stock bearing five per cent. interest, and redeemable at the end of fourteen years, the interest payable half-yearly at the treasury of the United States. . . .

SEC. 2. And, That all that portion of the Territory of the United States bounded as follows (boundaries) . . . is hereby erected into a temporary government, by the name of the Territory of New Mexico: Provided, That nothing in this act contained shall be construed to inhibit the government of the United States from dividing said Territory into two or more Territories, in such manner and at such times as Congress shall deem convenient and proper, or from attaching any portion thereof to any other Territory or State: And provided, further, That, when admitted as a State, the said Territory, or any portion of the same, shall be received into the Union, with our without slavery, as their constitution may prescribe at the time of their admission.

3. THE UTAH ACT

September 9, 1850

Be it enacted, That all that part of the territory of the United States included within the following limits, to wit: bounded on the west by the State of California, on the north by the Territory of Oregon, and on the east by the summit of the

Rocky Mountains, and on the south by the thirty-seventh parallel of north latitude, be, and the same is hereby, created into a temporary government, by the name of the Territory of Utah; and when admitted as a State, the said Territory, or any portion of the same, shall be received into the Union, with or without slavery, as their constitution may prescribe at the time of their admission: Provided, That nothing in this act contained shall be construed to inhibit the government of the United States from dividing said Territory into two or more Territories, in such manner and at such times as Congress shall deem convenient and proper, or from attaching any portion of said Territory to any other State or Territory of the United States. . . .

4. FUGITIVE SLAVE ACT

September 18, 1850

. . . SEC. 5. That it shall be the duty of all marshals and deputy marshals to obey and execute all warrants and precepts issued under the provisions of this act, when to them directed; and should any marshal or deputy marshal refuse to receive such warrant, or other process, when tendered, or to use all proper means diligently to execute the same, he shall, on conviction thereof, be fined in the sum of one thousand dollars, to the use of such claimant, . . . and after arrest of such fugitive, by such marshal or his deputy, or whilst at any time in his custody under the provisions of this act, should such fugitive escape, whether with or without the assent of such marshal or his deputy, such marshal shall be liable, on his official bond, to be prosecuted for the benefit of such claimant, for the full value of the service or labor of said fugitive in the State, Territory, or District whence he escaped: and the better to enable the said commissioners, when thus appointed, to execute their duties faithfully and efficiently, in conformity with the requirements of the Constitution of the United States and of this act, they are hereby authorized and empowered, within their counties respectively, to appoint, . . . any one or more suitable persons, from time to time, to execute all such warrants and other process as may be issued by them in the lawful performance of their respective duties; with authority to such commissioners, or the persons to be appointed by them, to execute process as aforesaid, to summon and call to their aid the bystanders, or *posse comitatus* of the proper county, when necessary to ensure a faithful observance of the clause of the Constitution referred to, in conformity with the provisions of this act; and all good citizens are hereby commanded to aid and assist in the prompt and efficient execution of this law, whenever their services may be required, as aforesaid, for that purpose; and said warrants shall run, and be executed by said officers, any where in the State within which they are issued.

SEC. 6. That when a person held to service or labor in any State or Territory of the United States, has heretofore or shall hereafter escape into another State or Territory of the United States, the person or persons to whom such service or labor may be due, . . . may pursue and reclaim such fugitive person, either by procuring a warrant from some one of the courts, judges, or commissioners aforesaid, of the proper circuit, district, or county, for the apprehension of such fugitive from service or labor, or be seizing and arresting such fugitive, where the same can be done without process, and by taking, or causing such person to be taken, forthwith before such court, judge, or commissioner, whose duty it shall be to hear and determine the case of such claimant in a summary manner; and upon satisfactory proof being made, by deposition or affidavit, in writing, to be taken and certified by such court, judge, or commissioner, or by other satisfactory testimony, duly taken and certified by some court, . . . and with proof, also by affidavit, of the identity of the person whose service or labor is claimed to be due as aforesaid, that the person so arrested does in fact owe service or labor to the person or persons claiming him or her, in the State or Territory from which such fugitive may have escaped as aforesaid, and that said person escaped, to make out and deliver to such claimant, his or her agent or attorney, a certificate setting forth the substantial facts as to the service or labor due from such fugitive to the claimant, and of his or her escape from the State or Territory in which he or she was arrested, with authority to such claimant, . . . to use such reasonable force and restraint as may be necessary, under the circumstances of the case, to take and remove such fugitive person back to the State or Territory whence he or she may have escaped as aforesaid. In no trial or hearing under this act shall the testimony of such alleged fugitive be admitted in evidence; and the certificates in this and the first [fourth] section mentioned, shall be conclusive of the right of the person or persons in whose favor granted, to remove such fugitive to the State or Territory from which he escaped, and shall prevent all molestation of such person or persons by any process issued by any court, judge, magistrate, or other person whomsoever.

SEC. 7. That any persons who shall knowingly and willingly obstruct, hinder, or prevent such claimant, his agent or attorney, or any person or persons lawfully assisting him, her, or them, from arresting such a fugitive from service or labor, either with or without process as aforesaid, or shall rescue, or attempt to rescue, such fugitive from service or labor, from the custody of such claimant, . . . or other person or persons lawfully assisting as aforesaid, when so arrested,

. . . or shall aid, abet, or assist such person so owing service or labor as aforesaid, directly or indirectly, to escape from such claimant, . . . or shall harbor or conceal such fugitive, so as to prevent the discovery and arrest of such person, after notice or knowledge of the fact that such person was a fugitive from service or labor . . . shall, for either of said offences, be subject to a fine not exceeding one thousand dollars, and imprisonment not exceeding six months . . . ; and shall moreover forfeit and pay, by way of civil damages to the party injured by such illegal conduct, the sum of one thousand dollars, for each fugitive so lost as aforesaid. . . .

SEC. 9. That, upon affidavit made by the claimant of such fugitive, . . . that he has reason to apprehend that such fugitive will be rescued by force from his or their possession before he can be taken beyond the limits of the State in which the arrest is made, it shall be the duty of the officer making the arrest to retain such fugitive in his custody, and to remove him to the State whence he fled, and there to deliver him to said claimant, his agent, or attorney. And to this end, the officer aforesaid is hereby authorized and required to employ so many persons as he may deem necessary to overcome such force, and to retain them in his service so long as circumstances may require. . . .

SEC. 10. That when any person held to service or labor in any State or Territory, or in the District of Columbia, shall escape therefrom, the party to whom such service or labor shall be due, . . . may apply to any court of record therein, . . . and make satisfactory proof to such court, . . . of the escape aforesaid, and that the person escaping owed service or labor to such party. Whereupon the court shall cause a record to be made of the matters so proved, and also a general description of the person so escaping, with such convenient certainty as may be; and a transcript of such record, . . . being produced in any other State, Territory, or district in which the person so escaping may be found, . . . shall be held and taken to be full and conclusive evidence of the fact of escape, and that the service or labor of the person escaping is due to the party in such record mentioned. And upon the production by the said party of other and further evidence if necessary, either oral or by affidavit, in addition to what is contained in the said record of the identity of the person escaping, he or she shall be delivered up to the claimant. And the said court, commissioner, judge, or other person authorized by this act to grant certificates to claimants of fugitives, shall, upon the production of the record and other evidences aforesaid, grant to such claimant a certificate of his right to take any such person identified and proved to be owing service or labor as aforesaid, which certificate shall authorize such claimant to seize or arrest and transport such person to the State or Territory from which he escaped. . . .

5. Act Abolishing the Slave Trade in the District of Columbia

September 20, 1850

Be enacted . . . , That from and after the first day of January, 1, 1851, it shall not be lawful to bring into the District of Columbia any slave whatever, for the purpose of being sold, or for the purpose of being placed in depot, to be subsequently transferred to any other State or place to be sold as merchandize. And if any slave shall be brought into the said District by its owner, or by the authority or consent of its owner, contrary to the provisions of this act, such slave shall thereupon become liberated and free.

SEC. 2. That it shall and may be lawful for each of the corporations of the cities of Washington and Georgetown, from time to time, and as often as may be necessary, to abate, break up, and abolish any depot or place of confinement of slaves brought into the said District as merchandize, contrary to the provisions of this act, by such appropriate means as may appear to either of the said corporations expedient and proper. And the same power is hereby vested in the Levy Court of Washington county, if any attempt shall be made, within its jurisdictional limits, to establish a depot or place of confinement for slaves brought into the said District as merchandize for sale contrary to this act.

The Seventh of March Speech

Daniel Webster   *March 7, 1850*

Since his famous debate with Senator Hayne in 1830, Daniel Webster had been recognized as the foremost advocate of national unity. In the 1840s he actively opposed both the war with Mexico and the acquisition of new territory. Nonetheless, he spoke in favor of Henry Clay's last attempt at compromise in a speech given on the floor of the Senate, March 7, 1850. As always for Webster, preservation of the Union took precedence.

MR. President,—I wish to speak to-day, not as a Massachusetts man, nor as a northern man, but as an American, and a member of the Senate of the United States. It is fortunate that there is a Senate of the United States; a body not yet moved from propriety, not lost to a just sense of its own dignity and its own high responsibilities, and a body to which the country looks, with confidence, for wise, moderate, patriotic, and healing counsels. It is not to be denied that we live in the midst of strong agitations, and are surrounded by very considerable dangers to our institutions and government. The imprisoned winds are let loose. The East, the West, the North, and the stormy South, all combine to throw the whole sea into commotion, to toss its billows to the skies, and disclose its profoundest depths. I do not affect to regard myself, Mr. President, as holding, or as fit to hold, the helm in this combat with the political elements; but I have a duty to perform, and I mean to perform it with fidelity—not without a sense of existing dangers, but not without hope. I have a part to act, not for my own security or safety, for I am looking out for no fragment upon which to float away from the wreck, if wreck there must be, but for the good of the whole, and the preservation of the whole; and there is that which will keep me to my duty during this struggle, whether the sun and the stars shall appear, or shall not appear for many days. I speak to-day for the preservation of the Union. "Hear me, for my cause." I speak to-day, out of a solicitous and anxious heart, for the restoration to the country of that quiet and that harmony which make the blessings of this union so rich and so dear to us all. These are the topics that I propose to myself to discuss; these are the motives, and the sole motives, that influence me in the wish to communicate my opinions to the Senate and the country; and if I can do anything, however little, for the promotion of these ends, I shall have accomplished all that I desire. . . .

Mr. President, I should much prefer to have heard, from every member on this floor, declarations of opinion that this Union could never be dissolved, than the declaration that in any case, under the pressure of circumstances, such a dissolution was possible. I hear with pain, and anguish, and distress, the word secession, especially when it falls from the lips of those who are eminently patriotic, and known to the country, and known all over the world, for their political services. Secession! Peaceable secession! Sir, your eyes and mine are never destined to see that miracle. The dismemberment of this vast country without convulsion! The breaking up of the fountains of the great deep without ruffling the surface! Who is so foolish—I beg every body's pardon—as to expect to see any such thing? Sir, he who sees these States, now revolving in harmony around a common centre, and expects to see them quit their places and fly off without convulsion, may look the next hour to see the heavenly bodies rush from their spheres, and jostle against each other in the realms of space, without producing the crush of the universe. There can be no such thing as a peaceable secession. Peaceable secession is an utter impossibility. Is the great Constitution under which we live—covering this whole country—is it to be thawed and melted away by secession, as the snows on the mountain melt under the influence of a vernal sun—disappear almost unobserved, and die off? No, sir! I will not state what might produce the disruption of the states; but, sir, I see it as plainly as I see the sun in heaven—I see that disruption must produce such a war as I will not describe, in its twofold characters. . . .

Sir, I may express myself too strongly, perhaps—but some things, some moral things, are almost as impossible, as other natural or physical things; and I hold the idea of a separation of these States—those that are free to form one government, and those that are slaveholding to form another—as a moral impossibility. We could not separate the States by any such line, if we were to draw it. We could not sit down here to-day and draw a line of separation, that would satisfy any five men in the country. There are natural causes that would keep and tie us together, and there are social and domestic relations which we could not break if we would, and which we should not, if we could. Sir, nobody can look over the face of this country at the present moment—nobody can see where its population is the most dense and growing—without being ready to admit, and compelled to admit, that ere long, America will be in the valley of the Mississippi. . . .

And now, Mr. President, instead of speaking of the possibility or utility of secession, instead of dwelling in these caverns of darkness, instead of groping with those ideas so full of all that is horrid and horrible, let us come out into the light of day; let us enjoy the fresh air of liberty and union; let us cherish those hopes which belong to us; let us devote ourselves to those great objects that are fit for our consideration and our action; let us raise our conceptions to the magnitude and the importance of the duties that devolve upon us; let our comprehension be as broad as the country for which we act, our aspirations as high as its certain destiny; let us not be pigmies in a case that calls for men. Never did there devolve, on any generation of men, higher trusts than now devolve upon us for the preservation of this Constitution and the harmony and peace of all who are destined to live under it. Let us make our generation one of the strongest and brightest links in that golden chain which is destined, I fully believe, to grapple the people of all the States to this Constitution, for ages to come. It is a great popular constitutional Government, guarded by legislation, law, and by judicature, and defended by the affections of the whole people. No monarchical throne presses the States together; no iron chain of military power encircles them; they live and stand upon a Government popular in its form, representative in its character, founded upon principles of equality, and calculated, we hope, as to last forever. In all its history, it has been beneficent; it has trodden down no man's liberty; it has crushed no State. Its daily respiration is liberty and patriotism; its yet youthful veins are full of enterprise, courage, and honorable love of glory and renown. Large before, the country has now, by recent events, become vastly larger. This republic now extends, with a vast breadth, across the whole continent. The two great seas of the world wash the one and the other shore. We realize on a mighty scale, the beautiful description of the ornamental border of the buckler of Achilles—

Now the broad shield complete the artist crowned,
With his last band, and poured the ocean round;
In living silver seemed the waves to roll,
And beat the buckler's verge, and bound the whole.

Ain't I a Woman?

Sojourner Truth   *May 29, 1851*

Sojourner Truth, born into slavery, became one of the great evangelist, abolitionist and feminist leaders of the nineteenth century. Born on a farm in New York in the late 1790s, the slave Isabella (her given name) spent her first three decades with several masters. Freed just before slavery was abolished in New York in 1827, she moved to New York City. There she became involved in an evangelistic missionary movement.

Taking the name Sojourner Truth, she left New York in 1843, following a call to "travel up and down the land," preaching the brotherhood of man, speaking out for abolition and fighting for women's rights. At a women's suffrage meeting in Akron, Ohio, in May 1851, she turned the tide of debate against the condescending arguments of male superiority. She rose on the second day of the convention, delivering a pointed defense of womanhood.

WELL, children, where there is so much racket there must be something out of kilter. I think that 'twixt the negroes of the South and the women at the

North, all talking about rights, the white men will be in a fix pretty soon. But what's all this here talking about?

That man over there says that women need to be helped into carriages, and lifted over ditches, and to have the best place everywhere. Nobody ever helps me into carriages, or over mud-puddles, or gives me any best place! And ain't I a woman? Look at me! Look at my arm! I have ploughed and planted, and gathered into barns, and no man could head me! And ain't I a woman? I could work as much and eat as much as a man—when I could get it—and bear the lash as well! And ain't I a woman? I have borne thirteen children, and seen them most all sold off to slavery, and when I cried out with my mother's grief, none but Jesus heard me! And ain't I a woman?

Then they talk about this thing in the head; what's this they call it? [Intellect, someone whispers.] That's it, honey. What's that got to do with women's rights or negro's rights? If my cup won't hold but a pint, and yours holds a quart, wouldn't you be mean not to let me have my little half-measure full?

Then that little man in black there, he says women can't have as much rights as men, 'cause Christ wasn't a woman! Where did your Christ come from? Where did your Christ come from? From God and a woman! Man had nothing to do with Him.

If the first woman God ever made was strong enough to turn the world upside down all alone, these women together ought to be able to turn it back, and get it right side up again! And now they is asking to do it, the men better let them.

Obliged to you for hearing me, and now old Sojourner ain't got nothing more to say.

KANSAS-NEBRASKA ACT

Stephen Douglas   *May 30, 1854*

---

*Popular sovereignty had helped to avert the crisis in
1850, but had yet to be tested. In 1854, the status of slavery in
the western territories once again became an issue. By this time
the "Great Triumvirate," Henry Clay, John C. Calhoun and
Daniel Webster, were all dead. A new generation of leaders had
arisen in the Senate, among them Stephen Douglas of Illinois.*

Hoping to avoid another divisive debate, Douglas introduced legislation to organize the territory of Nebraska on the basis of popular sovereignty. But to gain support for the bill, he had to give in to southern demands for an opportunity to compete territorially. The act was rewritten, dividing the territory along the fortieth parallel. The southern half, Kansas, was adjacent to slave-holding Missouri and open to an extension of the slave frontier, clearly violating the Missouri Compromise. The struggle for control of Kansas became the first violent conflict between North and South. By 1855, two rival territorial governments were in place and the first blood had been shed.

AN Act to Organize the Territories of Nebraska and Kansas.

Be it enacted. . . , That all that part of the territory of the United States included within the following limits, except such portions thereof as are hereinafter expressly exempted from the operations of this act, to wit: beginning at a point in the Missouri River where the fortieth parallel of north latitude crosses the same; thence west on said parallel to the east boundary of the Territory of Utah, on the summit of the Rocky Mountains; thence on said summit northward to the forty-ninth parallel of north latitude; thence east on said parallel to the western boundary of the territory of Minnesota; thence southward on said boundary to the Missouri River; thence down the main channel of said river to the place of beginning, be, and the same is hereby, created into a temporary government by the name of the Territory of Nebraska; and when admitted as a State or States, the said Territory, or any portion of the same, shall be received into the Union with or without slavery, as their constitution may prescribe at the time of their admission: . . .

SEC. 10. And be it further enacted that the provisions of an act entitled "An act respecting fugitives from justice, and persons escaping from the service of their masters," approved February 12, 1793, and the provisions of an act entitled "An act to amend and supplementary to, the aforesaid act," approved September 18, 1850, be, and the same are hereby declared to extend to and be in full force within the limits of said Territory of Nebraska. . . .

SEC. 14. And be it further enacted . . . That the Constitution, and all laws of the United States which are not locally inapplicable, shall have the same force and effect within the said Territory of Nebraska as elsewhere within the United States, except the eighth section of the act prepatory to the admission of Missouri into the Union, approved March 6, 1820, which, being inconsistent with the principle of non-intervention by Congress with slavery in the States and Territories, as recognized by the legislation of eighteen hundred and fifty, commonly called the Compromise Measures, is hereby declared inoperative and void; it being the true intent and meaning of this act not to legislate slavery into any Territory or State, nor to exclude it therefrom, but to leave the people thereof perfectly free to form and regulate their domestic institutions in their own way, subject only to the Constitution of the United States: Provided, That nothing herein contained shall be construed to revive or put in force any law or regulation which may have existed prior to the act of March 6, 1820, either protecting, establishing, prohibiting, or abolishing slavery. . . .

SEC. 19. And be it further enacted, That all that part of the Territory of the United States included within the following limits, except such portions thereof as are hereinafter expressly exempted from the operations of this act, to wit, beginning at a point on the western boundary of the State of Missouri, where the thirty-seventh parallel of north latitude crosses the same; thence west on said parallel to the eastern boundary of New Mexico; thence north on said boundary to latitude thirty-eight; thence following said boundary westward to the east boundary of the Territory of Utah, on the summit of the Rocky Mountains; thence northward on said summit to the fortieth parallel of latitude; thence east on said parallel to the western boundary of the State of Missouri; thence south with the western boundary of said State to the place of beginning, be, and the same is hereby, created into a temporary government by the name of the Territory of Kansas; and when admitted as a State or States, the said Territory, or any portion of the same, shall be received into the Union with or without slavery, as their constitution may prescribe at the time of their admission. . . .

DRED SCOTT V. SANDFORD

Roger Taney   *1857*

In 1834, Dred Scott's master, Dr. John Emerson, took him from St. Louis to an army post in Rock Island, Illinois, and, two years later, to Fort Snelling in Wisconsin Territory, returning to Missouri in 1838. In 1847, Scott sued for his freedom in the Missouri circuit court, on the grounds that his residence in a free state and a free territory had made him a free man. The circuit court judged in Scott's favor, but the decision was overturned in 1848 by the Missouri Supreme Court.

In the meantime, Scott's ownership had passed to John Sanford (Scott's petition misspelled the surname as Sandford). In 1853, Scott sued Sanford for damages, claiming illegal detention of himself and his family as slaves. Sanford's defense rested on the argument that Scott, as a slave, could not be a citizen, and therefore had no right to sue. Scott's plea was overruled, but he appealed to the Supreme Court of the United States.

The importance of Chief Justice Roger Taney's opinion goes far beyond the denial of Scott's legal rights. Taney went on to declare that residence in a free state or territory did not make a slave free, and, most significantly, that the prohibition of slavery in any of the western territories by the Missouri Compromise was unconstitutional. All at once, the Supreme Court had decided the issue of slavery for all the new territories. The Dred Scott decision seemed to indicate yet another victory for the South.

TANEY, C.J. . . . There are two leading questions presented by the record:

1. Had the Circuit Court of the United States jurisdiction to hear and determine the case between these parties? And,

2. If it has jurisdiction, is the judgment it has given erroneous or not?

The plaintiff in error, who was also the plaintiff in the court below, was, with his wife and children, held as slaves by the defendant, in the State of Missouri, and he brought this action in the Circuit Court of the United States for that district, to assert the title of himself and his family to freedom.

The declaration is in the form usually adopted in that state to try questions of this description . . . that he and the defendant are citizens of different States; that is, that he is a citizen of Missouri, and the defendant a citizen of New York.

The defendant pleaded in abatement to the jurisdiction of the court, that the plaintiff was not a citizen of the State of Missouri, as alleged in his declaration, being a negro of African descent whose ancestors were of pure African blood, and who were brought into this country and sold as slaves.

To this plea the plaintiff demurred, and the defendant joined in demurrer. . . .

Before we speak of the pleas in bar, it will be proper to dispose of the questions which have arisen on the plea in abatement.

That plea denies the right of the plaintiff to sue in a court of the United States, for the reasons therein stated.

If the question raised by it is legally before us, and the court should be of opinion that the facts stated in it disqualify the plaintiff from becoming a citizen, in the sense in which that word is used in the Constitution of the United States, then the judgment of the Circuit Court is erroneous, and must be reversed. . . .

And if the plea and demurrer, and judgment of the court below upon it, are before us upon this record, the question to be decided is, whether the facts stated in the plea are sufficient to show that the plaintiff is not entitled to sue as a citizen in a court of the United States.

This is certainly a very serious question, and one that now for the first time has been brought for decision before this court. But it is brought here by those who have a right to bring it, and it is our duty to meet it and decide it.

The question is simply this: Can a negro, whose ancestors were imported into this country, and sold as slaves, become a member of the political community formed and brought into existence by the Constitution of the United States, and as such become entitled to all the rights, and privileges, and immunities, guarantied by that instrument to the citizen? One of these rights is the privilege of suing in a court of the United States in the cases specified in the Constitution. . . .

In discussing this question, we must not confound the rights of citizenship which a state may confer within its own limits, and the rights of citizenship as a member of the Union. It does not by any means follow, because he has all the rights and privileges of a citizen of a State, that he must be a citizen of the United States. He may have all of the rights and privileges of the citizen of a State, and yet not be entitled to the rights and privileges of a citizen in any other State. For, previous to the adoption of the Constitution of the United States, every State had the undoubted right to confer on whomsoever it pleased the character of a citizen, and to endow him with all its rights. But this character, of course, was confined to the boundaries of the State, and gave him no rights or privileges in other States beyond those secured to him by the laws of nations and the comity of States. Nor have the several States surrendered the power of conferring these rights and privileges by adopting the Constitution of the United States. Each State may still confer them upon an alien, or any one it thinks proper, or upon any class or description of persons; yet he would not be a citizen in the sense in which that word is used in the Constitution of the United States, nor entitled to sue as such in one of its courts, nor to the privileges and immunities of a citizen in the other States. The rights which he would acquire would be restricted to the State which gave them. . . .

It is true, every person, and every class and description of persons, who were at the time of the adoption of the Constitution recognized as citizens in the several States, became also citizens of this new political body; but none other; it was formed by them, and for them and their posterity, but for no one else. And the personal rights and privileges guarantied to citizens of this new sovereignty were intended to embrace those only who were then members of the several state communities, or who should afterwards, by birthright or otherwise, become members, according to the provisions of the Constitution and the principles on which it was founded. . . .

It becomes necessary, therefore, to determine who were citizens of the several States when the Constitution was adopted. And in order to do this, we must recur to the governments and institutions of the thirteen Colonies, when they separated from Great Britain and formed new sovereignties . . . . We must inquire who, at that time, were recognized as the people or citizens of a State. . . .

In the opinion of the court, the legislation and histories of the times, and the language used in the Declaration of Independence, show, that neither the class of persons who had been imported as slaves, nor their descendants, whether they had become free or not, were then acknowledged as a part of the people, nor intended to be included in the general words used in that memorable instrument.

It is difficult at this day to realize the state of public opinion in relation to that unfortunate race, which prevailed in the civilized and enlightened portions of the world at the time of the Declaration of Independence, and when the Constitution of the United States was framed and adopted. . . .

They had for more than a century before been regarded as beings of an inferior order; and altogether unfit to associate with the white race, either in social or political relations; and so far inferior that they had no rights which the white man was bound to respect; and that the negro might justly and lawfully be reduced to slavery for his benefit. . . . This opinion was at that time fixed and universal in the civilized portion of the white race. It was regarded as an axiom in morals as well as in politics, which no one thought of disputing, or supposed to be open to dispute; and men in every grade and position in society daily and habitually acted upon it in their private pursuits, as well as in matters of public concern, without doubting for a moment the correctness of this opinion. . . .

The legislation of the different Colonies furnishes positive and undisputable proof of this fact. . . .

The language of the Declaration of Independence is equally conclusive. . . .

This state of public opinion had undergone no change when the Constitution was adopted, as is equally evident from its provisions and language. . . .

But there are two clauses in the Constitution which point directly and specifically to the negro race as a separate class of persons, and show clearly that they were not regarded as a portion of the people or citizens of the Government then formed.

One of these clauses reserves to each of the thirteen States the right to import slaves until the year 1808, if he thinks it proper. And the importation which it thus sanctions was unquestionably of persons of the race of which we are speaking, as the traffic in slaves in the United States has always been confined to them. And by the other provision the States pledge themselves to each other to maintain the right of property of the master, by delivering up to him any slave who may have escaped from his service, and be found within their respective territories. . . . And these two provisions show, conclusively, that neither the description of persons therein referred to, nor their descendants, were embraced in any of the other provisions of the Constitution; for certainly these two clauses were not intended to confer on them or their posterity the blessings of liberty, or any of the personal rights so carefully provided for the citizen. . . .

Indeed, when we look to the condition of this race in the several States at the time, it is impossible to believe that these rights and privileges were intended to be extended to them. . . .

And upon a full and careful consideration of the subject, the court is of opinion that, upon the facts stated in the plea in abatement, Dred Scott was not a citizen of Missouri within the meaning of the Constitution of the United States, and not entitled as such to sue in its courts; and, consequently, that the Circuit Court had no jurisdiction of the case, and that the judgment on the plea in abatement is erroneous. . . .

We proceed, therefore, to inquire whether the facts relied on by the plaintiff entitled him to his freedom. . . .

In considering this part of the controversy, two questions arise: 1st. Was he, together with his family, free in Missouri by reason of the stay in the territory of the United States hereinbefore mentioned? And 2d, If they were not, is Scott himself free by reason of his removal to Rock Island, in the State of Illinois, as stated in the above admissions?

We proceed to examine the first question.

The Act of Congress, upon which the plaintiff relies, declares that slavery and involuntary servitude, except as a punishment for crime, shall be forever prohibited in all that part of the territory ceded by France, under the name of Louisiana, which lies north of thirty-six degrees thirty minutes north latitude, and not included within the limits of Missouri. And the difficulty which meets us at the threshold of this part of the inquiry is, whether Congress was authorized to pass this law under any of the powers granted to it by the Constitution; for if the authority is not given by that instrument, it is the duty of this court to declare it void and inoperative, and incapable of conferring freedom upon any one who is held as a slave under the laws of any one of the States. . . .

But the power of Congress over the person or property of a citizen can never be a mere discretionary power under our Constitution and form of Government. The powers of the Government and the rights and privileges of the citizen are regulated and plainly defined by the Constitution itself. And when the Territory becomes a part of the United States, the Federal Government enters into possession in the character impressed upon it by those who created it. It enters upon it with its powers over the citizen strictly defined, and limited by the Constitution, from which it derives its own existence, and by virtue of which alone it continues to exist and act as a Government and sovereignty. It has no power of any kind beyond it; and it cannot, when it enters a Territory of the United States, put off its character, and assume discretionary or despotic powers which the Constitution has denied to it. It cannot create for itself a new character separated from the citizens of the United States, and the duties it owes them under the provisions of the Constitution. The Territory being a part of the United States, the Government and the citizen both enter it under the authority of the Constitution, with their respective rights defined and marked out; and the Federal Government can exercise no power over his person or property, beyond what that instrument confers, nor lawfully deny any right which it has reserved. . . .

The rights of private property have been guarded with equal care. Thus the rights of property are united with the rights of person, and placed on the same ground by the fifth amendment to the Constitution. . . . An Act of Congress which deprives a person of the United States of his liberty or property merely because he came himself or brought his property into a particular Territory of the United States, and who had committed no offense against the laws, could hardly be dignified with the name of due process of law. . . .

And this prohibition is not confined to the States, but the words are general, and extend to the whole territory over which the Constitution gives its power to legislate, including those portions of it remaining under territorial government, as well as that covered by States. . . .

Now . . . the right of property in a slave is distinctly and expressly affirmed in the Constitution. The right to traffic in it, like an ordinary article of merchandise and property, was guaranteed to the citizens of the United States, in every State that might desire it, for twenty years. And the Government in express terms is pledged to protect it in all future time, if the slave escapes from his owner. This is done in plain word—too plain to be misunderstood. And no word can be found in the Constitution which gives Congress a greater power over slave property, or which entitles property of that kind to less protection than property of any other description. The only power conferred is the power coupled with the duty of guarding and protecting the owner in his rights.

Upon these considerations, it is the opinion of the court that the Act of Congress which prohibited a citizen from holding and owning property of this kind in the territory of the United States north of the line therein mentioned, is not warranted by the Constitution, and is therefore void; and that neither Dred Scott himself, nor any of his family, were made free by being carried into this territory; even if they had been carried there by the owner, with the intention of becoming a permanent resident. . . .

Upon the whole, therefore, it is the judgment of this court, that it appears by the record before us that the plaintiff in error is not a citizen of Missouri, in the sense in which that word is used in the Constitution; and that the Circuit Court of the United States, for that reason, had no jurisdiction in the case, and could give no judgment in it.

Its judgment for the defendant must, consequently, be reversed, and a mandate issued directing the suit to be dismissed for want of jurisdiction.
Wayne, J., Nelson, J., Grier, J., Daniel, J., Campbell, J. and Catron, J., filed separate concurring opinions. McLean, J. and Curtis, J. dissented.

VI

CIVIL WAR

"HOUSE DIVIDED" SPEECH

Abraham Lincoln   *June 17, 1858*

Born February 12, 1809, Abraham Lincoln spent his first twenty-one years on frontier farms in Kentucky, Indiana and Illinois. In his young adulthood, he tried his hand at several occupations before eventually settling on the law.

Lincoln first became active in politics in the 1830s. From 1834 to 1842, he served as a Whig member of the Illinois state legislature. His legislative career was mostly involved in the promotion of economic enterprise, but in 1837 he helped draft a protest to an anti-abolition bill, maintaining that slavery was "both injustice and bad policy." Lincoln's distaste for slavery, though grounded in moral objections, stemmed mainly from its divisive effect on national politics. From 1847 to 1849, Lincoln served as the sole Whig in Illinois's congressional delegation. One of the few bills he introduced during his single term was a proposal for the gradual emancipation of slaves in the District of Columbia.

In 1856, Lincoln joined the new Republican Party and, due in part to his moderate views on slavery, soon rose to leadership among Illinois Republicans. He was chosen as the Republican candidate for the United States Senate in 1858. At

*the close of the state convention, he delivered a speech clearly
stating his belief that the nation could not continue to be
divided between two opposing economic and moral systems, a
speech that has been identified ever since by its biblical quota-
tion (Mark 3:25).*

MR. President and Gentlemen of the Convention: If we could first know where we are, and whither we are tending, we could better judge what to do, and how to do it. We are now far into the fifth year since a policy was initiated with the avowed object and confident promise of putting an end to slavery agitation. Under the operation of that policy, that agitation has not only not ceased, but has constantly augmented. In my opinion, it will not cease until a crisis shall have been reached and passed. "A house divided against itself cannot stand." I believe this government cannot endure permanently half slave and half free. I do not expect the Union to be dissolved; I do not expect the house to fall; but I do expect it will cease to be divided. It will become all one thing, or all the other. Either the opponents of slavery will arrest the further spread of it, and place it where the public mind shall rest in the belief that it is the course of ultimate extinction, or its advocates will push it forward till it shall become alike lawful in all the States, old as well as new, North as well as South.

Have we no tendency to the latter condition?

Let any one who doubts, carefully contemplate that now almost complete legal combination—piece of machinery, so to speak—compounded of the Nebraska doctrine and the Dred Scott decision. Let him consider, not only what work the machinery is adapted to do, and how well adapted, but also let him study the history of its construction and trace, if he can, or rather fail, if he can, to trace the evidences of design, and concert of action, among its chief architects, from the beginning.

The new year of 1854 found slavery excluded from more than half the States by State Constitutions, and from most of the National territory by Congressional prohibition. Four days later, commenced the struggle which ended in repealing that Congressional prohibition. This opened all the National territory to slavery, and was the first point gained. . . .

While the Nebraska Bill was passing through Congress, a law case, involving the question of a negro's freedom, by reason of his owner having voluntarily taken him first into a free State, and then into a territory covered by the Congressional prohibition, and held him as a slave for a long time in each, was passing through the United States Circuit Court for the District of Missouri; and both Nebraska Bill and lawsuit were brought to a decision in the same month of May, 1854. The negro's name was "Dred Scott," which name now designates the decision finally made in the case. Before the then next Presidential election, the law case came to, and was argued in, the Supreme Court of the United States; but the decision of it was deferred until after the election. Still, before the election, Senator Trumbull, on the floor of the Senate, requested the leading advocate of the Nebraska Bill to state his opinion whether the people of a Territory can constitutionally exclude slavery from their limits; and the latter answers: "That is a question for the Supreme Court."

Abraham Lincoln, photograph by Mathew Brady, 1864.

The election came. Mr. Buchanan was elected, and the indorsement, such as it was, secured. That was the second point gained. . . . The Presidential inauguration came, and still no decision of the court; but the incoming President, in his inaugural address, fervently exhorted the people to abide by the forthcoming decision, whatever it might be. Then, in a few days, came the decision.

The reputed author of the Nebraska Bill finds an early occasion to make a speech at this capital indorsing the Dred Scott decision, and vehemently denouncing all opposition to it. The new President, too, seizes the early occasion of the Silliman letter to indorse and strongly construe that decision, and to express his astonishment that any different view had ever been entertained!

At length a squabble springs up between the President and the author of the Nebraska Bill, on the mere question of fact, whether the Lecompton Constitution was or was not in any just sense made by the people of Kansas; and in that quarrel the latter declares that all he wants is a fair vote for the people, and that he cares not whether slavery be voted down or voted up. I do not understand his declaration, that he cares not whether slavery be voted down or voted up, to be intended by him other than as an apt definition of the policy he would impress upon the public mind. . . . That principle is the only shred left of his original Nebraska doctrine. Under the Dred Scott decision "squatter sovereignty" squatted out of existence, tumbled down like temporary scaffolding; like the mould at the foundry, served through one blast, and fell back into loose sand; helped to carry an election, and then was kicked to the winds. His late joint struggle with the Republicans, against the Lecompton Constitution, involves nothing of the original Nebraska doctrine. That struggle was made on a point—the right of a people to make their own constitution—upon which he and the Republicans have never differed.

The several points of the Dred Scott decision, in connection with Senator Douglas's "care not" policy, constitute the piece of machinery, in its present state of advancement. This was the third point gained. The working points of that machinery are:

Firstly, That no negro slave, imported as such from Africa, and no descendant of such slave, can ever be a citizen of any State, in the sense of that term as used in the Constitution of the United States. This point is made in order to deprive the negro, in every possible event, of the benefit of that provision of the United States Constitution which declares that "The citizens of each State shall be entitled to all privileges and immunities of citizens in the several States."

Secondly, That, "subject to the Constitution of the United States," neither Congress nor a Territorial Legislature can exclude slavery from any United States Territory. This point is made in order that individual men may fill up the Territories with slaves, without danger of losing them as property, and thus to enhance the chances of permanency to the institution through all the future.

Thirdly, That whether the holding a negro in actual slavery in a free State makes him free, as against the holder, the United States courts will not decide, but will leave to be decided by the courts of any slave State the negro may be forced into by the master. This point is made, not to be pressed immediately; but, if acquiesced in for a while, and apparently indorsed by the people at an election, then to sustain the logical conclusion that what Dred Scott's master might lawfully do with Dred Scott, in the free State of Illinois, every other master may lawfully do with any other one, or one thousand slaves, in Illinois, or in any other free State.

Auxiliary to all this, and working hand in hand with it, the Nebraska doctrine, or what is left of it, is to educate and mould public opinion, at least Northern public opinion, not to care whether slavery is voted down or voted up. This shows exactly where we now are; and partially, also, whither we are tending. . . .

Why was the amendment, expressly declaring the right of the people, voted down? Plainly enough now,—the adopting of it would have spoiled the niche for the Dred Scott decision. Why was the court decision held up? Why even a Senator's individual opinion withheld, till after the Presidential election? Plainly enough now,—the speaking out then would have damaged the "perfectly free" argument upon which the election was to be carried. Why was the outgoing President's felicitation on the indorsement? Why the delay of a reargument? Why the incoming President's advance exhortation in favor of the decision? These things look like the cautious patting and petting of a spirited horse preparatory to mounting him, when it is dreaded that he may give the rider a fall. And why the hasty after-indorsement of the decision by the President and others?

We cannot absolutely know that all these exact adaptations are the result of preconcert. But when we see a lot of framed timbers, different portions of which we know have been gotten out at different times and places and by different workmen,—Stephen, Franklin, Roger, and James, for instance,—and when we see these timbers joined together, and see they exactly make the frame of a house or a mill, all the tenons and mortises exactly fitting, and all the lengths and proportions of the different pieces exactly adapted to their respective places, and not a piece too many or too few,—not omitting even scaffolding,—or, if a single piece be lacking, we see the place in the frame exactly fitted and prepared yet to bring such piece in,—in such a case, we find it impossible not to believe that Stephen and Franklin and Roger and James all understood one another from the beginning, and all worked upon a common plan or draft drawn up before the first blow was struck. . . .

ADDRESS TO THE VIRGINIA COURT

John Brown   *November 2, 1859*

In the late 1840s John Brown, long a disciple of William Lloyd Garrison, became convinced that slavery could only be abolished through violent action. In 1855 he and his five sons set out for Kansas with a wagon load of guns and ammunition. For the next three years he played a leading role in the war for control of "Bleeding Kansas."

In 1858 Brown conceived the idea of forming a provisional government of freed slaves in the mountains of western Virginia and Maryland. On October 16, 1859, Brown led a raiding party into Harper's Ferry, taking the arsenal and sixty hostages. For a day and a night, Brown's army held out, but finally succumbed to an assault of United States Marines commanded by Colonel Robert E. Lee. Brown was arrested and tried for murder, insurrection and treason.

Brown's trial became a focal point of the slavery controversy. Northern editorialists lionized him; southerners saw him

*as a dangerous advocate of violence and the man who had
attempted to arm slaves. The high moral tone of his final
statement before the court immortalized him as a martyr for the
abolitionist cause. Though he failed to provoke the slave insurrection he had hoped for, Brown's raid and execution were instrumental in increasing hostility between North and South.*

I have, may it please the Court, a few words to say.

In the first place, I deny every thing but what I have already admitted, of
a design on my part to free Slaves. I intended, certainly, to have made a clean
thing of that matter, as I did last winter, when I went into Missouri, and there took
Slaves, without the snapping of a gun on either side, moving them through the
country, and finally leaving them in Canada. I desired to have done the same
thing again on a much larger scale. That was all I intended. I never did intend
murder, or treason, or the destruction of property, or to excite or incite Slaves
to rebellion, or to make insurrection.

I have another objection, and that is, that it is unjust that I should suffer
such a penalty. Had I interfered in the manner, and which I admit has been fairly
proved,—for I admire the truthfulness and candor of the greater portion of the
witnesses who have testified in this case,—had I so interfered in behalf of the
Rich, the Powerful, the Intelligent, the so-called Great, or in behalf of any of their
friends, either father, mother, brother, sister, wife, or children, or any of that class,
and suffered and sacrificed what I have in this interference, it would have been
all right. Every man in this Court would have deemed it an act worthy a reward,
rather than a punishment.

This Court acknowledges too, as I suppose, the validity of the Law of God.
I saw a book kissed, which I suppose to be the Bible, or at least the New
Testament, which teaches me that, "All things whatsoever I would that men
should do to me, I should do even so to them." It teaches me further, to
"Remember them that are in bonds, as bound with them." I endeavored to act
up to that instruction. I say I am yet too young to understand that God is any
respecter of persons. I believe that to have interfered as I have done, as I have
always freely admitted I have done, in behalf of his despised poor, I have done
no wrong, but right.

Now, if it is deemed necessary that I should forfeit my life, for the
furtherance of the ends of justice, and mingle my blood further with the blood
of my children, and with the blood of millions in this slave country, whose rights
are disregarded by wicked, cruel, and unjust enactments,—I say, let it be done.

Let me say one word further: I feel entirely satisfied with the treatment I have received on my trial. Considering all the circumstances, it has been more generous than I expected; but I feel no consciousness of guilt. I have stated from the first what was my intention, and what was not. I never had any design against the liberty of any person, nor any disposition to commit treason, or excite slaves to rebel, or make any general insurrection. I never encouraged any man to do so, but always discouraged any idea of that kind.

Let me say something, also, in regard to the statements made by some of those who were connected with me. I hear that it has been stated by some of them, that I have induced them to join me; but the contrary is true. I do not say this to injure them, but as regarding their weakness. Not one but joined me of his own accord, and the greater part at their own expense. A number of them I never saw and never had a word of conversation with, till the day they came to me, and that was for the purpose I have stated. Now I have done.

South Carolina Ordinance and Declaration of Causes of Secession

December 20–24, 1860

Abraham Lincoln's election as the Republican presidential candidate in 1860 was beyond the tolerance of radical southerners. South Carolina, ever the champion of states' rights, was the first to secede from the Union. As soon as Lincoln's election had been confirmed in the electoral college, a state convention was convened, unanimously adopting an ordinance of secession on December 20, 1860. A few days later, the convention passed a declaration of the causes justifying secession. Within weeks, six other states followed South Carolina out of the Union. In early February 1861, representatives met in Montgomery, Alabama, to form the Confederate States of America.

South Carolina Ordinance of Secession

December 20, 1860

AN Ordinance to Dissolve the Union between the State of South Carolina and other States united with her under the compact entitled the Constitution of the United States of America:

We, the people of the State of South Carolina, in Convention assembled, do declare and ordain, and it is hereby declared and ordained, that the ordinance adopted by us in Convention, on the 23d day of May, in the year of our Lord 1788, whereby the Constitution of the United States of America was ratified, and also all Acts and parts of Acts of the General Assembly of this State ratifying the amendments of the said Constitution, are hereby repealed, and that the union now subsisting between South Carolina and other States under the name of the United States of America is hereby dissolved.

South Carolina Declaration of Causes of Secession

December 24, 1860

The people of the State of South Carolina in Convention assembled, on the 2d day of April, A.D. 1852, declared that the frequent violations of the Constitution of the United States by the Federal Government, and its encroachments upon the reserved rights of the States, fully justified this State in their withdrawal from the Federal Union; but in deference to the opinions and wishes of the other Slaveholding States, she forbore at that time to exercise this right. Since that time these encroachments have continued to increase, and further forbearance ceases to be a virtue.

And now the State of South Carolina having resumed her separate and equal place among nations, deems it due to herself, to the remaining United States of America, and to the nations of the world, that she should declare the immediate causes which have led to this act.

In 1787, Deputies were appointed by the States to revise the articles of Confederation; and on 17th September, 1787, these Deputies recommended, for the adoption of the States, the Articles of Union, known as the Constitution of the United States.

. . . Thus was established by compact between the States, a Government with defined objects and powers, limited to the express words of the grant. . . . We hold that the Government thus established is subject to the two great principles asserted in the Declaration of Independence; and we hold further, that the mode of its formation subjects it to a third fundamental principle, namely, the law of compact. We maintain that in every compact between two or more parties, the obligation is mutual; that the failure of one of the contracting parties to perform a material part of the agreement, entirely releases the obligation of the other; and that, where no arbiter is provided, each party is remitted to his own judgment to determine the fact of failure, with all its consequences.

In the present case, that fact is established with certainty. We assert that fourteen of the States have deliberately refused for years past to fulfill their constitutional obligations, and we refer to their own statutes for the proof.

The Constitution of the United States, in its fourth Article, provides as follows:

"No person held to service or labor in one State under the laws thereof, escaping into another, shall, in consequence of any law or regulation therein, be discharged from such service or labor, but shall be delivered up, on claim of the party to whom such service or labor may be due."

This stipulation was so material to the compact that without it that compact would not have been made. The greater number of the contracting parties held slaves, and they had previously evinced their estimate of the value of such a stipulation by making it a condition in the Ordinance for the government of the territory ceded by Virginia, which obligations, and the laws of the General Government, have ceased to effect the objects of the Constitution. The States of Maine, New Hampshire, Vermont, Massachusetts, Connecticut, Rhode Island, New York, Pennsylvania, Illinois, Indiana, Michigan, Wisconsin and Iowa, have enacted laws which either nullify the acts of Congress, or render useless any attempt to execute them. In many of these States the fugitive is discharged from the service of labor claimed, and in none of them has the State Government complied with the stipulation made in the Constitution. The State of New Jersey, at an early day, passed a law in conformity with her constitutional obligation; but the current of Anti-Slavery feeling has led her more recently to enact laws which render inoperative the remedies provided by her own laws and by the laws of Congress. In the State of New York even the right of transit for a slave has been denied by her tribunals; and the States of Ohio and Iowa have refused to surrender to justice fugitives charged with murder, and with inciting servile insurrection in the State of Virginia. Thus the constitutional compact has been deliberately broken and disregarded by the non-slaveholding States; and the consequence follows that South Carolina is released from her obligation. . . .

We affirm that these ends for which this Government was instituted have been defeated, and the Government itself has been destructive of them by the action of the non-slaveholding States. Those States have assumed the right of deciding upon the propriety of our domestic institutions; and have denied the rights of property established in fifteen of the States and recognized by the Constitution; they have denounced as sinful the institution of Slavery; they have permitted the open establishment among them of societies, whose avowed object is to disturb the peace of and eloin the property of the citizens of other States. They have encouraged and assisted thousands of our slaves to leave their homes; and those who remain, have been incited by emissaries, books, and pictures, to servile insurrection.

For twenty-five years this agitation has been steadily increasing, until it has now secured to its aid the power of the common Government. Observing the forms of the Constitution, a sectional party has found within that article establishing the Executive Department, the means of subverting the Constitution itself. A geographical line has been drawn across the Union, and all the States north of that line have united in the election of a man to the high office of President of the United States whose opinions and purposes are hostile to Slavery. He is to be intrusted with the administration of the common Government, because he has declared that "Government cannot endure permanently half slave, half free," and that the public mind must rest in the belief that Slavery is in the course of ultimate extinction.

This sectional combination for the subversion of the Constitution has been aided, in some of the States, by elevating to citizenship persons who, by the supreme law of the land, are incapable of becoming citizens; and their votes have been used to inaugurate a new policy, hostile to the South, and destructive of its peace and safety.

On the 4th of March next this party will take possession of the Government. It has announced that the South shall be excluded from the common territory, that the Judicial tribunal shall be made sectional, and that a war must be waged against Slavery until it shall cease throughout the United States.

The guarantees of the Constitution will then no longer exist; the equal rights of the States will be lost. The Slaveholding States will no longer have the power of self-government, or self-protection, and the Federal Government will have become their enemy.

Sectional interest and animosity will deepen the irritation; and all hope of remedy is rendered vain, by the fact that the public opinion at the North has invested a great political error with the sanctions of a more erroneous religious belief.

We, therefore, the people of South Carolina, by our delegates in Convention assembled, appealing to the Supreme Judge of the world for the rectitude of our intentions, have solemnly declared that the Union heretofore existing between this State and the other States of North America is dissolved, and that the State of South Carolina has resumed her position among the nations of the world, as a separate and independent state, with full power to levy war, conclude peace, contract alliances, establish commerce, and to do all other acts and things which independent States may of right do.

First Inaugural Address

Abraham Lincoln   *March 4, 1861*

> *Dedicated to maintaining the Union, Abraham Lincoln was also determined to avoid open conflict if possible. After his election he tried to reassure southerners that he would not interfere with existing laws or institutions, and that change could occur only through due process with their participation and consent. He hoped conciliation would coax dissenters back into the Union.*
>
> *On the other hand, he clearly believed that the Union could not be dissolved. The Springfield lawyer was prepared to present several arguments against the legality or viability of secession. Beyond this, Lincoln could not accept separation as the solution to the crisis: the majority and minority could only resolve their differences by working together; otherwise, the majority would be forced to impose its will.*

FELLOW Citizens of the United States:

—In compliance with a custom as old as the Government itself, I appear before you to address you briefly, and to take in your presence the oath prescribed by the Constitution of the United States to be taken by the President "before he enters on the execution of his office." . . .

Apprehension seems to exist among the people of the Southern States that by the accession of a Republican administration their property and their peace and personal security are to be endangered. There has never been any reasonable cause for such apprehension. Indeed, the most ample evidence to the contrary has all the while existed and been open to their inspection. It is found in nearly all the published speeches of him who now addresses you. I do but quote from one of those speeches when I declare that "I have no purpose, directly or indirectly, to interfere with the institution of slavery in the States where it exists. I believe I have no lawful right to do so, and I have no inclination to do so." . . .

I now reiterate these sentiments; and, in doing so, I only press upon the public attention the most conclusive evidence of which the case is susceptible, that the property, peace and security of no section are to be in any wise endangered by the now incoming administration. I add, too, that all the protection which, consistently with the Constitution and the laws, can be given, will be cheerfully given to all the States when lawfully demanded, for whatever cause—as cheerfully to one section as to another. . . .

I take the official oath to-day with no mental reservations, and with no purpose to construe the Constitution or laws by any hypercritical rules. And, while I do not choose now to specify particular acts of Congress as proper to be enforced, I do suggest that it will be much safer for all, both in official and private stations, to conform to and abide by all those acts which stand unrepealed, than to violate any of them, trusting to find impunity in having them held to be unconstitutional. . . .

A disruption of the Federal Union, heretofore only menaced, is now formidably attempted.

I hold that, in contemplation of universal law and of the Constitution, the Union of these States is perpetual. Perpetuity is implied, if not expressed, in the fundamental law of all national governments. It is safe to assert that no government proper ever had a provision in its organic law for its own termination. Continue to execute all the express provisions of our national Constitution, and the Union will endure forever—it being impossible to destroy it except by some action not provided for in the instrument itself.

Again, if the United States be not a government proper, but an association of States in the nature of contract merely, can it as a contract be peaceably unmade by less than all the parties who made it? One party to a contract may violate it—break it, so to speak; but does it not require all to lawfully rescind it?

Descending from these general principles, we find the proposition that in legal contemplation the Union is perpetual confirmed by the history of the Union itself. The Union is much older than the Constitution. It was formed, in fact, by the Articles of Association in 1774. It was matured and continued by the Declaration of Independence in 1776. It was further matured, and the faith of all the then thirteen States expressly plighted and engaged that it should be perpetual, by the Articles of Confederation in 1778. And, finally, in 1787 one of the declared objects for ordaining and establishing the Constitution was "to form a more perfect Union."

But if the destruction of the Union by one or by a part only of the States be lawfully possible, the Union is less perfect than before the Constitution, having lost the vital element of perpetuity.

It follows from these views that no State upon its own mere motion can lawfully get out of the Union; that resolves and ordinances to that effect are legally void; and that acts of violence, within any State or States, against the authority of the United States, are insurrectionary or revolutionary, according to circumstances.

I therefore consider that, in view of the Constitution and the laws, the Union is unbroken; and to the extent of my ability I shall take care, as the Constitution itself expressly enjoins upon me, that the laws of the Union be faithfully executed in all the States. Doing this I deem to be only a simple duty on my part; and I shall perform it so far as practicable, unless my rightful masters, the American people, shall withhold the requisite means, or in some authoritative manner direct the contrary. I trust this will not be regarded as a menace, but only as the declared purpose of the Union that it will constitutionally defend and maintain itself.

In doing this there needs to be no bloodshed or violence; and there shall be none, unless it be forced upon the national authority. The power confided to me will be used to hold, occupy, and possess the property and places belonging to the Government, and to collect the duties and imposts; but beyond what may be necessary for these objects, there will be no invasion, no using of force against or among the people anywhere. Where hostility to the United States, in any interior locality, shall be so great and universal as to prevent competent resident citizens from holding the Federal offices, there will be no attempt to force obnoxious strangers among the people for that object. While the strict legal right may exist in the government to enforce the exercise of these offices, the attempt to do so would be so irritating, and so nearly impracticable withal, that I deem it better to forego for the time the uses of such offices.

The mails, unless repelled, will continue to be furnished in all parts of the Union. So far as possible, the people everywhere shall have that sense of perfect security which is most favorable to calm thought and reflection. The course here indicated will be followed unless current events and experience shall show a modification or change to be proper, and in every case and exigency my best discretion will be exercised according to circumstances actually existing, and with a view and a hope of a peaceful solution of the national troubles and the restoration of fraternal sympathies and affections.

That there are persons in one section or another who seek to destroy the

Union at all events, and are glad of any pretext to do it, I will neither affirm nor deny; but if there be such, I need address no word to them. To those, however, who really love the Union may I not speak?

Before entering upon so grave a matter as the destruction of our national fabric, with all its benefits, its memories, and its hopes, would it not be wise to ascertain precisely why we do it? Will you hazard so desperate a step while there is any possibility that any portion of the ills you fly from have no real existence? Will you, while the certain ills you fly to are greater than all the real ones you fly from—will you risk the commission of so fearful a mistake?

All profess to be content in the Union if all constitutional rights can be maintained. Is it true, then, that any right, plainly written in the Constitution, has been denied? I think not. Happily the human mind is so constituted that no party can reach to the audacity of doing this. Think, if you can, of a single instance in which a plainly written provision of the Constitution has ever been denied. If by the mere force of numbers a majority should deprive a minority of any clearly written constitutional right, it might, in a moral point of view, justify revolution— certainly would if such a right were a vital one. But such is not our case. All the vital rights of minorities and of individuals are so plainly assured to them by affirmations and negations, guaranties and prohibitions, in the Constitution, that controversies never arise concerning them. But no organic law can ever be framed with a provision specifically applicable to every question which may occur in practical administration. No foresight can anticipate, nor any document of reasonable length contain, express provisions for all possible questions. Shall fugitives from labor be surrendered by national or by State authority? The Constitution does not expressly say. May Congress prohibit slavery in the Territories? The Constitution does not expressly say. Must Congress protect slavery in the Territories? The Constitution does not expressly say.

From questions of this class spring all our constitutional controversies, and we divide upon them into majorities and minorities. If the minority will not acquiesce, the majority must, or the Government must cease. There is no other alternative; for continuing the Government is acquiescence on one side or the other.

If a minority in such a case will secede rather than acquiesce, they make a precedent which in turn will divide and ruin them; for a minority of their own will secede from them whenever a majority refuses to be controlled by such minority. For instance, why may not any portion of a new confederacy a year or two hence arbitrarily secede again, precisely as portions of the present Union now claim to secede from it? All who cherish disunion sentiments are now being educated to the exact temper of doing this.

Is there such perfect identity of interests among the States to compose a new Union as to produce harmony only, and prevent renewed secession?

Plainly, the central idea of secession is the essence of anarchy. A majority held in restraint by constitutional checks and limitations, and always changing easily with deliberate changes of popular opinions and sentiments, is the only true sovereign of a free people. Whoever rejects it does, of necessity, fly to anarchy or to despotism. Unanimity is impossible; the rule of a minority, as a permanent arrangement, is wholly inadmissible; so that, rejecting the majority principle, anarchy or despotism in some form is all that is left.

I do not forget the position assumed by some, that constitutional questions are to be decided by the Supreme Court; nor do I deny that such decisions must be binding, in any case, upon the parties to a suit, as to the object of that suit, while they are also entitled to a very high respect and consideration in all parallel cases by all other departments of the government. And, while it is obviously possible that such decision may be erroneous in any given case, still the evil effect following it, being limited to that particular case, with the chance that it may be overruled and never become a precedent for other cases, can better be borne than could the evils of a different practice. At the same time, the candid citizen must confess that if the policy of the government, upon vital questions affecting the whole people, is to be irrevocably fixed by decisions of the Supreme Court, the instant they are made, in ordinary litigation between parties in personal actions, the people will have ceased to be their own rulers, having to that extent practically resigned the government into the hands of that eminent tribunal. Nor is there in this view any assault upon the court or the judges. It is a duty from which they may not shrink to decide cases properly brought before them, and it is no fault of theirs if others seek to turn their decisions to political purposes.

One section of our country believes slavery is right, and ought to be extended, while the other believes it is wrong, and ought not to be extended. This is the only substantial dispute. The fugitive slave clause of the Constitution and the law for the suppression of the foreign slave trade are each as well enforced, perhaps, as any law can ever be in a community where the moral sense of the people imperfectly supports the law itself. The great body of the people abide by the dry legal obligation in both cases, and a few break over in each. This, I think, cannot be perfectly cured; and it would be worse in both cases after the separation of the sections than before. The foreign slave trade, now imperfectly suppressed, would be ultimately revived, without restriction, in one section, while fugitive slaves, now only partially surrendered, would not be surrendered at all by the other.

Physically speaking, we cannot separate. We cannot remove our respective sections from each other, nor build an impassable wall between them.

A husband and wife may be divorced and go out of the presence and beyond the reach of each other; but the different parts of our country cannot do this. They cannot but remain face to face, and intercourse, either amicable or hostile, must continue between them. Is it possible, then, to make that intercourse more advantageous or more satisfactory after separation than before? Can aliens make treaties easier than friends can make laws? Can treaties be more faithfully enforced between aliens than laws can among friends? Suppose you go to war, you cannot fight always; and when, after much loss on both sides, and no gain on either, you cease fighting, the identical old questions as to terms of intercourse are again upon you.

This country, with its institutions, belongs to the people who inhabit it. Whenever they shall grow weary of the existing government, they can exercise their constitutional right of amending it, or their revolutionary right to dismember or overthrow it. I cannot be ignorant of the fact that many worthy and patriotic citizens are desirous of having the national Constitution amended. While I make no recommendation of amendments, I fully recognize the rightful authority of the people over the whole subject, to be exercised in either of the modes prescribed in the instrument itself, and I should, under existing circumstances, favor rather than oppose a fair opportunity being afforded the people to act upon it. I will venture to add that to me the convention mode seems preferable, in that it allows amendments to originate with the people themselves, instead of only permitting them to take or reject propositions originated by others not especially chosen for the purpose, and which might not be precisely such as they would wish to either accept or refuse. I understand a proposed amendment to the Constitution—which amendment, however, I have not seen—has passed Congress, to the effect that the Federal Government shall never interfere with the domestic institutions of the States, including that of persons held to service. To avoid misconstruction of what I have said, I depart from my purpose not to speak of particular amendments so far as to say that, holding such a provision to now be implied constitutional law, I have no objection to its being made express and irrevocable. . . .

Why should there not be a patient confidence in the ultimate justice of the people? Is there any better or equal hope in the world? In our present differences is either party without faith of being in the right? If the Almighty Ruler of nations, with his eternal truth and justice, be on your side of the North, or on yours of the South, that truth and that justice will surely prevail by the judgment of this great tribunal of the American people.

By the frame of the government under which we live, this same people have wisely given their public servants but little power for mischief; and have, with equal wisdom, provided for the return of that little to their own hands at very short intervals. While the people retain their virtue and vigilance, no administration, by any extreme of wickedness or folly, can very seriously injure the government in the short space of four years.

My countrymen, one and all, think calmly and well upon this whole subject. Nothing valuable can be lost by taking time. If there be an object to hurry any of you in hot haste to a step which you would never take deliberately, that object will be frustrated by taking time; but no good object can be frustrated by it. Such of you as are now dissatisfied still have the old Constitution unimpaired, and, on the sensitive point, the laws of your own framing under it; while the new administration will have no immediate power, if it would, to change either. If it were admitted that you who are dissatisfied hold the right side in the dispute, there still is no single good reason for precipitate action. Intelligence, patriotism, Christianity, and a firm reliance on Him who has never yet forsaken this favored land, are still competent to adjust in the best way all our present difficulty.

In your hands, my dissatisfied fellow countrymen, and not in mine, is the momentous issue of civil war. The government will not assail you. You can have no conflict without being yourselves the aggressors. You have no oath registered in heaven to destroy the government, while I shall have the most solemn one to "preserve, protect, and defend" it.

I am loath to close. We are not enemies, but friends. We must not be enemies. Though passion may have strained, it must not break, our bonds of affection. The mystic chords of memory, stretching from every battle-field and patriot grave to every living heart and hearthstone all over this broad land, will yet swell the chorus of the Union when again touched, as surely they will be, by the better angels of our nature.

THE BATTLE HYMN OF THE REPUBLIC

Julia Ward Howe   *December 1861*

John Brown's execution for treason in 1859 galvanized abolitionist determination. After the outbreak of war, one of the most popular marching songs of the Union army commemorated his martyrdom:
>   *John Brown's body lies a-mouldering in the grave,*
>   *His soul is marching on.*
Many variations of this song, sung to the tune of an old

southern camp meeting hymn, appeared in the course of the war. Certainly the most famous was Julia Ward Howe's "Battle Hymn of the Republic," inspired when Howe witnessed a battle in December 1861. The poem was published in the Atlantic Monthly *in February 1862.*

Mine eyes have seen the glory of the coming of the Lord:
He is trampling out the vintage where the grapes of wrath are stored;
He hath loosed the fateful lightning of his terrible swift sword:
    His truth is marching on.

I have seen Him in the watch fires of a hundred circling camps;
They have builded Him an altar in the evening dews and damps;
I can read His righteous sentence by the dim and flaring lamps.
    His day is marching on.

I have read a fiery gospel writ in burnished rows of steel:
"As ye deal with my contemners, so with you my grace shall deal;
Let the Hero, born of woman, crush the serpent with his heel,
    Since God is marching on."

He has sounded forth the trumpet that shall never call retreat;
He is sifting out the hearts of men before his judgment seat:
Oh! be swift, my soul, to answer Him! be jubilant, my feet!
    Our God is marching on.

In the beauty of the lilies Christ was born across the sea,
With a glory in His bosom that transfigures you and me:
As He died to make men holy, let us die to make men free,
    While God is marching on.

THE HOMESTEAD ACT

May 20, 1862

Sales of public lands in the early years of the republic were intended primarily to help reduce the national debt, resulting in most lands being sold in large blocks to speculators. By 1835, though, the debt had been retired and pressure grew to provide lands freely from the public domain to hard-pressed tenant farmers and urban laborers. The Republican Party adopted the "homestead" proposal in 1856, tying it to a prohibition on slavery in the territories ("Free Men, Free Soil"). The Republican victory in 1860, and the consequent secession of the southern states, guaranteed a strong congressional majority favoring free farms. The Homestead Act was passed by the thirty-seventh Congress on May 20, 1862.

The act achieved only limited results, since little easily cultivated land remained available, and many farmers still had difficulty raising capital. By 1890, only a third of the homesteaders had actually obtained deeds. Nonetheless, the act did contribute to the development of the last agricultural frontiers in the Dakotas, Oklahoma and other western regions.

AN act to secure homesteads to actual settlers on the public domain.

Be it enacted, That any person who is the head of a family, or who has arrived at the age of twenty-one years, and is a citizen of the United States, or who shall have filed his declaration of intention to become such, as required by the naturalization laws of the United States, and who has never borne arms against the United States Government or given aid and comfort to its enemies, shall, from and after the first of January, eighteen hundred and sixty-three, be entitled to enter one quarter-section or a less quantity of unappropriated public lands, upon which said person may have filed a pre-emption claim, or which may, at the time the application is made, be subject to pre-emption at one dollar and twenty-five cents, or less, per acre; or eighty acres or less of such unappropriated lands, at two dollars and fifty cents per acre, to be located in a body, in conformity to the legal subdivisions of the public lands, and after the same shall have been surveyed: Provided, That any person owning or residing on land may, under the provisions of this act, enter other land lying contiguous to his or her said land, which shall not, with the land so already owned and occupied, exceed in the aggregate one hundred and sixty acres.

SEC. 2. That the person applying for the benefit of this act shall, upon application to the register of the land office in which he or she is about to make such entry, make affidavit before the said register or receiver that he or she is the head of a family, or is twenty-one or more years of age, or shall have performed service in the Army or Navy of the United States, and that he has never borne arms against the Government of the United States or given aid and comfort to its enemies, and that such application is made for his or her exclusive use and benefit, and that said entry is made for the purpose of actual settlement and

cultivation, and not, either directly or indirectly, for the use or benefit of any other person or persons whomsoever; and upon filing the said affidavit with the register or receiver, and on payment of ten dollars, he or she shall thereupon be permitted to enter the quantity of land specified: Provided, however, That no certificate shall be given or patent issued therefor until the expiration of five years from the date of such entry; and if, at the expiration of such time, or at any time within two years thereafter, the person making such entry—or if he be dead, his widow; or in case of her death, his heirs or devisee; or in case of a widow making such entry, her heirs or devisee, in case of her death—shall prove by two credible witnesses that he, she, or they have resided upon or cultivated the same for the term of five years immediately succeeding the time of filing the affidavit aforesaid, and shall make affidavit that no part of said land has been alienated, and that he has borne true allegiance to the Government of the United States; then, in such case, he, she, or they, if at that time a citizen of the United States, shall be entitled to a patent, as in other cases provided for by law: And provided, further, That in case of the death of both father and mother, leaving an infant child or children under twenty-one years of age, the right and fee shall insure to the benefit of said infant child or children; and the executor, administrator, or guardian may, at any time within two years after the death of the surviving parent, and in accordance with the laws of the State in which such children for the time being have their domicile, sell said land for the benefit of said infants, but for no other purpose; and the purchaser shall acquire the absolute title by the purchase, and be entitled to a patent from the United States, on payment of the office fees and sum of money herein specified. . . .

THE MORRILL ACT

July 2, 1862

The mechanic arts movement began with the founding of the Franklin Institute in Philadelphia in 1824. The object of creating a skilled labor class educated in the arts and sciences remained only partially achievable through privately funded institutions, however. The great leap forward in mechanical and agricultural education came only with passage of the Morrill Act.

Justin Morrill of Vermont, author of the act, served forty-three years in the House of Representatives and Senate. He was a fiscal conservative, and well known for his Tariff of 1861. But his most important legislative legacy was the Morrill Act of 1862, providing grants of federal land to state colleges. Today the "land grant" universities comprise some thirteen million acres, and include some of the leading educational institutions in the nation.

AN Act donating Public Lands to the several States and Territories which may provide Colleges for the Benefit of Agriculture and the Mechanic Arts.

Be it enacted by the Senate and House of Representatives of the United States of America in Congress assembled, That there be granted to the several States, for the purpose hereinafter mentioned, an amount of public land, to be apportioned to each State a quantity equal to thirty thousand acres for each senator and representative in Congress to which the States are respectively entitled by the apportionment under the census of eighteen hundred and sixty: Provided, That no mineral lands shall be selected or purchased under the provisions of this act.

SEC. 2. And be it further enacted, That the land aforesaid, after being surveyed, shall be apportioned to the several States in sections or subdivisions of sections, not less than one quarter of a section; and whenever there are public lands in a State subject to sale at private entry at one dollar and twenty-five cents per acre, the quantity to which said State shall be entitled shall be selected from such lands within the limits of such State, and the Secretary of the Interior is hereby directed to issue to each of the States in which there is not the quantity of public lands subject to sale at private entry at one dollar and twenty-five cents per acre, to which said State may be entitled under the provisions of this act, land scrip to the amount in acres for the deficiency of its distributive share: said scrip to be sold by said States and the proceeds thereof applied to the uses and purposes prescribed in this act, and for no other use or purpose whatsoever. . . .

SEC. 4. And be it further enacted, That all moneys derived from the sale of the lands aforesaid by the States to which the lands are apportioned, and from the sale of land scrip hereinbefore provided for, shall be invested in stocks of the United States, or of the States, or some other safe stocks, yielding not less than five per centum upon the par value of said stocks; and that the moneys so invested shall constitute a perpetual fund, the capital of which shall remain forever undiminished, (except so far as may be provided in section fifth of this act,) and the interest of which shall be inviolably appropriated, by each State which may take and claim the benefit of this act, to the endowment, support, and maintenance of at least one college where the leading object shall be, without excluding other scientific and classical studies, and including military tactics, to teach such branches of learning as are related to agriculture and mechanic arts, in such manner as the legislatures of the State may respectively prescribe, in order to promote the liberal and practical education of the industrial classes in the several pursuits and professions in life. . . .

SEC. 6. No State while in a condition of rebellion or insurrection against the government of the United States shall be entitled to the benefit of this Act. . . .

THE EMANCIPATION PROCLAMATION

Abraham Lincoln   *January 1, 1863*

Having been elected on a platform pledging nonin-
terference with slavery, Abraham Lincoln was reluctant at first
to adopt national abolitionist policies. Above all, his primary
concern at the beginning of the war was to keep the border
states in the Union.

But two summers of lackluster campaigning by the Army
of the Potomac, producing only a series of humiliating defeats
or standoffs, had instilled a grim determination to see the war

through to its conclusion. As it became apparent that no easy outcome was in sight, Lincoln could no longer avoid final settlement of the slavery issue. In September 1862, the Union army finally delivered a victory at Antietam. Lincoln took the opportunity to announce that, as of January 1, 1863, all slaves in the seceding states would be emancipated. Since the Emancipation Proclamation applied only to territories outside Union control, few slaves were directly affected. Its importance was largely symbolic and did help to gain support abroad for the Union cause.

WHEREAS on the 22d day of September, A.D. 1862, a proclamation was issued by the President of the United States, containing, among other things, the following, to wit:

"That on the 1st day of January, A.D. 1863, all persons held as slaves within any State or designated part of a State the people whereof shall then be in rebellion against the United States shall be then, thenceforward, and forever free; and the executive government of the United States, including the military and naval authority thereof, will recognize and maintain the freedom of such persons and will do no act or acts to repress such persons, or any of them, in any efforts they may make for their actual freedom.

"That the executive will on the 1st day of January aforesaid, by proclamation, designate the States and parts of States, if any, in which the people thereof, respectively, shall then be in rebellion against the United States; and the fact that any State or the people thereof shall on that day be in good faith represented in the Congress of the United States by members chosen thereto at elections wherein a majority of the qualified voters of such States shall have participated shall, in the absence of strong countervailing testimony, be deemed conclusive evidence that such State and the people thereof are not then in rebellion against the United States."

Now, therefore, I, Abraham Lincoln, President of the United States, by virtue of the power in me vested as Commander-in-Chief of the Army and Navy of the United States in time of actual armed rebellion against the authority and government of the United States, and as a fit and necessary war measure for suppressing said rebellion, do, on this 1st day of January, A.D. 1863, and in accordance with my purpose so to do, publicly proclaimed for the full period of one hundred days from the first day above mentioned, order and designate as the States and parts of States wherein the people thereof, respectively, are this day in rebellion against the United States the following, to wit:

Arkansas, Texas, Louisiana (except the parishes of St. Bernard, Plaquemines, Jefferson, St. John, St. Charles, St. James, Ascension, Assumption, Terrebonne, Lafourche, St. Mary, St. Martin, and Orleans, including the city of New Orleans), Mississippi, Alabama, Florida, Georgia, South Carolina, North Carolina, and Virginia (except the forty-eight counties designated as West Virginia, and also the counties of Berkeley, Accomac, Northampton, Elizabeth City, York, Princess Anne, and Norfolk, including the cities of Norfolk and Portsmouth), and which excepted parts are for the present left precisely as if this proclamation were not issued.

And by virtue of the power and for the purpose aforesaid, I do order and declare that all persons held as slaves within said designated States and parts of States are, and henceforward shall be, free; and that the Executive Government of the United States, including the military and naval authorities thereof, will recognize and maintain the freedom of said persons.

And I hereby enjoin upon the people so declared to be free to abstain from all violence, unless in necessary self-defense; and I recommend to them that, in all cases when allowed, they labor faithfully for reasonable wages.

And I further declare and make known that such persons of suitable condition will be received into the armed service of the United States to garrison forts, positions, stations, and other places, and to man vessels of all sorts in said service.

And upon this act, sincerely believed to be an act of justice, warranted by the Constitution upon military necessity, I invoke the considerate judgment of mankind and the gracious favor of Almighty God.

ADDRESS AT GETTYSBURG

Abraham Lincoln   *November 19, 1863*

On July 4, 1863, the Army of the Potomac watched as Robert E. Lee's Army of Northern Virginia retreated from the battlefield at Gettysburg, Pennsylvania. Three days of hard fighting had given the Union one of the greatest victories of the war. When, a few days later, news came of the fall of Vicksburg, Mississippi, Abraham Lincoln must have thought that finally things seemed to be going right.

A time for reflection had come. Called upon to deliver

remarks dedicating a cemetery at Gettysburg, Lincoln took the occasion to express his personal sorrow at the human costs of war and to revive faith in democracy and the Union.

FOUR score and seven years ago our fathers brought forth on this continent, a new nation, conceived in liberty, and dedicated to the proposition that all men are created equal.

Now we are engaged in a great civil war, testing whether that nation or any nation so conceived and so dedicated, can long endure. We are met on a great battle-field of that war. We have come to dedicate a portion of that field, as a final resting place for those who here gave their lives that that nation might live. It is altogether fitting and proper that we should do this.

But, in a larger sense, we can not dedicate—we can not consecrate—we can not hallow—this ground. The brave men, living and dead, who struggled here, have consecrated it, far above our poor power to add or detract. The world will little note, nor long remember what we say here, but it can never forget what they did here. It is for us the living, rather, to be dedicated here to the unfinished work which they who fought here have thus far so nobly advanced. It is rather for us to be here dedicated to the great task remaining before us—that from these honored dead we take increased devotion to that cause for which they gave the last full measure of devotion—that we here highly resolve that these dead shall not have died in vain—that this nation, under God, shall have a new birth of freedom—and that government of the people, by the people, for the people, shall not perish from the earth.

Wounded Soldier, date unknown, from the records of the Office of the Chief Signal Officer, photograph by Mathew Brady.

SECOND INAUGURAL ADDRESS

Abraham Lincoln   *March 4, 1865*

With victory imminent, President Abraham Lincoln used his second inaugural to set the tone for reconciliation and restoration of the nation. A freethinker, Lincoln never joined a church, yet his faith is evident in his message. There is also some sense of Lincoln's conviction that he was an instrument of Providence. Above all, his belief in the need for leniency was never better expressed than in the final paragraph of this speech.

FELLOW-Countrymen:—At this second appearing to take the oath of the presidential office there is less occasion for an extended address than there was at the first. Then a statement somewhat in detail of a course to be pursued seemed fitting and proper. Now, at the expiration of four years, during which public declarations have been constantly called forth on every point and phase of the great contest which still absorbs the attention and engrosses the energies of the nation, little that is new could be presented. The progress of our arms, upon which all else chiefly depends, is as well known to the public as to myself, and it is, I trust, reasonably satisfactory and encouraging to all. With high hope for the future, no prediction in regard to it is ventured.

On the occasion corresponding to this four years ago all thoughts were anxiously directed to an impending civil war. All dreaded it, all sought to avert it. While the inaugural address was being delivered from this place, devoted altogether to saving the Union without war, insurgent agents were in the city seeking to destroy it without war—seeking to dissolve the Union and divide effects by negotiation. Both parties deprecated war, but one of them would make war rather than let the nation survive, and the other would accept war rather than let it perish, and the war came.

One eighth of the whole population was colored slaves, not distributed generally over the Union, but localized in the southern part of it. These slaves constituted a peculiar and powerful interest. All knew that this interest was somehow the cause of the war. To strengthen, perpetuate, and extend this interest was the object for which the insurgents would rend the Union even by war, while the Government claimed no right to do more than to restrict the territorial enlargement of it. Neither party expected for the war the magnitude or the duration which it has already attained. Neither anticipated that the cause of the conflict might cease with or even before the conflict itself should cease. Each looked for an easier triumph, and a result less fundamental and astounding. Both read the same Bible and pray to the same God, and each invokes His aid against the other. It may seem strange that any men should dare to ask a just God's assistance in wringing their bread from the sweat of other men's faces, but let us judge not that we be not judged. The prayers of both could not be answered. That of neither has been answered fully. The Almighty has His own purposes. "Woe unto the world because of offenses; for it must needs be that offenses come, but woe to that man by whom the offense cometh." If we shall suppose that American slavery is one of those offenses which, in the providence of God, must needs come, but which, having continued through His appointed time, He now wills to remove, and that He gives to both North and South this terrible war as the woe due to those by whom the offense came, shall we discern therein any departure from those divine attributes which the believers in a living God always ascribe to Him? Fondly do we hope, fervently do we pray, that this mighty scourge of war may speedily pass away. Yet, if God wills that it continue until all the wealth piled by the bondsman's two hundred and fifty years of unrequited toil shall be sunk, and until every drop of blood drawn with the lash shall be paid by another drawn with the sword, as was said three thousand years ago, so still it must be said, "The judgments of the Lord are true and righteous altogether."

With malice towards none, with charity for all, with firmness in the right as God gives us to see the right, let us strive on to finish the work we are in, to bind up the nation's wounds, to care for him who shall have borne the battle and for his widow and his orphan, to do all which may achieve and cherish a just and lasting peace among ourselves and with all nations.

FAREWELL TO HIS ARMY

Robert E. Lee   *April 10, 1865*

Following the fall of the Confederate capital at Richmond, Virginia, April 2, 1865, Robert E. Lee led his army west, hoping to link up with General Joseph E. Johnston and establish a new base. After only a few days, he found himself boxed in and cut off from any supplies. He wrote General Ulysses Grant, asking for terms of surrender, and the two met at

*Appomattox Courthouse, Virginia, on April 9, 1865. The follow-
ing day he said goodbye to his troops, expressing his gratitude
and high regard for their valor.*

HEADQUARTERS, Army of Northern Virginia,

After four years of arduous service, marked by unsurpassed courage and fortitude, the Army of Northern Virginia has been compelled to yield to overwhelming numbers and resources. I need not tell the survivors of so many hard-fought battles, who have remained steadfast to the last, that I have consented to this result from no distrust of them; but, feeling that valour and devotion could accomplish nothing that could compensate for the loss that would have attended the continuation of the contest, I have determined to avoid the useless sacrifice of those whose past services have endeared them to their countrymen. By the terms of the agreement, officers and men can return to their homes and remain there until exchanged. You will take with you the satisfaction that proceeds from the consciousness of duty faithfully performed; and I earnestly pray that a merciful God will extend to you His blessing and protection. With an increasing admiration of your constancy and devotion to your country, and a grateful remembrance of your kind and generous consideration of myself, I bid you an affectionate farewell.

AMENDMENT XIII: SLAVERY ABOLISHED

December 18, 1865

---

*Proposed by Congress January 31, 1865, this amend-
ment's ratification was completed December 18, 1865. The
Emancipation Proclamation had been intended primarily as a
temporary exercise of presidential war powers. Abraham
Lincoln himself doubted its constitutionality and recognized the
need for a more permanent measure. At the 1864 Republican
convention, he urged the inclusion of a plank supporting a
constitutional amendment abolishing slavery. The sweeping
Republican victory that fall provided a mandate for the amendment, which Lincoln pushed through the lame duck Congress by
the end of the year. Though he did not live to see its final*

ratification, Lincoln's sponsorship of the Thirteenth Amendment cemented his reputation as the "Great Emancipator."

SEC. 1. Neither slavery nor involuntary servitude, except as a punishment for crime whereof the party shall have been duly convicted, shall exist within the United States, or any place subject to their jurisdiction.

SEC. 2. Congress shall have power to enforce this article by appropriate legislation.

THE IMPEACHMENT AND TRIAL OF PRESIDENT ANDREW JOHNSON

March 2–May 26, 1868

The Civil War was fought to preserve the Union and to end slavery. But radical Republicans feared that abolition alone would be insufficient, that the restructuring of southern society in order to guarantee former slaves' rights would be required to assure complete victory.

Had Abraham Lincoln survived his second term, his prestige and pragmatic approach might have been sufficient to moderate radical reconstruction. After Lincoln's assassination, Vice-President Andrew Johnson attempted to continue his program. Where a northern Republican might have succeeded, though, a southern Democrat was bound to fail since radicals suspected Johnson's loyalties and motives.

Johnson repeatedly vetoed radical civil rights bills and reconstruction programs, and campaigned vigorously in the 1866 elections, denouncing Republican congressional leadership. In 1867, Congress acted to limit presidential power through the Tenure of Office Act. When Johnson continued to block enforcement of reconstruction legislation, the radicals finally decided to remove him from office, but failed by a single vote.

ARTICLES exhibited by the House of Representatives of the United States, in the name of themselves and all the people of the United States, against Andrew Johnson, President of the United States, in maintenance and support of their impeachment against him for high crimes and misdemeanors in office.

ARTICLE I. That said Andrew Johnson, President of the United States, on the 21st day of February, A.D. 1868, at Washington, in the district of Columbia, unmindful of the high duties of his office, of his oath of office, and of the requirement of the Constitution that he should take care that the laws be faithfully executed, did unlawfully and in violation of the Constitution and laws of the United States issue an order in writing for the removal of Edwin M. Stanton from the office of Secretary for the Department of War, said Edwin M. Stanton having been theretofore duly appointed and commissioned, by and with the advice and consent of the Senate of the United States, as such Secretary; and said Andrew Johnson, President of the United States, on the 12th day of August, A.D. 1867, and during the recess of said Senate, having suspended by his order Edwin M. Stanton from said office, and within twenty days after the first day of the next meeting of said Senate—that is to say, on the 12th day of December, in the year last aforesaid—having reported to said Senate such suspension, with the evidence and reasons for his action in the case and the name of the person designated to perform the duties of such office temporarily until the next meeting of the Senate; and said Senate thereafterwards, on the 13th day of January, A.D. 1868, having duly considered the evidence and reasons reported by said Andrew Johnson for said suspension, and having refused to concur in said suspension, whereby and by force of the provisions of an act entitled "An Act regulating the tenure of certain civil offices," passed March 2, 1867, said Edwin M. Stanton did forthwith resume the functions of his office, whereof the said Andrew Johnson had then and there due notice; and said Edwin M. Stanton, by reason of the premises, on said 21st day of February, being lawfully entitled to hold said office of Secretary for the Department of War; which said order for the removal of said Edwin M. Stanton is in substance as follows; that is to say:

Executive Mansion,
Washington, D.C., February 21, 1868.

HON. EDWIN M. STANTON,
Washington, D.C.
SIR: By virtue of the power and authority vested in me as President by the Constitution and laws of the United States, you are hereby removed from office as Secretary for the Department of War, and your functions as such will terminate upon the receipt of this communication.

You will transfer to Brevet Major-General Lorenzo Thomas, Adjutant-General of the Army, who has this day been authorized and empowered to act as Secretary of War *ad interim*, all records, books, papers, and other public property now in your custody and charge.

Respectfully, yours,

ANDREW JOHNSON.

which order was unlawfully issued with intent then and there to violate the act entitled "An act regulating the tenure of certain civil offices," passed March 2, 1867 . . . whereby said Andrew Johnson, President of the United States, did then and there commit and was guilty of a high misdemeanor in office.

ART. II. That on said 21st day of February, A.D. 1868, at Washington, in the District of Columbia, said Andrew Johnson, President of the United States, . . . did, with intent to violate the Constitution of the United States and the act aforesaid, issue and deliver to one Lorenzo Thomas a letter of authority in substance as follows; that is to say:

Executive Mansion

Washington, D.C., February 21, 1868.

Brevet Major-General LORENZO THOMAS,

Adjutant-General United States Army,

Washington, D.C.

SIR: The Hon. Edwin M. Stanton having been this day removed from office as Secretary for the Department of War, you are hereby authorized and empowered to act as Secretary of War *ad interim*, and will immediately enter upon the discharge of the duties pertaining to that office.

Mr. Stanton has been instructed to transfer to you all the records, books, papers, and other public property now in his custody and charge.

Respectfully, yours,

ANDREW JOHNSON.

then and there being no vacancy in said office of Secretary for the Department of War; whereby said Andrew Johnson, President of the United States, did then and there commit and was guilty of a high misdemeanor in office.

ART. III. That said Andrew Johnson, President of the United States, on the 21st day of February, A.D. 1868, at Washington, in the District of Columbia, did commit and was guilty of a high misdemeanor in office in this, that without authority of law, while the Senate of the United States was then and there in session, he did appoint one Lorenzo Thomas to be Secretary for the Department of War *ad interim*, without the advice and consent of the Senate, and with intent to violate the Constitution of the United States, . . .

ART. IV. That said Andrew Johnson, President of the United States, . . . did unlawfully conspire with one Lorenzo Thomas, and with other persons to the House of Representatives unknown . . .

[Articles IV-IX specify in detail the nature of President Johnson's alleged conspiracy and crimes.]

March 3, 1868.

The following additional articles of impeachment were agreed to, *viz*:

ART. X. That said Andrew Johnson, President of the United States, unmindful of the high duties of his office and the dignity and proprieties thereof, and of the harmony and courtesies which ought to exist and be maintained between the executive and legislative branches of the Government of the United States, . . . did attempt to bring into disgrace, ridicule, hatred, contempt, and reproach the Congress of the United States and the several branches thereof, to impair and destroy the regard and respect of all the good people of the United States for the Congress and legislative power thereof (which all officers of the Government ought inviolably to preserve and maintain), and to excite the odium and resentment of all the good people of the United States against Congress and the laws by it duly and constitutionally enacted; and, in pursuance of his said design and intent, openly and publicly, and before diverse assemblages of the citizens of the United States, . . . did, on the 18th day of August, A.D. 1868, and on divers other days and times, . . . make and deliver with a loud voice certain intemperate, inflammatory, and scandalous harangues, and did therein utter loud threats and bitter menaces, as well against Congress as the laws of the United States, duly enacted thereby, amid the cries, jeers, and laughter of the multitudes then assembled and in hearing. . . [The bulk of Article X concerns specifications of occasions where President Johnson slandered Congress.]

ART. XI. That said Andrew Johnson, President of the United States, . . . did on the 18th day of August, A.D. 1866, at the city of Washington, in the District of Columbia, by public speech, declare and affirm in substance that the Thirty-ninth Congress of the United States was not a Congress of the United States authorized by the Constitution to exercise legislative power under the same, but, on the contrary, was a Congress of only part of the States; thereby denying and intending to deny that the legislation of said Congress was valid or obligatory upon him the said Andrew Johnson, except in so far as he saw fit to approve the same . . . in pursuance of said declaration the said Andrew Johnson, President of the United States, . . . on the 21st day of February, A.D. 1868, at the city of Washington, in the District of Columbia, did unlawfully, and in disregard of the requirement of the Constitution that he should take care that the laws be faithfully executed, attempt to prevent the execution of an act entitled "An act regulating the tenure of certain civil offices," passed March 2, 1867, by unlawfully devising and contriving, and attempting to devise and contrive, means by which he should prevent Edwin M. Stanton from forthwith resuming the functions of the office of Secretary for the Department of War, notwithstanding the refusal of the Senate to concur in the suspension theretofore by said Andrew Johnson of said Edwin M. Stanton from said office of Secretary for the Department of War, and also by further unlawfully devising and contriving, and attempting to devise and contrive, means then and there to prevent the execution of an act entitled "An act making appropriations for the support of the Army for the fiscal year ending June 30, 1868, and for other purposes," approved March 2, 1867, and also to prevent the execution of an act entitled "An act to provide for the more efficient government of the rebel States," passed March 2, 1867, whereby the said Andrew Johnson, President of the United States, did then, to wit, on the 21st day of February, A.D. 1868, at the city of Washington, commit and was guilty of a high misdemeanor in office.

Saturday, May 16, 1868.
The United States vs. Andrew Johnson, President.
        The Chief Justice stated that, in pursuance of the order of the Senate, he would first proceed to take the judgment of the Senate on the eleventh article. The roll of the Senate was called, with the following result: . . .
        The Chief Justice announced that upon this article thirty-five Senators had voted "guilty" and nineteen Senators "not guilty," and declared that two-thirds of the Senators present not having pronounced him guilty, Andrew Johnson, President of the United States, stood acquitted of the charges contained in the eleventh article of impeachment.

Tuesday, May 26, 1868.
The United States vs. Andrew Johnson, President.
        The Senate ordered that the vote be taken upon the second article of impeachment. The roll of the Senate was called, with the following result: . . .
        The Chief Justice announced that upon this article thirty-five Senators had voted "guilty" and nineteen Senators had voted "not guilty," and declared that two-thirds of the Senators present not having pronounced him guilty, Andrew Johnson, President of the United States, stood acquitted of the charges contained in the second article of impeachment.
        The Senate ordered that the vote be taken upon the third article of impeachment. The roll of the Senate was called, with the following result : . . .
        The Chief Justice announced that upon this article thirty-five Senators had

voted "guilty" and nineteen Senators had voted "not guilty," and declared that two-thirds of the Senators present not having pronounced him guilty, Andrew Johnson, President of the United States, stood acquitted of the charges contained in the third article.

No objection being made, the secretary, by direction of the Chief Justice, entered the judgment of the Senate upon the second, third, and eleventh articles, as follows:

The Senate having tried Andrew Johnson, President of the United States, upon articles of impeachment exhibited against him by the House of Representatives, and two-thirds of the Senators present not having found him guilty of the charges contained in the second, third, and eleventh articles of impeachment, it is therefore

Ordered and adjudged, That the said Andrew Johnson, President of the United States, be, and he is, acquitted of the charges in said articles made and set forth.

A motion "that the Senate sitting for the trial of the President upon articles of impeachment do now adjourn without delay" was adopted by a vote of 34 yeas to 16 nays. . . .

The Chief Justice declared the Senate sitting as a court of impeachment for the trial of Andrew Johnson, President of the United States, upon articles of impeachment exhibited against him by the House of Representatives, adjourned without delay.

AMENDMENT XIV: CITIZENSHIP RIGHTS NOT TO BE ABRIDGED

July 28, 1868

Proposed by Congress June 13, 1866, this amendment's ratification was completed July 28, 1868. The Civil Rights Act, passed over Andrew Johnson's veto on April 9, 1866, formally conferred citizenship on emancipated slaves. Extensive doubt as to the constitutionality of the act arose, though, especially considering the implications of the Dred Scott decision. In 1866, a joint committee of Congress formulated a constitutional amendment incorporating the act's provisions. At first rejected by southern legislatures, ratification of the amendment was made a precondition for readmission to the Union, thus assuring its adoption. The Fourteenth Amendment, for the first time, defined citizenship and guaranteed federal protection for citizen's rights against the powers of the states.

SEC. 1. All persons born or naturalized in the United States, and subject to the jurisdiction thereof, are citizens of the United States and of the State wherein they reside. No State shall make or enforce any law which shall abridge the privileges or immunities of citizens of the United States; nor shall any State deprive any person of life, liberty, or property, without due process of law; nor deny to any person within its jurisdiction the equal protection of the laws.

SEC. 2. Representatives shall be apportioned among the several States according to their respective numbers, counting the whole number of persons in each State, excluding Indians not taxed. But when the right to vote at any election for the choice of electors for President and Vice President of the United States, Representatives in Congress, the Executive and Judicial officers of a State, or the members of the Legislature thereof, is denied to any of the male inhabitants of such State, being twenty-one years of age, and citizens of the United States, or in any way abridged, except for participation in rebellion, or other crime, the basis of representation therein shall be reduced in the proportion which the number of such male citizens shall bear to the whole number of male citizens twenty-one years of age in such State.

SEC. 3. No person shall be a Senator or Representative in Congress, or elector of President and Vice President, or hold any office, civil or military, under the United States, or under any State, who, having previously taken an oath, as a member of Congress, or as an officer of the United States, or as a member of any State legislature, or as an executive or judicial officer of any State, to support the Constitution of the United States, shall have engaged in insurrection or rebellion against the same, or given aid or comfort to the enemies thereof. But Congress may be a vote of two-thirds of each House, remove such disability.

SEC. 4. The validity of the public debt of the United States, authorized by law, including debts incurred for payment of pensions and bounties for services in suppressing insurrection or rebellion, shall not be questioned. But neither the United States nor any State shall assume or pay any debt or obligation incurred in aid of insurrection or rebellion against the United States, or any claim for the loss or emancipation of any slave; but all such debts, obligations and claims, shall be held illegal and void.

SEC. 5. The Congress shall have power to enforce, by appropriate legislation, the provisions of this article.

AMENDMENT XV: RACE NO BAR TO VOTING RIGHTS

March 30, 1870

Proposed by Congress February 26, 1869, this amendment's ratification was completed March 30, 1870. The Fourteenth Amendment implied, but did not guarantee, black suffrage. A landslide Republican victory in the 1868 election gave the radicals a mandate to add the finishing touch to reconstruction. Some radicals would have liked to have gone further with the Fifteenth Amendment's provisions, forbidding the use of property or literacy qualifications. This was denied, though, since many northern and western states wanted to preserve these tactics to exclude immigrants.

SEC. 1. The right of citizens of the United States to vote shall not be denied or abridged by the United States or by any State on account of race, color, or previous condition of servitude—

SEC. 2. The congress shall have power to enforce this article by appropriate legislation—

VII

AMERICA
COMES OF AGE

ON WOMAN'S RIGHT TO SUFFRAGE

Susan B. Anthony   *1873*

    For a generation, the women's rights campaign had paralleled the abolition campaign. Logically, the granting of black citizenship implied full citizenship for women, too. The most radical feminist leaders, in fact, refused to support passage of the Fifteenth Amendment unless it was accompanied by a sixteenth amendment enfranchising women.

    One of the women's rights advocates was Susan B. Anthony, born February 15, 1820, in Adams, Massachusetts. She was the daughter of a Quaker abolitionist and, from the 1840s, active in the women's, abolition and temperance movements. In 1872 she led a group of women to the polls in Rochester, New York, and was arrested. At her trial the follow-ing year, she made this definitive statement on women's right to vote. Eventually convicted, she refused to pay her fine. Anthony continued her crusade, collaborating with Elizabeth Cady Stanton, Matilda Joslyn Gage and Ida Harper on four volumes

of the History of Woman Suffrage, *and helping to organize the*
National Woman Suffrage Association.

FRIENDS and Fellow Citizens:—I stand before you to-night under indictment for the alleged crime of having voted at the last presidential election,
without having a lawful right to vote. It shall be my work this evening to prove
to you that in thus voting, I not only committed no crime, but, instead, simply
exercised my citizen's rights, guaranteed to me and all United States citizens by
the National Constitution, beyond the power of any State to deny.

The preamble of the Federal Constitution says:

"We, the people of the United States, in order to form a more perfect
union, establish justice, insure domestic tranquility, provide for the common
defense, promote the general welfare, and secure the blessings of liberty to
ourselves and our posterity, do ordain and establish this Constitution for the
United States of America."

It was we, the people; not we, the white male citizens; nor yet we, the
male citizens; but we, the whole people, who formed the Union. And we formed
it, not to give the blessings of liberty, but to secure them; not to the half of
ourselves and the half of our posterity, but to the whole people—women as well
as men. And it is a downright mockery to talk to women of their enjoyment of
the blessings of liberty while they are denied the use of the only means of
securing them provided by this democratic-republican government—the ballot.

For any State to make sex a qualification that must ever result in the
disfranchisement of one entire half of the people is to pass a bill of attainder, or
an *ex post facto* law, and is therefore a violation of the supreme law of the land.
By it the blessings of liberty are for ever withheld from women and their female
posterity. To them this government has no just powers derived from the consent
of the governed. To them this government is not a democracy. It is not a republic.
It is an odious aristocracy; a hateful oligarchy of sex: the most hateful aristocracy
ever established on the face of the globe; an oligarchy of wealth, where the rich
govern the poor. An oligarchy of learning, where the educated govern the
ignorant, or even an oligarchy of race, where the Saxon rules the African, might
be endured; but this oligarchy of sex, which makes father, brothers, husband,
sons, the oligarchs over the mother and sisters, the wife and daughters of every
household—which ordains all men sovereigns, all women subjects, carries
dissension, discord and rebellion into every home of the nation.

Webster, Worcester and Bouvier all define a citizen to be a person in the
United States, entitled to vote and hold office.

The only question left to be settled now is: Are women persons? And I hardly believe any of our opponents will have the hardihood to say they are not. Being persons, then, women are citizens; and no State has a right to make any law, or to enforce any old law, that shall abridge their privileges or immunities. Hence, every discrimination against women in the constitutions and laws of the several States is to-day null and void, precisely as is every one against negroes.

REPORT ON THE LANDS
OF THE ARID REGION

John Wesley Powell   *1878*

> *John Wesley Powell was born in rural New York on March 24, 1834. He served in the United States Army during the Civil War, losing his right arm at Shiloh. Resigning his commission in 1865, he taught geology for a time in Illinois. From 1871 to 1879, he directed government surveys of public lands in the West, leading a series of expeditions to the Rocky Mountains and Great Basin. During the same period, he published three major works:* Exploration of the Colorado River and Its Tributaries *(1875),* An Introduction to the Study of Indian Languages *(1877) and* Report on the Lands of the Arid Region of the United States *(1878).*
>
> *The report for the first time analyzed the role of water in developing the West, and is a landmark statement regarding the importance of conservation and free access to resources. From 1881 to 1892, Powell directed the United States Geological Survey, working to map water resources and expand agricultural projects.*

. . . IF the whole of the Arid Region was yet unsettled, it might be wise for the Government to undertake the parceling of the lands and to employ skilled engineers to do the work, whose duties could be performed in advance of settlement. . . . Many of the lands surveyed along the minor streams have been entered, and the titles to these lands are in the hands of actual settlers. Many pasturage farms, or ranches, as they are called locally, have been established throughout the country. These remarks are true of every state and territory in the Arid Region. In the main these ranches or pasturage farms are on Government land, and the settlers are squatters, and some are not expecting to make permanent homes. . . . It is now too late for the Government to parcel the pasturage lands in advance of the wants of settlers in the most available way, so as to closely group residences and give water privileges to the several farms. Many of the farmers are actually on the ground, and are clamoring for some means by which they can obtain titles to pasturage farms of an extent adequate to their wants, and the tens of thousands of individual interests would make the problem a difficult one for the officers of the Government to solve. A system less arbitrary than that of the rectangular surveys now in vogue, and requiring unbiased judgment, overlooking the interests of single individuals and considering only the interests of the greatest number, would meet with local opposition. . . .

Under these circumstances it is believed that it is best to permit the people to divide their lands for themselves—not in a way by which each man may take what he pleases for himself, but by providing methods by which these settlers may organize and mutually protect each other from the rapacity of individuals. The lands, as lands, are of but slight value, as they cannot be used for ordinary agricultural purposes, i.e., the cultivation of crops; but their value consists in the scant grasses which they spontaneously produce, and these values can be made available only by the use of the waters necessary for the subsistence of stock, and that necessary for the small amount of irrigable land which should be attached to the several pasturage farms. Thus, practically, all values inherent in the water, and an equitable division of the waters can be made only by a wise system of parcelling the lands; and the people in organized bodies can well be trusted with this right, while individuals could not thus be trusted. These considerations have led to the plan suggested in the bill submitted for the organization of pasturage districts.

In like manner, in the bill designed for the purpose of suggesting a plan for the organization of irrigation districts, the same principle is involved, *viz*, that of permitting the settlers themselves to subdivide the lands into such tracts as they may desire.

The lands along the streams are not valuable for agricultural purposes in continuous bodies or squares, but only in irrigable tracts governed by the levels of the meandering canals which carry the water for irrigation, and it would be greatly to the advantage of every such district if the lands could be divided into parcels, governed solely by the conditions under which the water could be distributed over them; and such parcelling cannot be done prior to the occupancy of the lands, but can only be made *pari passu* with the adoption of a system of canals; and the people settling on these lands should be allowed the privilege of dividing the lands into such tracts as may be most available for such purposes, and they should not be hampered with the present arbitrary system of dividing tracts into rectangular tracts. . . .

The title to no tract of land should be conveyed from the Government to the individual until the proper survey of the same is made and the plat prepared for record. With this precaution, which the Government already invariably takes in disposing of its lands, no fear of uncertainty of identification need be entertained. . . .

. . . The general subject of water rights is one of great importance. In many places in the Arid Region irrigation companies are organized who obtain vested rights in the waters they control, and consequently the rights to such waters do not inhere in any particular tracts of land.

When the area to which it is possible to take the water of any given stream is much greater than the stream is competent to serve, if the land titles and water rights are severed, the owner of any tract of land is at the mercy of the owner of the water right. In general the lands greatly exceed the capacities of the streams. Thus the lands have no value without water. If the water rights fall into the hands of irrigating companies and the lands into the hands of individual farmers, the farmers then will be dependent upon the stock companies, and eventually the monopoly of water rights will be an intolerable burden to the people.

The magnitude of the interests involved must not be overlooked. All the present and future agriculture of more than four-tenths of the area of the United States is dependent upon irrigation, and practically all values for agricultural industries inhere, not in the lands, but in the water. Monopoly of land need not be feared. The question for legislators to solve is to devise some practical means by which water rights may be distributed among individual farmers and water monopolies prevented. . . .

The pioneer is fully engaged in the present with its hopes of immediate remuneration for labor. The present development of the country fully occupies him. For this reason every effort put forth to increase the area of the agricultural land by irrigation is welcomed. Every man who turns his attention to this department of industry is considered a public benefactor. But if in the eagerness for present development a land and water system shall grow up in which the practical control of agriculture shall fall into the hands of water companies, evils will result therefrom that generations may not be able to correct, and the very men who are now lauded as benefactors to the country will, in the ungovernable reaction which is sure to come, be denounced as oppressors of the people.

The right to use water should inhere in the land to be irrigated, and water rights should go with land titles.

Those unacquainted with the industrial institutions of the far west, involving the use of lands and waters, may without careful thought suppose that the long recognized principles of the common law are sufficient to prevent the severance of land and water rights; but other practices are obtaining which have, or eventually will have, all the force of common law because the necessities of the country require the change, and these practices are obtaining the color of right from state and territorial legislation, and to some extent by national legislation. In all that country the natural channels of the streams cannot be made to govern water rights without great injury to its agricultural and mining industries. For the great purposes of irrigation and hydraulic mining the water has no value in its natural channel. In general the water cannot be used for irrigation on the lands immediately contiguous to the streams—i.e., the flood plains or bottom valleys. . . . The waters must be taken to a greater or less extent on the bench lands to be used in irrigation. All the waters of all the arid lands will eventually be taken from their natural channels, and they can be utilized only to the extent to which they are thus removed, and water rights must of necessity be severed from the natural channels. There is another important factor to be considered. The water when used in irrigation is absorbed by the soil and reëvaporated to the heavens. It cannot be taken from its natural channel, used, and returned. Again, the water cannot in general be properly utilized in irrigation by requiring it to be taken from its natural channel within the limits ordinarily included in a single ownership. In order to conduct the water on the higher bench lands where it is to be used in irrigation, it is necessary to go up the stream until a level is reached from which the waters will flow to the lands to be redeemed. The exceptions to this are so small that the statement scarcely needs qualification. Thus, to use the water it must be diverted from its natural course often miles or scores of miles from where it is to be used.

The ancient principles of common law applying to the use of natural streams, so wise and equitable in a humid region, would, if applied to the Arid Region, practically prohibit the growth of its most important industries. Thus it is that a custom is springing up in the Arid Region which may or may not have color of authority in statutory or common law; on this I do not wish to express an opinion; but certain it is that water rights are practically being severed from the natural channels of the streams; and this must be done. In the change, it is to be feared that water rights will in many cases be separated from all land rights as the system is now forming. If this fear is not groundless, to the extent that such a separation is secured, water will become a property independent of the land, and this property will be gradually absorbed by a few. Monopolies of water will be secured, and the whole agriculture of the country will be tributary thereto— a condition of affairs which an American citizen having in view the interests of the largest number of the people cannot contemplate with favor.

Practically, in that country the right to water is acquired by priority of utilization, and this is as it should be from the necessities of the country. But two important qualifications are needed. The user right should attach to the land where used, not to the individual or company constructing the canals by which it is used; the priority of usage should secure the right. But this needs some slight modification. A farmer settling on a small tract, to be redeemed by irrigation, should be given a reasonable length of time in which to secure his water right by utilization, that he may secure it by his own labor, either directly by constructing the waterways himself, or indirectly by coöperating with his neighbours in constructing systems of waterways. Without this provision there is little inducement for poor men to commence farming operations, and men of ready capital only will engage in such enterprises. . . .

If there be any doubt of the ultimate legality of the practices of the people in the arid country relating to water and land rights, all such doubts should be speedily quieted through the enactment of appropriate laws by the national legislature. Perhaps an amplification by the courts of what has been designated as the natural right to the use of water may be made to cover the practices now obtaining; but it hardly seems wise to imperil interests so great by intrusting them to the possibility of some future court made law.

NARRATIVE

Chief Joseph   *April 1879*

By the late 1870s, nearly all the Native American population had been restricted to reservations. Only a few bands remained free: Sitting Bull's Lakota in Canada, Geronimo's Apache in Mexico, and, in the mountains of northeastern Oregon, a single band of the Nez Percé. In May 1877 all nontreaty Nez Percé were given an ultimatum to move to the Lapwai Reservation in Idaho. At first, In-mut-too-yah-lat-lat, called Chief Joseph by the whites, agreed. But, hearing that some of his young men had killed a few white squatters, he decided to escape north.

In a brilliant series of rearguard holding actions, 250 Nez Percé warriors managed to protect the band's retreat

*against four United States Army columns. After fleeing 1,600
miles across Oregon, Washington, Idaho and Montana, the
band was finally cornered only forty miles from the Canadian
border. On October 5, 1877, Joseph surrendered to General
Miles. In 1879, Chief Joseph traveled to Washington, D.C., to
state the Indians' case before President Hayes, several con-
gressmen and other government officials. His account recording his dealings with the government was published in the*
North American Review *in April 1879. Contrary to government promises, the Wallamwatkin band were sent to a barren
reservation in the Indian Territory and were not allowed to
return to the mountains of eastern Washington until 1885.*

MY friends, I have been asked to show you my heart. I am glad to have a chance to do so. I want the white people to understand my people. Some of you think an Indian is like a wild animal. This is a mistake. I will tell you all about our people, and then you can judge whether an Indian is a man or not. I believe much trouble and blood would be saved if we opened our hearts more. I will tell you in my way how the Indian sees things. The white man has more words to tell you how they look to him, but it does not require many words to speak the truth. What I have to say will come from my heart, and I will speak with a straight tongue. Ah-cum-kin-i-ma-me-hut [the Great Spirit] is looking at me, and will hear me.

My name is In-mut-too-yah-lat-lat [Thunder traveling over the mountains]. I am chief of the Wal-lam-wat-kin band of Chute-pa-lu, or Nez Percés. I was born in eastern Oregon, thirty-eight winters ago. My father was chief before me. When a young man, he was called Joseph by Mr. Spaulding, a missionary. He died a few years ago. There was no stain on his hands of the blood of a white man. He left a good name on the earth. He advised me well for my people.

Our fathers gave us many laws, which they had learned from their fathers. These laws were good. They told us to treat all men as they treated us; that we should never be the first to break a bargain; that it was a disgrace to tell a lie; that we should speak only the truth; that it was a shame for one man to take from another his wife, or his property without paying for it. We were taught to believe that the Great Spirit sees and hears everything, and that he never forgets; that hereafter he will give every man a spirit-home according to his deserts: if he has been a good man, he will have a good home; if he has been a bad man, he will have a bad home. This I believe, and all my people believe the same. . . .

The first white men of your people who came to our country were named

Lewis and Clarke. They also brought many things that our people had never seen. They talked straight, and our people gave them a great feast, as a proof that their hearts were friendly. These men were very kind. They made presents to our chiefs and our people made presents to them. We had a great many horses, of which we gave them what they needed, and they gave us guns and tobacco in return. All the Nez Percés made friends with Lewis and Clarke, and agreed to let them pass through their country, and never to make war on white men. This promise the Nez Percés have never broken. No white man can accuse them of bad faith, and speak with a straight tongue. It has always been the pride of the Nez Percés that they were the friends of the white men. . . .

For a short time we lived quietly. But this could not last. White men had found gold in the mountains around the land of winding water. They stole a great many horses from us, and we could not get them back because we were Indians. The white men told lies for each other. They drove off a great many of our cattle. Some white men branded our young cattle so they could claim them. We had no friend who would plead our cause before the law councils. It seemed to me that some of the white men in Wallowa were doing these things on purpose to get up a war. They knew that we were not strong enough to fight them. I labored hard to avoid trouble and bloodshed. We gave up some of our country to the white men, thinking that then we could have peace. We were mistaken. The white man would not let us alone. We could have avenged our wrongs many times, but we did not. Whenever the Government has asked us to help them against other Indians, we have never refused. When the white men were few and we were strong we could have killed them all off, but the Nez Percés wished to live at peace. . . .

I could see no other way to avoid a war. We moved over to White Bird Creek, sixteen miles away, and there encamped, intending to collect our stock before leaving; but the soldiers attacked us, and the first battle was fought. . . .

I could not bear to see my wounded men and women suffer any longer; we had lost enough already. General Miles had promised that we might return to our own country with what stock we had left. I thought we could start again. I believed General Miles, or I never would have surrendered. I have heard that he has been censured for making the promise to return us to Lapwai. He could not have made any other terms with me at that time. I would have held him in check until my friends came to my assistance, and then neither of the generals nor their soldiers would have ever left Bear Paw Mountain alive.

On the fifth day I went to General Miles and gave up my gun, and said, "From where the sun now stands I will fight no more." My people needed rest— we wanted peace. . . .

At last I was granted permission to come to Washington and bring my friend Yellow Bull and our interpreter with me. I am glad we came. I have shaken hands with a great many friends, but there are some things I want to know which no one seems able to explain. I can not understand how the Government sends a man out to fight us, as it did General Miles, and then breaks his word. Such a Government has something wrong about it. I can not understand why so many chiefs are allowed to talk so many different ways, and promise so many different things. I have seen the Great Father Chief [the President], the next Great Chief [Secretary of the Interior], the Commissioner Chief [Hayt], the Law Chief [General Butler], and many other law chiefs [Congressmen], and they all say they are my friends, and that I shall have justice, but while all their mouths talk right I do not understand why nothing is done for my people. I have heard talk and talk, but nothing is done. Good words do not last long unless they amount to something. Words do not pay for my dead people. They do not pay for my country, now overrun by white men. They do not protect my father's grave. They do not pay for all my horses and cattle. Good words will not give me back my children. Good words will not make good the promise of your War Chief General Miles. Good words will not give my people good health and stop them from dying. Good words will not get my people a home where they can live in peace and take care of themselves. I am tired of talk that comes to nothing. It makes my heart sick when I remember all the good words and all the broken promises. There has been too much talking by men who had no right to talk. Too many misinterpretations have been made, too many misunderstandings have come up between the white men about the Indians. If the white man wants to live in peace with the Indian he can live in peace. There need be no trouble. Treat all men alike. Give them the same laws. Give them all an even chance to live and grow. All men were made by the same Great Spirit Chief. They are all brothers. The earth is the mother of all people, and all people should have equal rights upon it. You might as well expect the rivers to run backward as that any man who was born a free man should be contented when penned up and denied liberty to go where he pleases. If you tie a horse to a stake, do you expect he will grow fat? If you pen an Indian up on a small spot of earth, and compel him to stay there, he will not be contented, nor will he grow and prosper. I have asked some of the great white chiefs where they get their authority to say to the Indian that he shall stay in one place, while he sees white men going where they please. They can not tell me.

I only ask of the Government to be treated as all other men are treated. If I can not go to my own home, let me have a home in a country where my people will not die so fast. I would like to go to Bitter Root Valley. There my people would be healthy; where they are now they are dying. Three have died since I left my camp to come to Washington.

When I think of our condition my heart is heavy. I see men of my race treated as outlaws and driven from country to country, or shot down like animals.

I know that my race must change. We cannot hold our own with the white men as we are. We only ask an even chance to live as other men live. We ask to be recognized as men. We ask that the same law shall work alike on all men. If an Indian breaks the law, punish him by the law. If a white man breaks the law, punish him also.

Let me be a free man—free to travel, free to stop, free to work, free to trade where I choose, free to choose my own teachers, free to follow the religion of my fathers, free to talk and think and act for myself—and I will obey every law, or submit to the penalty.

Whenever the white man treats the Indian as they treat each other, then we shall have no more wars. We shall be all alike—brothers of one father and mother, with one sky above us and one country around us, and one government for all. Then the Great Spirit Chief who rules above will smile upon this land, and send rain to wash out the bloody spots made by brothers' hands from the face of the earth. For this time the Indian race are waiting and praying. I hope that no more groans of wounded men and women will ever go to the ear of the Great Spirit Chief above, and that all people may be one people.

In-mut-too-yah-lat-lat has spoken for his people.

THE NEW COLOSSUS

Emma Lazarus   *1883*

---

*Following the Civil War, the French historian Edward
Laboulaye suggested a gift to the United States, commemorating
the friendship and shared ideals of the two nations. The Statue
of Liberty, by Frederic-Auguste Bartholdi, with an internal
framework designed by Gustave Eiffel, was completed in 1885
and shipped to New York. The pedestal was finished the following year and, on October 28, 1886, the statue was dedicated by
President Grover Cleveland. Inscribed on a bronze plaque
inside the base of the statue were lines from Emma Lazarus's
sonnet, "The New Colossus," first published in 1883.*

Not like the brazen giant of Greek fame,
With conquering limbs astride from land to land;
Here at our sea-washed, sunset gates shall stand
A mighty woman with a torch, whose flame
Is the imprisoned lightning, and her name
Mother of Exiles. From her beacon hand
Glows world-wide welcome; her mild eyes command
The air-bridged harbor that twin cities frame.

"Keep, ancient lands, your storied pomp!" cries she
With silent lips, "Give me your tired, your poor,
Your huddled masses yearning to breathe free,
The wretched refuse of your teeming shore.
Send these, the homeless, tempest-tost to me,
I lift my lamp beside the golden door!"

THE SHERMAN ANTI-TRUST ACT

July 2, 1890

The last three decades of the nineteenth century were a period of industrial revolution in the United States. The growth of American manufacturing was led by a few businessmen who established leadership in an industry and then attempted to create monopoly domination of the market. In 1882, John D. Rockefeller incorporated the Standard Oil Trust in Ohio. The trust was designed to control voting rights in competing corporations within a small group of "trustees," eliminating the risks, and benefits, of competition. By 1890, trusts had been established in half a dozen industries.

By this time, however, reform-minded journalists and politicians had determined to break up the trusts. Among these was Senator John Sherman of Ohio, younger brother of General William Tecumseh Sherman. Sherman was chairman of the Senate Finance Committee and author of the first legislative attempt to deter monopoly trade. Though weak and generally ineffective, the Anti-Trust Act did provide the groundwork for later legislation promoting a freer marketplace.

AN Act To protect trade and commerce against unlawful restraints and monopolies. . . .

Be it enacted

SEC. 1. Every contract, combination in the form of trust or otherwise, or conspiracy, in restraint of trade or commerce among the several States, or with foreign nations, is hereby declared to be illegal. Every person who shall make any such contract or engage in any such combination or conspiracy, shall be deemed guilty of a misdemeanor, and, on conviction thereof, shall be punished by fine not exceeding five thousand dollars, or by imprisonment not exceeding one year, or by both said punishments, in the discretion of the court.

SEC. 2. Every person who shall monopolize, or attempt to monopolize, or combine or conspire with any other person or persons, to monopolize any part of the trade or commerce among the several States, or with foreign nations, shall be deemed guilty of a misdemeanor, and, on conviction thereof, shall be punished by fine not exceeding five thousand dollars, or by imprisonment not exceeding one year, or by both said punishments, in the discretion of the court.

SEC. 3. Every contract, combination in form of trust or otherwise, or conspiracy, in restraint of trade or commerce in any Territory of the United States or of the District of Columbia, or in restraint of trade or commerce between any such Territory and another, or between any such Territory or Territories and any State or States or the District of Columbia, or with foreign nations, or between the District of Columbia and any State or States or foreign nations, is hereby declared illegal. Every person who shall make any such contract or engage in any such combination or conspiracy, shall be deemed guilty of a misdemeanor, and, on conviction thereof, shall be punished by fine not exceeding five thousand dollars, or by imprisonment not exceeding one year, or by both said punishments, in the discretion of the court.

SEC. 4. The several circuit courts of the United States are hereby invested with jurisdiction to prevent and restrain violations of this act; and it shall be the duty of the several district attorneys of the United States in their respective districts, under the direction of the Attorney-General, to institute proceedings in equity to prevent and restrain such violations. Such proceedings may be by way of petition setting forth the case and praying that such violation shall be enjoined or otherwise prohibited. When the parties complained of shall have been duly notified of such petition the courts shall proceed, as soon as may be, to the hearing and determination of the case; and pending such petition and before final decrees, the court may at any time make such temporary restraining order or prohibition as shall be deemed just in the premises.

SEC. 5. Whenever it shall appear to the court before which any proceeding under Section four of this act may be pending, that the ends of justice require that other parties should be brought before the court, the court may cause them to be summoned, whether they reside in the district in which the court is held or not; and subpoenas to that end may be served in any district by the marshal thereof.

SEC. 6. Any property owned under any contract or by any combination, or pursuant to any conspiracy (and being the subject thereof) mentioned in section one of this act, and being in the course of transportation from one State to another, or to a foreign country, shall be forfeited to the United States, and may be seized and condemned by like proceedings as those provided by law for the forfeiture, seizure, and condemnation of property imported into the United States contrary to law.

SEC. 7. Any person who shall be injured in his business or property by any other person or corporation by reason of anything forbidden or declared to be unlawful by this act, may sue therefor in any circuit court of the United States in the district in which the defendant resides or is found, without respect to the amount in controversy, and shall recover threefold the damages by him sustained, and the costs of suit, including a reasonable attorney's fee.

SEC. 8. That the word "person" or "persons," wherever used in this act shall be deemed to include corporations and associations existing under or authorized by the laws of either the United States, the laws of any of the Territories, the laws of any State, or the laws of any foreign country.

America the Beautiful

Katharine Lee Bates 1893

Katharine Lee Bates was an author and educator born in Falmouth, Massachusetts, on August 12, 1859. She received a degree from Wellesley College and remained to teach English literature from 1885 to 1925. Inspired by the view from the summit of Pikes Peak during a summer visit to Colorado, she composed her famous poem, "America the Beautiful." She also

*published several short stories and collections of children's
literature before her death in 1929.*

O beautiful for spacious skies,
　For amber waves of grain,
For purple mountain majesties
　Above the fruited plain!
　　America! America!
　God shed His grace on thee
And crown thy good with brotherhood
　From sea to shining sea!

O beautiful for pilgrim feet,
　Whose stern, impassioned stress
A thoroughfare for freedom beat
　Across the wilderness!
　　America! America!
　God mend thine every flaw,
Confirm thy soul in self-control,
　Thy liberty in law!

O beautiful for heroes proved
　In liberating strife,
Who more than self their country loved,
　And mercy more than life!
　　America! America!
　May God thy gold refine
Till all success be nobleness
　And every gain divine!

O beautiful for patriot dream
　That sees beyond the years
Thine alabaster cities gleam
　Undimmed by human tears!
　　America! America!
　God shed His grace on thee
And crown thy good with brotherhood
　From sea to shining sea!

ATLANTA EXPOSITION SPEECH

Booker T. Washington　　　　　　　　　　　　　　*1895*

---

　　*Despite the provisions of the Fourteenth and Fifteenth
Amendments, blacks remained semicitizens in the old Confederacy. Literacy requirements, "grandfather" clauses and
property restrictions ensured an exclusively white franchise. In
addition, brutal extralegal measures, including lynchings,
helped keep blacks "in their place."*
　　*Some black leaders, most notably Booker T. Washington,
felt that, under the circumstances, it was best to avoid conflict.
Washington urged accommodation and education in mechan-
ics and agriculture. He put this philosophy into practice after
becoming the first president of the Tuskegee Institute in 1881.*

Through thrift and hard work, he thought blacks could earn the respect of whites, and, in the long run, full citizenship. While welcomed by many, Washington's advice was challenged by some black intellectuals and led indirectly to the foundation of the Niagara Movement by Washington's leading critic, W.E.B. Du Bois. In the summer of 1895 Washington delivered his views on black advancement to an integrated audience at the Atlanta Exposition, a fair celebrating the recovery of the South from the devastations of war and reconstruction.

MR. President and Gentlemen of the Board of Directors and Citizens:

One-third of the population of the South is of the Negro race. No enterprise seeking the material, civil, or moral welfare of this section can disregard this element of our population and reach the highest success. I but convey to you, Mr. President and Directors, the sentiment of the masses of my race when I say that in no way have the value and manhood of the American Negro been more fittingly and generously recognized than by the managers of this magnificent exposition at every stage of its progress. It is a recognition that will do more to cement the friendship of the two races than any occurrence since the dawn of our freedom.

Not only this, but the opportunity here afforded will awaken among us a new era of industrial progress. Ignorant and inexperienced, it is not strange that in the first years of our new life we began at the top instead of at the bottom; that a seat in Congress or the state legislature was more sought than real estate or industrial skill; that the political convention or stump speaking had more attractions than starting a dairy farm or a truck garden.

A ship lost at sea for many days suddenly sighted a friendly vessel. From the mast of the unfortunate vessel was seen a signal, "Water, water; we die of thirst!" The answer from the friendly vessel at once came back, "Cast down your buckets where you are." A second time the signal, "Water, water; send us water!" ran up from the distressed vessel, and was answered, "Cast down your buckets where you are." A third and fourth signal for water was answered, "Cast down your buckets where you are." The captain of the distressed vessel, at last heeding the injunction, cast down his bucket, and it came up full of fresh, sparkling water from the mouth of the Amazon River. To those of my race who depend on bettering their condition in a foreign land or who underestimate the importance of cultivating friendly relations with the Southern white man, who is their next-door neighbor, I would say: "Cast down your bucket where you are"—cast it down in making friends in every manly way of the people of all races by whom we are surrounded.

To those of the white race who look to the incoming of those of foreign birth and strange tongue and habits for the prosperity of the South, were I permitted I would repeat what I say to my own race, "Cast down your bucket where you are." Cast it down among the eight millions of Negroes whose habits you know, whose fidelity and love you have tested in days when to have proved treacherous meant the ruin of your firesides. Cast down your bucket among these people who have, without strikes and labor wars, tilled your fields, cleared your forests, built your railroads and cit-ies, and brought forth treasures from the bowels of the earth, and helped make possible this magnificent repre-sentation of the progress of the South. Casting down your bucket among my people, helping and encouraging them as you are doing on these grounds, and to education of head, hand, and heart, you will find that they will buy your surplus land, make blossom the waste places in your fields, and run your factories. While doing this, you can be sure in the future, as in the past, that you and your families will be sur-rounded by the most patient, faithful, law-abiding, and unresentful people that the world has seen. As we have proved our loyalty to you in the past, in nursing your children, watching by the sickbed of your mothers and fathers, and often following them with tear-dimmed eyes to their graves, so in the future, in our humble way, we shall stand by you with a devotion that no foreigner can approach, ready to lay down our lives, if need be, in defense of yours, interlacing our industrial, commercial, civil, and religious life with yours in a way that shall make the interests of both races one. In all things that are purely social we can be as separate as the fingers, yet one as the hand in all things essential to mu-tual progress.

Booker T. Washington and his wife, Margaret, photographer unknown.

There is no defense or security for any of us except in the highest intelligence and development of all. If anywhere there are efforts tending to curtail the fullest growth of the Negro, let these efforts be turned into stimulating, encouraging, and making him the most useful and intelligent citizen. Effort or means so invested will pay a thousand per cent interest. These efforts will be twice blessed—"blessing him that gives and him that takes."

There is no escape through law of man or God from the inevitable:—

> The laws of changeless justice bind
> Oppressor with oppressed;
> And close as sin and suffering joined
> We march to fate abreast.

Nearly sixteen millions of hands will aid you in pulling the load upward, or they will pull against you the load downward. We shall constitute one-third and more of the ignorance and crime of the South, or one-third its intelligence and progress; we shall contribute one-third to the business and industrial prosperity of the South, or we shall prove a veritable body of death, stagnating, depressing, retarding every effort to advance the body politic.

Gentlemen of the Exposition, as we present to you our humble effort at an exhibition of our progress, you must not expect overmuch. Starting thirty years ago with ownership here and there in a few quilts and pumpkins and chickens (gathered from miscellaneous sources), remember the path that has led from these to the inventions and production of agricultural implements, buggies, steam-engines, newspapers, books, statuary, carving, paintings, the management of drugstores and banks, has not been trodden without contact with thorns and thistles. While we take pride in what we exhibit as a result of our independent efforts, we do not for a moment forget that our part in this exhibition would fall far short of your expectations but for the constant help that has come to our educational life, not only from the southern states, but especially from northern philanthropists, who have made their gifts a constant stream of blessing and encouragement.

The wisest among my race understand that the agitation of questions of social equality is the extremest folly, and that progress in the environment of all the privileges that will come to us must be the result of severe and constant struggle rather than of artificial forcing. No race that has anything to contribute to the markets of the world is long in any degree ostracized. It is important and right that all privileges of the law be ours, but it is vastly more important that we be prepared for the exercises of these privileges. The opportunity to earn a dollar in a factory just now is worth infinitely more than the opportunity to spend a dollar in an opera house.

In conclusion, may I repeat that nothing in thirty years has given us more hope and encouragement and drawn us so near to you of the white race, as this opportunity offered by the Exposition; and here bending, as it were, over the altar that represents the results of the struggles of your race and mine, both starting practically empty-handed three decades ago, I pledge that in your effort to work out the great and intricate problem which God has laid at the doors of the South, you shall have at all times the patient, sympathetic help of my race. Only let this be constantly in mind: that, while from representations in these buildings of the product of field, of forest, of mine, of factory, letters, and art much good will come, yet far above and beyond material benefits will be that higher good, that, let us pray God, will come, in a blotting out of sectional differences and racial animosities and suspicions, in a determination to administer absolute justice, in a willing obedience among all classes to the mandates of law. This, coupled with our material prosperity, will bring into our beloved South a new heaven and a new earth.

CROSS OF GOLD SPEECH

William Jennings Bryan   *July 8, 1896*

The United States operated on a bimetallic standard until adoption of the gold standard in 1873. The Populist movement of the 1880s and 1890s arose in part from demands to return to bimetallism after the discoveries of large silver deposits in Nevada and Arizona. Abundant currency and higher inflation favored farmers with debts and hopes for higher commodity prices.

The Populist Party was the beneficiary of a dramatic political realignment as the Democrats lost a third of their congressional seats in the 1894 election. The "silver wing" of the Democratic Party gained strength after this disaster, and at the 1896 national convention managed to win nomination of a relatively unknown congressman from Nebraska, William Jennings Bryan. Only thirty-six years old, Bryan had electrified the convention with his attack on the gold standard. The Democrats identified themselves as the free silver party and absorbed nearly all the Populists' strength in the poorer West and South, though solid middle class support assured Republi-

*can victory in the electoral college. Bryan went on to run twice
more for the presidency, but never again came as close as he
had in 1896.*

I would be presumptuous, indeed, to present myself against the distinguished gentlemen to whom you have listened if this were a mere measuring of abilities; but this is not a contest between persons. The humblest citizen in all the land, when clad in the armor of a righteous cause, is stronger than all the hosts of error. I come to speak to you in defense of a cause as holy as the cause of liberty—the cause of humanity.

When this debate is concluded, a motion will be made to lay upon the table the resolution offered in commendation of the Administration, and also, the resolution offered in condemnation of the Administration. We object to bringing this question down to the level of persons. The individual is but an atom; he is born, he acts, he dies; but principles are eternal; and this has been a contest over a principle.

Never before in the history of this country has there been witnessed such a contest as that through which we have just passed. Never before in the history of American politics has a great issue been fought out as this issue has been, by the voters of a great party. On the fourth of March 1893, a few Democrats, most of them members of Congress, issued an address to the Democrats of the nation, asserting that the money question was the paramount issue of the hour; declaring that a majority of the Democratic party has the right to control the action of the party on this paramount issue; and concluding with the request that the believers in the free coinage of silver in the Democratic party should organize, take charge of, and control the policy of the Democratic party. Three months later, at Memphis, an organization was perfected, and the silver Democrats went forth openly and courageously proclaiming their belief, and declaring that, if successful, they would crystallize into a platform the declaration which they had made. Then began the struggle. With a zeal approaching the zeal which inspired the Crusaders who followed Peter the Hermit, our silver Democrats went forth from victory unto victory until they are now assembled, not to discuss, not to debate, but to enter up the judgement already rendered by the plain people of this country. In this contest brother has been arrayed against brother, father against son. The warmest ties of love, acquaintance, and association have been disregarded; old leaders have been cast aside when they have refused to give expression to the sentiments of those whom they would lead, and new leaders have sprung up to give direction to this cause of truth. Thus has the contest been waged, and we have assembled here under as binding and solemn instructions as were ever imposed upon representatives of the people.

We do not come as individuals. As individuals we might have been glad to compliment the gentleman from New York [Senator Hill], but we know that the people for whom we speak would never be willing to put him in a position where he could thwart the will of the Democratic party. I saw it was not a question of persons; it was a question of principle, and it is not with gladness, my friends, that we find ourselves brought into conflict with those who are now arrayed on the other side. . . .

When you come before us and tell us that we are about to disturb your business interests, we reply that you have disturbed our business interests by your course.

We say to you that you have made the definition of a business man too limited in its application. The man who is employed for wages is as much a business man as his employer; the attorney in a country town is as much a business man as the corporation counsel in a great metropolis; the merchant at the cross-roads store is as much a business man as the merchant of New York; the farmer who goes forth in the morning and toils all day, who begins in the spring and toils all summer, and who by the application of brain and muscle to the natural resources of the country creates wealth, is as much a business man as the man who goes upon the Board of Trade and bets upon the price of grain; the miners who go down a thousand feet into the earth, or climb two thousand feet upon the cliffs, and bring forth from their hiding places the precious metals to be poured into the channels of trade are as much business men as the few financial magnates who, in a back room, corner the money of the world. We come to speak of this broader class of business men.

Ah, my friends, we say not one word against those who live upon the Atlantic Coast, but the hardy pioneers who have braved all the dangers of the wilderness, who have made the desert to bloom as the rose—the pioneers away out there who rear their children near to Nature's heart, where they can mingle their voices with the voices of the birds—out there where they have erected schoolhouses for the education of their young, churches where they praise their Creator, and cemeteries where rest the ashes of their dead—these people, we say, are as deserving of the consideration of our party as any people in this country. It is for these that we speak. We do not come as aggressors. Our war is not a war of conquest; we are fighting in the defense of our homes, our families, and posterity. We have petitioned, and our petitions have been scorned; we have entreated, and our entreaties have been disregarded; we have begged, and they have mocked when our calamity came. We beg no longer; we entreat no more; we petition no more. We defy them!

The gentleman from Wisconsin [Vilas] has said that he fears a Robespierre.

My friends, in this land of the free you need not fear that a tyrant will spring up from among the people. What we need is an Andrew Jackson to stand, as Jackson stood, against the encroachments of organized wealth.

They tell us that this platform was made to catch votes. We reply to them that changing conditions make new issues; that the principles upon which Democracy rests are as everlasting as the hills, but they must be applied to new conditions as they arise. Conditions have arisen, and we are here to meet those conditions. They tell us that the income tax ought not to be brought in here; that it is a new idea. They criticize us for our criticism of the Supreme Court of the United States. My friends, we have not criticized; we have simply called attention to what you already know. If you want criticisms read the dissenting opinions of the court. There you will find criticisms. They say that we passed an unconstitutional law; we deny it. The income tax was not unconstitutional when it was passed; it was not unconstitutional when it went before the Supreme Court for the first time; it did not become unconstitutional until one of the judges changed his mind, and we cannot be expected to know when a judge will change his mind. The income tax is just. It simply intends to put the burden of government justly upon the backs of the people. I am in favor of an income tax. When I find a man who is not willing to bear his share of the burdens of the government which protects him, I find a man who is unworthy to enjoy the blessings of a government like ours.

They say that we are opposing national bank currency; it is true. If you will read what Thomas Benton said, you will find he said that, in searching history, he could find but one parallel to Andrew Jackson; that was Cicero, he destroyed the conspiracy of Cataline and saved Rome. Benton said that Cicero only did for Rome what Jackson did for us when he destroyed the bank conspiracy and saved America. We say in our platform we believe that the right to coin and issue money is a function of government. We believe it. We believe that it is a part of sovereignty, and can no more with safety be delegated to private individuals than we could afford to delegate to private individuals the power to make penal statutes or levy taxes. Mr. Jefferson, who was once regarded as good Democratic authority, seems to have differed in opinion from the gentleman who has addressed us on the part of the minority. Those who are opposed to this proposition tell us that the issue of paper money is a function of the banks, and that the government ought to go out of the banking business. I stand with Jefferson rather than with them, and tell them, as he did, that the issue of money is a function of government, and that the banks ought to go out of the government business.

They complain about the plank which declares against life tenure in office. They have tried to strain it to mean that which it does not mean. What we oppose by that plank is the life tenure which is being built up in Washington, and which excludes from participation in official benefits the humbler members of society. . . .

And now, my friends, let me come to the paramount issue. If they ask us why it is that we say more on the money question than we say upon the tariff question, I reply that, if protection has slain its thousands, the gold standard has slain its tens of thousands. If they ask us why we do not embody in our platforms all the things that we believe in, we reply that when we have restored the money of the Constitution, all other necessary reform will be possible; but that until this is done, there is no other reform that can be accomplished.

Why is it that within three months such a change has come over the country? Three months ago when it was confidently asserted that those who believed in the gold standard would frame our platform and nominate our candidates, even the advocates of the gold standard did not think that we could elect a President. And they had good reason for their doubt, because there is scarcely a State here today asking for the gold standard which is not in the absolute control of the Republican Party. But note the change. Mr. McKinley was nominated at St. Louis upon a platform which declared for the maintenance of the gold standard until it can be changed into bimetallism by international agreement. Mr. McKinley was the most popular man among the Republicans, and three months ago everybody in the Republican Party prophesied his election. How is it today? Why, the man who was once pleased to think that he looked like Napoleon—that man shudders today when he remembers that he was nominated on the anniversary of the battle of Waterloo.

Not only that, but as he listens, he can hear with ever-increasing distinctness the sound of the waves as they beat upon the lonely shores of St. Helena.

Why this change? Ah, my friends, is not the reason for the change evident to any one who will look at the matter? No private character, however pure, no personal popularity, however great, can protect from the avenging wrath of an indignant people a man who will declare that he is in favor of fastening the gold standard upon this country, or who is willing to surrender the right of self-government and place the legislative control of our affairs in the hands of foreign potentates and powers.

We go forth confident that we shall win. Why? Because upon the paramount issue of this campaign there is not a spot of ground upon which the enemy will dare to challenge battle. If they tell us that the gold standard is a good thing, we shall point to their platform and tell them that their platform pledges the party to get rid of the gold standard and substitute bimetallism. If the gold standard is a good thing why try to get rid of it? I call your attention to the fact that some of the very people who are in this Convention today and who tell us that we ought to declare in favor of international bimetallism—thereby declaring that the gold standard is wrong and that the principle of bimetallism is better—these very people four months ago were open and avowed advocates of the gold standard, and were then telling us that we could not legislate two metals together, even with the aid of all the world. If the gold standard is a good thing, we ought to declare in favor of its retention and not in favor of abandoning it; and if the gold standard is a bad thing why should we wait until other nations are willing to help us to let go? Here is the line of battle, and we care not upon which issue they force the fight; we are prepared to meet them on either issue or on both. If they tell us that the gold standard is the standard of civilization, we reply to them that this, the most enlightened of all the nations of the earth, has never declared for a gold standard and that both the great parties this year are declaring against it. If the gold standard is the standard of civilization, why, my friends, should we not have it? If they come to meet us on that issue we can present the history of our nation. More than that; we can tell them that they will search the pages of history in vain to find a single instance where the common people of any land have ever declared themselves in favor of the gold standard. They can find where the holders of fixed investments have declared for a gold standard, but not where the masses have. Mr. Carlisle said in 1878 that this was a struggle between the "idle holders of idle capital" and "the struggling masses, who produce the wealth and pay the taxes of the country," and, my friends, the question we are to decide is: Upon which side will the Democratic party fight; upon the side of "the idle holders of idle capital" or upon the side of "the struggling masses"? That is the question which the party must answer first, and then it must be answered by each individual hereafter. The sympathies of the Democratic party, as shown by the platform, are on the side of the struggling masses who have ever been the foundation of the Democratic party. There are two ideas of government. There are those who believe that if you will only legislate to make the well-to-do prosperous, their prosperity will leak through on those below. The Democratic idea, however, has been that if you make the masses prosperous, their prosperity will find its way up through every class which rests upon them.

You come to us and tell us that the great cities are in favor of the gold standard; we reply that the great cities rest upon our broad and fertile prairies. Burn down your cities and leave our farms, and your cities will spring up again as if by magic; but destroy our farms and the grass will grow in the streets of every city in the country.

My friends, we declare that this nation is able to legislate for its own people on every question, without waiting for the aid or consent of any other nation on earth; and upon that issue we expect to carry every state in the Union.

I shall not slander the inhabitants of the fair state of Massachusetts nor the inhabitants of the state of New York by saying that, when they are confronted with the proposition, they will declare that this nation is not able to attend to its own business. It is the issue of 1776 over again. Our ancestors, when but three million in number, had the courage to declare their political independence of every other nation; shall we, their descendants, when we have grown to seventy millions, declare that we are less independent than our forefathers?

No, my friends, that will never be the verdict of our people. Therefore, we care not upon what lines the battle is fought. If they say bimetallism is good, but that we cannot have it until other nations help us, we reply, that instead of having a gold standard because England has, we will restore bimetallism, and then let England have bimetallism because the United States has it. If they dare to come out in the open field and defend the gold standard as a good thing, we will fight them to the uttermost. Having behind us the producing masses of this nation and the world, supported by the commercial interests, the laboring interests and the toilers everywhere, we will answer their demand for a gold standard by saying to them: You shall not press down upon the brow of labor this crown of thorns, you shall not crucify mankind upon a cross of gold.

PLESSY V. FERGUSON

Henry B. Brown   *1896*

---

*Polling places were not the only places excluded to blacks.
In the 1880s and 1890s a series of "Jim Crow" laws completed
the color line in nearly all public spheres. This lawful separation
was endorsed by the Supreme Court in 1896. Homer Plessy, a
black man (who was in fact seven-eighths white) was arrested
for sitting in a "whites only" car on a Louisiana train. The
Supreme Court upheld his conviction on the grounds that
"separate but equal" facilities did not violate the Fourteenth
Amendment. In the lone dissenting opinion, Justice John
Marshall Harlan pointed out the inconsistencies and troubling
implications of legal segregation and argued against any regulation of civil liberties. The ruling was not reversed until the landmark Brown v. Board of Education of Topeka decision in 1954.*

BROWN, J. This case turns upon the constitutionality of an act of the general assembly of the state of Louisiana, passed in 1890, providing for separate railway carriages for the white and colored races. . . .

The constitutionality of this act is attacked upon the ground that it conflicts both with the 13th Amendment of the Constitution, abolishing slavery, and the 14th Amendment, which prohibits certain restrictive legislation on the part of the states.

1. That it does not conflict with the 13th Amendment, which abolished slavery and involuntary servitude, except as a punishment for crime, is too clear for argument. . . .

A statute which implies merely a legal distinction between the white and colored races—a distinction which is founded in the color of the two races, and which must always exist so long as white men are distinguished from the other race by color—has no tendency to destroy the legal equality of the two races, or re-establish a state of involuntary servitude. Indeed, we do not understand that the 13th Amendment is strenuously relied upon by the plaintiff in error in this connection. . . .

The object of the amendment was undoubtedly to enforce the absolute equality of the two races before the law, but in the nature of things it could not have been intended to abolish distinctions based upon color, or to enforce social, as distinguished from political, equality, or a commingling of the two races upon terms unsatisfactory to either. Laws permitting, and even requiring their separation in places where they are liable to be brought into contact do not necessarily imply the inferiority of either race to the other, and have been generally, if not universally, recognized as within the competency of the state legislatures in the exercise of their police power. The most common instance of this is connected with the establishment of separate schools for white and colored children, which have been held to be a valid exercise of the legislative power even by courts of states where the political rights of the colored race have been longest and most earnestly enforced. . . .

It is claimed by the plaintiff in error that, in any mixed community, the reputation of belonging to the dominant race, in this instance the white race is property, in the same sense that a right of action, or of inheritance, is property. Conceding this to be so, for the purposes of this case, we are unable to see how this statute deprives him of, or in any way affects his right to, such property. If he be a white man and assigned to a colored coach, he may have his action for damages against the company for being deprived of his so-called property. Upon the other hand, if he be a colored man and be so assigned, he has been deprived of no property, since he is not lawfully entitled to the reputation of being a white man. . . .

So far, then, as a conflict with the 14th Amendment is concerned, the case reduces itself to the question whether the statute of Louisiana is a reasonable regulation, and with respect to this there must necessarily be a large discretion on the part of the legislature. In determining the question of reasonableness it is at liberty to act with reference to the established usages, customs, and traditions of the people, and with a view to the promotion of their comfort, and the preservation of the public peace and good order. Gauged by this standard, we cannot say that a law which authorizes or even requires the separation of the two races in public conveyances is unreasonable or more obnoxious to the 14th Amendment than the acts of Congress requiring separate schools for colored children in the District of Columbia, the constitutionality of which does not seem to have been questioned, or the corresponding acts of state legislatures.

We consider the underlying fallacy of the plaintiff's argument to consist in the assumption that the enforced separation of the two races stamps the colored race with a badge of inferiority. If this be so, it is not by reason of anything found in the act, but solely because the colored race chooses to put that construction upon it. The argument necessarily assumes that if, as has been more than once the case, and is not unlikely to be so again, the colored race should become the dominant power in the state legislature, and should enact a law in precisely similar terms, it would thereby relegate the white race to an inferior position. We imagine that the white race, at least, would not acquiesce in this assumption. The argument also assumes that social prejudice may be overcome by legislation, and that equal rights cannot be secured to the Negro except by an enforced commingling of the two races. We cannot accept this proposition. If the two races are to meet on terms of social equality, it must be the result of natural affinities, a mutual appreciation of each other's merits and a voluntary consent of individuals. . . . Legislation is powerless to eradicate racial instincts or to abolish distinctions based upon physical differences, and the attempt to do so can only result in accentuating the difficulties of the present situation. If the civil and political right of both races be equal, one cannot be inferior . . . to the other civilly or politically. If one race be inferior to the other socially, the Constitution of the United States cannot put them upon the same plane.

Justice Harlan, dissenting: It was said in argument that the statute of Louisiana does not discriminate against either race, but prescribes a rule applicable alike to white and colored citizens. But the argument does not meet the difficulty. Every one knows that the statute in question had its origin in the purpose, not so much to exclude white persons from railroad cars occupied by blacks, as to exclude colored people from coaches occupied by or assigned to white persons. . . .

If a State can prescribe, as a rule of civil conduct, that whites and blacks shall not travel as passengers in the same railroad coach, why may it not so regulate the use of the streets of its cities and towns as to compel white citizens to keep on one side of a street and black citizens to keep on the other? . . . Further, if this statute of Louisiana is consistent with the personal liberty of citizens, why may not the State require the separation in railroad coaches of native and naturalized citizens of the United States, or of Protestants and Roman Catholics? . . .

In respect of civil rights, common to all citizens, the Constitution of the United States does not, I think, permit any public authority to know the race of those entitled to be protected in the enjoyment of such rights. Every true man has pride of race, and under appropriate circumstances, when the rights of others, his equals before the law, are not to be affected, it is his privilege to express such pride and to take such action based upon it as to him seems proper. But I deny that any legislative body or judicial tribunal may have regard to the race of citizens when the civil rights of those citizens are involved. Indeed such legislation as that here in question is inconsistent, not only with that equality of rights which pertains to citizenship, national and state, but with the personal liberty enjoyed by every one within the United States. . . .

In my opinion, the judgment this day rendered will, in time, prove to be quite as pernicious as the decision made by this tribunal in the Dred Scott Case. It was adjudged in that case that the descendants of Africans who were imported into this country and sold as slaves were not included nor intended to be included under the word "citizens" in the Constitution, and could not claim any of the rights and privileges which that instrument provided for and secured to citizens of the United States; that at the time of the adoption of the Constitution they were "considered as a subordinate and inferior class of beings, who had been subjugated by the dominant race, and, whether emancipated or not, yet remained subject to their authority, and had no rights or privileges but such as those who held the power and the government might choose to grant them." The recent amendments of the Constitution, it was supposed, had eradicated these principles from our institutions. But it seems that we have yet, in some of the states, a dominant race, a superior class of citizens, which assumes to regulate the enjoyment of civil rights, common to all citizens, upon the basis of race. The present decision, it may well be apprehended, will not only stimulate aggressions, more or less brutal and irritating, upon the admitted rights of colored citizens, but will encourage the belief that it is possible, by means of state enactments, to defeat the beneficent purposes which the people of the United States had in view when they adopted the recent amendments of the Constitution, by one of which the blacks of this country were made citizens of the United States and of the states in which they respectively reside and whose privileges and immunities, as citizens, the states are forbidden to abridge. Sixty millions of whites are in no danger from the presence here of eight millions of blacks. The destinies of the two races in this country are indissolubly linked together, and the interests of both require that the common government of all shall not permit the seeds of race hate to be planted under the sanction of law. What can more certainly arouse race hate, what more certainly create and perpetuate a feeling of distrust between these races, than state enactments which in fact proceed on the ground that colored citizens are so inferior and degraded that they cannot be allowed to sit in public coaches occupied by white citizens? That, as all will admit, is the real meaning of such legislation as was enacted in Louisiana. . . .

The sure guarantee of the peace and security of each race is the clear, distinct, unconditional recognition by our governments, national and state, of every right that inheres in civil freedom, and of the equality before the law of all citizens of the United States without regard to race. . . .

If evils will result from the commingling of the two races upon public highways established for the benefit of all, they will be infinitely less than those that will surely come from state legislation regulating the enjoyment of civil rights upon the basis of race. We boast of the freedom enjoyed by our people above all other peoples. But it is difficult to reconcile that boast with a state of the law which, practically, puts the brand of servitude and degradation upon a large class of our fellow citizens, our equals before the law. The thin disguise of "equal" accommodations for passengers in railroad coaches will not mislead anyone, or atone for the wrong this day done. . . .

I am of opinion that the statute of Louisiana is inconsistent with the personal liberty of citizens, white and black, in that state, and hostile to both the spirit and letter of the Constitution of the United States. If laws of like character should be enacted in the several states of the Union, the effect would be in the highest degree mischievous. Slavery as an institution tolerated by law would, it is true, have disappeared from our country, but there would remain a power in the states, by sinister legislation, to interfere with the full enjoyment of the blessings of freedom; to regulate civil rights, common to all citizens, upon the basis of race; and to place in a condition of legal inferiority a large body of American citizens, now constituting a part of the political community, called the people of the United States, for whom and by whom, through representatives, our government is administered. Such a system is inconsistent with the guarantee given by the Constitution to each state of a republican form of government, and may be stricken down by Congressional action, or by the courts in the discharge of their solemn duty to maintain the supreme law of the land, anything in the

Constitution or laws of any state to the contrary notwithstanding.

For the reasons stated, I am constrained to withhold my assent from the opinion and judgment of the majority.

LETTER TO BOOKER T. WASHINGTON

Susan B. Anthony   *December 19, 1898*

Though sometimes conflicting, the campaigns for black and women's civil rights continued their close association through the end of the nineteenth century. Following a visit by President William McKinley to the Tuskegee Institute, Susan B. Anthony wrote this letter to Booker T. Washington, praising his work, and urging him to support both women's and Asian suffrage in the newly acquired territory of Hawaii.

MY Dear Friends:—

I am despatching to you a set of my biography, both for yourself and for the library of your splendid school.

I should very much like to have been present when you were escorting the President through the different departments of your institution. It must have made him and the members of the cabinet realize something of the work you are doing for the education and elevation of the colored people of the South.

You have of course noticed the proscription of the Chinese and Japanese from citizenship in the proposed government of the new Territory of Hawaii, and I hope you have also noticed the invidious shutting out of all women from the right to vote or hold office there. Both propositions, I hope, will be repudiated by Congress, and if not I shall hope that President McKinley will veto the bill on the ground of the preliminary constitution violation of the fundamental principles of our government.

I trust that you are well, and that your family and your school are all prospering. Please accept my kind regards and Christmas greetings for all who abide with you.

Very sincerely yours,
Susan B. Anthony

Open Door Circular Letter

John Hay   *September 6, 1899*

The long decline of the Chinese Qing Dynasty became apparent after China's defeat by the Japanese in 1895. As the Japanese and European imperialists moved in for the final carving up of the Middle Kingdom, Great Britain and the United States became increasingly concerned, not as much for the fate of China as for maintenance of British and American trading rights. In March 1898, the British ambassador proposed a joint action to protect the integrity of China (and, of course, British and American interests), eventually leading to the formulation of the famous "Open Door" policy. In September 1899, Secretary of State John Hay announced this policy in a circular note to United States ambassadors at Berlin, London and St. Petersburg.

While the replies of the various powers were far from the support Hay hoped to obtain, he chose to interpret them as acceptance, announcing their assent in a second circular note. When the Boxer Rebellion broke out in 1900, the United States joined the campaign to raise the siege of foreign legations at Beijing, taking the opportunity to assert China's territorial integrity. As long as an "independent" China survived, so would United States claims to equal access to the Chinese market.

MR. Hay to Mr. White
Department of State
Sir: At the time when the Government of the United States was informed by that of Germany that it had leased from His Majesty the Emperor of China the port of Kiao-chao and the adjacent territory in the province of Shantung, assurances were given to the ambassador of the United States at Berlin by the Imperial German minister for foreign affairs that the rights and privileges insured by treaties with China to citizens of the United States would not thereby suffer or be in anywise impaired within the area over which Germany has thus obtained control.

More recently, however, the British Government recognized by a formal agreement with Germany the exclusive right of the latter country to enjoy in said leased area and the contiguous "sphere of influence or interest" certain privileges, more especially those relating to railroads and mining enterprises; but, as the exact nature and extent of the rights thus recognized have not been clearly defined, it is possible that serious conflicts of interest may at any time arise, not only between British and German subjects within said area, but that the interests of our citizens may also be jeopardized thereby.

Earnestly desirous to remove any cause of irritation and to insure at the same time to the commerce of all nations in China the undoubted benefits which should accrue from a formal recognition by the various powers claiming "spheres of interest" that they shall enjoy perfect equality of treatment for their commerce and navigation within such "spheres," the Government of the United States would be pleased to see His German Majesty's Government give formal assurances and lend its coöperation in securing like assurances from the other interested powers that each within its respective sphere of whatever influence—

First. Will in no way interfere with any treaty port or any vested interest within any so-called "sphere of interest" or leased territory it may have in China.

Second. That the Chinese treaty tariff of the time being shall apply to all merchandise landed or shipped to all such ports as are within said "sphere of interest" (unless they be "free ports"), no matter to what nationality it may belong, and that duties so leviable shall be collected by the Chinese Government.

Third. That it will levy no higher harbor dues on vessels of another nationality frequenting any port in such "sphere" than shall be levied on vessels of its own nationality, and no higher railroad charges over lines built, controlled, or operated within its "sphere" on merchandise belonging to citizens or subjects of other nationalities transported through such "sphere" than shall be levied on similar merchandise belonging to its own nationals transported over equal distances.

The liberal policy pursued by His Imperial German Majesty in declaring Kiao-chao a free port and in aiding the Chinese Government in the establishment there of a custom-house are so clearly in line with the proposition which this Government is anxious to see recognized that it entertains the strongest hope that Germany will give its acceptance and hearty support.

The recent case of His Majesty the Emperor of Russia declaring the port of Talien-wan open during the whole of the lease under which it is held from China, to the merchant ships of all nations, coupled with the categorical assurances made to this Government by His Imperial Majesty's representative at this capital at the time, and since repeated to me by the present Russian ambassador, seem to insure the support of the Emperor to the proposed measure. Our ambassador at the Court of St. Petersburg has, in consequence, been instructed to submit it to the Russian Government and to request their early consideration of it. A copy of my instruction on the subject to Mr. Tower is herewith inclosed for your confidential information.

The commercial interests of Great Britain and Japan will be so clearly served by the desired declaration of intentions, and the views of the Governments of these countries as to the desirability of the adoption of measures insuring the benefits of equality of treatment of all foreign trade throughout China are so similar to those entertained by the United States, that their acceptance of the propositions herein outlined and their cooperation in advocating their adoption by the other powers can be confidently expected. I inclose herewith copy of the instruction which I have sent to Mr. Choate on the subject.

In view of the present favorable conditions, you are instructed to submit the above considerations to His Imperial German Majesty's minister for foreign affairs, and to request his early consideration of the subject.

Copy of this instruction is sent to our ambassadors at London and at St. Petersburg for their information.

FOURTH ANNUAL MESSAGE TO CONGRESS

Theodore Roosevelt   *December 6, 1904*

Theodore Roosevelt served two terms as president of the United States (1901-1909) and ran for a third. Roosevelt's dedication to furthering the United States' international role, especially in the Western Hemisphere, marked a departure from the isolationism of the nineteenth century. Roosevelt received a Nobel Peace Prize for his mediation of the Russo-Japanese War in 1905. His fourth annual message to Congress outlines his view of the responsibilities of the United States to keep its neighbors "stable, orderly, and prosperous." Roosevelt advocated United States military intervention and occupation when necessary to uphold the ideals of the Monroe Doctrine.

. . . IT is not true that the United States feels any land hunger or entertains any projects as regards the other nations of the Western Hemisphere save such as are for their welfare. All that this country desires is to see the neighboring countries stable, orderly, and prosperous. Any country whose people conduct themselves well can count upon our hearty friendship. If a nation shows that it knows how to act with reasonable efficiency and decency in social and political matters, if it keeps order and pays its obligations, it need fear no interference from the United States. Chronic wrongdoing, or an impotence which results in a general loosening of the ties of civilized society, may in America, as elsewhere, ultimately require intervention by some civilized nation, and in the Western Hemisphere the adherence of the United States to the Monroe Doctrine may force the United States, however reluctantly, in flagrant cases of such wrongdoing or impotence, to the exercise of an international police power. If every country washed by the Caribbean Sea would show the progress in stable and just civilization which with the aid of the Platt amendment Cuba has shown since our troops left the island, and which so many of the republics in both Americas are constantly and brilliantly showing, all question of interference by this Nation with their affairs would be at an end. Our interests and those of our southern neighbors are in reality identical. They have great natural riches, and if within their borders the reign of law and justice obtains, prosperity is sure to come to them. While they thus obey the primary laws of civilized society they may rest assured that they will be treated by us in a spirit of cordial and helpful sympathy. We would interfere with them only in the last resort, and then only if it became evident that their inability or unwillingness to do justice at home and abroad had violated the rights of the United States or had invited foreign aggression to the detriment of the entire body of American nations. It is a mere truism to say that every nation, whether in America or anywhere else, which desires to maintain its freedom, its independence, must ultimately realize that the right of such independence can not be separated from the responsibility of making good use of it.

In asserting the Monroe Doctrine, in taking such steps as we have taken in regard to Cuba, Venezuela, and Panama, and in endeavoring to circumscribe the theater of war in the Far East, and to secure the open door in China, we have acted in our own interest as well as in the interest of humanity at large. There are, however, cases in which, while our own interests are not greatly involved, strong appeal is made to our sympathies. . . . But in extreme cases action may be justifiable and proper. What form the action shall take must depend upon the circumstances of the case; that is, upon the degree of the atrocity and upon our power to remedy it. The cases in which we could interfere by force of arms as we interfered to put a stop to intolerable conditions in Cuba are necessarily very few.

Seventh Annual Message to Congress

Theodore Roosevelt   *December 3, 1907*

> *Theodore Roosevelt brought the Progressive ideals of the
> need for government regulation with him to the White House;
> his efforts to control the growth of corporations earned him the
> nickname "Trust Buster." With his chief advisor on natural
> resources, Gifford Pinchot, Roosevelt implemented a program of
> conservation of public lands and resources for use, as opposed
> to preservation, and spearheaded government regulation of
> natural resources. In his seventh annual message to Congress,
> Roosevelt stated the necessity of federal government involvement
> to ensure the continued availability of the nation's wilderness
> lands and natural resources.*

TO the Senate and House of Representatives:

. . . The conservation of our natural resources and their proper use constitute the fundamental problem which underlies almost every other problem of our national life. . . . As a nation we not only enjoy a wonderful measure of present prosperity but if this prosperity is used aright it is an earnest of future success such as no other nation will have. The reward of foresight for this nation is great and easily foretold. But there must be the look ahead, there must be a realization of the fact that to waste, to destroy, our natural resources, to skin and exhaust the land instead of using it so as to increase its usefulness, will result in undermining in the days of our children the very prosperity which we ought by right to hand down to them amplified and developed. For the last few years, through several agencies, the government has been endeavoring to get our people to look ahead and to substitute a planned and orderly development of our resources in place of a haphazard striving for immediate profit. Our great river systems should be developed as national water highways, the Mississippi, with its tributaries, standing first in importance, and the Columbia second, although there are many others of importance on the Pacific, the Atlantic, and the Gulf slopes. The National Government should undertake this work, and I hope a beginning will be made in the present Congress; and the greatest of all our rivers, the Mississippi, should receive special attention. From the Great Lakes to the mouth of the Mississippi there should be a deep waterway, with deep waterways leading from it to the East and the West. Such a waterway would practically mean the extension of our coastline into the very heart of our country. It would be of incalculable benefit to our people. If begun at once it can be carried through in time appreciably to relieve the congestion of our great freight-carrying lines of railroads. The work should be systematically and continuously carried forward in accordance with some well-conceived plan. The main streams should be improved to the highest point of efficiency before the improvement of the branches is attempted; and the work should be kept free from every taint of recklessness or jobbery. The inland waterways which lie just back of the whole

Theodore Roosevelt.

Eastern and Southern coasts should likewise be developed. Moreover, the development of our waterways involves many other important water problems, all of which should be considered as part of the same general scheme. The government dams should be used to produce hundreds of thousands of horse-power as an incident to improving navigation; for the annual value of the unused water-power of the United States perhaps exceeds the annual value of the products of all our mines. As an incident to creating the deep waterways down the Mississippi, the government should build along its whole lower length levees which, taken together with the control of the headwaters, will at once and forever put a complete stop to all threat of floods in the immensely fertile delta region. The territory lying adjacent to the Mississippi along its lower course will thereby become one of the most prosperous and populous, as it already is one of the most fertile, farming regions in all the world. I have appointed an inland waterways commission to study and outline a comprehensive scheme of development along all the lines indicated. Later I shall lay its report before the Congress.

Irrigation should be far more extensively developed than at present, not only in the States of the great plains and the Rocky Mountains, but in many others, as, for instance, in large portions of the South Atlantic and Gulf States, where it should go hand in hand with the reclamation of swampland. The Federal Government should seriously devote itself to this task, realizing that utilization of waterways and water-power, forestry, irrigation, and the reclamation of lands threatened with overflow, are all interdependent parts of the same problem. The work of the Reclamation Service in developing the larger opportunities of the Western half of our country for irrigation is more important than almost any other movement. The constant purpose of the government in connection with the Reclamation Service has been to use the water resources of the public lands for the ultimate greatest good of the greatest number; in other words, to put upon the land permanent home-makers, to use and develop it for themselves and for their children and children's children. . . .

The effort of the government to deal with the public land has been based upon the same principle as that of the Reclamation Service. The land law system which was designed to meet the needs of the fertile and well-watered regions of the Middle West has largely broken down when applied to the drier regions of the great plains, the mountains, and much of the Pacific slope, where a farm of 160 acres is inadequate for self-support. . . .

Some such legislation as that proposed is essential in order to preserve the great stretches of public grazing-land which are unfit for cultivation under present methods and are valuable only for the forage which they supply. These stretches amount in all to some 300,000,000 acres, and are open to the free grazing of cattle, sheep, horses, and goats, without restriction. Such a system, or lack of system, means that the range is not so much used as wasted by abuse. As the West settles, the range becomes more and more overgrazed. Much of it cannot be used to advantage unless it is fenced, for fencing is the only way by which to keep in check the owners of nomad flocks which roam hither and thither, utterly destroying the pastures and leaving a waste behind so that their presence is incompatible with the presence of home-makers. The existing fences are all illegal. . . . All these fences, those that are hurtful and those that are beneficial, are alike illegal and must come down. But it is outrage that the law should necessitate such action on the part of the Administration. The unlawful fencing of public lands for private grazing must be stopped, but the necessity which occasioned it must be provided for. The Federal Government should have control of the range, whether by permit or lease, as local necessities may determine. Such control could secure the great benefit of legitimate fencing, while at the same time securing and promoting the settlement of the country. . . . The government should part with its title only to the actual home-maker, not to the profit-maker who does not care to make a home. Our prime object is to secure the rights and guard the interests of the small ranchman, the man who ploughs and pitches hay for himself. It is this small ranchman, this actual settler and home-maker, who in the long run is most hurt by permitting thefts of the public land in whatever form.

Optimism is a good characteristic, but if carried to an excess it becomes foolishness. We are prone to speak of the resources of this country as inexhaustible; this is not so. The mineral wealth of the country, the coal, iron, oil, gas, and the like, does not reproduce itself, and therefore is certain to be exhausted ultimately; and wastefulness in dealing with it today means that our descendants will feel the exhaustion a generation or two before they otherwise would. But there are certain other forms of waste which could be entirely stopped—the waste of soil by washing, for instance, which is among the most dangerous of all wastes now in progress in the United States, is easily preventable, so that this present enormous loss of fertility is entirely unnecessary. The preservation or replacement of the forests is one of the most important means of preventing this loss. We have made a beginning in forest preservation, but . . . so rapid has been the rate of exhaustion of timber in the United States in the past, and so rapidly is the remainder being exhausted, that the country is unquestionably on the verge of a timber famine which will be felt in every household in the land. . . . The present annual consumption of lumber is certainly three times as great as the annual growth; and if the consumption and growth continue unchanged, practically all our lumber will be exhausted in another generation, while long before the limit to complete exhaustion is reached the growing scarcity will make itself felt in many blighting ways upon our national welfare. About twenty per cent of our forested territory is now reserved in national forests; but these do not include the most valuable timberlands, and in any event the proportion is too small to expect that the reserves can accomplish more than a mitigation of the trouble which is ahead for the nation. . . . We should acquire in the Appalachian and White Mountain regions all the forest-lands that it is possible to acquire for the use of the nation. These lands, because they form a national asset, are as emphatically national as the rivers which they feed, and which flow through so many States before they reach the ocean. . . .

DECLARATION OF THE
CONSERVATION CONFERENCE

U.S. Governors   *May 15, 1908*

―――――――――――

In response to President Theodore Roosevelt's 1907
address on the need for federal laws governing natural re-
sources and national lands, a conference of United States state
and territorial governors met in 1908 to discuss the states' role

*in conservation. At this Conservation Conference, the governors
issued a declaration on May 15, 1908, which called for judicious use of American lands to preserve their productivity as
well as their beauty. The governors called for swift action by the
United States Congress to conserve American water and land,
and promised that the states themselves would also endeavor to
protect the environment. In a moment of rare concert, all state
and territorial governors signed the measure.*

WE the Governors of the States and Territories of the United States of
America, in Conference assembled, do hereby declare the conviction that the
great prosperity of our country rests upon the abundant resources of the land
chosen by our forefathers for their homes and where they laid the foundation
of this great Nation.

We look upon these resources as a heritage to be made use of in establishing and promoting the comfort, prosperity, and happiness of the American
People, but not to be wasted, deteriorated, or needlessly destroyed.

We agree that our country's future is involved in this; that the great natural
resources supply the material basis on which our civilization must continue to
depend, and on which the perpetuity of the Nation itself rests.

We agree, in the light of facts brought to our knowledge and from
information received from sources which we can not doubt, that this material
basis is threatened with exhaustion. Even as each succeeding generation from
the birth of the Nation has performed its part in promoting the progress and
development of the Republic, so do we in this generation recognize it as a high
duty to perform our part; and this duty in large degrees lies in the adoption of
measures for the conservation of the natural wealth of the country.

We declare our firm conviction that this conservation of our natural
resources is a subject of transcendent importance, which should engage
unremittingly the attention of the Nation, the States, and the People in earnest
cooperation. These natural resources include the land on which we live and
which yields our food; the living waters which fertilize the soil, supply power,
and form great avenues of commerce; the forests which yield the materials for
our homes, prevent erosion of the soil, and conserve the navigation and other
uses of our streams; and the minerals which form the basis of our industrial life,
and supply us with heat, light, and power.

We agree that the land should be so used that erosion and soil-wash shall
cease; that there should be reclamation of arid and semi-arid regions by means
of irrigation, and of swamp and overflowed regions by means of drainage; that

the waters should be so conserved and used as to promote navigation, to enable the arid regions to be reclaimed by irrigation, and to develop power in the interests of the People; that the forests which regulate our rivers, support our industries, and promote the fertility and productiveness of the soil should be preserved and perpetuated; that the minerals found so abundantly beneath the surface should be so used as to prolong their utility; that the beauty, healthfulness, and habitability of our country should be preserved and increased; that the sources of national wealth exist for the benefit of the People, and that monopoly thereof should not be tolerated.

We commend the wise forethought of the President in sounding the note of warning as to the waste and exhaustion of the natural resources of the country, and signify our high appreciation of his action in calling this Conference to consider the same and to seek remedies therefor through cooperation of the Nation and the States.

We agree that this cooperation should find expression in suitable action by the Congress within the limits of and coextensive with the national jurisdiction of the subject, and, complementary thereto, by the legislatures of the several States within the limits of and coextensive with their jurisdiction.

We declare the conviction that in the use of the natural resources our independent States are interdependent and bound together by ties of mutual benefits, responsibilities and duties.

We agree in the wisdom of future conferences between the President, Members of Congress, and the Governors of States on the conservation of our natural resources with a view of continued cooperation and action on the lines suggested; and to this end we advise that from time to time, as in his judgment may seem wise, the President call the Governors of the States and Members of Congress and others into conference.

We agree that further action is advisable to ascertain the present condition of our natural resources and to promote the conservation of the same; and to that end we recommend the appointment by each State of a Commission on the Conservation of Natural Resources, to cooperate with each other and with any similar commission of the Federal Government.

We urge the continuation and extension of forest policies adapted to secure the husbanding and renewal of our diminishing timber supply, the prevention of soil erosion, the protection of headwaters, and the maintenance of the purity and navigability of our streams. We recognize that the private ownership of forest lands entails responsibilities in the interests of all the People, and we favor the enactment of laws looking to the protection and replacement of privately owned forests.

We recognize in our waters a most valuable asset of the People of the

United States, and we recommend the enactment of laws looking to the conservation of water resources for irrigation, water supply, power, and navigation, to the end that navigable and source streams may be brought under complete control and fully utilized for every purpose. We especially urge on the Federal Congress the immediate adoption of a wise, active, and thorough waterway policy, providing for the prompt improvement of our streams and the conservation of their watersheds required for the uses of commerce and the protection of the interests of our People.

We recommend the enactment of laws looking to the prevention of waste in the mining and extraction of coal, oil, gas, and other minerals with a view to their wise conservation for the use of the People, and to the protection of human life in the mines.

Let us conserve the foundations of our prosperity.

[SIGNATURES]

Amendment XVI
Income Tax Authorized

February 25, 1913

Proposed by Congress July 12, 1909, its ratification was completed February 25, 1913.

THE Congress shall have power to lay and collect taxes on incomes, from whatever source derived, without apportionment among the several States and without regard to any census or enumeration.

Amendment XVII
Direct Popular Election of Senators

May 31, 1913

Proposed by Congress May 16, 1912, its ratification was completed May 31, 1913.

THE Senate of the United States shall be composed of two senators from each State, elected by the people thereof, for six years; and each Senator shall have one vote. The electors in each State shall have the qualifications requisite for electors of the most numerous branch of the State legislature.

When vacancies happen in the representation of any State in the Senate, the executive authority of such State shall issue writs of election to fill such vacancies: Provided, That the legislature of any State may empower the executive thereof to make temporary appointments until the people fill the vacancies by election as the legislature may direct.

This amendment shall not be so construed as to affect the election or term of any senator chosen before it becomes valid as part of the Constitution.

VIII
TWO WARS AND
A DEPRESSION

WOMEN AND WAR

Jane Addams   *May 1915*

———————

Jane Addams was a Progressive reformer who championed the causes of peace, women's rights and social justice. In May 1915, Addams addressed the International Congress of Women at The Hague on the subject of "Women and War." Addams argued that women, by virtue of their innate devotion to the preservation of life and civilization, were the natural enemies of violence and warfare. From this congress, Addams and other women pacifists founded the Women's International League for Peace and Freedom (WILPF) in May 1919 in reaction against World War I. Addams served as the president of the WILPF from its founding to her death in 1935. Her address at The Hague served to crystallize women's opposition to war, and she became the standard bearer for the international peace movement. She shared the Nobel Peace Prize in 1931.

———————

AT this last evening of the International Congress of Women, now drawing to its successful conclusion, its president wishes first to express her sincere admiration for the women who have come here from the belligerent nations. They have come from home at a moment when the national consciousness is so welling up from each heart and overflowing into the consciousness of others that the individual loses, not only all concern for his personal welfare, but for his convictions as well and gladly merges all he has into his country's existence.

It is a high and precious moment in human experience; war is too great a price to pay for it but it is worth almost anything else. I therefore venture to call the journey of these women, many of them heartsick and sorrowful, to this Congress, little short of an act of heroism. Even to appear to differ from those she loves in the hour of their affliction or exaltation, has ever been the supreme test of woman's conscience.

For the women coming from neutral nations there have also been supreme difficulties. In some of these countries, woman has a large measure of political responsibility and, in all of them, women for long months have been sensitive to the complicated political conditions which may also easily compromise a neutral nation and jeopardize the peace and safety of its people. At a Congress such as this, an exaggerated word may easily be spoken or reported as spoken which would make a difficult situation still more difficult; but these women have bravely taken that risk and made the moral venture. We from the United States, who have made the longest journey and are therefore freest from these entanglements, can speak out our admiration for these fine women from the neutral as well as from the fighting nations.

Why then were women from both the warring and the neutral nations ready to come to this Congress to the number of 1500? By what profound and spiritual forces were they impelled, at this moment when the spirit of Internationalism is apparently broken down, to believe that the solidarity of women would hold fast and that through them, as through a precious instrument, they would be able to declare the reality of those basic human experiences ever perpetuating and cherishing the race, and courageously to set them over against the superficial and hot impulses which have so often led to warfare.

Those great underlying forces, in response to which so many women have come here, belong to the human race as a whole and constitute a spiritual internationalism which surrounds and completes our national life, even as our national life itself surrounds and completes our family life; they do not conflict with patriotism on one side any more than family devotion conflicts with it upon the other.

We have come to this International Congress of women not only to protest from our hearts and with the utmost patience we can command, unaffrighted even by the "difficult and technical," to study this complicated modern world of ours now so sadly at war itself; but furthermore we would fain suggest ways by which this large internationalism may find itself and dig new channels through which it may flow.

At moments it appears as if the excessive nationalistic feeling expressing itself during these fateful months through the exaltation of warfare in so many of the great nations, is due to the accumulation within their own borders of those higher human affections which should have had an outlet into the larger life of the world but could not, because no international devices had been provided for such expression. No great central authority could deal with this sum of human will, as a scientist deals with the body of knowledge in his subject irrespective of its national origins, and the nations themselves became congested, as it were, and inevitably grew confused between what was legitimate patriotism and those universal emotions which have nothing to do with national frontiers.

We are happy that the Congress has met at The Hague. Thirty years ago I came to this beautiful city, full fifteen years before the plans for international organization had found expression here. If I can look back to such wonderful beginnings in my own lifetime, who shall say that the younger women on this platform may not see the completion of an international organization which shall make war impossible because good will and just dealing between nations shall have found an ordered method of expression?

We have many evidences at the present moment that, inchoate and unorganized as it is, it may be found even in the midst of this war constantly breaking through its national bounds. The very soldiers in the opposing trenches have to be moved about from time to time lest they come to know each other, not as the enemy but as individuals, and a sense of comradeship overwhelm their power to fight.

This totally unnecessary conflict between the great issues of internationalism and of patriotism rages all about us even in our own minds so that we wage a veritable civil war within ourselves. These two great affections should never have been set one against the other; it is too late in the day for war. For decades, the lives of all the peoples of the world have been revealed to us through the products of commerce, news agencies, through popular songs and novels, through photographers and cinematographs, and last of all through the interpretations of the poets and artists.

Suddenly all these wonderful agencies are applied to the hideous business of uncovering the details of warfare.

Never before has the world known so fearfully and so minutely what war means to the soldier himself, to women and children, to that civilization which is the common heritage of all mankind. All this intimate and realistic knowledge of war is recorded upon human hearts more highly sensitized than ever before in the history of man and filled with a new and avid hunger for brotherhood.

In the shadow of this intolerable knowledge, we, the women of this International Congress, have come together to make our solemn protest against that of which we know.

Our protest may be feeble but the world progresses, in the slow and halting manner in which it does progress, only in proportion to the moral energy exerted by the men and women living in it; social advance must be pushed forward by the human will and understanding united for conscious ends. The slow progress towards juster international relations may be traced to the distinguished jurist of the Netherlands, Grotius, whose honored grave is but a few miles from here; to the great German, Immanuel Kant, who lifted the subject of "Eternal Peace" high above even philosophical controversy; to Count Tolstoy, of Russia, who so trenchantly set forth in our own day, and so on from one country to another.

Each in his own time, because he placed law above force, was called a dreamer and a coward, but each did his utmost to express clearly the truth that was in him and beyond that human effort can not go.

These mighty names are but the outstanding witnesses among the host of men and women who have made their obscure contributions to the same great end.

Conscious of our own shortcomings and not without a sense of complicity in the present war, we women have met in earnestness and in sorrow to add what we may to this swelling tide of purpose.

It is possible that the appeal for the organization of the world upon peaceful lines has been made too exclusively to man's reason and sense of justice, quite as the eighteenth century enthusiasm for humanity was prematurely founded on intellectual sentiment. Reason is only a part of the human endowment; emotion and deep-set racial impulses must be utilized as well— those primitive human urgings to foster life and to protect the hopeless, of which women were the earliest custodians, and even the social and gregarious instincts that we share with the animals themselves. These universal desires must be given opportunities to expand and the most highly trained intellects must serve them rather than the technique of war and diplomacy.

They tell us that wounded lads lying in helpless pain and waiting too long for the field ambulance, call out constantly for their mothers, impotently beseeching them for help; during this Congress we have been told of soldiers who say to their hospital nurses, "We can do nothing for ourselves, but go back to the trenches again and again so long as we are able. Can not the women do something about this war? Are you kind to us only when we are wounded?"

The time may come when the exhausted survivors of the war may well reproach women for their inaction during this terrible time. It is possible they will then say that when devotion to the ideals of patriotism drove thousands of men into international warfare, the women refused to accept the challenge and in that moment of terror failed to assert clearly and courageously the sanctity of human life, the reality of things of the spirit.

For three days we have met together, so conscious of the bloodshed and desolation surrounding us, that all irrelevant and temporary matters fell away and we spoke solemnly to each other of the great and eternal issues, as do those who meet around the bedside of the dying.

We have formulated our message and given it to the world to heed when it will, confident that at last the great Court of International Opinion will pass righteous judgment upon all human affairs.

ADDRESS TO THE
UNITED STATES SENATE

Woodrow Wilson   *January 22, 1917*

Woodrow Wilson was president of the United States from 1913 to 1921. As a Progressive, Wilson opposed America's entry into World War I, which he viewed as a primarily European conflict over colonial power. However, in February 1917, Germany renewed unrestricted submarine warfare and the British intercepted the "Zimmerman note," which promised Mexico the return of Texas and California in exchange for the formation of a German-Mexican alliance against the United States. These events polarized American public opinion against the Central Powers, and Wilson entered the war on the side of Britain and France. Wilson believed that United States involvement would make it possible for America to play a decisive role in the peace, in order to "make the world safe for democracy," and to ensure that World War I would be the "war to end all wars." To these ends, Wilson proposed a "peace without victory" in a 1917 address to the Senate of the United States.

GENTLEMEN of the Senate: . . .

. . . I have sought this opportunity to address you because I thought that I owed it to you, as the counsel associated with me in the final determination of our international obligations, to disclose to you without reserve the thought and purpose that have been taking form in my mind in regard to the duty of our Government in the days to come when it will be necessary to lay afresh and upon a new plan the foundations of peace among the nations.

It is inconceivable that the people of the United States should play no part in that great enterprise. . . . They cannot in honor withhold the service to which they are now about to be challenged. They do not wish to withhold it. But they owe it to themselves and to the other nations of the world to state the conditions under which they will feel free to render it.

That service is nothing less than this, to add their authority and their power to the authority and force of other nations to guarantee peace and justice throughout the world. Such a settlement cannot now be long postponed. It is right that before it comes this Government should frankly formulate the conditions upon which it would feel justified in asking our people to approve its formal and solemn adherence to a League for Peace. I am here to attempt to state those conditions.

The present war must first be ended; but we owe it to candor and to a just regard for the opinion of mankind to say that, so far as our participation in guarantees of future peace is concerned, it makes a great deal of difference in what way and upon what terms it is ended. The treaties and agreements which bring it to an end must embody terms which will create a peace that is worth guaranteeing and preserving, a peace that will win the approval of mankind, not merely a peace that will serve the several interests and immediate aims of the nations engaged. . . .

No covenant of co-operative peace that does not include the peoples of the New World can suffice to keep the future safe against war; and yet there is only one sort of peace that the peoples of America could join in guaranteeing. The elements of that peace must be elements that engage the confidence and satisfy the principles of the American governments, elements consistent with their political faith and with the practical convictions which the peoples of America have once for all embraced and undertaken to defend. . . .

It will be absolutely necessary that a force be created as a guarantor of the permanency of the settlement so much greater than the force of any nation now engaged or any alliance hitherto formed or projected that no nation, no probable combination of nations could face or withstand it. If the peace presently to be made is to endure, it must be a peace made secure by the organized major force of mankind.

The terms of the immediate peace agreed upon will determine whether it is a peace for which such a guarantee can be secured. The question upon which the whole future peace and policy of the world depends is this: Is the present war a struggle for a just and secure peace, or only for a new balance of power? If it be only a struggle for a new balance of power, who will guarantee, who can guarantee the stable equilibrium of the new arrangement? Only a tranquil Europe can be a stable Europe. There must be, not a balance of power, but a community of power; not organized rivalries, but an organized common peace.

Fortunately we have received very explicit assurances on this point. . . . I think it will be serviceable if I attempt to set forth what we understand them to be.

They imply, first of all, that it must be a peace without victory. It is not pleasant to say this. I beg that I may be permitted to put my own interpretation upon it and that it may be understood that no other interpretation was in my thought. I am seeking only to face realities and to face them without soft concealments. Victory would mean peace forced upon the loser, a victor's terms imposed upon the vanquished. It would be accepted in humiliation, under duress, at an intolerable sacrifice, and would leave a sting, a resentment, a bitter memory upon which terms of peace would rest, not permanently, but only as upon quicksand. Only a peace between equals can last. Only a peace the very principle of which is equality and a common participation in a common benefit. The right state of mind, the right feeling between nations, is as necessary for a lasting peace as is the just settlement of vexed questions of territory or of racial and national allegiance.

The equality of nations upon which peace must be founded if it is to last must be an equality of rights; the guarantees exchanged must neither recognize nor imply a difference between big nations and small, between those that are powerful and those that are weak. Right must be based upon the common strength, not upon the individual strength, of the nations upon whose concert peace will depend. Equality of territory or of resources there of course cannot be; nor any sort of equality not gained in the ordinary peaceful and legitimate development of the peoples themselves. But no one asks or expects anything more than an equality of rights. Mankind is looking now for freedom of life, not for equipoises of power.

And there is a deeper thing involved than even equality of right among organized nations. No peace can last, or ought to last, which does not recognize and accept the principle that governments derive all their just powers from the consent of the governed, and that no right anywhere exists to hand peoples about from sovereignty to sovereignty as if they were property. I take it for granted, for instance, if I may venture upon a single example, that statesmen everywhere are agreed that there should be a united, independent, and autonomous Poland, and that henceforth inviolable security of life, of worship, and of industrial and social development should be guaranteed to all peoples who have lived hitherto under the power of governments devoted to a faith and purpose hostile to their own. . . .

So far as practicable, moreover, every great people now struggling towards a full development of its resources and of its powers should be assured a direct outlet to the great highways of the sea. Where this cannot be done by the cession of territory, it can no doubt be done by the neutralization of direct rights of way under the general guarantee which will assure the peace itself. With a right comity of arrangement no nation need be shut away from free access to the open paths of the world's commerce.

And the paths of the sea must alike in law and in fact be free. The freedom of the seas is the *sine qua non* of peace, equality, and co-operation. No doubt a somewhat radical reconsideration of many of the rules of international practice hitherto thought to be established may be necessary in order to make the seas indeed free and common in practically all circumstances for the use of mankind, but the motive for such changes is convincing and compelling. There can be no trust or intimacy between the peoples of the world without them. The free, constant, unthreatened intercourse of nations is an essential part of the process of peace and of development. It need not be difficult either to define or to secure the freedom of the seas if the governments of the world sincerely desire to come to an agreement concerning it.

It is a problem closely connected with the limitation of naval armaments and the co-operation of the navies of the world in keeping the seas at once free and safe. And the question of limiting naval armaments opens the wider and perhaps more difficult question of the limitation of armies and of all programs of military preparation. Difficult and delicate as these questions are, they must be faced with the utmost candor and decided in a spirit of real accommodation if peace is to come with healing in its wings, and come to stay. Peace cannot be had without concession and sacrifice. There can be no sense of safety and equality among the nations if great preponderating armaments are henceforth to continue here and there to be built up and maintained. The statesmen of the world must plan for peace and nations must adjust and accommodate their policy to it as they have planned for war and made ready for pitiless contest and rivalry. The question of armaments, whether on land or sea, is the most immediately and intensely practical question connected with the future fortunes of nations and of mankind.

I have spoken upon these great matters without reserve and with the utmost explicitness because it has seemed to me to be necessary if the world's yearning desire for peace was anywhere to find free voice and utterance. Perhaps I am the only person in high authority amongst all the peoples of the world who is at liberty to speak and hold nothing back. I am speaking as an individual, and yet I am speaking also, of course, as the responsible head of a great government, and I feel confident that I have said what the people of the United States would wish me to say. . . .

I am proposing, as it were, that the nations should with one accord adopt the doctrine of President Monroe as the doctrine of the world: that no nation should seek to extend its polity over any other nation or people, but that every people should be left free to determine its own polity, its own way of development, unhindered, unthreatened, unafraid, the little along with the great and powerful.

I am proposing that all nations henceforth avoid entangling alliances which would draw them into competitions of power; catch them in a net of intrigue and selfish rivalry, and disturb their own affairs with influences intruded from without. There is no entangling alliance in a concert of power. When all unite to act in the same sense and with the same purpose all act in the common interest and are free to live their own lives under a common protection.

I am proposing government by the consent of the governed; that freedom of the seas which in international conference after conference representatives of the United States have urged with the eloquence of those who are the most convinced disciples of liberty; and that moderation of armaments which makes of armies and navies a power for order merely, not an instrument of aggression or of selfish violence.

These are American principles, American policies. We could stand for no others. And they are also the principles and policies of forward looking men and women everywhere, of every modern nation, of every enlightened community. They are the principles of mankind and must prevail.

THE FOURTEEN POINTS

Woodrow Wilson   *January 8, 1918*

---

*President Woodrow Wilson presented his plan for the
postwar world in the Fourteen Points that he wished to include
in the Treaty of Versailles. Wilson argued for self-determination
of liberated colonies, open diplomatic negotiations among all*

countries, and, most important, a League of Nations which
would enforce liberal ideals and protect the peace. Significantly,
several of Wilson's points were omitted from the Treaty of
Versailles. Georges Clemençeau, the French Premier, criticized
Wilson's Fourteen Points by saying, "Even God Almighty only
has ten." Wilson's idealism also went unappreciated at home.
Not only did the isolationist Senate refuse to allow the United
States to join the League of Nations, but it also denied rat-
ification of the Treaty of Versailles, necessitating a separate
peace with Germany. Wilson's frantic drive to garner public
support for the treaty and the League ended when he suffered a
debilitating stroke in Pueblo, Colorado, in September 1919.

GENTLEMEN of the Congress: . . . It will be our wish and purpose that the processes of peace, when they are begun, shall be absolutely open and that they shall involve and permit henceforth no secret understandings of any kind. The day of conquest and aggrandizement is gone by; so is also the day of secret covenants entered into in the interest of particular governments and likely at some unlooked-for moment to upset the peace of the world. It is this happy fact, now clear to the view of every public man whose thoughts do not still linger in an age that is dead and gone, which makes it possible for every nation whose purposes are consistent with justice and the peace of the world to avow now or at any other time the objects it has in view.

We entered this war because violations of right had occurred which touched us to the quick and made the life of our own people impossible unless they were corrected and the world secured once for all against their recurrence. What we demand in this war, therefore, is nothing peculiar to ourselves. It is that the world be made fit and safe to live in; and particularly that it be made safe for every peace-loving nation which, like our own, wishes to live its own life, determine its own institutions, be assured of justice and fair dealing by the other peoples of the world as against force and selfish aggression. All the peoples of the world are in effect partners in this interest, and for our own part we see very clearly that unless justice be done to others it will not be done to us. The program of the world's peace, therefore, is our program; and that program, the only possible program, as we see it, is this:

I. Open covenants of peace, openly arrived at, after which there shall be no private international understandings of any kind but diplomacy shall proceed always frankly and in the public view.

II. Absolute freedom of navigation upon the seas, outside territorial waters, alike in peace and in war, except as the seas may be closed in whole or in part by international action for the enforcement of international covenants.

III. The removal, so far as possible, of all economic barriers and the establishment of an equality of trade conditions among all the nations consenting to the peace and associating themselves for its maintenance.

IV. Adequate guarantees given and taken that national armaments will be reduced to the lowest point consistent with domestic safety.

V. A free, open-minded, and absolutely impartial adjustment of all colonial claims, based upon a strict observance of the principle that in determining all such questions of sovereignty the interests of the population concerned must have equal weight with the equitable claims of the government whose title is to be determined.

VI. The evacuation of all Russian territory and such a settlement of all questions affecting Russia as will secure the best and freest coöperation of the other nations of the world in obtaining for her an unhampered and unembarrassed opportunity for the independent determination of her own political development and national policy and assure her of a sincere welcome into the society of free nations under institutions of her own choosing; and, more than a welcome, assistance also of every kind that she may need and may herself desire. The treatment accorded Russia by her sister nations in the months to come will be the acid test of their good will, of their comprehension of her needs as distinguished from their own interests, and of their intelligent and unselfish sympathy.

VII. Belgium, the whole world will agree, must be evacuated and restored, without any attempt to limit the sovereignty which she enjoys in common with all other free nations. No other single act will serve as this will serve to restore confidence among the nations in the laws which they have themselves set and determined for the government of their relations with one another. Without this healing act the whole structure and validity of international law is forever impaired.

VIII. All French territory should be freed and the invaded portions restored, and the wrong done to France by Prussia in 1871 in the matter of Alsace-Lorraine, which has unsettled the peace of the world for nearly fifty years, should be righted, in order that peace may once more be made secure in the interest of all.

IX. A readjustment of the frontiers of Italy should be effected along clearly recognizable lines of nationality.

X. The peoples of Austria-Hungary, whose place among the nations we wish to see safeguarded and assured, should be accorded the freest opportunity of autonomous development.

XI. Rumania, Serbia, and Montenegro should be evacuated; occupied territories restored; Serbia accorded free and secure access to the sea; and the relations of the several Balkan states to one another determined by friendly counsel along historically established lines of allegiance and nationality; and international guaranties of the political and economic independence and territorial integrity of the several Balkan states should be entered into.

XII. The Turkish portions of the present Ottoman Empire should be assured a secure sovereignty, but the other nationalities which are now under Turkish rule should be assured an undoubted security of life and an absolutely unmolested opportunity of autonomous development, and the Dardanelles should be permanently opened as a free passage to the ships and commerce of all nations under international guarantees.

XIII. An independent Polish state should be erected which should include the territories inhabited by indisputably Polish populations, which should be assured a free and secure access to the sea, and whose political and economic independence and territorial integrity should be guaranteed by international covenant.

XIV. A general association of nations must be formed under specific covenants for the purpose of affording mutual guaranties of political independence and territorial integrity to great and small states alike.

In regard to these essential rectifications of wrong and assertions of right we feel ourselves to be intimate partners of all the governments and peoples associated together against the Imperialists. We cannot be separated in interest or divided in purpose. We stand together until the end.

For such arrangements and covenants we are willing to fight and to continue to fight until they are achieved; but only because we wish the right to prevail and desire a just and stable peace such as can be secured only by removing the chief provocations to war, which this program does not remove. We have no jealousy of German greatness, and there is nothing in this program that impairs it. We grudge her no achievement or distinction of learning or of pacific enterprise such as have made her record very bright and enviable. We do not wish to injure her or to block in any way her legitimate influence or power. We do not wish to fight her either with arms or with hostile arrangements of trade if she is willing to associate herself with us and the other peace-loving nations of the world in covenants of justice and law and fair dealing. We wish her only to accept a place of equality among the peoples of the world,—the new world in which we now live,—instead of a place of mastery.

Neither do we presume to suggest to her any alteration or modification of her institutions. But it is necessary, we must frankly say, and necessary as a preliminary to any intelligent dealings with her on our part, that we should know whom her spokesmen speak for when they speak to us, whether for the Reichstag majority or for the military party and the men whose creed is imperial domination.

We have spoken now, surely, in terms too concrete to admit of any further doubt or question. An evident principle runs through the whole program I have outlined. It is the principle of justice to all peoples and nationalities, and their right to live on equal terms of liberty and safety with one another, whether they be strong or weak. Unless this principle be made its foundation no part of the structure of international justice can stand. The people of the United States could act upon no other principle, and to the vindication of this principle they are ready to devote their lives, their honor, and everything that they possess. The moral climax of this the culminating and final war for human liberty has come, and they are ready to put their own strength, their own highest purpose, their own integrity and devotion to the test.

Amendment XVIII
Liquor Prohibition

January 16, 1919

Proposed by Congress December 18, 1917, its ratification was completed January 16, 1919.

AFTER one year from the ratification of this article, the manufacture, sale or transportation of intoxicating liquors within, the importation thereof into, or the exportation thereof from the United States and all territory subject to the jurisdiction thereof for beverage purposes is hereby prohibited.

The Congress and the several States shall have concurrent power to enforce this article by appropriate legislation.

This article shall be inoperative unless it shall have been ratified as an amendment to the Constitution by the legislatures of the several States, as provided in the Constitution, within seven years from the date of the submission hereof to the States by Congress.

AMENDMENT XIX
NATIONAL WOMAN SUFFRAGE

August 26, 1920

Proposed by Congress June 4, 1919, this amendment's ratification was completed August 26, 1920. Women had won the right to vote in Wyoming in 1869 and in several other western states in the late nineteenth century. The long battle for women's right to vote nationally was finally won with the passage of the Nineteenth Amendment.

THE right of citizens of the United States to vote shall not be denied or abridged by the United States or by any States on account of sex.

The Congress shall have power by appropriate legislation to enforce the provisions of this article.

THE PHILOSOPHY OF
RUGGED INDIVIDUALISM

Herbert Hoover   *October 22, 1928*

In the course of his 1928 presidential campaign, Herbert Hoover appealed to the profound faith of most Americans in the American economy and way of life. Although a few intellectuals and farmers pointed out the precariousness of the United States economy, Americans generally saw a bright and prosperous future ahead. Hoover's definition of Liberalism appealed to this majority with the argument that government regulation could only hinder economic prosperity, and he won the election. Ironically, on October 24, 1929, one year and two days after

Hoover gave this speech in New York City, the Stock Market Crash marked the onset of the Great Depression.

THIS campaign now draws near a close. The platforms of the two parties defining principles and offering solutions of various national problems have been presented and are being earnestly considered by our people. . . .

In my acceptance speech I endeavored to outline the spirit and ideals by which I would be guided in carrying that platform into administration. Tonight I will not deal with the multitude of issues which have been already well canvassed. I intend rather to discuss some of those more fundamental principles and ideals upon which I believe the government of the United States should be conducted. . . .

After the war, when the Republican party assumed administration of the country, we were faced with the problem of determination of the very nature of our national life. During one hundred and fifty years we have built up a form of self-government and a social system which is peculiarly our own. It differs essentially from all others in the world. It is the American system. It is just as definite and positive a political and social system as has ever been developed on earth. It is founded upon a particular conception of self-government in which de-centralized local responsibility is the very base. Further than this, it is founded upon the conception that only through ordered liberty, freedom, and equal opportunity to the individual will his initiative and enterprise spur on the march of progress. And in our insistence upon equality of opportunity has our system advanced beyond all the world.

During the war we necessarily turned to the government to solve every difficult economic problem. The government having absorbed every energy of our people for war, there was no other solution. For the preservation of the state the Federal Government became a centralized despotism which undertook unprecedented responsibilities, assumed autocratic powers, and took over the business of citizens. To a large degree we regimented our whole people temporarily into a socialistic state. However justified in time of war if continued in peace-time it would destroy not only our American system but with it our progress and freedom as well.

When the war closed, the most vital of all issues both in our country and throughout the world was whether governments should continue their wartime ownership and operation of many instrumentalities of production and distribution. We were challenged with a peace-time choice between the American system of rugged individualism and a European philosophy of diametrically opposed doctrines—doctrines of paternalism and state socialism. The acceptance of these ideas would have meant the destruction of self-government through centralization of government. It would have meant the undermining of the individual initiative and enterprise through which our people have grown to unparalleled greatness. . . .

The Republican Party from the beginning resolutely turned its face away from these ideas and these war practices. . . . When the Republican Party came into full power it went at once resolutely back to our fundamental conception of the state and the rights and responsibilities of the individual. Thereby it restored confidence and hope in the American people, it freed and stimulated enterprise, it restored the government to its position as an umpire instead of a player in the economic game. For these reasons the American people have gone forward in progress while the rest of the world has halted, and some countries have even gone backwards. If anyone will study the causes of retarded recuperation in Europe, he will find much of it due to stifling of private initiative on one hand, and overloading of the government with business on the other.

There has been revived in this campaign, however, a series of proposals which, if adopted, would be a long step toward the abandonment of our American system and a surrender to the destructive operation of governmental conduct of commercial business. Because the country is faced with difficulty and doubt over certain national problems—that is prohibition, farm relief, and electrical power—our opponents propose that we must thrust government a long way into the businesses which give rise to these problems. In effect, they abandon the tenets of their own party and turn to state socialism as a solution for the difficulties presented by all three. It is proposed that we shall change from prohibition to the state purchase and sale of liquor. If their agricultural relief program means anything, it means that the government shall directly or indirectly buy and sell and fix prices of agricultural products. And we are to go into the hydroelectric power business. In other words, we are confronted with a huge program of government in business.

There is, therefore, submitted to the American people a question of fundamental principle. That is: shall we depart from the principles of our American political and economic system, upon which we have advanced beyond all the rest of the world, in order to adopt methods based on principles destructive of its very foundations? And I wish to emphasize the seriousness of these proposals. I wish to make my position clear; for this goes to the very roots of American life and progress.

I should like to state to you the effect that this projection of government in business would have upon our system of self-government and our economic system. That effect would reach to the daily life of every man and woman. It would impair the very basis of liberty and freedom not only for those left outside the fold of expanded bureaucracy but for those embraced within it.

Let us first see the effect upon self-government. When the Federal Government undertakes to go into commercial business it must at once set up the organization and administration of that business, and it immediately finds itself in a labyrinth, every alley of which leads to the destruction of self-government.

Commercial business requires a concentration of responsibility. Self-government requires decentralization and many checks and balances to safeguard liberty. Our Government to succeed in business would need to become in effect a despotism. There at once begins the destruction of self-government. . . .

It is a false liberalism that interprets itself into the government operation of commercial business. Every step of bureaucratizing of the business of our country poisons the very roots of liberalism—that is, political equality, free speech, free assembly, free press, and equality of opportunity. It is the road not to more liberty, but to less liberty. Liberalism should be found not striving to spread bureaucracy but striving to set bounds to it. True liberalism seeks all legitimate freedom first in the confident belief that without such freedom the pursuit of all other blessings and benefits is vain. That belief is the foundation of all American progress, political as well as economic.

Liberalism is a force truly of the spirit, a force proceeding from the deep realization that economic freedom cannot be sacrificed if political freedom is to be preserved. Even if Governmental conduct of business could give us more efficiency instead of less efficiency, the fundamental objection to it would remain unaltered and unabated. It would destroy political equality. It would increase rather than decrease abuse and corruption. It would stifle initiative and invention. It would undermine the development of leadership. It would cramp and cripple the mental and spiritual energies of our people. It would extinguish equality and opportunity. It would dry up the spirit of liberty and progress. For these reasons primarily it must be resisted. For a hundred and fifty years liberalism has found its true spirit in the American system, not in the European systems.

I do not wish to be misunderstood in this statement. I am defining a general policy. It does not mean that our government is to part with one iota of its national resources without complete protection to the public interest. I have already stated that where the government is engaged in public works for purposes of flood control, of navigation, of irrigation, of scientific research or national defense, or in pioneering a new art, it will at times necessarily produce power or commodities as a by-product. But they must be a by-product of the major purpose, not the major purpose itself.

Nor do I wish to be misinterpreted as believing that the United States is free-for-all and devil-take-the-hindmost. The very essence of equality of opportunity and of American individualism is that there shall be no domination by any group or combination in this republic, whether it be business or political. On the contrary, it demands economic justice as well as political and social justice. It is no system of *laissez faire*.

I feel deeply on this subject because during the war I had some practical experience with governmental operation and control. I have witnessed not only at home but abroad the many failures of government in business. I have seen its tyrannies, its injustices, its destructions of self-government, its undermining of the very instincts which carry our people forward to progress. I have witnessed the lack of advance, the lowered standards of living, the depressed spirits of people working under such a system. My objection is based not upon theory or upon a failure to recognize wrong or abuse, but I know the adoption of such methods would strike at the very roots of American life and would destroy the very basis of American progress.

Our people have the right to know whether we can continue to solve our great problems without abandonment of our American system. I know we can. . . .

And what have been the results of the American system? Our country has become the land of opportunity to those born without inheritance, not merely because of the wealth of its resources and industry but because of this freedom of initiative and enterprise. Russia has natural resources equal to ours. Her people are equally industrious, but she has not had the blessings of one hundred and fifty years of our form of government and our social system.

By adherence to the principles of decentralized self-government, ordered liberty, equal opportunity, and freedom to the individual, our American experiment in human welfare has yielded a degree of well-being unparalleled in all the world. It has come nearer to the abolition of poverty, to the abolition of fear of want, than humanity has ever reached before. Progress of the past seven years is the proof of it. This alone furnishes the answer to our opponents, who ask us to introduce destructive elements into the system by which this has been accomplished. . . .

I have endeavored to present to you that the greatness of America has grown out of a political and social system and a method of control of economic forces distinctly its own—our American system—which has carried this great experiment in human welfare farther than ever before in all history. We are nearer today to the ideal of the abolition of poverty and fear from the lives of men and women than ever before in any land. And I again repeat that the departure from our American system by injecting principles destructive to it which our opponents propose, will jeopardize the very liberty and freedom of our people, and will destroy equality of opportunity not alone to ourselves but to our children. . . .

Amendment XX: Beginning of Presidential Terms, Congressional Sessions

January 23, 1933

Proposed by Congress March 2, 1932, its ratification was completed January 23, 1933.

SEC. 1. The terms of the President and Vice-President shall end at noon on the twentieth day of January, and the terms of Senators and Representatives at noon on the third day of January, of the years in which such terms would have ended if this article had not been ratified; and the terms of their successors shall then begin.

SEC. 2. The Congress shall assemble at least once in every year, and such meeting shall begin at noon on the third day of January, unless they shall by law appoint a different day.

SEC. 3. If, at the time fixed for the beginning of the term of the President, the President-elect shall have died, the Vice-President-elect shall become President. If a President shall not have been chosen before the time fixed for the beginning of his term, or if the President-elect shall have failed to qualify, then the Vice-President-elect shall act as President until a President shall have qualified; and the Congress may by law provide for the case wherein neither a President-elect nor a Vice-President-elect shall have qualified, declaring who shall then act as President, or the manner in which one who is to act shall be selected, and such person shall act accordingly until a President or Vice-President shall have qualified.

SEC. 4. The Congress may by law provide for the case of the death of any of the persons from whom the House of Representatives may choose a President whenever the right of choice shall have devolved upon them, and for the case of the death of any of the persons from whom the Senate may choose a Vice-President whenever the right of choice shall have devolved upon them.

SEC. 5. Sections 1 and 2 shall take effect on the 15th day of October following the ratification of this article.

SEC. 6. This article shall be inoperative unless it shall have been ratified as an amendment to the Constitution by the legislatures of three-fourths of the several States within seven years from the date of its submission.

First Inaugural Address

Franklin Delano Roosevelt   *March 4, 1933*

Franklin Delano Roosevelt was elected president of the United States for an unprecedented four terms (1933-1945) and saw the United States through the Great Depression and World War II. On the eve of his first inauguration in March 1933, the nation's banking system collapsed as millions of panicked depositors attempted to withdraw savings that banks had invested in long-term loans. Roosevelt spoke to this crisis in his inaugural address on March 4, 1933, telling Americans "the only thing we have to fear is fear itself." Soon Roosevelt closed American banks by proclamation and summoned a special session of Congress to pass emergency banking legislation. Roosevelt's response to the banking crisis marked the beginning of what was termed the "New Deal," an extensive series of social and economic programs aimed at economic recovery.

PRESIDENT Hoover, Mr. Chief Justice, my friends:

This is a day of national consecration, and I am certain that my fellow-Americans expect that on my induction into the Presidency I will address them with a candor and a decision which the present situation of our nation impels.

This is pre-eminently the time to speak the truth, the whole truth, frankly and boldly. Nor need we shrink from honestly facing conditions in our country today. This great nation will endure as it has endured, will revive and will prosper.

So first of all let me assert my firm belief that the only thing we have to fear is fear itself—nameless, unreasoning, unjustified terror which paralyzes needed efforts to convert retreat into advance.

In every dark hour of our national life a leadership of frankness and vigor has met with that understanding and support of the people themselves which is essential to victory. I am convinced that you will again give that support to leadership in these critical days.

In such a spirit on my part and on yours we face our common difficulties. They concern, thank God, only material things. Values have shrunken to fantastic levels; taxes have risen; our ability to pay has fallen, government of all kinds is faced by serious curtailment of income; the means of exchange are frozen in the currents of trade; the withered leaves of industrial enterprise lie on every side; farmers find no markets for their produce; the savings of many years in thousands of families are gone.

More important, a host of unemployed citizens face the grim problem of existence, and an equally great number toil with little return. Only a foolish optimist can deny the dark realities of the moment.

Yet our distress comes from no failure of substance. We are stricken by no plague of locusts. Compared with the perils which our forefathers conquered because they believed and were not afraid, we have still much to be thankful for. Nature still offers her bounty and human efforts have multiplied it. Plenty is at our doorstep, but a generous use of it languishes in the very sight of the supply.

Primarily, this is because the rulers of the exchange of mankind's goods have failed through their own stubbornness and their own incompetence, have admitted their failure and abdicated. Practices of the unscrupulous money changers stand indicted in the court of public opinion, rejected by the hearts and minds of men.

True, they have tried, but their efforts have been cast in the pattern of an outworn tradition. Faced by failure of credit, they have proposed only the lending of more money.

Stripped of the lure of profit by which to induce our people to follow their false leadership, they have resorted to exhortations, pleading tearfully for restored confidence. They know only the rules of a generation of self-seekers.

They have no vision, and when there is no vision the people perish.

The money changers have fled from their high seats in the temple of our civilization. We may now restore that temple to the ancient truths.

The measure of the restoration lies in the extent to which we apply social values more noble than mere monetary profit.

Happiness lies not in the mere possession of money; it lies in the joy of achievement, in the thrill of creative effort.

The joy and moral stimulation of work no longer must be forgotten in the mad chase of evanescent profits. These dark days will be worth all they cost us if they teach us that our true destiny is not to be ministered unto but to minister to ourselves and to our fellow-men.

Recognition of the falsity of material wealth as the standard of success goes hand in hand with the abandonment of the false belief that public office and high political position are to be valued only by the standards of pride of place and personal profit; and there must be an end to a conduct in banking and in business which too often has given to a sacred trust the likeness of callous and selfish wrongdoing.

Small wonder that confidence languishes, for it thrives only on honesty, on honor, on the sacredness of obligations, on faithful protection, on unselfish performance. Without them it cannot live.

Restoration calls, however, not for changes in ethics alone. This nation asks for action, and action now.

Our greatest primary task is to put people to work. This is no unsolvable problem if we face it wisely and courageously.

It can be accomplished in part by direct recruiting by the government itself, treating the task as we would treat the emergency of a war, but at the same time, through this employment, accomplishing greatly needed projects to stimulate and reorganize the use of our natural resources.

Hand in hand with this, we must frankly recognize the overbalance of population in our industrial centers and, by engaging on a national scale in the redistribution, endeavor to provide a better use of the land for those best fitted for the land.

The task can be helped by definite efforts to raise the values of agricultural products and with this the power to purchase the output of our cities.

It can be helped by preventing realistically the tragedy of the growing loss, through foreclosure, of our small homes and our farms.

It can be helped by insistence that the Federal, State and local governments act forthwith on the demand that their cost be drastically reduced.

It can be helped by the unifying of relief activities which today are often scattered, uneconomical and unequal. It can be helped by national planning for and supervision of all forms of transportation and of communications and other utilities which have a definitely public character.

There are many ways in which it can be helped, but it can never be helped merely by talking about it. We must act, and act quickly.

Finally, in our progress toward a resumption of work we require two safeguards against a return of the evils of the old order; there must be a strict supervision of all banking and credits and investments; there must be an end to speculation with other people's money, and there must be provision for an adequate but sound currency.

These are the lines of attack. I shall presently urge upon a new Congress in special session detailed measures for their fulfillment, and I shall seek the immediate assistance of the several States.

Through this program of action we address ourselves to putting our own national house in order and making income balance outgo.

Our international trade relations, though vastly important, are, in point of time and necessity, secondary to the establishment of a sound national economy.

I favor as a practical policy the putting of first things first. I shall spare no effort to restore world trade by international economic readjustment, but the emergency at home cannot wait on that accomplishment.

The basic thought that guides these specific means of national recovery is not narrowly nationalistic.

It is the insistence, as a first consideration, upon the interdependence of the various elements in, and parts of, the United States—a recognition of the old and permanently important manifestation of the American spirit of the pioneer.

It is the way to recovery. It is the immediate way. It is the strongest assurance that the recovery will endure.

In the field of world policy I would dedicate this nation to the policy of the good neighbor—the neighbor who resolutely respects himself and, because he does so, respects the rights of others—the neighbor who respects his obligations and respects the sanctity of his agreements in and with a world of neighbors.

If I read the temper of our people correctly, we now realize as we have never before, our interdependence on each other; that we cannot merely take, but we must give as well; that if we are to go forward we must move as a trained and loyal army willing to sacrifice for the good of a common discipline, because, without such discipline, no progress is made, no leadership becomes effective.

We are, I know, ready and willing to submit our lives and property to such discipline because it makes possible a leadership which aims at a larger good.

This I propose to offer, pledging that the larger purposes will bind upon us all as a sacred obligation with a unity of duty hitherto evoked only in time of armed strife.

With this pledge taken, I assume unhesitatingly the leadership of this great army of our people, dedicated to a disciplined attack upon our common problems.

Action in this image and to this end is feasible under the form of government which we have inherited from our ancestors.

Our Constitution is so simple and practical that it is possible always to meet extraordinary needs by changes in emphasis and arrangement without loss of essential form.

That is why our constitutional system has proved itself the most superbly enduring political mechanism the modern world has produced. It has met every stress of vast expansion of territory, of foreign wars, of bitter internal strife, of world relations.

It is to be hoped that the normal balance of executive and legislative authority may be wholly adequate to meet the unprecedented task before us. But it may be that an unprecedented demand and need for undelayed action may call for temporary departure from that normal balance of public procedure.

I am prepared under my constitutional duty to recommend the measures that a stricken nation in the midst of a stricken world may require.

Franklin D. Roosevelt, portrait by Frank O. Salisbury.

These measures, or such other measures as the Congress may build out of its experience and wisdom, I shall seek, within my constitutional authority, to bring to speedy adoption.

But in the event that the Congress shall fail to take one of these two courses, and in the event that the national emergency is still critical, I shall not evade the clear course of duty that will then confront me.

I shall ask the Congress for the one remaining instrument to meet the crisis—broad executive power to wage a war against the emergency as great as the power that would be given me if we were in fact invaded by a foreign foe.

For the trust reposed in me I will return the courage and the devotion that befit the time. I can do no less.

We face the arduous days that lie before us in the warm courage of national unity; with the clear consciousness of seeking old and precious moral values; with the clean satisfaction that comes from the stern performance of duty by old and young alike.

We aim at the assurance of a rounded and permanent national life.

We do not distrust the future of essential democracy. The people of the United States have not failed. In their need they have registered a mandate that they want direct, vigorous action.

They have asked for discipline and direction under leadership. They have made me the present instrument of their wishes. In the spirit of the gift I take it.

In this dedication of a nation we humbly ask the blessing of God. May He protect each and every one of us! May He guide me in the days to come!

AMENDMENT XXI
REPEAL OF AMENDMENT XVIII

December 5, 1933

Proposed by Congress February 20, 1933, its ratification was completed December 5, 1933.

SEC. 1. The eighteenth article of amendment to the Constitution of the United States is hereby repealed.

SEC. 2. The transportation or importation into any State, Territory, or Possession of the United States for delivery or use therein of intoxicating liquors, in violation of the laws thereof, is hereby prohibited.

SEC. 3. This article shall be inoperative unless it shall have been ratified as an amendment to the Constitution by conventions in the several States, as provided in the Constitution, within seven years from the date of the submission hereof to the States by the Congress.

FOUR FREEDOMS SPEECH

Franklin Delano Roosevelt   *January 6, 1941*

As 1941 began, Nazi Germany controlled the European continent from the Arctic to the Pyrenees. From America it seemed that only Great Britain stood between Hitler and the United States. Still, the isolationism of Congress and the American public remained firm.

Franklin Roosevelt had been elected for his third term with promises to keep the United States out of the war in Europe. Despite this vow, he looked on events in Europe with great concern. On January 6, 1941, Roosevelt addressed a joint session of Congress to discuss the seriousness of the European situation and to draw attention to the need for Americans to defend liberty.

TO the Congress of the United States:

I address you, the Members of the Seventy-Seventh Congress, at a moment unprecedented in the history of the Union. I use the word "unprecedented," because at no previous time has American security been as seriously threatened from without as it is today. . . .

It is true that prior to 1914 the United States often had been disturbed by events in other Continents. We had even engaged in two wars with European nations and in a number of undeclared wars in the West Indies, in the Mediterranean and in the Pacific for the maintenance of American rights and for the principles of peaceful commerce. In no case, however, had a serious threat been raised against our national safety or our independence.

What I seek to convey is the historic truth that the United States as a nation has at all times maintained opposition to any attempt to lock us in behind an ancient Chinese wall while the procession of civilization went past. Today, thinking of our children and their children, we oppose enforced isolation for ourselves or for any part of the Americas.

Even when the World War broke out in 1914, it seemed to contain only small threat of danger to our own American future. But, as time went on, the American people began to visualize what the downfall of democratic nations might mean to our own democracy.

We need not over-emphasize imperfections in the Peace of Versailles. We need not harp on failure of the democracies to deal with problems of world deconstruction. We should remember that the Peace of 1919 was far less unjust than the kind of "pacification" which began even before Munich, and which is being carried on under the new order of tyranny that seeks to spread over every continent today. The American people have unalterably set their faces against that tyranny.

Every realist knows that the democratic way of life is at this moment being directly assailed in every part of the world—assailed either by arms, or by secret spreading of poisonous propaganda by those who seek to destroy unity and promote discord in nations still at peace. During sixteen months this assault has blotted out the whole pattern of democratic life in an appalling number of independent nations, great and small. The assailants are still on the march, threatening other nations, great and small.

Therefore, as your President, performing my constitutional duty to "give to the Congress information of the state of the Union," I find it necessary to report that the future and the safety of our country and of our democracy are overwhelmingly involved in events far beyond our borders.

Armed defense of democratic existence is now being gallantly waged in four continents. If that defense fails, all the population and all the resources of Europe, Asia, Africa and Australia will be dominated by the conquerors. The total of those populations and their resources greatly exceeds the sum total of the population and resources of the whole of the Western Hemisphere—many times over.

In times like these it is immature—and incidentally untrue—for anybody to brag that an unprepared America, single-handed, and with one hand tied behind its back, can hold off the whole world.

No realistic American can expect from a dictator's peace international generosity, or return of true independence, or world disarmament, or freedom of expression, or freedom of religion—or even good business. Such a peace would bring no security for us or for our neighbors. "Those, who would give up essential liberty to purchase a little temporary safety, deserve neither liberty nor safety." As a nation we may take pride in the fact that we are soft-hearted; but we cannot afford to be soft-hearted. We must always be wary of those who with sounding brass and a tinkling cymbal preach the "ism" of appeasement. We must especially beware of that small group of selfish men who would clip the wings of the American eagle in order to feather their own nests.

I have recently pointed out how quickly the tempo of modern warfare could bring into our very midst the physical attack which we must expect if the dictator nations win this war.

There is much loose talk of our immunity from immediate and direct invasion from across the seas. Obviously, as long as the British Navy retains its power, no such danger exists. Even if there were no British Navy, it is not probable that any enemy would be stupid enough to attack us by landing troops in the United States from across thousands of miles of ocean, until it had acquired strategic bases from which to operate. But we learn much from the lessons of the past years in Europe—particularly the lesson of Norway, whose essential seaports were captured by treachery and surprise built up over a series of years. The first phase of the invasion of this Hemisphere would not be the landing of regular troops. The necessary strategic points would be occupied by secret agents and their dupes—and great numbers of them are already here, and in Latin America.

As long as the aggressor nations maintain the offensive, they—not we—will choose the time and the place and the method of their attack. That is why the future of all American Republics is today in serious danger. That is why this Annual Message to the Congress is unique in our history. That is why every member of the Executive branch of the government and every member of the Congress face great responsibility—and great accountability.

The need of the moment is that our actions and our policy should be devoted primarily—almost exclusively—to meeting the foreign peril. For all our domestic problems are now a part of the great emergency. Just as our national policy in internal affairs has been based upon a decent respect for the rights and dignity of all our fellowmen within our gates, so our national policy in foreign affairs has been based on a decent respect for the rights and dignity of all nations, large and small. And the justice of morality must and will win in the end.

Our national policy is this.

First, by an impressive expression of the public will and without regard to partisanship, we are committed to all-inclusive national defense.

Second, by an impressive expression of the public will and without regard to partisanship, we are committed to full support of all those resolute peoples, everywhere, who are resisting aggression and are thereby keeping war away from our Hemisphere. By this support, we express our determination that the democratic cause shall prevail; and we strengthen the defense and security of our own nation.

Third, by an impressive expression of the public will and without regard to partisanship we are committed to the proposition that principles of morality and considerations for our own security will never permit us to acquiesce in a peace dictated by aggressors and sponsored by appeasers. We know that enduring peace cannot be bought at the cost of other people's freedom.

In the recent national election there was no substantial difference between the two great parties in respect to that national policy. No issue was fought out on this line before the American electorate. Today, it is abundantly evident that American citizens everywhere are demanding and supporting speedy and complete action in recognition of obvious danger. Therefore, the immediate need is a swift and driving increase in our armament production. . . .

Our most useful and immediate role is to act as an arsenal for them as well as for ourselves. They do not need man power. They do need billions of dollars worth of the weapons of defense. . . .

Let us say to the democracies: "We Americans are vitally concerned in your defense of freedom. We are putting forth our energies, our resources and our organizing powers to give you the strength to regain and maintain a free world. We shall send you, in ever-increasing numbers, ships, planes, tanks, guns. This is our purpose and our pledge." In fulfillment of this purpose we will not be intimidated by the threats of dictators that they will regard as a breach of international law and as an act of war our aid to the democracies which dare to resist their aggression. Such aid is not an act of war, even if a dictator should unilaterally proclaim it so to be. When the dictators are ready to make war upon us, they will not wait for an act of war on our part. They did not wait for Norway or Belgium or the Netherlands to commit an act of war. Their only interest is in a new one-way international law, which lacks mutuality in its observance, and, therefore, becomes an instrument of oppression.

The happiness of future generations of Americans may well depend upon how effective and how immediate we can make our aid felt. No one can tell the exact character of the emergency situations that we may be called upon to meet. The Nation's hands must not be tied when the Nation's life is in danger. We must all prepare to make the sacrifices that the emergency—as serious as war itself—demands. Whatever stands in the way of speed and efficiency in defense preparations must give way to the national need.

A free nation has the right to expect full cooperation from all groups. A free nation has the right to look to the leaders of business, of labor, and of agriculture to take the lead in stimulating effort, not among other groups but within their own groups. The best way of dealing with the few slackers and trouble makers in our midst is, first, to shame them by patriotic example, and, if that fails, to use the sovereignty of government to save government.

As men do not live by bread alone, they do not fight by armaments alone. Those who man our defenses, and those behind them who build our defenses, must have the stamina and courage which come from an unshakable belief in the manner of life which they are defending. The mighty action which we are calling for cannot be based on a disregard of all things worth fighting for.

The Nation takes great satisfaction and much strength from the things which have been done to make its people conscious of their individual stake in the preservation of democratic life in America. Those things have toughened the fibre of our people, have renewed their faith and strengthened their devotion to the institutions we make ready to protect. Certainly this is no time to stop thinking about the social and economic problems which are the root cause of the social revolution which is today a supreme factor in the world.

There is nothing mysterious about the foundations of a healthy and strong democracy. The basic things expected by our people of their political and economic systems are simple. They are: equality of opportunity for youth and for others; jobs for those who can work; security for those who need it; the ending of special privilege for the few; the preservation of civil liberties for all; the enjoyment of the fruits of scientific progress in a wider and constantly rising standard of living.

These are the simple and basic things that must never be lost sight of in the turmoil and unbelievable complexity of our modern world. The inner and abiding strength of our economic and political systems is dependent upon the degree to which they fulfill these expectations.

Many subjects connected with our social economy call for immediate improvement. As examples: We should bring more citizens under the coverage of old age pensions and unemployment insurance. We should widen the opportunities for adequate medical care. We should plan a better system by which persons deserving or needing gainful employment may obtain it.

I have called for personal sacrifice. I am assured of the willingness of almost all Americans to respond to that call. . . .

In the future days, which we seek to make secure, we look forward to a world founded upon four essential human freedoms.

The first is freedom of speech and expression—everywhere in the world.

The second is freedom of every person to worship God in his own way—everywhere in the world.

The third is freedom from want—which, translated into world terms, means economic understandings which will secure to every nation a healthy peace time life for its inhabitants—everywhere in the world.

The fourth is freedom from fear—which, translated into world terms, means a world-wide reduction of armaments to such a point and in such a thorough fashion that no nation will be in a position to commit an act of physical aggression against any neighbor—anywhere in the world.

That is no vision of a distant millenium. It is a definite basis for a kind of world attainable in our own time and generation. That kind of world is the very antithesis of the so-called new order of tyranny which the dictators seek to create with the crash of a bomb.

To that new order we oppose the greater conception—the moral order. A good society is able to face schemes of world domination and foreign revolutions alike without fear.

Since the beginning of our American history we have been engaged in change—in a perpetual peaceful revolution—a revolution which goes on steadily, quietly adjusting itself to changing conditions—without the concentration camp or the quick-lime in the ditch. The world order which we seek is the cooperation of free countries, working together in a friendly, civilized society.

This nation has placed its destiny in the hands and heads and hearts of its millions of free men and women; and its faith in freedom under the guidance of God. Freedom means the supremacy of human rights everywhere. Our support goes to those who struggle to gain those rights or keep them. Our strength is in our unity of purpose.

To that high concept there can be no end save victory.

THE ATLANTIC CHARTER

Franklin Delano Roosevelt   *August 14, 1941*
and Winston Churchill

---

*In August 1941, President Roosevelt and British Prime
Minister Winston Churchill met for four days off the coast of
Newfoundland. At this meeting they discussed how the United
States might support the British war effort and delineated war
aims and the shape of the postwar world. Echoing Woodrow
Wilson's Fourteen Points, the Atlantic Charter called for collective security, disarmament, self-determination, economic
cooperation and freedom of the seas. It also provided the basis
for the United Nations Organization, which was chartered in
1945.*

THE President of the United States of America and the Prime Minister, Mr.
Churchill, representing His Majesty's Government in the United Kingdom, being
met together, deem it right to make known certain common principles in the
national policies of their respective countries on which they base their hopes for
a better future for the world.

First, their countries seek no aggrandizement, territorial or other;

Second, they desire to see no territorial changes that do not accord with
the freely expressed wishes of the peoples concerned;

Third, they respect the right of all peoples to choose the form of
government under which they will live; and they wish to see sovereign rights and
self government restored to those who have been forcibly deprived of them;

Fourth, they will endeavor, with due respect for their existing obligations,
to further the enjoyment by all States, great or small, victor or vanquished, of
access, on equal terms, to the trade and to the raw materials of the world which
are needed for their economic prosperity;

Fifth, they desire to bring about the fullest collaboration between all
nations in the economic field with the object of securing, for all, improved labor
standards, economic advancement and social security;

Sixth, after the final destruction of the Nazi tyranny, they hope to see
established a peace which will afford to all nations the means of dwelling in safety

within their own boundaries, and which will afford assurance that all the men in all the lands may live out their lives in freedom from fear and want;

Seventh, such a peace should enable all men to traverse the high seas and oceans without hindrance;

Eighth, they believe that all of the nations of the world, for realistic as well as spiritual reasons must come to the abandonment of the use of force. Since no future peace can be maintained if land, sea or air armaments continue to be employed by nations which threaten, or may threaten, aggression outside of their frontiers, they believe, pending the establishment of a wider and permanent system of general security, that the disarmament of such nations is essential. They will likewise aid and encourage all other practicable measures which will lighten for peace-loving peoples the crushing burden of armaments.

Franklin D. Roosevelt
Winston S. Churchill

DECLARATION OF WAR

Franklin Delano Roosevelt   *December 8, 1941*

> *By the fall of 1941 relations between the United States and Japan had strained to the breaking point. Protesting continued Japanese expansion in Asia as well as Japanese membership in the Rome–Berlin–Tokyo Axis, the United States froze Japanese assets in the United States and placed a trade embargo on oil shipments to Japan. America's refusal to lift the embargo convinced the Japanese government that war with the United States was inevitable. Fearing that they could not win a protracted war against the United States, the Japanese planned a massive attack on the Philippines and Hawaii to paralyze the American Pacific fleet. On the morning of December 7, 1941, Japanese planes attacked the unsuspecting American naval base at Pearl Harbor, killing more than 2,500 people, sinking several battleships and destroying aircraft.*
>
> *The following day, President Franklin Delano Roosevelt captured the shock and grief of a nation in his address announcing the attack and asking for a declaration of war.*

YESTERDAY, December 7, 1941—a date which will live in infamy—the United States of America was suddenly and deliberately attacked by naval and air forces of the Empire of Japan.

The United States was at peace with that nation and, at the solicitation of Japan, was still in conversation with its Government and its Emperor looking toward the maintenance of peace in the Pacific. Indeed, one hour after Japanese air squadrons had commenced bombing in Oahu, the Japanese Ambassador to the United States and his colleague delivered to the Secretary of State a formal reply to a recent American message. While this reply stated that it seemed useless to continue the existing diplomatic negotiations, it contained no threat or hint of war or armed attack.

It will be recorded that the distance of Hawaii from Japan makes it obvious that the attack was deliberately planned many days or even weeks ago. During the intervening time the Japanese Government has deliberately sought to deceive the United States by false statements and expressions of hope for continued peace.

The attack yesterday on the Hawaiian Islands has caused severe damage to American naval and military forces. Very many American lives have been lost. In addition American ships have been reported torpedoed on the high seas between San Francisco and Honolulu.

Yesterday the Japanese Government also launched an attack against Malaya. Last night Japanese forces attacked Hong Kong. Last night Japanese forces attacked Guam. Last night Japanese forces attacked the Philippine Islands. Last night the Japanese attacked Wake Island. This morning the Japanese attacked Midway Island.

Japan has, therefore, undertaken a surprise offensive extending throughout the Pacific area. The facts of yesterday speak for themselves. The people of the United States have already formed their opinions and well understand the implications to the very life and safety of our nation.

As Commander-in-Chief of the Army and Navy, I have directed that all measures be taken for our defense.

Always will we remember the character of the onslaught against us.

No matter how long it may take us to overcome this premeditated invasion, the American people in their righteous might will win through to absolute victory.

I believe I interpret the will of the Congress and of the people when I assert that we will not only defend ourselves to the uttermost but will make very certain that this form of treachery shall never endanger us again.

Hostilities exist. There is no blinking at the fact that our people, our territory and our interests are in grave danger.

With confidence in our armed forces—with the unbonded determination of our people—we will gain the inevitable triumph—so help us God.

I ask that the Congress declare that since the unprovoked and dastardly attack by Japan on Sunday, December seventh, a state of war has existed between the United States and the Japanese Empire.

EXECUTIVE ORDER 9066

Franklin Delano Roosevelt   *February 19, 1942*

The shock of the Japanese attack on Pearl Harbor made deep impressions on the nation. It combined with the lack of American understanding of Japanese culture to encourage fear of all people of Japanese ancestry, and especially of those who had come to settle in the western United States. In February 1942, Japanese-Americans were stripped of their rights of citizenship and subjected to curfews, forced to abandon their property, and interned in relocation camps away from the West Coast.

Almost immediately Nisei (Japanese-Americans born in the United States) protested for their rights in the courts and attempted to prove their loyalty to America. In January 1943, Secretary of War Henry Stimson gave in to pressures from Nisei to form a Nisei fighting unit to serve in the European theater; from this came the 442nd Regimental Combat Team, the most decorated American unit in World War II, made up of Nisei volunteers and the federalized Hawaiian National Guard.

WHEREAS the successful prosecution of the war requires every possible protection against espionage and against sabotage to national-defense materials, national-defense premises, and national-defense utilities. . . .

Now, therefore, by virtue of the authority vested in me as President of the United States, and Commander in Chief of the Army and Navy, I hereby authorize and direct the Secretary of War, and the Military Commanders whom he may from time to time designate, whenever he or any designated Commander deems such action necessary or desirable, to prescribe military areas in such places and of such extent as he or the appropriate Military Commander may determine, from which any or all persons may be excluded, and with respect to which, the right of any person to enter, remain in, or leave shall be subject to whatever restrictions the Secretary of War or the appropriate Military Commander may impose in his discretion. The Secretary of War is hereby authorized to provide for residents of any such area who are excluded therefrom, such transportation, food, shelter, and other accommodations as may be necessary, in the judgment of the Secretary of War or the said Military Commander, and until other arrangements are made, to accomplish the purpose of this order. The designation of military areas in any region or locality shall supersede designations of prohibited and restricted areas by the Attorney General under the Proclamations of December 7 and 8, 1941, and shall supersede the responsibility and authority of the Attorney General under the said Proclamations in respect of such prohibited and restricted areas.

I hereby further authorize and direct the Secretary of War and the said Military Commanders to take such other steps as he or the appropriate Military Commander may deem advisable to enforce compliance with the restrictions applicable to each Military area hereinabove authorized to be designated, including the use of Federal troops and other Federal Agencies, with authority to accept assistance of state and local agencies.

I hereby further authorize and direct all Executive Departments, independent establishments and other Federal Agencies, to assist the Secretary of War or the said Military Commanders in carrying out this Executive Order, including the furnishing of medical aid, hospitalization, food, clothing, transportation, use of land, shelter, and other supplies, equipment, utilities, facilities, and services. . . .

Members of the Mochida Family awaiting evacuation bus in Hayward, California, 1942. From the records of the War Relocation Authority, photograph by Dorothea Lange.

Victory, uncontrollable exuberance displayed by men of Service Squadron 10 anchored in the western Pacific as news of Japan's willingness to surrender spread through the fleet, August 10, 1945. From the general records of the Department of the Navy, photographer unknown.

IX

THE UNITED STATES AND WORLD POWER

THE UNITED NATIONS CONFERENCE

Harry S. Truman   *June 26, 1945*

Vice-President Harry S. Truman, who became president upon the death of Franklin Roosevelt, had come to prominence in the early 1940s as a senator from Missouri. After Roosevelt died unexpectedly in April 1945, Truman tried to carry on the policies of his predecessor as closely as possible in the first years of his own administration. Early in the war the Allies had discussed the formation of a new international organization. As early as the Atlantic Charter, Roosevelt and Churchill had delineated what the goals and functions of such a body should be. In 1943 at the Teheran Conference, Roosevelt had proposed an institution controlled by the "Four Policemen": the United States, Great Britain, the Soviet Union, and China. The following year at Dumbarton Oaks, representatives of the four countries approved a preliminary charter for what was then called the United Nations Organization. In April 1945 the United Nations Conference assembled in San Francisco, California, to approve a final charter. On June 26, President Truman ad-

dressed this organization and pledged the support promised by the late President Roosevelt.

MR. Chairman and Delegates to the United Nations Conference on International Organization:

I deeply regret that the press of circumstances when this Conference opened made it impossible for me to be here to greet you in person. I have asked for the privilege of coming today, to express on behalf of the people of the United States our thanks for what you have done here, and to wish you Godspeed on your journeys home.

Somewhere in this broad country, every one of you can find some of our citizens who are sons and daughters, or descendants in some degree of your own native land. All our people are glad and proud that this historic meeting and its accomplishments have taken place in our country. And that includes the millions of loyal and patriotic Americans who stem from the countries not represented at this Conference.

We are grateful to you for coming. We hope you have enjoyed your stay, and that you will come again.

You assembled in San Francisco nine weeks ago with the high hope and confidence of peace-loving people the world over.

Their confidence in you has been justified.

The Charter of the United Nations which you have just signed is a solid structure upon which we can build a better world. History will honor you for it. Between the victory in Europe and the final victory in Japan, in this most destructive of all wars, you have won a victory against war itself.

It was the hope of such a Charter that helped sustain the courage of stricken peoples through the darkest days of the war. For it is a declaration of great faith by the nations of the earth—faith that war is not inevitable, faith that peace can be maintained.

If we had had this Charter a few years ago—and above all, the will to use it—millions now dead would be alive. If we should falter in the future in our will to use it, millions now living will surely die.

It has already been said by many that this is only a first step to a lasting peace. That is true. The important thing is that all our thinking and all our actions be based on the realization that it is in fact only a first step. Let us all have it firmly in mind that we start today from a good beginning and, with our eye always on the final objective, let us march forward.

The Constitution of my own country came from a Convention which—like this one—was made up of delegates with many different views. Like this

Charter, our Constitution came from a free and sometimes bitter exchange of conflicting opinions. When it was adopted, no one regarded it as a perfect document. But it grew and developed and expanded. And upon it there was built a bigger, a better, a more perfect union.

This Charter, like our own Constitution, will be expanded and improved as time goes on. No one claims that it is now a final or a perfect instrument. It has not been poured into any fixed mold. Changing world conditions will require readjustments—but they will be the readjustments of peace and not of war.

That we now have this Charter at all is a great wonder. It is also a cause for profound thanksgiving to Almighty God, who has brought us so far in our search for peace through world organization.

There were many who doubted that agreement could ever be reached by these fifty countries differing so much in race and religion, in language and culture. But these differences were all forgotten in one unshakable unity of determination—to find a way to end wars. . . .

We have tested the principle of cooperation in this war and have found that it works. Through the pooling of resources, through joint and combined military command, through constant staff meetings, we have shown what united strength can do in war. That united strength forced Germany to surrender. United strength will force Japan to surrender.

The United Nations have also had experience, even while the fighting was still going on, in reaching economic agreements for times of peace. What was done on the subject of relief at Atlantic City, food at Hot Springs, finance at Bretton Woods, aviation at Chicago, was a fair test of what can be done by nations determined to live cooperatively in a world where they cannot live peacefully any other way.

What you have accomplished in San Francisco shows how well these lessons of military and economic cooperation have been learned. You have created a great instrument for peace and security and human progress in the world.

The world must now use it! . . .

There is a time for making plans—and there is a time for action. The time for action is now! Let us, therefore, each in his own nation and according to its own way, seek immediate approval of this Charter—and make it a living thing.

I shall send this Charter to the United States Senate at once. I am sure that the overwhelming sentiment of the people of my country and of their representatives in the Senate is in favor of immediate ratification.

A just and lasting peace cannot be attained by diplomatic agreement alone, or by military cooperation alone. Experience has shown how deeply the seeds of war are planted by economic rivalry and by social injustice. The Charter recognizes this fact for it has provided for economic and social cooperation as well. It has provided for this cooperation as part of the very heart of the entire compact.

It has set up machinery of international cooperation which men and nations of good will can use to help correct economic and social causes for conflict.

Harry S. Truman, portrait by Martha G. Kempton, 1947.

Artificial and uneconomic trade barriers should be removed—to the end that the standard of living of as many people as possible throughout the world may be raised. For Freedom from Want is one of the basic Four Freedoms toward which we all strive. The large and powerful nations of the world must assume leadership in this economic field as in all others.

Under this document we have good reason to expect the framing of an international bill of rights, acceptable to all the nations involved. That bill of rights will be as much a part of international life as our own Bill of Rights is a part of our Constitution. The Charter is dedicated to the achievement and observance of human rights and fundamental freedoms. Unless we can attain those objectives for all men and women everywhere—without regard to race, language or religion—we cannot have permanent peace and security.

With this Charter the world can begin to look forward to the time when all worthy human beings may be permitted to live decently as free people.

The world has learned again that nations, like individuals, must know the truth if they would be free—must read and hear the truth, learn and teach the truth.

We must set up an effective agency for constant and thorough interchange of thought and ideas. For there lies the road to a better and more tolerant understanding among nations and among peoples.

All Fascism did not die with Mussolini. Hitler is finished—but the seeds spread by his disordered mind have firm root in too many fanatical brains. It is easier to remove tyrants and destroy concentration camps than it is to kill the ideas which gave them birth and strength. Victory on the battlefield was essential, but it was not enough. For a good peace, a lasting peace, the decent peoples of the earth must remain determined to strike down the evil spirit which has hung over the world for the last decade. . . .

THE TRUMAN DOCTRINE

Harry S. Truman   *March 12, 1947*

---

*Relations between the United States and the Soviet Union
had begun to deteriorate in 1942 over the United States' delay
in opening a second front in Europe. Conflicts over the disposition of Allied-conquered territories in Eastern Europe, and
Germany especially, had led American policymakers to conclude that the Soviet Union was by nature expansionistic and
that it would have to be contained.*

*As early as 1944 a civil war had raged in Greece
between the sitting monarchist government, supported by Great
Britain, and Communist rebels. President Truman saw in
Greece his worst nightmare: a capitalist country threatened by
what he believed to be a U.S.S.R.-sponsored Communist insurrection. In reality the Communist rebels in Greece were na-
tionalists supported by the Yugoslavian leader, Marshal Tito,
against Stalin's wishes. In 1947, in response to the spread of
Soviet influence, Truman proclaimed a program of economic
aid for Greece and any other nation threatened by Communist
expansion or insurrection.*

THE gravity of the situation which confronts the world today necessitates my appearance before a joint session of the Congress. The foreign policy and the national security of this country are involved.

One aspect of the present situation, which I wish to present to you at this time for your consideration and decision, concerns Greece and Turkey.

The United States has received from the Greek Government an urgent appeal for financial and economic assistance. Preliminary reports from the American Economic Mission now in Greece and reports from the American Ambassador in Greece corroborate the statement of the Greek Government that assistance is imperative if Greece is to survive as a free nation.

I do not believe that the American people and the Congress wish to turn a deaf ear to the appeal of the Greek Government.

The very existence of the Greek state is today threatened by the terrorist activities of several thousand armed men, led by Communists, who defy the

Government's authority at a number of points, particularly along the northern boundaries. A commission appointed by the United Nations Security Council is at present investigating disturbed conditions in Northern Greece and alleged border violations along the frontiers between Greece on the one hand and Albania, Bulgaria and Yugoslavia on the other.

Meanwhile, the Greek Government is unable to cope with the situation. The Greek Army is small and poorly equipped. It needs supplies and equipment if it is to restore the authority to the Government throughout Greek territory.

Greece must have assistance if it is to become a self-supporting and self-respecting democracy. The United States must supply this assistance. We have already extended to Greece certain types of relief and economic aid but these are inadequate. There is no other country to which democratic Greece can turn. No other nation is willing and able to provide the necessary support for a democratic Greek Government.

The British Government, which has been helping Greece, can give no further financial or economic aid after March 31. Great Britain finds itself under the necessity of reducing or liquidating its commitments in several parts of the world, including Greece.

We have considered how the United Nations might assist in this crisis. But the situation is an urgent one requiring immediate action, and the United Nations and its related organizations are not in a position to extend help of the kind that is required. . . .

Greece's neighbor, Turkey, also deserves our attention. The future of Turkey as an independent and economically sound state is clearly no less important to the freedom-loving peoples of the world than the future of Greece. The circumstances in which Turkey finds itself today are considerably different from those of Greece. Turkey has been spared the disasters that have beset Greece. And during the war, the United States and Great Britain furnished Turkey with material aid. Nevertheless, Turkey now needs our support.

Since the war Turkey has sought additional financial assistance from Great Britain and the United States for the purpose of effecting the modernization necessary for the maintenance of its national integrity. That integrity is essential to the preservation of order in the Middle East.

The British Government has informed us that, owing to its own difficulties, it can no longer extend financial or economic aid to Turkey. As in the case of Greece, if Turkey is to have the assistance it needs, the United States must supply it. We are the only country able to provide that help.

I am fully aware of the broad implications involved if the United States extends assistance to Greece and Turkey, and I shall discuss these implications with you at this time.

One of the primary objectives of the foreign policy of the United States is the creation of conditions in which we and other nations will be able to work out a way of life free from coercion. This was a fundamental issue in the war with Germany and Japan. Our victory was won over countries which sought to impose their will, and their way of life, upon other nations.

To ensure the peaceful development of nations, free from coercion, the United States has taken a leading part in establishing the United Nations. The United Nations is designed to make possible lasting freedom and independence for all its members. We shall not realize our objectives, however, unless we are willing to help free peoples to maintain their free institutions and their national integrity against aggressive movements that seek to impose on them totalitarian regimes. This is no more than a frank recognition that totalitarian regimes imposed on free peoples, by direct or indirect aggression, undermine the foundations of international peace and hence the security of the United States.

The peoples of a number of countries of the world have recently had totalitarian regimes forced upon them against their will. The Government of the United States had made frequent protests against coercion and intimidation, in violation of the Yalta Agreement, in Poland, Rumania and Bulgaria. I must also state that in a number of other countries there have been similar developments.

At the present moment in world history nearly every nation must choose between alternative ways of life. The choice is too often not a free one.

One way of life is based upon the will of the majority, and is distinguished by free institutions, representative government, free elections, guarantees of individual liberty, freedom of speech and religion, and freedom from political oppression.

The second way of life is based upon the will of the minority forcibly imposed upon the majority. It relies upon terror and oppression, a controlled press and radio, fixed elections, and the suppression of personal freedoms.

I believe that it must be the policy of the United States to support free peoples who are resisting attempted subjugation by armed minorities or by outside pressures.

I believe that we must assist free peoples to work out their own destinies in their own way.

I believe that our help should be primarily through economic and financial aid which is essential to economic stability and orderly political processes.

The world is not static, and the status quo is not sacred. But we cannot allow changes in the status quo in violation of the charter of the United Nations by such methods as coercion, or by such subterfuges as political infiltration. In helping free and independent nations to maintain their freedom, the United

States will be giving effect to the principles of the charter of the United Nations.

It is necessary only to glance at a map to realize that the survival and integrity of the Greek nation are of grave importance in a much wider situation. If Greece should fall under the control of an armed minority, the effect upon its neighbor, Turkey, would be immediate and serious. Confusion and disorder might well spread throughout the entire Middle East.

Moreover, the disappearance of Greece as an independent state would have a profound effect upon those countries in Europe whose peoples are struggling against great difficulties to maintain their freedoms and their independence while they repair the damages of war.

It would be an unspeakable tragedy if these countries, which have struggled so long against overwhelming odds, should lose that victory for which they sacrificed so much. Collapse of free institutions and loss of independence would be disastrous not only for them but for the world. Discouragement and possibly failure would quickly be the lot of neighboring peoples striving to maintain their freedom and independence.

Should we fail to aid Greece and Turkey in this fateful hour, the effect will be far reaching to the west as well as to the east. We must take immediate and resolute action.

I therefore ask the Congress to provide authority for assistance to Greece and Turkey in the amount of $400,000,000 for the period ending June 30, 1948.

In addition to funds, I ask the Congress to authorize the detail of American civilian and military personnel to Greece and Turkey, at the request of those countries, to assist in the tasks of reconstruction, and for the purpose of supervising the use of such financial and material assistance as may be furnished. I recommend that authority also be provided for the instruction and training of selected Greek and Turkish personnel.

Finally, I ask that the Congress provide authority which will permit the speediest and most effective use, in terms of needed commodities, supplies, and equipment, of such funds as may be authorized. . . .

The seeds of totalitarian regimes are nurtured by misery and want. They spread and grow in the evil soil of poverty and strife. They reach their full growth when the hope of a people for a better life has died. We must keep that hope alive. The free peoples of the world look to us for support in maintaining their freedoms.

If we falter in our leadership, we may endanger the peace of the world— and we shall surely endanger the welfare of this nation.

Great responsibilities have been placed upon us by the swift movement of events. I am confident that the Congress will face these responsibilities squarely.

THE MARSHALL PLAN

George C. Marshall   *June 5, 1947*

---

*George C. Marshall, who had been chief of the American
staff during World War II, served as President Harry Truman's
secretary of state from 1947 to 1949. Marshall realized that the
economic devastation of the European continent after the war
made governments there unstable and, Marshall believed,
susceptible to overthrow or invasion by Communists.*

*In an address at Harvard University, Marshall an-
nounced the European Recovery Plan, or as it came to be
called, the Marshall Plan. Marshall pledged United States
economic and technical assistance to reconstruct the European
economy. The Soviet Union and other Eastern European
countries were also invited to take part, but they declined.
Sixteen western European countries and West Germany formed
the Organization of Economic Cooperation to coordinate the
program, and from 1948 to 1952 the participating countries
received over $12 billion in aid from the United States.*

I need not tell you gentlemen that the world situation is very serious. That
must be apparent to all intelligent people. I think one difficulty is that the problem
is one of such enormous complexity that the very mass of facts presented to the
public by press and radio make it exceedingly difficult for the man in the street
to reach a clear appraisement of the situation. Futhermore, the people of this
country are distant from the troubled areas of the earth and it is hard for them
to comprehend the plight and consequent reactions of the long-suffering
peoples, and the effect of those reactions on their governments in connection
with our efforts to promote peace in the world.

In considering the requirements for the rehabilitation of Europe the
physical loss of life, the visible destruction of cities, factories, mines, and railroads
was correctly estimated, but it has become obvious during recent months that
this visible destruction was probably less serious than the dislocation of the entire
fabric of European economy. For the past ten years conditions have been highly
abnormal. The feverish preparation for war and the more feverish maintenance
of the war effort engulfed all aspects of national economies. Machinery has fallen

into disrepair or is entirely obsolete. Under the arbitrary and destructive Nazi rule, virtually every possible enterprise was geared into the German war machine. Long-standing commercial ties, private institutions, banks, insurance companies and shipping companies disappeared, through loss of capital, absorption through nationalization or by simple destruction. In many countries, confidence in the local currency has been severely shaken. The breakdown of the business structure of Europe during the war was complete. Recovery has been seriously retarded by the fact that two years after the close of hostilities a peace settlement with Germany and Austria has not been agreed upon. But even given a more prompt solution of these difficult problems, the rehabilitation of the economic structure of Europe quite evidently will require a much longer time and greater effort than had been foreseen.

There is a phase of this matter which is both interesting and serious. The farmer has always produced the foodstuffs to exchange with the city dweller for the other necessities of life. This division of labor is the basis of modern civilization. At the present time it is threatened with breakdown. The town and city industries are not producing adequate goods to exchange with the food-producing farmer. Raw materials and fuel are in short supply. Machinery is lacking or worn out. The farmer or the peasant cannot find the goods for sale which he desires to purchase. So the sale of his farm produce for money which he cannot use seems to him an unprofitable transaction. He, therefore, has withdrawn many fields from crop cultivation and is using them for grazing. He feeds more grain to stock and finds for himself and his family an ample supply of food, however short he may be on clothing and the other ordinary gadgets of civilization. Meanwhile people in the cities are short of food and fuel. So the governments are forced to use their foreign money and credits to procure these necessities abroad. This process exhausts funds which are urgently needed for reconstruction. Thus a very serious situation is rapidly developing which bodes no good for the world. The modern system of the division of labor upon which the exchange of products is based is in danger of breaking down.

The truth of the matter is that Europe's requirements for the next three or four years of foreign food and other essential products—principally from America—are so much greater than her present ability to pay that she must have substantial additional help, or face economic, social, and political deterioration of a very grave character.

The remedy lies in breaking the vicious circle and restoring the confidence of the European people in the economic future of their own countries and of Europe as a whole. The manufacturer and the farmer throughout wide areas must be able and willing to exchange their products for currencies the continuing value of which is not open to question.

Aside from the demoralizing effect on the world at large and the possibilities of disturbances arising as a result of the desperation of the people concerned, the consequences to the economy of the United States should be apparent to all. It is logical that the United States should do whatever it is able to do to assist in the return of normal economic health in the world, without which there can be no political stability and no assured peace. Our policy is directed not against any country or doctrine but against hunger, poverty, desperation, and chaos. Its purpose should be the revival of a working economy in the world so as to permit the emergence of political and social conditions in which free institutions can exist. Such assistance, I am convinced, must not be on a piecemeal basis as various crises develop. Any assistance that this Government may render in the future should provide a cure rather than a mere palliative. Any government that is willing to assist in the task of recovery will find full cooperation, I am sure, on the part of the United States Government. Any government which maneuvers to block the recovery of other countries cannot expect help from us. Furthermore, governments, political parties, or groups which seek to perpetuate human misery in order to profit therefrom politically or otherwise will encounter the opposition of the United States.

It is already evident that, before the United States Government can proceed much further in its efforts to alleviate the situation and help start the European world on its way to recovery, there must be some agreement among the countries of Europe as to the requirements of the situation and the part those countries themselves will take in order to give proper effect to whatever action might be undertaken by this Government. It would be neither fitting nor efficacious for this Government to undertake to draw up unilaterally a program designed to place Europe on its feet economically. This is the business of the Europeans. The initiative, I think, must come from Europe. The role of this country should consist of friendly aid in the drafting of a European program and of later support of such a program so far as it may be practical for us to do so. The program should be a joint one, agreed to by a number, if not all European nations.

An essential part of any successful action on the part of the United States is an understanding on the part of the people of America of the character of the problem and the remedies to be applied. Political passion and prejudice should have no part. With foresight, and a willingness on the part of our people to face up to the vast responsibility which history has clearly placed upon our country, the difficulties I have outlined can and will be overcome.

Inaugural Address

Harry S. Truman   *January 19, 1949*

---

*President Harry Truman inherited his predecessor's deep
involvement in international affairs but was also very concerned with domestic matters. Truman's legacy includes the
Fair Deal as well as the desegregation of the armed forces in
1947. In foreign affairs Truman's outlook consisted mainly of
containing Soviet expansion and supporting those who opposed
the Soviet Union and rejected the Communist system. To these
ends the Truman administration presented a statement of
policy, titled NSC-68, a complete reorganization of the American defense system which formed the United States Air Force,
founded the National Security Council and created the Central
Intelligence Agency. Domestically, Truman strove to maintain
agreement on the importance of social programs in the tradition
of the New Deal. President Truman's inaugural address, given
on January 19, 1949, reflects these simultaneous concerns.*

. . . IN the coming years, our program for peace and freedom will emphasize four major courses of action.

First, we will continue to give unfaltering support to the United Nations and related agencies, and we will continue to search for ways to strengthen their authority and increase their effectiveness. We believe that the United Nations will be strengthened by the new nations which are being formed in lands now advancing toward self-government under democratic principles.

Second, we will continue our programs for world economic recovery.

This means, first of all, that we must keep our full weight behind the European Recovery Program. We are confident of the success of this major venture in world recovery. We believe that our partners in this effort will achieve the status of self-supporting nations once again.

In addition, we must carry out our plans for reducing the barriers to world trade and increasing its volume. Economic recovery and peace itself depend on increased world trade.

Third, we will strengthen freedom-loving nations against the dangers of aggression.

We are now working out with a number of countries a joint agreement designed to strengthen the security of the North Atlantic area. Such an agreement would take the form of a collective defense arrangement within the terms of the United Nations Charter.

We have already established such a defense pact for the Western Hemisphere by the treaty of Rio de Janeiro.

The primary purpose of these agreements is to provide unmistakable proof of the joint determination of the free countries to resist armed attack from any quarter. Each country participating in these arrangements must contribute all it can to the common defense.

If we can make it sufficiently clear, in advance, that any armed attack affecting our national security would be met with overwhelming force, the armed attack might never occur.

I hope soon to send to the Senate a treaty respecting the North Atlantic security plan.

In addition, we will provide military advice and equipment to free nations which will cooperate with us in the maintenance of peace and security.

Fourth, we must embark on a bold new program for making the benefits of our scientific advances and industrial progress available for the improvement and growth of under-developed areas.

More than half the people of the world are living in conditions approaching misery. Their food is inadequate. They are victims of disease. Their economic life is primitive and stagnant. Their poverty is a handicap and a threat both to them and to more prosperous areas.

For the first time in history, humanity possesses the knowledge and the skill to relieve the suffering of these people.

The United States is pre-eminent among nations in the development of industrial and scientific techniques. The material resources which we can afford to use for the assistance of other peoples are limited. But our imponderable resources in technical knowledge are constantly growing and are inexhaustible.

I believe that we should make available to peace-loving peoples the benefits of our store of technical knowledge in order to help them realize their aspirations for a better life. And, in cooperation with other nations, we should foster capital investment in areas needing development.

Our aim should be to help the free peoples of the world, through their own efforts, to produce more food, more clothing, more materials for housing, and more mechanical power to lighten their burdens.

We invite other countries to pool their technological resources in this undertaking. Their contributions will be warmly welcomed. This should be a cooperative enterprise in which all nations work together through the United

Nations and its specialized agencies wherever practicable. It must be a world wide effort for the achievement of peace, plenty, and freedom.

With the cooperation of business, private capital, agriculture, and labor in this country, this program can greatly increase the industrial activity in other nations and can raise substantially their standards of living.

Such new economic developments must be devised and controlled to benefit the peoples of the areas in which they are established. Guarantees to the investor must be balanced by guarantees in the interest of the people whose resources and whose labor go into these developments.

The old imperialism—exploitation for foreign profit—has no place in our plans. What we envisage is a program of development based on the concepts of democratic fair-dealing.

All countries, including our own, will greatly benefit from a constructive program for the better use of the world's human and natural resources. Experience shows that our commerce with other countries expands as they progress industrially and economically.

Greater production is the key to prosperity and peace. And the key to greater production is a wider and more vigorous application of modern scientific and technical knowledge.

Only by helping the least fortunate of its members to help themselves can the human family achieve the decent, satisfying life that is the right of all people.

Democracy alone can supply the vitalizing force to stir the peoples of the world into triumphant action, not only against their human oppressors, but also against their ancient enemies—hunger, misery, and despair.

On the basis of these four major courses of action we hope to help create the conditions that will lead eventually to personal freedom and happiness for all mankind.

If we are to be successful in carrying out these policies, it is clear that we must have continued prosperity in this country and we must keep ourselves strong.

Slowly but surely we are weaving a world fabric of international security and growing prosperity.

We are aided by all who wish to live in freedom from fear—even by those who live today in fear under their own governments.

We are aided by all who want relief from the lies of propaganda—who desire truth and sincerity.

We are aided by all who desire self-government and a voice in deciding their own affairs.

We are aided by all who long for economic security—for the security and abundance that men in free societies can enjoy.

We are aided by all who desire freedom of speech, freedom of religion, and freedom to live their own lives for useful ends.

Our allies are the millions who hunger and thirst after righteousness.

In due time, as our stability becomes manifest, as more and more nations come to know the benefits of democracy and to participate in growing abundance, I believe that those countries which now oppose us will abandon their delusions and join with the free nations of the world in a just settlement of international differences.

Events have brought our American democracy to new influence and new responsibilities. They will test our courage, our devotion to duty, and our concept of liberty.

But I say to all men, what we have achieved in liberty, we will surpass in greater liberty.

Steadfast in our faith in the Almighty, we will advance toward a world where man's freedom is secure.

To that end we will devote our strength, our resources, and our firmness of resolve. With God's help, the future of mankind will be assured in a world of justice, harmony, and peace.

Amendment XXII
Limit Two Terms for President

February 27, 1951

Proposed by Congress March 24, 1947, its ratification was completed February 27, 1951.

SEC. 1. No person shall be elected to the office of the President more than twice, and no person who has held the office of President, or acted as President, for more than two years of a term to which some other person was elected President shall be elected to the office of the President more than once. But this Article shall not apply to any person holding the office of President when this Article was proposed by the Congress, and shall not prevent any person who may be holding the office of President, or acting as President, during the term within which this Article becomes operative from holding the office of President or acting as President during the remainder of such term.

Brown v. the Board of Education of Topeka, Kansas

Earl Warren 1954

---

*Earl Warren, former governor of California, was ap-
pointed chief justice of the Supreme Court by President Dwight
D. Eisenhower in 1953. Although Warren had a reputation as a
staunch conservative, Warren's court handed down some of the
most liberal decisions in the history of the court.* Miranda v.
Arizona, Gideon v. Wainwright, *and* Brown v. the Board of
Education of Topeka *were the most famous of these. Warren resigned as chief justice in 1969 and was replaced by Warren
Berger.*

*The Brown case came before the Supreme Court in 1952
as a test case supported by the National Association for the
Advancement of Colored People (NAACP). The Brown family
and the NAACP challenged the 1896* Plessy v. Ferguson *decision, which held that separate but equal facilities for blacks and
whites were constitutional.* Brown v. the Board of Education of
Topeka *overturned the 1896 decision, and Warren, in this
unanimous opinion, stated that separate but equal facilities in
public education were inherently unequal. This decision
marked a major victory for the American civil rights movement.*

APPEAL from the U.S. Dist. Court, District of Kansas.

Warren, C.J. These cases come to us from the States of Kansas, South
Carolina, Virginia, and Delaware. They are premised on different facts and
different local conditions, but a common legal question justifies their consideration together in this consolidated opinion.

In each of the cases, minors of the Negro race, through their legal
representatives, seek the aid of the courts in obtaining admission to the public
schools of their community on a nonsegregated basis. In each instance, they have
been denied admission to schools attended by white children under laws
requiring or permitting segregation according to race. This segregation was
alleged to deprive the plaintiffs of the equal protection of the laws under the

Fourteenth Amendment. In each of the cases other than the Delaware case, a three-judge federal district court denied relief to the plaintiffs on the so-called "separate but equal" doctrine announced by this Court in *Plessy v. Ferguson,* 163 U.S. 537. Under that doctrine, equality of treatment is accorded when the races are provided substantially equal facilities, even though these facilities be separate. In the Delaware case, the Supreme Court of Delaware adhered to that doctrine, but ordered that the plaintiffs be admitted to the white schools because of their superiority to the Negro schools.

The plaintiffs contend that segregated public schools are not "equal" and cannot be made "equal," and that hence they are deprived of the equal protection of the laws. Because of the obvious importance of the question presented, the Court took jurisdiction. Argument was heard in the 1952 Term, and reargument was heard this Term on certain questions propounded by the Court.

Reargument was largely devoted to the circumstances surrounding the adoption of the Fourteenth Amendment in 1868. It covered exhaustively consideration of the Amendment in Congress, ratification by the states, then existing practices in racial segregation, and the views of proponents and opponents of the Amendment. This discussion and our own investigation convince us that, although these sources cast some light, it is not enough to resolve the problem with which we are faced. At best, they are inconclusive. The most avid proponents of the post-War Amendments undoubtedly intended them to remove all legal distinctions among "all persons born or naturalized in the United States." Their opponents, just as certainly, were antagonistic to both the letter and the spirit of the Amendments and wished them to have the most limited effect. What others in Congress and the state legislatures had in mind cannot be determined with any degree of certainty.

An additional reason for the inconclusive nature of the Amendment's history, with respect to segregated schools, is the status of public education at that time. In the South, the movement toward free common schools, supported by general taxation, had not yet taken hold. Education of white children was largely in the hands of private groups. Education of Negroes was almost nonexistent, and practically all of the race were illiterate. In fact, any education of Negroes was forbidden by law in some states. Today, in contrast, many Negroes have achieved outstanding success in the arts and sciences as well as in the business and professional world. It is true that public education had already advanced further in the North, but the effect of the Amendment on Northern States was generally ignored in the congressional debates. Even in the North, the conditions of public education did not approximate those existing today. The curriculum was usually rudimentary; ungraded schools were common in rural areas; the school term was but three months a year in many states; and compulsory school attendance was virtually unknown. As a consequence, it is not surprising that there should be so little in the history of the Fourteenth Amendment relating to its intended effect on public education.

In the first cases in this Court construing the Fourteenth Amendment, decided shortly after its adoption, the Court interpreted it as proscribing all state-imposed discriminations against the Negro race. The doctrine of "separate but equal" did not make its appearance in this Court until 1896 in the case of *Plessy v. Ferguson, supra,* involving not education but transportation. American courts have since labored with the doctrine for over half a century. In this Court, there have been six cases involving the "separate but equal" doctrine in the field of public education. . . .

In approaching this problem, we cannot turn the clock back to 1868 when the Amendment was adopted, or even to 1896 when *Plessy v. Ferguson* was written. We must consider public education in the light of its full development and its present place in American life throughout the Nation. Only in this way can it be determined if segregation in public schools deprives these plaintiffs of the equal protection of the laws.

Today, education is perhaps the most important function of state and local governments. Compulsory school attendance laws and the great expenditures for education both demonstrate our recognition of the importance of education to our democratic society. It is required in the performance of our most basic public responsibilities, even service in the armed forces. It is the very foundation of good citizenship. Today it is a principal instrument in awakening the child to cultural values, in preparing him for later professional training, and in helping him to adjust normally to his environment. In these days, it is doubtful that any child may reasonably be expected to succeed in life if he is denied the opportunity of an education. Such an opportunity, where the state has undertaken to provide it, is a right which must be made available to all on equal terms.

We come then to the question presented: Does segregation of children in public schools solely on the basis of race, even though the physical facilities and other "tangible" factors may be equal, deprive the children of the minority group of equal educational opportunities? We believe that it does.

In *Sweatt v. Painter, supra* [339 U.S. 629, 70 S.Ct. 850], in finding that a segregated law school for Negroes could not provide them equal educational opportunities, this Court relied in large part on "those qualities which are incapable of objective measurement but which make for greatness in a law school." In *McLaurin v. Oklahoma State Regents, supra* [339 U.S. 637, 70 S.Ct. 853], the Court, in requiring that a Negro admitted to a white graduate school be treated like all other students, again resorted to intangible considerations: ". . . his ability to study, to engage in discussions and exchange views with other students, and, in general, to learn his profession." Such considerations apply with added force to children in grade and high schools. To separate them from others of similar age and qualifications solely because of their race generates a feeling of inferiority as to their state in the community that may affect their hearts and minds in a way unlikely ever to be undone. . . .

Whatever may have been the extent of psychological knowledge at the time of *Plessy v. Ferguson*, this finding is amply supported by modern authority. Any language in *Plessy v. Ferguson* contrary to this finding is rejected.

We conclude that in the field of public education the doctrine of "separate but equal" has no place. Separate educational facilities are inherently unequal. Therefore, we hold that the plaintiffs and others similarly situated for whom the actions have been brought are, by reason of the segregation complained of, deprived of the equal protection of the laws guaranteed by the Fourteenth Amendment. This deposition makes unnecessary any discussion whether such segregation also violates the Due Process Clause of the Fourteenth Amendment.

Because these are class actions, because of the wide applicability of this decision, and because of the great variety of local conditions, the formulation of decrees in these cases presents problems of considerable complexity. On reargument, the consideration of appropriate relief was necessarily subordinated to the primary question—the constitutionality of segregation in public education. We have now announced that such segregation is a denial of the equal protection of the laws. In order that we may have the full assistance of the parties in formulating decrees, the cases will be restored to the docket, and the parties are requested to present further argument. . . . The Attorney General of the United States is again invited to participate. The Attorneys General of the states requiring or permitting segregation in public education will also be permitted to appear as *amici curiae* upon request to do so by September 15, 1954, and submission of briefs by October 1, 1954.

It is so ordered.

FAREWELL ADDRESS

Dwight D. Eisenhower   *January 17, 1961*

Dwight D. Eisenhower served as president from 1953 to 1961. During World War II, Eisenhower had been the Supreme Commander of the Allied Expeditionary Force that landed at

Normandy and swept through Europe in 1944 and 1945. As a result of his war experiences, Eisenhower repeatedly criticized American readiness to send United States troops abroad. His 1952 campaign stated that Eisenhower would go to Korea and bring home American soldiers involved in the war there. His farewell address, given January 17, 1961, indicates the level of Eisenhower's commitment to the prevention of serious aggression and "hot war" involving the United States. Eisenhower warned the American people against the "military-industrial complex," the conjunction of interests and the great potential influence wielded by a large military establishment together with a large arms industry.

MY fellow Americans:

Three days from now, after half a century in the service of our country, I shall lay down the responsibilities of office as, in traditional and solemn ceremony, the authority of the Presidency is vested in my successor. . . .

We now stand ten years past the midpoint of a century that has witnessed four major wars among great nations. Three of them involved our own country. Despite these holocausts America is today the strongest, the most influential and most productive nation in the world. Understandably proud of this pre-eminence we yet realize that America's leadership and prestige depend, not merely upon our unmatched material progress, riches and military strength, but on how we use our power in the interests of world peace and human betterment.

Throughout America's adventure in free government, our basic purposes have been to keep the peace; to foster progress in human achievement, and to enhance liberty, dignity and integrity among people and among nations. To strive for less would be unworthy of a free and religious people. Any failure traceable to arrogance, or our lack of comprehension or readiness to sacrifice would inflict upon us grievous hurt both at home and abroad.

Progress toward these noble goals is persistently threatened by the conflict now engulfing the world. It commands our whole attention, absorbs our very beings. We face a hostile ideology—global in scope, atheistic in character, ruthless in purpose, and insidious in method. Unhappily the danger it poses promises to be of indefinite duration. To meet it successfully, there is called for, not so much the emotional and transitory sacrifices of crisis, but rather those which enable us to carry forward steadily, surely, and without complaint the burdens of a prolonged and complex struggle—with liberty the stake. Only thus shall we remain, despite every provocation, on our charted course toward permanent peace and human betterment. . . .

A vital element in keeping the peace is our military establishment. Our arms must be mighty, ready for instant action, so that no potential aggressor may be tempted to risk his own destruction.

Our military organization today bears little relation to that known by any of my predecessors in peacetime, or indeed by the fighting men of World War II or Korea.

Until the latest of our world conflicts, the United States had no armaments industry. American makers of plowshares could, with time and as required, make swords as well. But now we can no longer risk emergency improvisation of national defense; we have been compelled to create a permanent armaments industry of vast proportions. Added to this, three and a half million men and women are directly engaged in the defense establishment. We annually spend on military security more than the net income of all United States corporations.

This conjunction of an immense military establishment and a large arms industry is new in the American experience. The total influence—economic, political, even spiritual—is felt in every city, every statehouse, every office of the federal government. We recognize the imperative need for this development. Yet we must not fail to comprehend its grave implications. Our toil, resources, and livelihood are all involved; so is the very structure of our society.

In the councils of government, we must guard against the acquisition of unwarranted influence, whether sought or unsought, by the military-industrial complex. The potential for the disastrous rise of misplaced power exists and will persist.

We must never let the weight of this combination endanger our liberties or democratic processes. We should take nothing for granted. Only an alert and knowledgeable citizenry can compel the proper meshing of the huge industrial and military machinery of defense with our peaceful methods and goals, so that security and liberty may prosper together.

Akin to, and largely responsible for the sweeping changes in our in-dustrial-military posture, has been the technological revolution during recent decades.

In this revolution, research has become central; it also becomes more formalized, complex, and costly. A steadily increasing share is conducted for, by, or at the direction of, the federal government. . . .

The prospect of domination of the nation's scholars by federal employ-ment, project allocations, and the power of money is ever present—and is gravely to be regarded.

Yet, in holding scientific research and discovery in respect, as we should, we must also be alert to the equal and opposite danger that public policy could itself become the captive of a scientific-technological elite.

It is the task of statesmanship to mold, to balance, and to integrate these and other forces, new and old, within the principles of our democratic system—ever aiming toward the supreme goals of our free society.

Another factor in maintaining balance involves the element of time. As we peer into society's future, we—you and I, and our government—must avoid

Dwight D. Eisenhower, portrait by J. Anthony Wills.

the impulse to live only for today, plundering, for our own ease and convenience, the precious resources of tomorrow. We cannot mortgage the material assets of our grandchildren without risking the loss also of their political and spiritual heritage. We want democracy to survive for all generations to come, not to become the insolvent phantom of tomorrow.

Down the long lane of the history yet to be written America knows that this world of ours, ever growing smaller, must avoid becoming a community of dreadful fear and hate, and be, instead, a proud confederation of mutual trust and respect.

Such a confederation must be one of equals. The weakest must come to the conference table with the same confidence as do we, protected as we are by our moral, economic, and military strength. That table, though scarred by many past frustrations, cannot be abandoned for the certain agony of the battlefield.

Disarmament, with mutual honor and confidence, is a continuing imperative. Together we must learn how to compose differences, not with arms, but with intellect and decent purpose. Because this need is so sharp and apparent I confess that I lay down my official responsibilities in this field with a definite sense of disappointment. As one who has witnessed the horror and the lingering sadness of war—as one who knows that another war could utterly destroy this civilization which has been so slowly and painfully built over thousands of years—I wish I could say tonight that a lasting peace is in sight.

Happily, I can say that war has been avoided. Steady progress toward our ultimate goal has been made. But, so much remains to be done. As a private citizen, I shall never cease to do what little I can to help the world advance along that road. . . .

Inaugural Address

John F. Kennedy   *January 20, 1961*

---

*John Fitzgerald Kennedy served as president from 1961
to his assassination in 1963. Kennedy rose to political prominence as a senator from Massachusetts. In 1960 Kennedy ran
against the sitting vice-president, Richard Nixon, and won with
the narrowest of margins on the strength of the great personal
charisma he showed in the presidential debates.*

*In his inaugural address on January 20, 1961, perhaps
one of the most famous in American history, Kennedy captured
the spirit of "the New Frontier." With great enthusiasm he
outlined both the rights and the responsibilities of American
citizenship in a troubled world. For many Americans, Kennedy's statement, "Ask not what your country can do for you—
ask what you can do for your country," embodied the idealism
of the early 1960s.*

VICE-President Johnson, Mr. Speaker, Mr. Chief Justice, President Eisenhower, Vice-President Nixon, President Truman, Reverend Clergy, Fellow
Citizens:

We observe today not a victory of party but a celebration of freedom—
symbolizing an end as well as a beginning—signifying renewal as well as change.
For I have sworn before you and Almighty God the same solemn oath our
forebears prescribed nearly a century and three-quarters ago.

The world is very different now. For man holds in his mortal hands the
power to abolish all forms of human poverty and all forms of human life. And
yet the same revolutionary beliefs for which our forebears fought are still at issue
around the globe—the belief that the rights of man come not from the generosity
of the state but from the hand of God.

We dare not forget today that we are the heirs of that first revolution. Let
the word go forth from this time and place, to friend and foe alike, that the torch
has been passed to a new generation of Americans—born in this century,
tempered by war, disciplined by a hard and bitter peace, proud of our ancient
heritage—and unwilling to witness or permit the slow undoing of those human
rights to which this nation has always been committed, and to which we are

committed today at home and around the world.

Let every nation know, whether it wishes us well or ill, that we shall pay any price, bear any burden, meet any hardship, support any friend, oppose any foe to assure the survival and the success of liberty.

This much we pledge—and more.

To those old allies whose cultural and spiritual origins we share, we pledge the loyalty of faithful friends. United, there is little we cannot do in a host of co-operative ventures. Divided, there is little we can do—for we dare not meet a powerful challenge at odds and split asunder.

To those new states whom we welcome to the ranks of the free, we pledge our word that one form of colonial control shall not have passed away merely to be replaced by a far more iron tyranny. We shall not always expect to find them supporting our view. But we shall always hope to find them strongly supporting their own freedom—and to remember that, in the past, those who foolishly sought power by riding the back of the tiger ended up inside.

To those people in the huts and villages of half the globe struggling to break the bonds of mass misery, we pledge our best efforts to help them help themselves, for whatever period is required—not because the Communists may be doing it, not because we seek their votes, but because it is right. If a free society cannot help the many who are poor, it cannot save the few who are rich.

To our sister republics south of our border, we offer a special pledge— to convert our good words into good deeds—in a new alliance for progress— to assist free men and free governments in casting off the chains of poverty. But this peaceful revolution of hope cannot become the prey of hostile powers. Let all our neighbors know that we shall join with them to oppose aggression or subversion anywhere in the Americas. And let every other power know that this hemisphere intends to remain the master of its own house.

To that world assembly of sovereign states, the United Nations, our last best hope in an age where the instruments of war have far outpaced the instruments of peace, we renew our pledge of support—to prevent it from becoming merely a forum for invective—to strengthen its shield of the new and the weak—and to enlarge the area in which its writ may run.

Finally, to those nations who would make themselves our adversary, we offer not a pledge but a request: that both sides begin anew the quest for peace, before the dark powers of destruction unleashed by science engulf all humanity in planned or accidental self-destruction.

We dare not tempt them with weakness. For only when our arms are sufficient beyond doubt can we be certain beyond doubt that they will never be employed.

But neither can two great and powerful groups of nations take comfort from our present course—both sides overburdened by the cost of modern weapons, both rightly alarmed by the steady spread of the deadly atom, yet both racing to alter that uncertain balance of terror that stays the hand of mankind's final war.

So let us begin anew—remembering on both sides that civility is not a sign of weakness, and sincerity is always subject to proof. Let us never negotiate out of fear. But let us never fear to negotiate.

Let both sides explore what problems unite us instead of belaboring those problems which divide us.

Let both sides, for the first time, formulate serious and precise proposals for the inspection and control of arms—and bring the absolute power to destroy other nations under the absolute control of all nations.

Let both sides seek to invoke the wonders of science instead of its terrors. Together let us explore the stars, conquer the deserts, eradicate diseases, tap the ocean depths, and encourage the arts and commerce.

Let both sides unite to heed in all corners of the earth the command of Isaiah—to "undo the heavy burdens . . . and let the oppressed go free."

And if a beachhead of co-operation may push back the jungle of suspicion, let both sides join in creating a new endeavor, not a new balance of power, but a new world of law, where the strong are just and the weak secure and the peace preserved.

All this will not be finished in the first one hundred days. Nor will it be finished in the first one thousand days, nor in the life of this administration, nor even perhaps in our lifetime on this planet. But let us begin.

In your hands, my fellow citizens, more than mine, will rest the final success or failure of our course. Since this country was founded, each generation of Americans has been summoned to give testimony to its national loyalty. The graves of young Americans who answered the call to service surround the globe.

Now the trumpet summons us again—not as a call to bear arms, though arms we need—not as a call to battle, though embattled we are—but a call to bear the burden of a long twilight struggle, year in and year out, "rejoicing in hope, patient in tribulation"—a struggle against the common enemies of man: tyranny, poverty, disease, and war itself.

Can we forge against these enemies a grand and global alliance, North and South, East and West, that can assure a more fruitful life for all mankind? Will you join in that historic effort?

In the long history of the world, only a few generations have been granted the role of defending freedom in its hour of maximum danger. I do not shrink from this responsibility—I welcome it. I do not believe that any of us would exchange places with any other people or any other generation. The energy, the faith, the devotion which we bring to this endeavor will light our country and all who serve it—and the glow from that fire can truly light the world.

And so, my fellow Americans: ask not what your country can do for you—ask what you can do for your country.

My fellow citizens of the world: ask not what America will do for you, but what together we can do for the freedom of man.

Finally, whether you are citizens of America or citizens of the world, ask of us here the same high standards of strength and sacrifice which we ask of you. With a good conscience our only sure reward, with history the final judge of our deeds, let us go forth to lead the land we love, asking His blessing and His help, but knowing that here on earth God's work must truly be our own.

AMENDMENT XXIII: PRESIDENTIAL VOTE FOR DISTRICT OF COLUMBIA

March 29, 1961

Proposed by Congress June 16, 1960, its ratification was completed March 29, 1961.

SEC. 1. The District constituting the seat of Government of the United States shall appoint in such manner as the Congress may direct:

A number of electors of President and Vice-President equal to the whole number of Senators and Representatives in Congress to which the District would be entitled if it were a State, but in no event more than the least populous State; they shall be in addition to those appointed by the States, but they shall be considered, for the purposes of the election of President and Vice-President, to be electors appointed by a State; and they shall meet in the District and perform such duties as provided by the twelfth article of amendment.

SEC. 2. The Congress shall have power to enforce this article by appropriate legislation.

DECLARATION OF INDIAN PURPOSE

June 1961

---

*In the 1960s the federal government proposed to deal
with problems of Indian poverty by a program of economic
development of the reservations. In many ways this plan simply
built upon John Collier's unrealized Indian New Deal of the
1930s.*

*In June 1961, over 450 Indian delegates representing
ninety tribes gathered at the University of Chicago to make
recommendations on the future of the Indian in America. In its
formal "Declaration of Indian Purpose," the gathering called for
ending the "so-called termination policy of the last administration," referring to the Eisenhower administration's policy of
abolishment of tribes and forced Indian assimilation.*

CREED

We believe in the inherent right of all people to retain spiritual and
cultural values, and that the free exercise of these values is necessary to the
normal development of any people. Indians exercised this inherent right to live
their own lives for thousands of years before the white man came and took their
lands. It is a more complex world in which Indians live today, but the Indian
people who first settled the New World and built the great civilizations which
only now are being dug out of the past, long ago demonstrated that they could
master complexity.

We believe that the history and development of America show that the
Indian has been subjected to duress, undue influence, unwarranted pressures,
and policies which have produced uncertainty, frustration, and despair. Only
when the public understands these conditions and is moved to take action
toward the formulation and adoption of sound and consistent policies and
programs will these destroying factors be removed and the Indian resume his
normal growth and make his maximum contribution to modern society.

We believe in the future of a greater America, an America which we were
first to love, where life, liberty, and the pursuit of happiness will be a reality. In
such a future, with Indians and all other Americans cooperating, a cultural climate

will be created in which the Indian people will grow and develop as members of a free society.

LEGISLATIVE AND REGULATORY PROPOSALS

In order that basic objectives may be restated and that action to accomplish these objectives may be continuous and may be pursued in a spirit of public dedication, it is proposed that recommendations be adopted to strengthen the principles of the Indian Reorganization Act and to accomplish other purposes. These recommendations would be comparable in scope and purpose to the Indian Trade and Intercourse Act of June 30, 1834, the Act of the same date establishing the Bureau of Indian Affairs, and the Indian Reorganization Act of June 18, 1934, which recognized the inherent powers of Indian Tribes.

The recommendations we propose would redefine the responsibilities of the United States toward the Indian people in terms of a positive national obligation to modify or remove the conditions which produce the poverty and lack of social adjustment as these prevail as the outstanding attributes of Indian life today. . . .

The basic principle involves the desire on the part of Indians to participate in developing their own programs with help and guidance as needed and requested, from a local decentralized technical and administrative staff, preferably located conveniently to the people it serves. Also in recent years certain technical and professional people of Indian descent are becoming better qualified and available to work with and for their own people in determining their own programs and needs. The Indians as responsible individual citizens, as responsible tribal representatives, and as responsible Tribal Councils want to participate, want to contribute to their own personal and tribal improvements and want to cooperate with their Government on how best to solve the many problems in a business-like, efficient and economical manner as rapidly as possible. . . .

CONCLUDING STATEMENT

To complete our Declaration, we point out that in the beginning the people of the New World, called Indians by accident of geography, were possessed of a continent and a way of life. In the course of many years, our people had adjusted to every climate and condition from the Arctic to the torrid zones. In their livelihood and family relationships, their ceremonial observances, they reflected the diversity of the physical world they occupied.

The conditions in which Indians live today reflect a world in which every basic aspect of life has been transformed. Even the physical world is no longer the controlling factor in determining where and under what conditions men may live. In region after region, Indian groups found their means of existence either totally destroyed or materially modified. Newly introduced diseases swept away or reduced regional populations. These changes were followed by major shifts in the internal life of tribe and family.

The time came when the Indian people were no longer the masters of their situation. Their life ways survived subject to the will of a dominant sovereign power. This is said, not in a spirit of complaint; we understand that in the lives of all nations of people, there are times of plenty and times of famine. But we do speak out in a plea for understanding.

When we go before the American people, as we do in this Declaration, and ask for material assistance in developing our resources and developing our opportunities, we pose a moral problem which cannot be left unanswered. For the problem we raise affects the standing which our nation sustains before world opinion.

Our situation cannot be relieved by appropriated funds alone, though it is equally obvious that without capital investment and funded services, solutions will be delayed. Nor will the passage of time lessen the complexities which beset a people moving toward new meaning and purpose.

The answers we seek are not commodities to be purchased, neither are they evolved automatically through the passing of time.

The effort to place social adjustment on a money-time interval scale which has characterized Indian administration, has resulted in unwanted pressure and frustration.

When Indians speak of the continent they yielded, they are not referring only to the loss of some millions of acres in real estate. They have in mind that the land supported a universe of things they knew, valued, and loved.

With that continent gone, except for the few poor parcels they still retain, the basis of life is precariously held, but they mean to hold the scraps and parcels as earnestly as any small nation or ethnic group was ever determined to hold to identity and survival.

What we ask of America is not charity, not paternalism, even when benevolent. We ask only that the nature of our situation be recognized and made the basis of policy and action.

In short, the Indians ask for assistance, technical and financial, for the time needed, however long that may be, to regain in the America of the space age some measure of the adjustment they enjoyed as the original possessors of their native land.

CIVIL RIGHTS SPEECH

Martin Luther King, Jr.   *August 28, 1963*

> *Martin Luther King, Jr., first came to national promi-*
> *nence as the spokesman for the Selma bus boycott in 1955. The*
> *son of a Baptist minister and an ordained minister himself,*
> *King advocated nonviolent civil disobedience on the part of*
> *black Americans to overcome segregation. In 1960 King became*
> *president of the Southern Christian Leadership Conference*
> *(SCLC), a position he held until his assassination in 1968.*
>
> *In August 1963, King, the SCLC and several other civil*
> *rights groups organized a march on Washington, which*
> *culminated in a mass meeting on August 28. There on the steps*
> *of the Lincoln Memorial, at the feet of the statue of the "Great*
> *Emancipator," civil rights activists addressed the crowd of more*
> *than 200,000 people. At the end of the program King rose to*
> *give what was to be a brief address. In his "I Have a Dream"*
> *speech, he "subpoenaed the conscience of the nation before the*
> *judgment seat of morality."*

FIVESCORE years ago, a great American, in whose symbolic shadow we stand today, signed the Emancipation Proclamation. This momentous decree came as a great beacon light of hope to millions of Negro slaves who had been seared in the flames of withering injustice. It came as a joyous daybreak to end the long night of their captivity.

But one hundred years later, the Negro still is not free; one hundred years later, the life of the Negro is still sadly crippled by the manacles of segregation and the chains of discrimination; one hundred years later, the Negro lives on a lonely island of poverty in the midst of a vast ocean of material prosperity; one hundred years later, the Negro is still languished in the corners of American society and finds himself in exile in his own land.

So we've come here today to dramatize a shameful condition. In a sense we've come to our nation's capital to cash a check. When the architects of our republic wrote the magnificent words of the Constitution and the Declaration of Independence, they were signing a promissory note to which every American was to fall heir. This note was the promise that all men, yes, black men as well as white men, would be guaranteed the unalienable rights of life, liberty, and the pursuit of happiness.

It is obvious today that America has defaulted on this promissory note in so far as her citizens of color are concerned. Instead of honoring this sacred obligation, America has given the Negro people a bad check; a check which has come back marked "insufficient funds." We refuse to believe that there are insufficient funds in the great vaults of opportunity of this nation. And so we've come to cash this check, a check that will give us upon demand the riches of freedom and the security of justice.

We have also come to this hallowed spot to remind America of the fierce urgency of now. This is no time to engage in the luxury of cooling off or to take the tranquilizing drug of gradualism. Now is the time to make real the promises of democracy; now is the time to rise from the dark and desolate valley of segregation to the sunlit path of racial justice; now is the time to lift our nation from the quicksands of racial injustice to the solid rock of brotherhood; now is the time to make justice a reality for all God's children. It would be fatal for the nation to overlook the urgency of the moment. This sweltering summer of the Negro's legitimate discontent will not pass until there is an invigorating autumn of freedom and equality.

Nineteen sixty-three is not an end, but a beginning. And those who hope that the Negro needed to blow off steam and will now be content, will have a rude awakening if the nation returns to business as usual.

There will be neither rest nor tranquility in America until the Negro is granted his citizenship rights. The whirlwinds of revolt will continue to shake the foundations of our nation until the bright day of justice emerges.

But there is something that I must say to my people who stand on the warm threshold which leads into the palace of justice. In the process of gaining our rightful place we must not be guilty of wrongful deeds.

Let us not seek to satisfy our thirst for freedom by drinking from the cup of bitterness and hatred. We must forever conduct our struggle on the high plane of dignity and discipline. We must not allow our creative protest to degenerate into physical violence. Again and again we must rise to the majestic heights of meeting physical force with soul force.

The marvelous new militancy which has engulfed the Negro community must not lead us to a distrust of all white people, for many of our white brothers, as evidenced by their presence here today, have come to realize that their destiny is tied up with our destiny and they have come to realize that their freedom is inextricably bound to our freedom. This offense we share mounted to storm the battlements of injustice must be carried forth by a biracial army. We cannot walk alone.

And as we walk, we must make the pledge that we shall always march ahead. We cannot turn back. There are those who are asking the devotees of civil rights, "When will you be satisfied?" We can never be satisfied as long as the Negro is the victim of the unspeakable horrors of police brutality.

We can never be satisfied as long as our bodies, heavy with fatigue of travel, cannot gain lodging in the motels of the highways and the hotels of the cities. We cannot be satisfied as long as the Negro's basic mobility is from a smaller ghetto to a larger one.

We can never be satisfied as long as our children are stripped of their selfhood and robbed of their dignity by signs stating "for whites only." We cannot be satisfied as long as a Negro in Mississippi cannot vote and a Negro in New York believes he has nothing for which to vote. No, we are not satisfied, and we will not be satisfied until justice rolls down like waters and righteousness like a mighty stream.

I am not unmindful that some of you have come here out of excessive trials and tribulation. Some of you have come fresh from narrow jail cells. Some of you have come from areas where your quest for freedom left you battered by the storms of persecution and staggered by the winds of police brutality. You have been the veterans of creative suffering. Continue to work with the faith that unearned suffering is redemptive.

Go back to Mississippi; go back to Alabama; go back to South Carolina; go back to Georgia; go back to Louisiana; go back to the slums and ghettos of the northern cities, knowing that somehow this situation can, and will be changed. Let us not wallow in the valley of despair.

So I say to you, my friends, that even though we must face the difficulties of today and tomorrow, I still have a dream. It is a dream deeply rooted in the American dream that one day this nation will rise up and live out the true meaning of its creed—we hold these truths to be self-evident, that all men are created equal.

I have a dream that one day on the red hills of Georgia, sons of former slaves and sons of former slave-owners will be able to sit down together at the table of brotherhood.

I have a dream that one day, even the state of Mississippi, a state sweltering with the heat of injustice, sweltering with the heat of oppression, will be transformed into an oasis of freedom and justice.

I have a dream my four little children will one day live in a nation where they will not be judged by the color of their skin but by the content of their character. I have a dream today!

I have a dream that one day, down in Alabama, with its vicious racists, with its governor having his lips dripping with the words of interposition and nullification, that one day, right there in Alabama, little black boys and black girls will be able to join hands with little white boys and white girls as sisters and brothers. I have a dream today!

I have a dream that one day every valley shall be exalted, every hill and mountain shall be made low, the rough places shall be made plain, and the crooked places shall be made straight and the glory of the Lord will be revealed and all flesh shall see it together.

This is our hope. This is the faith that I go back to the South with.

With this faith we will be able to hew out of the mountain of despair a stone of hope. With this faith we will be able to transform the jangling discords of our nation into a beautiful symphony of brotherhood.

With this faith we will be able to work together, to pray together, to struggle together, to go to jail together, to stand up for freedom together, knowing that we will be free one day. This will be the day when all of God's children will be able to sing with new meaning—"my country 'tis of thee; sweet land of liberty; of thee I sing; land where my fathers died, land of the pilgrim's pride; from every mountain side, let freedom ring"—and if America is to be a great nation, this must become true.

Martin Luther King, Jr., artist unknown.

So let freedom ring from the prodigious hilltops of New Hampshire.

Let freedom ring from the mighty mountains of New York.

Let freedom ring from the heightening Alleghenies of Pennsylvania.

Let freedom ring from the snow-capped Rockies of Colorado.

Let freedom ring from the curvaceous slopes of California.

But not only that.

Let freedom ring from Stone Mountain of Georgia.

Let freedom ring from Lookout Mountain of Tennessee.

Let freedom ring from every hill and molehill of Mississippi, from every mountainside, let freedom ring.

And when we allow freedom to ring, when we let it ring from every village and hamlet, from every state and city, we will be able to speed up that day when all of God's children—black men and white men, Jews and Gentiles, Catholics and Protestants—will be able to join hands and to sing in the words of the old Negro spiritual, "Free at last, free at last; thank God Almighty, we are free at last."

ADDRESS TO A
JOINT SESSION OF CONGRESS

Lyndon Baines Johnson   *November 27, 1963*

Lyndon Baines Johnson became president in 1963 upon the assassination of President John F. Kennedy. Before becoming Kennedy's vice-president in 1961, Johnson had served as Senate majority leader and senator and congressman from Texas.

As the nation grieved over the shocking death of President Kennedy, Johnson addressed Congress for the first time as president on November 27. He stressed the Kennedy legacy and asked Congress to pass the pending civil rights legislation in memoriam to the dead president.

MR. Speaker, Mr. President, Members of the House, Members of the Senate, My Fellow Americans:

All I have I would have given gladly not to be standing here today.

The greatest leader of our time has been struck down by the foulest deed of our time. Today John Fitzgerald Kennedy lives on in the immortal words and works that he left behind. He lives on in the mind and memories of mankind. He lives on in the hearts of his countrymen.

No words are sad enough to express our sense of loss. No words are strong enough to express our determination to continue the forward thrust of America that he began.

The dream of conquering the vastness of space—the dream of partnership across the Atlantic, and across the Pacific as well—the dream of a Peace Corps in less-developed nations—the dream of education for all of our children—the dream of jobs for all who seek them and need them—the dream of care for our elderly—the dream of an all-out attack on mental illness—and, above all, the dream of equal rights for all Americans, whatever their race or color—these and other American dreams have been vitalized by his drive and by his dedication.

Now the ideas and ideals which he so nobly represented must and will be translated into effective action.

Under John Kennedy's leadership, this nation has demonstrated that it has the courage to seek peace and it has the fortitude to risk war. We have proved that we are a good and reliable friend to those who seek peace and freedom. We have shown that we can also be a formidable foe to those who reject the path of peace and those who seek to impose upon us or our allies the yoke of tyranny.

This nation will keep its commitments from South Vietnam to West Berlin. We will be unceasing in the search for peace; resourceful in our pursuit of areas of agreement, even with those with whom we differ; and generous and loyal to those who join with us in common cause.

In this age, when there can be no losers in peace and no victors in war, we must recognize the obligation to match national strength with national restraint. We must be prepared at one and the same time for both the confrontation of power and the limitation of power. We must be ready to defend the national interest and to negotiate the common interest. This is the path that we shall continue to pursue. Those who test our courage will find it strong and those who seek our friendship will find it honorable. We will demonstrate anew that the strong can be just in the use of strength—and the just can be strong in the defense of justice. And let all know we will extend no special privilege and impose no persecution.

We will carry on the fight against poverty and misery, ignorance and disease—in other lands and in our own. We will serve all of the nation, not one section or one sector, or one group, but all Americans. These are the United States—a united people with a united purpose.

Our American unity does not depend upon unanimity. We have differences; but now, as in the past, we can derive from those differences strength, not weakness, wisdom, not despair. Both as a people and as a government we can unite upon a program, a program which is wise, just, enlightened, and constructive.

For thirty-two years Capitol Hill has been my home. I have shared many moments of pride with you—pride in the ability of the Congress of the United States to act; to meet any crisis; to distill from our differences strong programs of national action.

An assassin's bullet has thrust upon me the awesome burden of the presidency. I am here today to say I need your help, I cannot bear this burden alone. I need the help of all Americans, in all America. This nation has experienced a profound shock, and in this critical moment it is our duty—yours and mine—as the government of the United States—to do away with uncertainty and doubt and delay and to show that we are capable of decisive action—that from the brutal loss of our leader we will derive not weakness but strength, that we can and will act and act now.

From this chamber of representative government let all the world know, and none misunderstand, that I rededicate this government to the unswerving support of the United Nations, to the honorable and determined execution of our commitments to our allies, to the maintenance of military strength second to none, to the defense of the strength and the stability of the dollar, to the expansion of our foreign trade, to the reinforcement of our programs of mutual assistance and cooperation in Asia and Africa, and to our Alliance for Progress in this hemisphere.

On the 20th day of January, in 1961, John F. Kennedy told his countrymen that our national work would not be finished "in the first thousand days, nor in the life of this administration, nor even perhaps in our lifetime on this planet. But"—he said—"let us begin." Today in this moment of new resolve, I would say to all my fellow Americans, let us continue.

This is our challenge—not to hesitate, not to pause, not to turn about and linger over this evil moment, but to continue on our course so that we may fulfill the destiny that history has set for us. Our most immediate tasks are here on this Hill.

First, no memorial oration or eulogy could more eloquently honor President Kennedy's memory than the earliest possible passage of the Civil Rights Bill for which he fought so long. We have talked long enough in this country about equal rights. We have talked for 100 years or more. It is time now to write the next chapter—and to write it in the books of law.

I urge you again, as I did in 1957 and again in 1960, to enact a civil rights law so that we can move forward to eliminate from this nation every trace of discrimination and oppression that is based upon race or color. There could be no greater source of strength to this nation both at home and abroad.

And, second, no act of ours could more fittingly continue the work of President Kennedy than the early passage of the tax bill for which he fought all this long year. This is a bill designed to increase our national income and federal revenues, and to provide insurance against recession. That bill, if passed without delay, means more security for those now working, more jobs for those now without them, and more incentive for our economy.

In short, this is no time for delay. It is time for action—strong, forward-looking action on the pending education bills to help bring the light of learning to every home and hamlet in America; strong, forward-looking action on youth employment opportunities; strong, forward-looking action on the pending foreign aid bill, making clear that we are not forfeiting our responsibilities to this hemisphere or to the world, nor erasing executive flexibility in the conduct of our foreign affairs; and strong, prompt, and forward-looking action on the remaining appropriation bills.

In this new spirit of action, the Congress can expect the full cooperation and support of the executive branch. And in particular I pledge that the expenditures of your government will be administered with the utmost thrift and frugality. I will insist that the government get a dollar's value for a dollar spent. The government will set an example of prudence and economy. This does not mean that we will not meet our unfilled needs or that we will not honor our commitments. We will do both.

As one who has long served in both houses of the Congress, I firmly believe in the independence and the integrity of the legislative branch. I promise you that I shall always respect this. It is deep in the marrow of my bones. With equal firmness, I believe in the capacity and I believe in the ability of the Congress, despite the divisions of opinion which characterize our nation, to act—to act wisely, to act vigorously, to act speedily when the need arises.

The need is here. The need is now.

We meet in grief; but let us also meet in renewed dedication and renewed vigor. Let us meet in action, in tolerance, and in mutual understanding.

John Kennedy's death commands what his life conveyed—that America must move forward. The time has come for Americans of all races and creeds and political beliefs to understand and to respect one another. So let us put an end to the teaching and the preaching of hate and evil and violence. Let us turn away from the fanatics of the far left and the far right, from the apostles of bitterness and bigotry, from those defiant of law and those who pour venom into our nation's bloodstream.

Lyndon B. Johnson, portrait by Elizabeth Shoumatoff, 1968.

I profoundly hope that the tragedy and the torment of these terrible days will bind us together in new fellowship, making us one people in our hour of sorrow. So let us here highly resolve that John Fitzgerald Kennedy did not live—or die—in vain. And on this Thanksgiving Eve, as we gather together to ask the Lord's blessing and give Him our thanks, let us unite in those familiar and cherished words:

> America, America,
> God shed His grace on thee,
> And crown thy good
> With brotherhood
> From sea to shining sea.

Amendment XXIV
Banned Poll Tax in Federal Elections

January 23, 1964

Proposed by Congress August 27, 1962, its ratification was completed January 23, 1964.

SEC. 1. The right of citizens of the United States to vote in any primary or other election for President or Vice-President, for electors for President or Vice-President, or for Senator or Representative in Congress, shall not be denied or abridged by the United States or any State by reason of failure to pay any poll tax or other tax.

SEC. 2. The Congress shall have power to enforce this article by appropriate legislation.

The Civil Rights Act

July 2, 1964

When Lyndon Johnson came to the presidency following the assassination of John F. Kennedy, he made civil rights a top priority. "No memorial oration or eulogy," he told a joint session of Congress on November 27, "could more eloquently honor President Kennedy's memory than the earliest possible passage of the Civil Rights Bill." The 1964 Civil Rights Bill passed just months later outlawed not only segregation in all public accommodations, but also job discrimination on the basis of race or national origin. As an enforcement measure, the act authorized the federal government to withhold funding from public agencies that discriminated on the basis of race, and gave the attorney general specific powers to guarantee voting rights and to end school segregation.

AN Act to enforce the constitutional right to vote, to confer jurisdiction upon the district courts of the United States to provide injunctive relief against discrimination in public accommodations, to authorize the Attorney General to institute suits to protect constitutional rights in public facilities and public education, to extend the Commission on Civil Rights, to prevent discrimination in federally assisted programs, to establish a Commission on Equal Opportunity, and for other purposes.

TITLE I—VOTING RIGHTS

(2) No person acting under color of law shall—

(A) in determining whether any individual is qualified under State law or laws to vote in any Federal election, apply any standard, practice, or procedure different from the standards, practices, or procedures applied under such law or laws to other individuals within the same county, parish, or similar political subdivision who have been found by State officials to be qualified to vote. . . .

(C) employ any literacy test as a qualification for voting in any Federal election unless (i) such test is administered to each individual and is conducted wholly in writing; and (ii) a certified copy of the test and of the answers given by the individual is furnished to him within twenty-five days of the submission of his request. . . .

TITLE II—INJUNCTIVE RELIEF AGAINST DISCRIMINATION IN PLACES OF PUBLIC ACCOMMODATION

SEC. 201. (a) All persons shall be entitled to the full and equal enjoyment of the goods, services, facilities, privileges, advantages, and accommodations of any place of public accommodation, as defined in this section, without discrimination or segregation on the ground of race, color, religion, or national origin.

(b) Each of the following establishments which serves the public is a place of public accommodation within the meaning of this title if its operations affect commerce, or if discrimination or segregation by it is supported by State action:

(1) any inn, hotel, motel or other establishment which provides lodging to transient guests, other than an establishment located within a building which contains not more than five rooms for rent or hire and which is actually occupied by the proprietor of such establishment as his residence;

(2) any restaurant, cafeteria, lunchroom, lunch counter, soda fountain, or other facility principally engaged in selling food for consumption on the premises. . . .

(3) any motion picture house, theater, concert hall, sports arena, stadium or other place of exhibition or entertainment. . . .

SEC. 202. All persons shall be entitled to be free, at any establishment or place, from discrimination or segregation of any kind on the ground of race, color, religion, or national origin, if such discrimination or segregation is or purports to be required by any law, statute, ordinance, regulation, rule, or order of a State or any agency or political subdivision thereof. . . .

SEC. 206. (a) Whenever the Attorney General has reasonable cause to believe that any person or group of persons is engaged in a pattern or practice of resistance to the full enjoyment of any of the rights secured by this title, . . . the Attorney General may bring a civil action in the appropriate district court of the United States. . . .

TITLE VI—NONDISCRIMINATION IN FEDERALLY ASSISTED PROGRAMS

SEC. 601. No person in the United States shall, on the ground of race, color, or national origin, be excluded from participation in, be denied the benefits of, or be subjected to discrimination under any program or activity receiving Federal financial assistance. . . .

GULF OF TONKIN RESOLUTION

August 24, 1964

On August 5, 1964, President Lyndon Johnson requested congressional authorization of broad presidential powers to allow the executive to respond directly to attacks on American forces. This measure, the Gulf of Tonkin Resolution, became the basis for deepening United States involvement in the war in Vietnam, and ultimately served as the "declaration of war" in the undeclared war there. The resolution was passed by both houses of Congress two days later with only two no votes, from Senators Wayne Morse and Ernest Gruening. The measure responded to attacks earlier in August on the United States ships C. Turner Joy *and* Maddox *by North Vietnamese torpedo boats in the Gulf of Tonkin.*

As Congress became critical of the conduct of the war in Vietnam, dissatisfaction over the passage of the resolution grew. Its main supporter in 1964, Senator J. William Fulbright, became one of its most vocal critics in the late 1960s. In 1967 Fulbright, as head of the Senate Foreign Relations Committee, launched a full-scale investigation of the circumstances leading to the passage of the measure. In 1970 Congress repealed the Gulf of Tonkin Resolution.

WHEREAS naval units of the Communist regime in Vietnam, in violation of the principles of the Charter of the United Nations and of international law, have deliberately and repeatedly attacked United States naval vessels lawfully present in international waters, and have thereby created a serious threat to international peace; and

Whereas those attacks are part of a deliberate and systematic campaign of aggression that the Communist regime in North Vietnam has been waging against its neighbors and the nations joined with them in the collective defense of their freedom; and

Whereas the United States is assisting the peoples of Southeast Asia to protect their freedom and has no territorial, military or political ambitions in that area, but desires only that these peoples should be left in peace to work out their own destinies in their own way: Now, therefore, be it

Resolved by the Senate and House of Representatives of the United States of American in Congress assembled, That the Congress approves and supports the determination of the President, as Commander in Chief, to take all necessary measures to repel any armed attack against the forces of the United States and to prevent further aggression.

SEC. 2. The United States regards as vital to its national interest and to world peace the maintenance of international peace and security in southeast Asia. Consonant with the Constitution of the United States and the Charter of the United Nations and in accordance with its obligations under the Southeast Asia Collective Defense Treaty, the United States is, therefore, prepared, as the President determines, to take all necessary steps, including the use of armed force, to assist any member [Britain, France, Australia, New Zealand, the Philippines, Thailand and Pakistan] or protocol state [South Vietnam, Laos and Cambodia] of the Southeast Asia Collective Defense Treaty requesting assistance in defense of its freedom.

SEC. 3. This resolution shall expire when the President shall determine that the peace and security of the area is reasonably assured by international conditions created by action of the United Nations or otherwise, except that it may be terminated earlier by concurrent resolution of the Congress.

Amendment XXV
Presidential Disability and Succession

February 10, 1967

Proposed by Congress July 6, 1965, its ratification was completed February 10, 1967.

SEC. 1. In case of the removal of the President from office or of his death or resignation, the Vice-President shall become President.

SEC. 2. Whenever there is a vacancy in the office of the Vice-President, the President shall nominate a Vice-President who shall take office upon confirmation by a majority vote of both houses of Congress.

SEC. 3. Whenever the President transmits to the President *pro tempore* of the Senate and the Speaker of the House of Representatives his written declaration that he is unable to discharge the powers and duties of his office, and until he transmits to them a written declaration to the contrary, such powers and duties shall be discharged by the Vice-President as Acting President.

SEC. 4. Whenever the Vice-President and a majority of either the principal officers of the executive departments, or of such other body as Congress may by law provide, transmit to the President *pro tempore* of the Senate and the Speaker of the House of Representatives their written declaration that the President is unable to discharge the powers and duties of his office, the Vice-President shall immediately assume the powers and duties of the office as Acting President.

Thereafter, when the President transmits to the President *pro tempore* of the Senate and the Speaker of the House of Representatives his written declaration that no inability exists, he shall resume the powers and duties of his office unless the Vice-President and a majority of either the principal officers of the executive department, or of such other body as Congress may by law provide, transmit within four days to the President *pro tempore* of the Senate and the Speaker of the House of Representatives their written declaration that the President is unable to discharge the powers and duties of his office. Thereupon Congress shall decide the issue, assembling within forty-eight hours for that purpose if not in session. If the Congress, within twenty-one days after receipt of the latter written declaration, or, if Congress is not in session, within twenty-one days after Congress is required to assemble, determines by two-thirds vote of both houses that the President is unable to discharge the powers and duties of his office, the Vice-President shall continue to discharge the same as Acting President; otherwise, the President shall resume the powers and duties of his office.

AMENDMENT XXVI
LOWERED VOTING AGE TO EIGHTEEN YEARS

July 1, 1971

Proposed by Congress March 8, 1971, its ratification was completed July 1, 1971.

SEC. 1. The right of citizens of the United States, who are eighteen years of age or older, to vote shall not be denied or abridged by the United States or by any State on account of age.

SEC. 2. The Congress shall have power to enforce this article by appropriate legislation.

THE EQUAL RIGHTS AMENDMENT

March 22, 1972

Proposed by Congress March 22, 1972, this amendment was never ratified. After women won the right to vote with the Nineteenth Amendment in 1920, many suffragists claimed that the vote was not enough to end what they saw as the repression of women. As a result, Alice Paul, leader of the National Woman's Party, wrote an Equal Rights Amendment in 1922. The proposed amendment, which called for an end to discrimination on the basis of sex, included an enforcement clause that required the federal government to act to uphold

*equal rights. During the 1930s and 1940s, the ERA ratification
had effectively failed.*

*The ERA came back to life in 1966 with the founding of
the National Organization for Women (NOW), inspired in part
by Betty Friedan's book,* The Feminine Mystique *(1963).
Friedan argued that women in the home had lost their identi-
ties outside of their roles as mothers and wives. Working
women, it was argued, faced job discrimination, unequal pay
for equal work and a lack of professional opportunities. An
Equal Rights Amendment would allow them to fight these
handicaps in the courts and in Congress. In 1972, after a
large-scale campaign by NOW and other feminist groups,
Congress passed the Equal Rights Amendment and sent it to the
states for ratification. At the state level the ERA campaign
encountered strong opposition from several groups, especially
the antifeminist or "profamily" movement. After passing
through thirty-five state legislatures in the late 1970s, in 1982
the ERA faltered three votes short of the required three-fourths
majority.*

RESOLVED by the Senate and House of Representatives of the United
States of America in Congress assembled (two-thirds of each House concurring
therein), That the following article is
proposed as an amendment to the
Constitution of the United States, which
shall be valid to all intents and purposes as part of the Constitution when
ratified by the legislatures of three-
fourths of the several States within
seven years from the date of its submission by the Congress:

Equal Rights March on Washington, photographer unknown 1978.

SEC. 1. Equality of rights under
the law shall not be denied or abridged
by the United States or by any State on
account of sex.

SEC. 2. The Congress shall have the power to enforce, by appropriate
legislation, the provisions of this article.

SEC. 3. This amendment shall take effect two years after the date of
ratification.

ROE ET AL. V. WADE

Harry Blackmun   *1973*

---

*In the early 1970s American women argued that control
over their bodies and their reproductive capacities was a basic
right guaranteed them in the Constitution. They argued that
state and federal statutes that limited women's access to
abortions abrogated this right. In 1972, two tests challenged
state governments' abilities to restrict women's legal access to
abortion:* Roe et al. v. Wade *and* Doe v. Bolton.

*On January 22, 1973, Justice Harry Blackmun read the
majority decision of the Supreme Court in the case of* Roe et al.
v. Wade. *The court ruled that state laws that criminalized abortion were unconstitutional, as they violated women's right to
privacy and impinged upon women's decisions whether or not
to enter pregnancy. As a result abortion became legal through
the second trimester of pregnancy. In the dissenting opinion,
Justice William Rehnquist argued that although one plaintiff
could argue for his or her own constitutional rights, "he may
not seek vindication for the rights of others."*

The Roe et al. v. Wade *decision was one of the court's
most controversial decisions in the 1970s; it remains controversial in the 1980s and 1990s, as it continues to be addressed in
cases before the Supreme Court.*

MR. Justice Blackmun delivered the opinion of the Court.

This Texas federal appeal [presents a constitutional challenge] to state
criminal abortion legislation. The Texas statutes under attack here are typical of
those that have been in effect in many States for approximately a century. The
Georgia statutes, in contrast, have a modern cast and are a legislative product
that, to an extent at least, obviously reflects the influences of recent attitudinal
change, of advancing medical knowledge and techniques, and of new thinking
about an old issue.

We forthwith acknowledge our awareness of the sensitive and emotional
nature of the abortion controversy, of the vigorous opposing views, even among
physicians, and of the deep and seemingly absolute convictions that the subject

inspires. One's philosophy, one's experiences, one's exposure to the raw edges of human existence, one's religious training, one's attitudes toward life and family and their values, and the moral standards one establishes and seeks to observe, are all likely to influence and to color one's thinking and conclusions about abortion.

In addition, population growth, pollution, poverty, and racial overtones tend to complicate and not to simplify the problem.

Our task, of course, is to resolve the issue by constitutional measurement, free of emotion and of predilection. We seek earnestly to do this, and, because we do, we have inquired into, and in this opinion place some emphasis upon, medical and medical-legal history and what that history reveals about man's attitudes toward the abortion procedure over the centuries. We bear in mind, too, Mr. Justice Holmes's admonition in his now-vindicated dissent in *Lochner v. New York,* 198 U.S. 45, 76 (1905):

"[The Constitution] is made for people of fundamentally differing views, and the accident of our finding certain opinions natural and familiar or novel and even shocking ought not to conclude our judgment upon the question whether statutes embodying them conflict with the Constitution of the United States."

I. The Texas statutes that concern us here are Arts. 1191-1194 and 1196 of the State's Penal Code. These make it a crime to "procure an abortion," as therein defined, or to attempt one, except with respect to "an abortion procured or attempted by medical advice for the purpose of saving the life of the mother." Similar statutes are in existence in a majority of the States. . . .

II. Jane Roe, a single woman who was residing in Dallas County, Texas, instituted this federal action in March 1970 against the District Attorney of the county. She sought a declaratory judgment that the Texas criminal abortion statutes were unconstitutional on their face, and an injunction restraining the defendant from enforcing the statutes.

Roe alleged that she was unmarried and pregnant; that she wished to terminate her pregnancy by an abortion "performed by a competent, licensed physician, under safe, clinical conditions"; that she was unable to get a "legal" abortion in Texas because her life did not appear to be threatened by the continuation of her pregnancy; and that she could not afford to travel to another jurisdiction in order to secure a legal abortion under safe conditions. She claimed that the Texas statutes were unconstitutionally vague and that they abridged her right of personal privacy, protected by the First, Fourth, Fifth, Ninth, and Fourteenth Amendments. . . .

V. The principal thrust of appellant's attack on the Texas statutes is that they improperly invade a right, said to be possessed by the pregnant woman, to choose to terminate her pregnancy. Appellant would discover this right in the concept of personal "liberty" embodied in the Fourteenth Amendment's Due Process Clause; or in personal, marital, familial, and sexual privacy said to be protected by the Bill of Rights. . . . Before addressing this claim, we feel it desirable briefly to survey, in several aspects, the history of abortion, for such insight as that history may afford us, and then to examine the state purposes and interests behind the criminal abortion laws.

VI. It perhaps is not generally appreciated that the restrictive criminal abortion laws in effect in a majority of States today are of relatively recent vintage. Those laws, generally proscribing abortion or its attempt at any time during pregnancy except when necessary to preserve the pregnant woman's life, are not of ancient or even of common-law origin. Instead, they derive from statutory changes effected, for the most part, in the latter half of the 19th century. . . . [There follows a review of ancient attitudes on abortion, the Hippocratic Oath, the English common law, the English statutory law, the American law, and the positions of the American Medical Association, the American Public Health Association, and the American Bar Association.]

VII. . . . The prevalence of high mortality rates at illegal "abortion mills" strengthens, rather than weakens, the State's interest in regulating the conditions under which abortions are performed. Moreover, the risk to the woman increases as her pregnancy continues. Thus, the State retains a definite interest in protecting the woman's own health and safety when an abortion is proposed at a late stage of pregnancy.

The third reason is the State's interest—some phrase it in terms of duty—in protecting prenatal life. Some of the argument for this justification rests on the theory that a new human life is present from the moment of conception. The State's interest and general obligation to protect life then extends, it is argued, to prenatal life. Only when the life of the pregnant mother herself is at stake, balanced against the life she carries within her, should the interest of the embryo or fetus not prevail. Logically, of course, a legitimate state interest in this area need not stand or fall on acceptance of the belief that life begins at conception or at some other point prior to live birth. In assessing the State's interest, recognition may be given to the less rigid claim that as long as at least potential life is involved, the State may assert interests beyond the protection of the pregnant woman alone.

Parties challenging state abortion laws have sharply disputed in some courts the contention that a purpose of these laws, when enacted, was to protect prenatal life. Pointing to the absence of legislative history to support the contention, they claim that most state laws were designed solely to protect the woman. Because medical advances have lessened this concern, at least with respect to abortion in early pregnancy, they argue that with respect to such abortions the laws can no longer be justified by any state interest. . . .

It is with these interests, and the weight to be attached to them, that this case is concerned.

VIII. The Constitution does not explicitly mention any right of privacy. In a line of decisions, however, going back perhaps as far as *Union Pacific R. Co. v. Botsford*, 141 U.S. 250, 251 (1891), the Court has recognized that a right of personal privacy, or a guarantee of certain areas or zones of privacy, does exist under the Constitution. . . .

This right of privacy, whether it be founded in the Fourteenth Amendment's concept of personal liberty and restrictions upon state action, as we feel it is, or, as the District Court determined, in the Ninth Amendment's reservation of rights to the people, is broad enough to encompass a woman's decision whether or not to terminate her pregnancy. The detriment that the State would impose upon the pregnant woman by denying this choice altogether is apparent. Specific and direct harm medically diagnosable even in early pregnancy may be involved. Maternity, or additional offspring, may force upon the woman a distressful life and future. Psychological harm may be imminent. Mental and physical health may be taxed by child care. There is also the distress, for all concerned, associated with the unwanted child, and there is the problem of bringing a child into a family already unable, psychologically and otherwise, to care for it. In other cases, as in this one, the additional difficulties and continuing stigma of unwed motherhood may be involved. All these are factors the woman and her responsible physician necessarily will consider in consultation.

On the basis of elements such as these, appellant and some *amici* argue that the woman's right is absolute and that she is entitled to terminate her pregnancy at whatever time, in whatever way, and for whatever reason she alone chooses. With this we do not agree. Appellant's arguments that Texas either has no valid interest at all in regulating the abortion decision, or no interest strong enough to support any limitation upon the woman's sole determination, are unpersuasive. The Court's decisions recognizing a right of privacy also acknowledge that some state regulation in areas protected by that right is appropriate. As noted above, a State may properly assert important interests in safeguarding health, in maintaining medical standards, and in protecting potential life. At some point in pregnancy, these respective interests become sufficiently compelling to sustain regulation of the factors that govern the abortion decision. The privacy right involved, therefore, cannot be said to be absolute. In fact, it is not clear to us that the claim asserted by some *amici* that one has an unlimited right to do with one's body as one pleases bears a close relationship to the right of privacy previously articulated in the Court's decisions. . . .

We, therefore, conclude that the right of personal privacy includes the abortion decision, but that this right is not unqualified and must be considered against important state interests in regulation.

We note that those federal and state courts that have recently considered abortion law challenges have reached the same conclusion. . . . Although the results are divided, most of these courts have agreed that the right of privacy, however based, is broad enough to cover the abortion decision; that the right, nonetheless, is not absolute and is subject to some limitations, and that at some point the state interests as to protection of health, medical standards, and prenatal life, become dominant. We agree with this approach. . . .

XI. To summarize and to repeat:

1. A state criminal abortion statute of the current Texas type, that excepts from criminality only a lifesaving procedure on behalf of the mother, without regard to pregnancy stage and without recognition of the interests involved, is violative of the Due Process Clause of the Fourteenth Amendment.

(a) For the stage prior to approximately the end of the first trimester, the abortion decision and its effectuation must be left to the medical judgment of the pregnant woman's attending physician.

(b) For the stage subsequent to approximately the end of the first trimester, the State, in promoting its interest in the health of the mother, may, if it chooses, regulate the abortion procedure in ways that are reasonably related to maternal health.

(c) For the stage subsequent to viability, the State in promoting its interest in the potentiality of human life may, if it chooses, regulate, and even proscribe, abortion except where it is necessary, in appropriate medical judgment, for the preservation of the life or health of the mother. . . .

This holding, we feel, is consistent with the relative weights of the respective interests involved, with the lessons and examples of medical and legal history, with the lenity of the common law, and with the demands of the profound problems of the present day. The decision leaves the State free to place increasing restrictions on abortion as the period of pregnancy lengthens, so long as these restrictions are tailored to the recognized state interests. . . .

Mr. Justice Rehnquist, dissenting:

The Court's opinion brings to the decision of this troubling question both extensive historical fact and a wealth of legal scholarship. While the opinion commands my respect, I find myself nonetheless in fundamental disagreement with those parts of it that invalidate the Texas statute in question, and therefore dissent. . . .

THE WAR POWERS ACT

November 7, 1973

---

*In 1973 Congress passed the War Powers Act, which
severely limited the powers of the president to become involved in
undeclared wars such as those in Vietnam and Korea. In part
the War Powers Act was a reaction against the Gulf of Tonkin
Resolution, which itself had been repealed in 1970. The War
Powers Act can also be seen as a restrictive measure against
President Nixon, who had been elected in 1968. Significantly,
the vote for passage of the act came immediately after the infamous "Saturday Night Massacre," Nixon's firing of special
Watergate Prosecutor Archibald Cox. Although President Nixon
vetoed the act, Congress was able to override.*

*In recent years the War Powers Act has been criticized for
not being enforceable and for leaving the president too much
leeway in the short-term insertion of troops in war zones. Its
ultimate constitutionality has also been questioned. Congress
invoked the War Powers Act for the first time in 1983 following
an attack on United States Marines stationed in Beirut, Lebanon,
as part of a multinational peacekeeping force. President Ronald
Reagan, wishing to avoid a constitutional battle over the issue,
agreed to the invocation after Congress agreed to an eighteen-
month extension of the troops' deployment.*

RESOLVED by the Senate and House of Representatives of the United
States of America in Congress assembled,

SECTION 1. This joint resolution may be cited as the "War Powers
Resolution."

SEC. 2. (a) It is the purpose of this joint resolution to fulfill the intent of
the framers of the Constitution of the United States and insure that the collective
judgment of both the Congress and the President will apply to the introduction
of United States Armed Forces into hostilities, or into situations where imminent
involvement in hostilities is clearly indicated by the circumstances, and to the
continued use of such forces in hostilities or in such situations.

(b) Under article I, section 8, of the Constitution, it is specifically provided that the Congress shall have the power to make all laws necessary and proper for carrying into execution, not only its own powers but also all other powers vested by the Constitution in the Government of the United States, or in any department or officer thereof.

(c) The constitutional powers of the President as Commander-in-Chief to introduce United States Armed Forces into hostilities, or into situations where imminent involvement in hostilities is clearly indicated by the circumstances, are exercised only pursuant to (1) a declaration of war, (2) specific statutory authorization, or (3) a national emergency created by attack upon the United States, its territories or possessions, or its armed forces.

SEC. 3. The President in every possible instance shall consult with Congress before introducing United States Armed Forces into hostilities or into situations where imminent involvement in hostilities is clearly indicated by the circumstances, and after every such introduction shall consult regularly with the Congress until United States Armed Forces are no longer engaged in hostilities or have been removed from such situations.

SEC. 4. (a) In the absence of a declaration of war, in any case in which United States Armed Forces are introduced—

(1) into hostilities or into situations where imminent involvement in hostilities is clearly indicated by the circumstances;

(2) into the territory, airspace or waters of a foreign nation, while equipped for combat, except for deployments which relate solely to supply, replacement, repair, or training of such forces; or

(3) in numbers which substantially enlarge United States Armed Forces equipped for combat already located in a foreign nation;

the President shall submit within 48 hours to the Speaker of the House of Representatives and to the President *pro tempore* of the Senate a report, in writing, setting forth—

(A) the circumstances necessitating the introduction of United States Armed Forces;

(B) the constitutional and legislative authority under which such introduction took place; and

(C) the estimated scope and duration of the hostilities or involvement.

(b) The President shall provide such other information as the Congress may request in the fulfillment of its constitutional responsibilities with respect to committing the Nation to war and to the use of United States Armed Forces abroad.

(c) Whenever United States Armed Forces are introduced into hostilities or into any situation described in subsection (a) of this section, the President shall, so long as such armed forces continue to be engaged in such hostilities or situation, report to the Congress periodically on the status of such hostilities or situation as well as on the scope and duration of such hostilities or situation, but in no event shall he report to the Congress less often than once every six months. . . .

RESIGNATION SPEECH

Richard M. Nixon   *August 8, 1974*

---

*In the 1972 presidential election, President Richard M.
Nixon swept to an overwhelming victory over his Democratic
challenger, Senator George McGovern. Almost immediately,
however, the Nixon presidency faced charges of criminality.
During the campaign, a group working for the Committee to Re-
elect the President broke into Democratic National Committee
headquarters at the Watergate office building in Washington,
D.C., apparently in search of political intelligence. Attempts by
the White House to stop or frustrate the ensuing investigations
ultimately failed when Nixon's own White House tape recordings revealed that the president and his assistants had repeatedly discussed the matter. As revelations mounted, Nixon
became preoccupied with preserving his presidency. The
Supreme Court, in a unanimous decision, required Nixon to
supply Special Prosecutor Leon Jaworski with tape recordings of
conversations with his advisors. In response to the content of
these tapes, the House Judiciary Committee voted to recommend
approval by the full House of three articles of impeachment
against President Nixon. Nine days later, on August 9, 1974,
Nixon resigned his office and was succeeded by Vice-President
Gerald Ford. One month later Ford pardoned Nixon; Nixon
accepted the pardon, but maintained that his mistakes were
personal and political, not criminal.*

GOOD evening.
This is the 37th time I have spoken to you from this office, where so many

decisions have been made that shaped the history of this Nation. Each time I have done so to discuss with you some matter that I believe affected the national interest.

In all the decisions I have made in my public life, I have always tried to do what was best for the Nation. Throughout the long and difficult period of Watergate, I have felt it was my duty to persevere, to make every possible effort to complete the term of office to which you elected me.

In the past few days, however, it has become evident to me that I no longer have a strong enough political base in the Congress to justify continuing that effort. As long as there was such a base, I felt strongly that it was necessary to see the constitutional process through to its conclusion, that to do otherwise would be unfaithful to the spirit of that deliberately difficult process and a dangerously destabilizing precedent for the future.

But with the disappearance of that base, I now believe that the constitutional purpose has been served, and there is no longer a need for the process to be prolonged.

I would have preferred to carry through to the finish whatever the personal agony it would have involved, and my family unanimously urged me to do so. But the interest of the Nation must always come before any personal considerations.

From the discussions I have had with Congressional and other leaders, I have concluded that because of the Watergate matter I might not have the support of the Congress that I would consider necessary to back the very difficult decisions and carry out the duties of this office in the way the interests of the Nation would require.

I have never been a quitter. To leave office before my term is completed is abhorrent to every instinct in my body. But as President, I must put the interest of America first. America needs a full-time President and a full-time Congress, particularly at this time with the problems we face at home and abroad.

To continue to fight through the months ahead for my personal vindication would almost totally absorb the time and attention of both the President and the Congress in a period when our entire focus should be on the great issues of peace abroad and prosperity without inflation at home.

Therefore, I shall resign the Presidency effective at noon tomorrow. Vice President Ford will be sworn in as President at that hour in this office.

As I recall the high hopes for America with which we began this second term, I feel a great sadness that I will not be here in this office working on your behalf to achieve those hopes in the next 2 1/2 years. But in turning over direction of the Government to Vice President Ford, I know, as I told the Nation when I nominated him for that office 10 months ago, that the leadership of America will be in good hands.

In passing this office to the Vice President, I also do so with the profound sense of the weight of responsibility that will fall on his shoulders tomorrow and, therefore, of the understanding, the patience, the cooperation he will need from all Americans.

As he assumes that responsibility, he will deserve the help and the support of all of us. As we look to the future, the first essential is to begin healing the wounds of this Nation, to put the bitterness and the divisions of the recent past behind us, and to rediscover those shared ideals that lie at the heart of our strength and unity as a great and as a free people.

By taking this action, I hope that I will have hastened the start of that process of healing which is so desperately needed in America.

I regret deeply any injuries that may have been done in the course of the events that led to this decision. I would say only that if some of my judgments were wrong, and some were wrong, they were made in what I believed at the time to be the best interest of the Nation.

To those who have stood with me during these past difficult months, to my family, my friends, to many others who joined in supporting my cause because they believed it was right, I will be eternally grateful for your support.

And to those who have not felt able to give me your support, let me say I leave with no bitterness toward those who have opposed me, because all of us, in the final analysis, have been concerned with the good of the country, however our judgments might differ.

So, let us all now join together in affirming that common commitment and in helping our new President succeed for the benefit of all Americans.

I shall leave this office with regret at not completing my term, but with gratitude for the privilege of serving as your President for the past 5 1/2 years. These years have been a momentous time in the history of our Nation and the world. They have been a time of achievement in which we can all be proud, achievements that represent the shared efforts of the Administration, the Congress, and the people.

But the challenges ahead are equally great, and they, too, will require the support and the efforts of the Congress and the people working in cooperation with the new Administration.

We have ended America's longest war, but in the work of securing a lasting peace in the world, the goals ahead are even more far-reaching and more difficult. We must complete a structure of peace so that it will be said of this generation, our generation of Americans, by the people of all nations, not only that we ended one war but that we prevented future wars.

We have unlocked the doors that for a quarter of a century stood between the United States and the People's Republic of China.

We must now ensure that the one quarter of the world's people who live in the People's Republic of China will be and remain not our enemies but our friends.

In the Middle East, 100 million people in the Arab countries, many of whom have considered us their enemy for nearly 20 years, now look on us as their friends. We must continue to build on that friendship so that peace can settle at last over the Middle East and so that the cradle of civilization will not become its grave.

Together with the Soviet Union we have made the crucial breakthroughs that have begun the process of limiting nuclear arms. But we must set as our goal not just limiting but reducing and finally destroying these terrible weapons so that they cannot destroy civilization and so that the threat of nuclear war will no longer hang over the world and the people.

We have opened the new relation with the Soviet Union. We must continue to develop and expand that new relationship so that the two strongest nations of the world will live together in cooperation rather than confrontation.

Around the world, in Asia, in Africa, in Latin America, in the Middle East, there are millions of people who live in terrible poverty, even starvation. We must keep as our goal turning away from production for war and expanding production for peace so that people everywhere on this earth can at least look forward in their children's time, if not in our own time, to having the necessities for a decent life.

Here in America, we are fortunate that most of our people have not only the blessings of liberty, but also the means to live full and good and, by the world's standards, even abundant lives. We must press on, however, to a goal of not only more and better jobs, but of full opportunity for every American and of what we are striving so hard right now to achieve, prosperity without inflation.

For more than a quarter of a century in public life I have shared in the turbulent history of this era. I have fought for what I believed in. I have tried to the best of my ability to discharge those duties and meet those responsibilities that were entrusted to me.

Sometimes I have succeeded and sometimes I have failed, but always I have taken heart from what Theodore Roosevelt once said about the man in the arena, "whose face is marred by dust and sweat and blood, who strives valiantly, who errs and comes short again and again because there is not effort without error and shortcoming, but who does actually strive to do the deed, who knows the great enthusiasms, the great devotions, who spends himself in a worthy cause, who at the best knows in the end the triumphs of high achievements and who at the worst, if he fails, at least fails while daring greatly."

I pledge to you tonight that as long as I have a breath of life in my body, I shall continue in that spirit. I shall continue to work for the great causes to which I have been dedicated throughout my years as a Congressman, a Senator, a Vice President, and President, the cause of peace not just for America but among all nations, prosperity, justice, and opportunity for all of our people.

There is one cause above all to which I have been devoted and to which I shall always be devoted for as long as I live.

When I first took the oath of office as President 5 1/2 years ago, I made this sacred commitment, to "consecrate my office, my energies, and all the wisdom I can summon to the cause of peace among nations."

I have done my very best in all these days since to be true to that pledge. As a result of these efforts, I am confident that the world is a safer place today, not only for the people of America, but for the people of all nations, and that all of our children have a better chance than before of living in peace rather than dying in war.

This, more than anything, is what I hoped to achieve when I sought the Presidency. This, more than anything, is what I hope will be my legacy to you, to our country, as I leave the Presidency.

To have served in this office is to have felt a very personal sense of kinship with each and every American. In leaving it, I do so with this prayer: May God's grace be with you in all the days ahead.

SOURCES

Full texts of the documents included in *Soul of America* can be found in the following sources.

I. COLONIAL AMERICA

Privileges and Prerogatives Granted to Columbus. Francis N. Thorpe, ed., *The Federal and State Constitutions, Colonial Charters, and Other Organic Laws of the States, Territories, and Colonies Now or Heretofore Forming the United States of America* (7 vols.; Washington, D.C.: Government Printing Office, 1909), vol. 1.

Letter from Francisco Vazquez de Coronado to His Majesty. George Parker Winship, ed., *The Journey of Coronado, 1540–1542* (New York: A. S. Barnes, 1904).

The Mayflower Compact. George B. Cheever, ed., *The Journal of the Pilgrims at Plymouth, in New England, in 1620* (New York, 1848).

Ordinance for the Virginia House of Burgesses. Thorpe, ed., *Federal and State Constitutions*, vol. 7.

History of Plymouth Plantation. *Bradford's History "Of Plimoth Plantation"* (Boston: Wright and Potter, State Printers, 1899).

Massachusetts School Law. *The Charters and General Laws of the Colony and Provence of Massachusetts Bay* (1814).

The Bloody Tenet of Persecution. E. B. O'Callaghan, ed., *Documents Relative to the Colonial History of the State of New-York* (15 vols.; Albany: Weed and Parsons, 1853–87).

The Great Case of Liberty of Conscience. *The Select Works of William Penn*, 3d. ed. (5 vols.; London: J. Phillips, 1782), vol. 3.

Resolution of the Germantown Mennonites. Milton Meltzer, ed., *Milestones to American Liberty: The Foundations of the Republic* (New York: Crowell, 1961).

Penn's Plan of Union. O'Callaghan, ed., *Documents Relative to the Colonial History*, vol. 9.

The Albany Plan of Union. Jared Sparks, ed., *The Works of Benjamin Franklin* (10 vols.; Boston: Charles Tappan, 1847), vol. 3.

II. THE AMERICAN REVOLUTION

Resolutions of the Stamp Act Congress. *Journals of the First Congress of the American*

Colonies (New York: E. Winchester, 1845).

The Association. Worthington C. Ford, et al., eds., *Journals of the Continental Congress, 1774–1789* (34 vols.; Washington, D.C.: Government Printing Office, 1904–37), vol. 1.

Speech in Virginia Convention. William Wirt Henry, ed., *Patrick Henry: Life, Correspondence, and Speeches* (3 vols.; New York: Charles Scribner's Sons, 1891).

The Battles of Lexington and Concord. Hezekiah Niles, *Principles and Acts of the Revolution in America* (Baltimore: W. O. Niles, 1822).

Letter to John Adams and Response. C. F. Adams, ed., *Familiar Letters of John Adams and His Wife Abigail Adams during the Revolution* (New York: Hurd and Houghton, 1876).

The Virginia Bill of Rights. Thorpe, ed., *Federal and State Constitutions*, vol. 7.

The Declaration of Independence. Ibid., vol. 1.

Speech on American Independence. Saul K. Padover, ed., *The World of the Founding Fathers* (New York: T. Yoseloff, 1960).

From *Common Sense*—American Affairs. Moncure Conway, ed., *The Writings of Thomas Paine* (4 vols.; New York: G. P. Putnam's Sons, 1894–96), vol. 1.

Resolution of Congress on Public Lands. Ford, et al., eds., *Journals of the Continental Congress*, vol. 18.

The Articles of Confederation. Benjamin P. Poore, comp., *The Federal and State Constitutions, Colonial Charters, and Other Organic Laws of the United States* (2 vols.; Washington, D.C.: Government Printing Office, 1877), vol. 1.

Notes on the State of Virginia—Religion. Thomas Jefferson, *Notes on the State of Virginia* (London: John Stockdale, 1787).

To Those Who Would Remove to America. Sparks, ed., *Works of Benjamin Franklin*, vol. 2.

What Is an American? Michel Guillaume St. Jean de Crèvecoeur, *Letters from an American Farmer* (London: Printed for T. Davies, 1782).

III. FORGING A NEW NATION

Report of Government for the Western Territory. *Journals of the American Congress from 1774 to 1788* (4 vols.; Washington, D.C.: Way and Gideon, 1823), vol. 4.

Virginia Statute of Religious Freedom. Henry A. Washington, ed., *The Writings of Thomas Jefferson* (9 vols.; Washington, D.C.: Taylor and Maury, 1853–54), vol. 8.

The Northwest Ordinance. Poore, comp., *Federal and State Constitutions*, vol. 1.

The Constitution of the United States. Edward S. Corwin, *The Constitution and What It Means Today*, 13th ed. (Princeton: Princeton University Press, 1973).

Speech before Federal Convention. Sparks, ed., *Works of Benjamin Franklin*, vol. 5.

The Federalist No. 1. Henry Cabot Lodge, ed., *The Federalist* (New York: G.P. Putnam's Sons, 1888).

The Federalist No. 2. Ibid.

The Federalist No. 51. Ibid.

On the Constitutionality of a National Bank. John C. Hamilton, ed., *The Works of Alexander Hamilton* (7 vols.; New York: J. F. Trow, 1850–51), vol. 4.

Amendments I–X: The Bill of Rights. Corwin, *The Constitution.*

Amendment XI: Judicial Powers Construed. Ibid.

Farewell Address. Jared Sparks, ed., *The Writings of George Washington* (12 vols.; Boston: Charles Tappan, 1846), vol. 12.

IV. THE YOUNG REPUBLIC

Inaugural Address. *A Compilation of the Messages and Papers of the Presidents* (20 vols.; New York: Bureau of National Literature, 1897–1917), vol. 1.

The Virginia Resolutions. Jonathan Elliot, ed., *Debates in the Several State Conventions on the Adoption of the Federal Constitution* (5 vols.; Washington, D.C.: Printed for the editor, 1836–45), vol. 4.

First Inaugural Address. Washington, ed., *Writings of Thomas Jefferson*, vol. 8.

The Louisiana Purchase. William M. Malloy, ed., *Treaties, Conventions, International Acts, Protocols, and Agreements between the United States of America and Other Powers* (2 vols.; Washington, D.C.: Government Printing Office, 1910).

Instructions to Meriwether Lewis. Paul Leicester Ford, ed., *The Writings of Thomas Jefferson* (10 vols.; New York: G. P. Putnam's Sons, 1892–99), vol. 7.

Marbury v. Madison. *Supreme Court Reports*, 1 Cranch 137 (1803).

Amendment XII: Choosing President and Vice-President. Corwin, *The Constitution.*

Speech to the Iroquois Six Nations. Edmund C. Stedman and Ellen Mackay Hutchinson, eds., *A Library of American Literature* (11 vols.; New York: C. L. Webster and Co., 1887–90), vol. 4.

Letter to Jefferson on the Expedition. Donald Jackson, ed., *Letters of the Lewis and Clark Expedition, with Related Documents, 1783–1854*, 2d ed. (2 vols.; Urbana: University of Illinois Press, 1978), vol. 1.

Speech to Governor Harrison. *The Book of the Indians of North America* (Boston: Josiah Drake, 1832).

The Star Spangled Banner. Oscar G. T. Sonneck, *The Star Spangled Banner* (Washington, D.C.: Government Printing Office, 1914).

Letter to Samuel Kercheval. Ford, ed., *Writings of Thomas Jefferson*, vol. 10.

McCulloch v. Maryland. *Supreme Court Reports*, 4 Wheaton 316 (1819).

Missouri Compromise Acts. *U.S. Statutes at Large*, 16th Cong., 1st sess., 1819–20, vol. 3.

Annual Message to Congress—The Monroe Doctrine. *Messages and Papers*, vol. 2.

V. A GATHERING STORM

South Carolina Exposition and Protest. Thomas Cooper, ed., *The Statutes at Large of South Carolina* (Columbia, 1836), vol. 1.

Second Reply to Hayne. *The Writings and Speeches of Daniel Webster* (18 vols.; Boston: Little, Brown, 1903), vol. 6.

To the Public. *The Liberator,* January 1, 1831.

Cherokee Nation v. Georgia. *Supreme Court Reports,* 5 Peters 1 (1831).

Veto of the Bank Bill. *Messages and Papers,* vol. 3.

Memorial and Protest of the Cherokee Nation. Meltzer, *Milestones.*

Civil Disobedience. *The Writings of Henry David Thoreau* (10 vols.; Cambridge: Riverside Press, 1893), vol. 10.

Treaty of Guadalupe Hidalgo. *U.S. Statutes at Large,* 1845–51, Treaties, vol. 9.

Seneca Falls Declaration of Sentiments and Resolutions. Elizabeth Cady Stanton, et al., eds., *History of Woman Suffrage* (6 vols.; New York: Fowler and Wells, 1881–1922). vol. 1.

Letter to Thomas Auld, His Former Master. Patricia W. Romero, comp., *I Too Am America: Documents from 1619 to the Present* (New York: Publishers Co., 1968).

Resolutions; The Compromise of 1850. *U.S. Statutes at Large,* 1845–51, vol. 9.

The Seventh of March Speech. *Congressional Globe,* 31st Cong., 1st sess., 1850.

Ain't I a Woman? *Narrative of Sojourner Truth* (1878; New York: Arno Press, 1968).

Kansas-Nebraska Act. *U.S. Statutes at Large,* 33d Cong., 1st sess., 1854, vol. 10.

Dred Scott v. Sandford. *Supreme Court Reports,* 19 Howard 393 (1857).

VI. Civil War

"House Divided" Speech. Alonzo T. Jones, ed., *Political Speeches and Debates of Abraham Lincoln and Stephen A. Douglas, 1854–1861* (Battle Creek, Mich.: International Tract Society, 1895).

Address to the Virginia Court. John D. Lawson, ed., *American State Trials* (17 vols.; St. Louis: Thomas Law Book Co., 1914–36), vol. 6.

South Carolina Ordinance and Declaration of Causes of Secession. Frank Moore, ed., *The Rebellion Record* (11 vols.; New York: G. P. Putnam and D. Van Nostrand, 1861–68), vol. 1.

First Inaugural Address. *Messages and Papers,* vol. 7.

The Battle Hymn of the Republic. *Atlantic Monthly,* February 1862.

The Homestead Act. *U.S. Statutes at Large,* 37th Cong., 2d sess., 1862, vol. 12.

The Morrill Act. Ibid.

The Emancipation Proclamation. Roy P. Basler, ed., *The Collected Works of Abraham Lincoln* (8 vols.; New Brunswick: Rutgers University Press, 1953), vol. 6.

Address at Gettysburg. Ibid., vol. 7.

Second Inaugural Address. Ibid., vol. 8.

Farewell to His Army. Armistead L. Long, *Memoirs of Robert E. Lee* (New York: J.M. Stoddart and Co., 1886).

Amendment XIII: Slavery Abolished. Corwin, *The Constitution.*

The Impeachment and Trial of President Andrew Johnson. Benjamin P. Poore, ed., *Trial of Andrew Johnson* (Washington, D.C.: Government Printing Office, 1868).

Amendment XIV: Citizenship Rights Not to Be Abridged. Corwin, *The Constitution.*

Amendment XV: Race No Bar to Voting Rights. Ibid.

VII. America Comes of Age

On Woman's Right to Suffrage. Ida Harper, *The Life and Work of Susan B. Anthony* (3 vols.; Indianapolis: Bowen–Merrill, 1898–1908), vol. 1.

Report on the Lands of the Arid Region. John Wesley Powell, *Report on the Lands of the Arid Region of the United States* (Washington, D.C.: Government Printing Office, 1878).

Narrative. Virginia Irving Armstrong, ed., *I Have Spoken: American History through the Voices of the Indians* (Chicago: Swallow Press, 1971).

The New Colossus. *The Poems of Emma Lazarus* (New York: Houghton Mifflin, 1889).

The Sherman Anti-Trust Act. *U.S. Statutes at Large*, 51st Cong., 1st sess., 1890, vol. 26.

America the Beautiful. Helen K. Johnson and Frederic Dean, eds., *Famous Songs and Those Who Made Them* (New York: Bryan, Taylor and Co., 1895).

Atlanta Exposition Speech. Booker T. Washington, *Up from Slavery: An Autobiography* (New York: Doubleday and Page, 1901).

Cross of Gold Speech. William Jennings Bryan, *The First Battle* (Chicago: W. B. Conkey Co., 1896).

Plessy v. Ferguson. *Supreme Court Reports*, 163 U.S. 537 (1896).

Letter to Booker T. Washington. Louis R. Harlan, et al., eds., *The Booker T. Washington Papers* (14 vols.; Urbana: University of Illinois Press, 1972–88), vol. 4.

Open Door Circular Letter. Malloy, ed., *Treaties, Conventions, International Acts*, vol. 1.

Fourth Annual Message to Congress. *Messages and Papers*, vol. 15.

Seventh Annual Message to Congress. Ibid.

Declaration of the Conservation Conference. *Proceedings of a Conference of Governors in the White House, Washington, D.C., May 13–15, 1908* (Washington, D.C.: Government Printing Office, 1909).

Amendment XVI: Income Tax Authorized. Corwin, *The Constitution.*

Amendment XVII: Direct Popular Election of Senators. Ibid.

VIII. Two Wars and a Depression

Women and War. Jane Addams, *Peace and Bread in Time of War* (New York: Macmillan, 1922).

Address to the United States Senate. 64th Cong., 2d sess., 1917, S. Doc. 685.

The Fourteen Points. *Messages and Papers,* vol. 18.

Amendment XVIII: Liquor Prohibition. Corwin, *The Constitution.*

Amendment XIX: National Woman Suffrage. Ibid.

The Philosophy of Rugged Individualism. *The New Day: Campaign Speeches of Herbert Hoover* (Palo Alto: Stanford University Press, 1928).

Amendment XX: Beginning of Presidential Terms, Congressional Sessions. Corwin, *The Constitution.*

First Inaugural Address. *Congressional Record*, 73d Cong., Special Session of the Senate, 1933.

Amendment XXI: Repeal of Amendment XVIII. Corwin, *The Constitution.*
Four Freedoms Speech. *Congressional Record,* 77th Cong., 1st sess., 1941.
The Atlantic Charter. 77th Cong., 1st sess., 1941, H. Doc. 358.
Declaration of War. *Congressional Record,* 77th Cong., 1st sess., 1941.
Executive Order 9066. *Federal Register,* vol. 7, 1942.

IX. THE UNITED STATES AND WORLD POWER

The United Nations Conference. *Public Papers of the Presidents of the United States: Harry
    S. Truman . . . 1945* (Washington, D.C.: Government Printing Office, 1961).
The Truman Doctrine. *Congressional Record,* 80th Cong., 1st sess., 1947.
The Marshall Plan. *Congressional Record,* 80th Cong., 1st sess., 1947, Appendix.
Inaugural Address. *Public Papers of the Presidents of the United States: Harry S. Truman
    . . . 1949* (Washington, D.C.: Government Printing Office, 1964).
Amendment XXII: Limit Two Terms for President. Corwin, *The Constitution.*
Brown v. the Board of Education of Topeka, Kansas. *Supreme Court Reports,* 347 U.S. 483
    (1954).
Farewell Address. *Department of State Bulletin,* February 6, 1961.
Inaugural Address. *Public Papers of the Presidents of the United States: John F. Kennedy
    . . . 1961* (Washington, D.C.: Government Printing Office, 1962).
Amendment XXIII: Presidential Vote for District of Columbia. Corwin, *The Constitution.*
Declaration of Indian Purpose. Francis Paul Prucha, ed., *Documents of United States
    Indian Policy* (Lincoln: University of Nebraska Press, 1975).
Civil Rights Speech. Coretta Scott King, comp., *The Words of Martin Luther King, Jr.* (New
    York: Newmarket Press, 1987).
Address to a Joint Session of Congress. *Public Papers of the Presidents of the United States:
    Lyndon B. Johnson . . . 1963–64* (Washington, D.C.: Government Printing Office,
    1965).
Amendment XXIV: Banned Poll Tax in Federal Elections. Corwin, *The Constitution.*
The Civil Rights Act. *U.S. Statutes at Large,* 1964, vol. 78, Public Law 88–352.
Gulf of Tonkin Resolution. *Department of State Bulletin,* August 24, 1964.
Amendment XXV: Presidential Disability and Succession. Corwin, *The Constitution.*
Amendment XXVI: Lowered Voting Age to Eighteen Years. Ibid.
The Equal Rights Amendment. Leslie F. Goldstein, *The Constitutional Rights of Women:
    Cases in Law and Social Change* (Madison: University of Wisconsin Press, 1988).
Roe et al. v. Wade. *Supreme Court Reports,* 410 U.S. 113 (1973).
The War Powers Act. *U.S. Statutes at Large,* 1973, vol. 87, Public Law 93–148.
Resignation Speech. *Public Papers of the Presidents of the United States: Richard Nixon .
    . . 1974* (Washington, D.C.: Government Printing Office, 1975).

BIBLIOGRAPHY

COLLECTIONS OF DOCUMENTS

The Annals of America. 22 vols. Chicago: Encyclopedia Britannica, 1968–.

Barrett, Edward L., Jr., and William Cohen. *Constitutional Law: Cases and Materials.* 7th ed. Mineola, N.Y.: Foundation Press, 1985.

Commager, Henry Steele, ed. *Documents of American History.* 9th ed. New York: Meredith Corporation, 1973.

A Compilation of the Messages and Papers of the Presidents. 20 vols. New York: Bureau of National Literature, 1897–1917.

Documentary History of the Constitution of the United States of America, 1787–1870. 5 vols. Washington, D.C.: Department of State, 1894–1905.

Elliot, Jonathan, ed. *Debates in the Several State Conventions on the Adoption of the Federal Constitution.* 5 vols. Washington, D.C.: Printed for the editor, 1836–45.

Glusker, Irwin, and Richard M. Ketchum, eds. *American Testament: Fifty Great Documents in American History.* New York: American Heritage Publishing Co., 1971.

Historical Statistics of the United States: Colonial Times to 1970. 2 vols. Washington, D.C.: U.S. Department of Commerce, 1975.

Israel, Fred L. *State of the Union Messages of the Presidents, 1790–1966.* 3 vols. New York: Chelsea House Publishers, 1967.

Journals of the American Congress from 1774 to 1788. 4 vols. Washington, D.C.: Way and Gideon, 1823.

MacDonald, H. Malcolm, et al. *Outside Readings in American Government.* New York: Crowell, 1957.

MacDonald, William, ed. *Select Documents Illustrative of the History of the United States, 1776–1861.* 1898. Reprint. New York: Burt Franklin, 1968.

Malloy, William M., ed. *Treaties, Conventions, International Acts, Protocols, and Agreements between the United States of America and Other Powers.* 2 vols. Washington, D.C.: Government Printing Office, 1910.

Meltzer, Milton, ed. *Milestones to American Liberty: The Foundations of the Republic.* New York: Crowell, 1961.

Millett, Stephen M. *A Selected Bibliography of American Constitutional History.* Santa Barbara: Clio Books, 1975.

Moquin, Wayne, and Charles van Doren, comps. *Great Documents in American Indian History.* New York: Praeger, 1973.

Morison, Samuel Eliot, ed. *Sources and Documents Illustrating the American Revolution, 1764–1788, and the Formation of the Federal Constitution.* Oxford: The Clarendon Press, 1923.

Morris, Richard B., ed. *Basic Documents in American History.* Princeton: D. Van Nostrand Co., 1965.

Morris, Richard B., and Jeffrey B. Morris, eds. *Great Presidential Decisions: State Papers That Changed the Course of History, from Washington to Reagan.* Rev. ed. New York: Richardson, Steirman and Black, 1988.

O'Callaghan, E. B., ed. *Documents Relative to the Colonial History of the State of New-York.* 15 vols. Albany: Weed and Parsons, 1853–87.

Poore, Benjamin P., comp. *The Federal and State Constitutions, Colonial Charters, and Other Organic Laws of the United States.* 2 vols. Washington, D.C.: Government Printing Office, 1877.

Romero, Patricia W., comp. *I Too Am America: Documents from 1619 to the Present.* New York: Publishers Co., 1968.

Scott, E. H., ed. *The Federalist and Other Constitutional Papers by Hamilton, Jay, Madison and Other Statesmen of Their Time.* 2 vols. Chicago: Albert, Scott and Co., 1894.

Tansill, C. C., ed. *Documents Illustrative of the Formation of the Union of the American States.* Washington, D.C.: Government Printing Office, 1927.

Thorpe, Francis N., ed. *The Federal and State Constitutions, Colonial Charters, and Other Organic Laws of the States, Territories, and Colonies Now or Heretofore Forming the United States of America.* 7 vols. Washington, D.C.: Government Printing Office, 1909.

THE PAPERS OF THE FOUNDING FATHERS

The Works of John Adams, Charles Francis Adams, ed. 10 vols. Boston: Little, Brown, 1850–56.

The Adams Papers, Lyman Butterfield, et al., eds. 32 vols.–. Cambridge: Harvard University Press, 1961–.

The Papers of Benjamin Franklin, Leonard W. Labaree, et al., eds. 27 vols.–. New Haven: Yale University Press, 1959–.

The Papers of Alexander Hamilton, Harold C. Syrett, ed. 27 vols. New York: Columbia University Press, 1961–87.

The Papers of Thomas Jefferson, Julian P. Boyd, et al., eds. 23 vols.–. Princeton: Princeton University Press, 1950–.

The Writings of Thomas Jefferson, Paul Leicester Ford, ed. 10 vols. New York: G. P. Putnam's Sons, 1892–99.

The Papers of James Madison, William T. Hutchinson, et al., eds. 16 vols.–. Chicago and Charlottesville: University of Chicago Press and University Press of Virginia, 1962–.

The Papers of George Washington, Donald Jackson, et al., eds. 15 vols.–. Charlottesville: University Press of Virginia, 1976–.

Additional Reading

I. Colonial America

Adams, James Truslow. *The Founding of New England*. Boston: Atlantic Monthly Press, 1921.

Baron, Robert C., ed. *America: One Land, One People*. Golden: Fulcrum, 1987.

Boorstin, Daniel J. T*he Americans: The Colonial Experience*. New York: Random House, 1958.

Craven, Wesley Frank. *The Southern Colonies in the Seventeenth Century, 1607–1689*. Baton Rouge: Louisiana State University Press, 1949.

DeVoto, Bernard. *The Course of Empire*. Boston: Houghton Mifflin, 1952.

Hofstadter, Richard. *America at 1750: A Social History*. New York: Knopf, 1971.

Meadows, Denis. *Five Remarkable Englishmen*. New York: Devin-Adair, 1961.

Morison, Samuel Eliot. *Builders of the Bay Colony*. Boston: Houghton Mifflin, 1930.

Morison, Samuel Eliot. *The Oxford History of the American People*. New York: Oxford University Press, 1965.

Nash, Gary. *Red, White and Black: The Peoples of Early America*. Englewood Cliffs: Prentice-Hall, 1974.

Parkman, Francis. *A Half Century of Conflict: France and England in North America*. 2 vols. Boston: Little, Brown, 1910.

Vaughan, Alden T. *American Genesis: Captain John Smith and the Founding of Virginia*. Boston: Little, Brown, 1975.

II. The American Revolution

Bailyn, Bernard. *The Ideological Origins of the American Revolution*. Cambridge: Harvard University Press, 1967.

Bemis, Samuel Flagg. *Diplomacy of the American Revolution*. New York: D. Appleton-Century Co., 1935.

Catton, Bruce, and William B. Catton. *The Bold and Magnificent Dream: America's Founding Years, 1492–1815*. Garden City: Doubleday, 1978.

Dabney, Virginius, ed. *The Patriots: The American Revolution Generation of Genius*. New York: Atheneum, 1975.

Franklin, Benjamin. *The Autobiography of Benjamin Franklin*. Edited by Leonard Labaree, et al. New Haven: Yale University Press, 1964.

Isaac, Rhys. *The Transformation of Virginia, 1740–1790*. Chapel Hill: University of North Carolina Press, 1982.

Jefferson, Thomas. *Notes on the State of Virginia*. 1787. Edited by William Peden. Chapel Hill: University of North Carolina Press, 1955.

Kerber, Linda K. *Women of the Republic: Intellect and Ideology in Revolutionary America*. Chapel Hill: Published for the Institute of Early American History and Culture by the University of North Carolina Press, 1980.

Malone, Dumas. *Jefferson the Virginian*. Boston: Little, Brown, 1948.

Malone, Dumas. *Jefferson and the Rights of Man*. Boston: Little, Brown, 1951.

Paine, Thomas. *Common Sense*. 1776. London: Penguin Books, 1976.

Tuchman, Barbara. *The First Salute: A View of the American Revolution*. New York: Knopf, 1988.

Van Doren, Carl. *Benjamin Franklin*. New York: Viking, 1938.

Wills, Gary. *Inventing America: Jefferson's Declaration of Independence*. Garden City: Doubleday, 1978.

Wood, Gordon S. *The Creation of the American Republic, 1776–1787*. New York: W.W. Norton and Co., 1969.

III. Forging a New Nation

Alden, John R. *The American Revolution, 1775–1783*. New York: Harper, 1954.

Bowen, Catherine. *Miracle at Philadelphia: The Story of the Constitutional Convention, May to September, 1787*. Boston: Little, Brown, 1966.

Bryce, James. *The American Commonwealth*. 2d ed. 2 vols. London: Macmillan, 1891.

Crèvecoeur, Michel Guillaume St. Jean de. *Letters from an American Farmer*. 1782. Reprint. New York: E.P. Dutton, 1957.

Flexner, James Thomas. *Washington, the Indispensable Man*. Boston: Little, Brown, 1974.

Freeman, Douglas S. *George Washington: A Biography*. 7 vols. New York: Scribner, 1948–57.

Malone, Dumas. *Jefferson and the Ordeal of Liberty*. Boston: Little, Brown, 1962.

Miller, J.C. *The Federalist Era, 1789–1801*. New York: Harper and Row, 1960.

Nettels, Curtis P. *George Washington and American Independence*. Boston: Little, Brown, 1951.

Norton, Mary Beth. *Liberty's Daughters: The Revolutionary Experience of American Women, 1750–1800*. Boston: Little, Brown, 1980.

Peterson, Merrill D. *Thomas Jefferson and the New Nation*. New York: Oxford University Press, 1970.

Rossiter, Clinton, ed. *The Federalist Papers*. New York: New American Library, 1961.

IV. The Young Republic

Adams, Henry. *The United States in 1800*. 1889. Reprint. Ithaca, N.Y.: Great Seal Books, 1955.

Bemis, Samuel Flagg. *John Quincy Adams and the Foundations of American Foreign Policy*. New York: Knopf, 1949.

Benson, Maxine, ed. *From Pittsburgh to the Rocky Mountains: Major Stephen Long's Expedition, 1819–1820*. Golden: Fulcrum, 1988.

Buley, R. Carlyle. *The Old Northwest: Pioneer Period, 1815–1840*. Bloomington: Indiana University Press, 1951.

Corwin, Edward S. *John Marshall and the Constitution: A Chronicle of the Supreme Court*. New Haven: Yale University Press, 1919.

Cott, Nancy F. *The Bonds of Womanhood: "Woman's Sphere" in New England, 1780–1835*. New Haven: Yale University Press, 1977.

Dangerfield, George. *The Era of Good Feelings*. New York: Harcourt Brace, 1952.

DeVoto, Bernard, ed. *The Journals of Lewis and Clark*. Boston: Houghton Mifflin, 1953.

Hansen, Marcus Lee. *The Atlantic Migration, 1607–1860: A History of the Continuing Settlement of the United States*. Cambridge: Harvard University Press, 1940.

Koch, Adrienne. *Jefferson and Madison: The Great Collaboration*. New York: Knopf, 1950.

Malone, Dumas. *Jefferson the President: First Term, 1801–1805*. Boston: Little, Brown, 1970.

Malone, Dumas. *Jefferson the President: Second Term, 1805–1809*. Boston: Little, Brown, 1974.

Malone, Dumas. *The Sage of Monticello*. Boston: Little, Brown, 1981.

May, Ernest R. *The Making of the Monroe Doctrine*. Cambridge: Harvard University Press, 1975.

V. A Gathering Storm

Clinton, Catherine. *The Other Civil War: American Women in the Nineteenth Century*. New York: Hill and Wang, 1984.

DeVoto, Bernard. *The Year of Decision: 1846*. Boston: Little, Brown, 1943.

Douglass, Frederick. *My Bondage and My Freedom*. Edited by William L. Andrews. Urbana: University of Illinois Press, 1988.

Eisenhower, John S.D. *So Far from God: The U.S. War with Mexico*. New York: Random House, 1989.

Filler, Louis. *The Crusade against Slavery*. New York: Harper and Row, 1960.

Josephy, Alvin. *The Patriot Chiefs: A Chronicle of American Indian Resistance*. New York: Penguin, 1969.

Kennedy, John F. *Profiles in Courage*. New York: Harper and Row, 1956.

Litwack, Leon. *North of Slavery: The Negro in the Free States, 1790–1860*. Chicago: University of Chicago Press, 1961.

Melder, Keith. *Beginnings of Sisterhood: The American Women's Rights Movement, 1800–1850*. New York: Schocken Books, 1977.

Moore, Glover. *The Missouri Controversy, 1819–1821*. Lexington: University of Kentucky Press, 1953.

Peterson, Merrill D. *The Great Triumvirate: Webster, Clay and Calhoun*. New York: Oxford University Press, 1987.

Potter, David M. *The Impending Crisis, 1848–1861*. New York: Harper and Row, 1976.

Schlesinger, Arthur M., Jr. *The Age of Jackson*. Boston: Little, Brown, 1945.

Tocqueville, Alexis de. *Democracy in America*. 1835. Edited by Henry Steele Commager. London: Oxford University Press, 1946.

Tyler, Alice Felt. *Freedom's Ferment: Phases of American Social History from the Colonial Period to the Outbreak of the Civil War*. Minneapolis: University of Minnesota Press, 1944.

VI. Civil War

Basler, Roy P., ed. *The Collected Works of Abraham Lincoln*. 8 vols. New Brunswick: Rutgers University Press, 1953.

Catton, Bruce. *The Centennial History of the Civil War.* 3 vols. Garden City: Doubleday, 1961–65.

Catton, Bruce. *A Stillness at Appomattox.* Garden City: Doubleday, 1953.

Foner, Eric. *Reconstruction: America's Unfinished Revolution, 1863–1877.* New York: Harper and Row, 1988.

Foote, Shelby. *The Civil War: A Narrative.* 3 vols. New York: Random House, 1958–74.

Freeman, Douglas S. *Lee's Lieutenants: A Study in Command.* 3 vols. New York: Charles Scribner's Sons, 1942–44.

Freeman, Douglas S. *Robert E. Lee.* 4 vols. New York: Charles Scribner's Sons, 1934–35.

McPherson, James M. B*attle Cry of Freedom: The Civil War Era.* New York: Oxford University Press, 1988.

Myers, Robert Manson, ed. *The Children of Pride: A True Story of Georgia and the Civil War.* New Haven: Yale University Press, 1972.

Nevins, Allan. *Ordeal of the Union.* New York: Charles Scribner's Sons, 1947.

Sandburg, Carl. *Abraham Lincoln: The War Years.* 4 vols. New York: Harcourt, Brace, 1939.

Williams, T. Harry. *Lincoln and His Generals.* New York: Random House, 1967.

Woodward, C. Vann, ed. *Mary Chesnut's Civil War.* New Haven: Yale University Press, 1981.

VII. America Comes of Age

Beale, Howard K. *Theodore Roosevelt and the Rise of America to World Power.* Baltimore: Johns Hopkins University Press, 1956.

Boorstin, Daniel J. *The Americans: The Democratic Experience.* New York: Random House, 1973.

Commager, Henry Steele. *The American Mind.* New Haven: Yale University Press, 1950.

Du Bois, W. E. B. *Black Reconstruction in America: 1860–1880.* 1935. Reprint. New York: Russell and Russell, 1962.

Goodwyn, Lawrence. *Democratic Promise: The Populist Movement in America.* New York: Oxford University Press, 1976.

Handlin, Oscar. *The Uprooted: The Epic Story of the Great Migrations That Made the American People.* Boston: Little, Brown, 1951.

Hofstadter, Richard. *The Age of Reform: From Bryan to F.D.R.* New York: Knopf, 1955.

Josephson, Matthew. *Robber Barons: The Great American Capitalists, 1861–1901.* New York: Harcourt, Brace, 1934.

Link, Arthur S. *Woodrow Wilson and the Progressive Era, 1910–1917.* New York: Harper and Row, 1954.

McPherson, James M. *The Abolitionist Legacy: From Reconstruction to the N.A.A.C.P.* Princeton: Princeton University Press, 1975.

Turner, Frederick Jackson. *The Frontier in American History.* 1920. Reprint. Tucson: University of Arizona Press, 1985.

Washington, Booker T. *Up from Slavery: An Autobiography.* New York: Doubleday and Page, 1901.

Williams, William A. *The Tragedy of American Diplomacy*. New York: Dell Publishing, 1959.

VIII. Two Wars and a Depression

Allen, Frederick Lewis. *Only Yesterday: An Informal History of the Nineteen Twenties*. New York: Harper and Brothers, 1931.

Cott, Nancy. *The Grounding of Modern Feminism*. New Haven: Yale University Press, 1987.

Eisenhower, Dwight D. *Crusade in Europe*. Garden City: Doubleday, 1948.

Hoover, Herbert. *The Ordeal of Woodrow Wilson*. New York: McGraw-Hill, 1958.

Hurt, R. Douglas. *The Dust Bowl: An Agricultural and Social History*. Chicago: Nelson–Hall, 1981.

Kennedy, David. *Over Here: The First World War and American Society*. New York: Oxford University Press, 1980.

Leuchtenburg, William E. *Franklin D. Roosevelt and the New Deal, 1932–1940*. New York: Harper and Row, 1963.

Link, Arthur S. *American Epoch: A History of the United States since the 1890s*. 5th ed. New York: Knopf, 1980.

Schulzinger, Robert D. *American Diplomacy in the Twentieth Century*. New York: Oxford University Press, 1984.

Soule, George. *Prosperity Decade: From War to Depression, 1917–1929*. New York: Rinehart, 1947.

Terkel, Studs. *"The Good War": An Oral History of World War II*. New York: Pantheon Books, 1984.

IX. The United States and World Power

Alexander, Charles C. *Holding the Line: The Eisenhower Era, 1952–1961*. Bloomington: Indiana University Press, 1975.

Cox, Archibald. *The Court and the Constitution*. Boston: Houghton Mifflin, 1987.

Gilbert, James. *Another Chance: Postwar America, 1945–1968*. Philadelphia: Temple University Press, 1981.

Goldman, Eric. *The Crucial Decade: America, 1945–1955*. New York: Knopf, 1956.

Herring, George C. *America's Longest War: The United States in Vietnam, 1950–1975*. New York: Knopf, 1979.

Hodgson, Godfrey. *America in Our Time: From World War II to Nixon*. Garden City: Doubleday, 1976.

Miller, Merle. *Plain Speaking: An Oral Biography of Harry S. Truman*. New York: Berkeley Publishing Corp., 1974.

Oates, Stephen B. *Let the Trumpet Sound: The Life of Martin Luther King, Jr*. New York: Harper and Row, 1982.

O'Neill, William L. *Coming Apart: An Informal History of the 1960s*. New York: Quadrangle, 1971.

Pollak, Louis H. *The Constitution and the Supreme Court: A Documentary History*. Cleveland: World Publishing Co., 1966.

Prucha, Francis Paul. *The Indians in American Society: From the Revolutionary War to the Present.* Berkeley: University of California Press, 1985.

Schlesinger, Arthur M., Jr. *A Thousand Days: John F. Kennedy in the White House.* Boston: Houghton Mifflin, 1965.

White, Theodore H. *America in Search of Itself: The Making of the President, 1956–1980.* New York: Harper and Row, 1982.

INDEX